SUNY series in Afro-American Studies
John R. Howard and Robert C. Smith, Editors

The
Shifting Wind

The Supreme Court and
Civil Rights from
Reconstruction to Brown

John R. Howard

State University of New York Press

Cover photo: Franz Jantzen, Collection of the Supreme Court of the United States.

Published by
State University of New York Press, Albany

For information, address State University of New York
Press, State University Plaza, Albany, N.Y., 12246

Production by E. Moore
Marketing by Dana Yanulavich

Library of Congress Cataloging-in-Publication Data

Howard, John R., 1933–
    the shifting wind : the Supreme Court and civil rights from
Reconstruction to Brown / John R. Howard.
        p.   cm. — (SUNY series in Afro-American studies)
    Includes bibliographical references and index.
    ISBN 0-7914-4089-3 (hc : alk. paper). — ISBN 0-7914-4090-7 (pbk.
: alk. paper)
    1. Afro-Americans—Civil rights—History. 2. Civil rights—United
States—History. 3. United States. Supreme Court—History.
I. Title. II. Series.
KF4757.H69 1999
342.73'085—dc21   98-23656
                                                                          CIP

10 9 8 7 6 5 4 3 2 1

Contents

Acknowledgments

A number of people provided counsel and assistance in the completion of this book. I would like to thank Sheldon Grebstein, former president of State University of New York at Purchase for a travel grant allowing me to make the trip to Washington, D.C., for the initial research at the National Archives and the Library of Congress. Joan Howard Jackson's hospitality made the numerous subsequent trips to Washington feasible. My colleagues Bill Baskin and Al Hunt provided feedback on earlier drafts of particular chapters, and my long-time friend and colleague Bob Smith provided valuable commentary. I am also greatful to the editors and staff of State University of New York Press for securing insightful and useful outside reviews on a very tight schedule. I would also like to thank Valencia Wallace for technical assistance in transferring the written word to computer disk. Finally I would like to thank my wife Mary Howard and my daughter Leigh Howard for providing an environment in which the long, hard, lonely work of writing a book could be successfully carried out.

Chapter 1

❧◇❧

Introduction:
The Supreme Court and Civil Rights

In the late Summer of 1868 three bodies were found in a cabin in rural Lewis County, Kentucky. The victims, all of whom were black, were members of the same family. Jack Foster lay sprawled in the doorway of the cabin, his wife Sallie nearby. Sallie's mother, Lucy Armstrong, blind and nearly ninety, lay dead on a bed. In the words of one of the first men on the scene, Jack and Sallie Foster "were cut in several places, almost to pieces."

A trail of blood led from the cabin out through the woods toward a nearby cabin. The fourth victim, eleven-year-old Richard Foster, badly wounded, had crawled away from the scene of the carnage toward the nearest refuge. Testimony offered later at trial indicated that "Mr. Nichols (the cabin's occupant) had retired to bed but being aroused by the call of Richard, he got up and went to the door and when he found Richard in a wounded and exhausted condition . . . took him in and went for help."

The men summoned by Nichols discovered the bodies in the cabin, still warm. They also found a lone survivor hiding under a bed, a few feet away from the blood and wreckage, twelve-year-old Laura Foster. Her brother Richard was mortally injured and would barely survive the night. Hence, in the coming proceedings against the assailants Laura Foster was to be the only living witness.

The immediate question posed by the sheriff's men who had found the bodies related to the identity of the attackers. Who had massacred the family and why? A dying declaration was sought from Richard as to the horrific events which had transpired in the Foster cabin. At the end of his statement, which was taken down word for word, he affixed his *X*. Laura Foster was also questioned as to who had come to the cabin and what had happened. Dying brother and terrified sister recounted the same story.

Some time after nightfall, perhaps around nine o'clock, two young white men, local residents, John Blyew and George Kennard, had come to the cabin, the dogs barking as they had come over a fence and approached the front door. Lucy Armstrong was preparing to go to bed. Sallie Foster was sewing a patch in a pair of britches. Blyew and Kennard were in the cabin only a short while before the assault started. Richard was the first victim. "Blyew struck me, but I do not know with what, about that time I think that George Kennard ran out of the house, and John Blyew was still killing us. I thought at this time I heard my Pap holler 'Oh.'"

Shortly after sunrise deputies descended on the Blyew cabin, there finding John Blyew and George Kennard. They also found two pair of freshly washed trousers and a pair of muddy boots. It was also determined that a short time before the killings Kennard had told Blyew that he believed there would soon be another war about the "niggers" and when it came he intended "to go to killing niggers." Indeed he was not sure that he would not "begin his work of killing them before the war should actually commence."

The arrests of Blyew and Kennard commenced the criminal proceedings. The trousers, boots, and statements constituted important but inconclusive evidence. Freshly washed trousers, muddy boots, and angry statements do not prove participation in mass murder. They constituted the kind of evidence used in a criminal proceeding to corroborate the testimony of a principal witness. Standing alone they were insufficient to secure an indictment, much less a conviction. Under most circumstances the testimony of an eye witness to the commission of the crime and a dying declaration by the victim of the violent act would have been sufficient to secure a conviction. The facts attending the murder of the Foster family presented an insurmountable problem however.

Under Kentucky law a person of African descent could not give testimony in a criminal proceeding against a white defendant. The language was convoluted but the meaning was clear. Under section 1, chapter 107 of the Revised Statutes of Kentucky a "negro or indian" could be a competent witness in cases involving "only negroes or indians . . . but in no other case." In other words, in a state criminal proceeding neither the eyewitness testimony of

Laura Foster nor the dying declaration of Richard Foster would be admissible against Blyew and Kennard. There was no way in which prosecution in a state court could result in a conviction.

Two years earlier however Congress had passed the first civil rights law in the history of the Republic. The Civil Rights Act of 1866 had been drafted in reaction to the so-called black codes, laws enacted in a number of states of the defeated confederacy having the intent and effect of restoring domination over the newly freed black population via such devices as "labor contracts" imposing a type of peonage.

A key provision of the Civil Rights Act of 1866 gave jurisdiction to federal courts for "all causes, civil and criminal, affecting persons who are denied or cannot enforce in the courts or judicial tribunals of the State, or locality, where they may be, any of the rights secured to them" for reasons of race. The language of this clause provided the basis for the assumption of federal jurisdiction over the case, and allowed the prosecution of Blyew and Kennard to proceed under federal jurisdiction in a federal court.

Laura Foster testified against the assailants, recounting the details of the bloody slaughter and responding to the prosecution's query for in-court identification of the attackers. Over defense objections the written account of Richard Foster's dying declaration with his X affixed was introduced into evidence. All of the other testimony, corroborative in nature, came from white witnesses. A pair of britches, a patch half sewn into them, was found near Sallie Foster's body. It did appear that Lucy Armstrong was about to turn in when struck down. Freshly washed trousers and muddy boots were found in the Blyew cabin the morning after the attack.

The jury brought back two guilty verdicts and on December 5, 1868, sentence was pronounced. John Blyew and George Kennard were to be "taken to the common jail of Jefferson County and there safely kept, until Friday, January twenty second, in the year of our Lord Eighteen Hundred and Sixty-nine, on which day between sunrise and sunset, the Marshall" was to hang them by the neck until dead.

On January 9, 1869, two weeks before the scheduled executions, the attorneys for the condemned men filed an appeal, setting the case on the road to the Supreme Court.

The pursuit of an appeal following a criminal conviction requires the defendant's appellate counsel to argue that substantial error in the proceedings against the accused violated one or more constitutionally protected rights and resulted in the conviction. An appeal directed to the nation's highest court requires as a threshold condition that the defendant allege error relative to a right protected under the United States Constitution. Hence, in the Writ of Error setting the case of *Blyew v. United States* on the road to the Supreme Court, Whitaker and Jackson, the attorneys for the condemned men, contended that the offense done to the rights of John Blyew and George Kennard had been of constitutional dimensions.

The United States Supreme Court sets its own docket in that it determines which cases it will hear and which cases it will not hear. Irrespective of appellate counsel's vigorous and impassioned contention that a case presents issues of constitutional importance, certiorari may not be granted. The granting of certiorari—literally, an agreement to review the record from below, including the record of any intermediate appellate court proceedings—allows appellate and opposing counsel to submit substantial written arguments to the court in the form of briefs, and on a scheduled date to appear before the court for oral argument.

Bland Ballard, the judge before whom Blyew and Kennard's attorneys appeared to initiate the appeals process, recognized that the case was "both new and important." And indeed it had excited great interest throughout the state. A joint resolution of the Kentucky General Assembly directed the governor to seek state entry on behalf of Blyew and Kennard, Kentucky contending that the removal of the case to federal court constituted a usurpation by the federal government of the state's authority to deal with a criminal matter.

It was the first case in which the full court would construe those provisions of the Civil Rights Act of 1866 which seemed to provide federal protection against state abuse, and it was also the first civil rights case ever heard by the Supreme Court.

In the fall of 1870 a full nine-member court met. The turmoil of the preceding decade had also brought turmoil to the Court. Within weeks of the outbreak of the Civil War in 1861 John Campbell of Georgia had resigned his seat and joined the confederacy. Abraham Lincoln had made four appointments, seeking justices who would be sympathetic to the federal government's enormous expansion of power as it pursued the war effort. The Court had fluctuated in size, finally being affixed at nine by Congress. The expansion in number allowed President Ulysses Grant to nominate two new justices, William Strong and Joseph Bradley, whom he hoped would side with the federal government in various challenges to the validity of the paper money it had issued during the war.

In December of 1871 one of those new associate justices, William Strong, handed down the court's decision in the case of *Blyew v. United States*. It was a split decision, Strong speaking for the majority. He began by reviewing the exact language of the relevant provisions of the Civil Rights Act of 1866, then recounted the grisly details of the murders. He then stated that counsel for Blyew and Kennard and for the State of Kentucky had raised a number of points on appeal of which one had come to be paramount, "Whether the Circuit Court had jurisdiction of the offence charged in the indictment." Both sides had focused on this issue in oral argument, and it was the focus of the majority holding.

That holding can be summarized as follows: The language of the Civil Rights Act provided federal jurisdiction for all causes civil and criminal affecting persons denied their rights because of race. In a criminal proceeding the only parties affected are the government, in the sense that the government wins a conviction or it does not, and the accused party, in the sense that the accused party is exonerated and goes free or is convicted and made subject to punishment. "Obviously the only parties to such a cause (a criminal proceeding) are the government and the person indicted. They alone can be reached by any judgment pronounced."

The victim of a homicide may be the subject of a criminal proceeding but cannot be said to be affected by the outcome of the proceeding. Thus with regard to, for example, ninety-year-old Lucy Armstrong. "In no sense can she be said to be affected by the cause (the criminal proceeding). Manifestly the act refers to persons in existence."

Neither are witnesses affected parties in a criminal proceeding. "Those who may possibly be witnesses . . . are no more affected by it than is every other person, for any one may be called as a witness." If the mere fact that one or more of the witnesses to a proceeding happened to be black was sufficient to justify federal jurisdiction then any case in which there was a black witness could be removed from state to federal court. Surely that was not the intention of the Act.

These propositions yielded the conclusion: "(T)he Circuit Court had not jurisdiction of the crime of murder committed in the district of Kentucky, merely because two persons who witnessed the murder were citizens of the African race, and for that reason incompetent by the law of Kentucky to testify in the courts of that state. They are not persons affected by the cause."[1]

The two dissenters, Joseph Bradley and Noah Swayne, went

directly to the heart of the majority holding. "Suppose that, in any State, assault and battery, mayhem—nay, murder itself, could be perpetrated upon a colored man with impunity, no law being provided for punishing the offender, would not that be a case of denial of rights to the colored population of that State? Would not the clause of the civil rights bill now under consideration give jurisdiction to the United States. . . . Yet, if an indictment should be found . . . the technical parties to the record would only be the United States as plaintiff and the criminal as defendant."[2]

In other words, under the logic of the majority holding there was no circumstance, no matter how outrageous the criminal act, under which federal jurisdiction could be assumed. Had it not been a crime at all under Kentucky law for a white man to kill a black man, federal jurisdiction could not be assumed upon commission of a slaying. If the witnesses were white there would be no statutory basis for federal jurisdiction, and if the witnesses were black they would be deemed parties not affected by the outcome of the proceedings. The dissenters argued that the majority had taken an approach to the law "too narrow, too technical, and too forgetful of the liberal objectives it had in view."[3]

On April 1, 1872 the Supreme Court issued the final document in its first civil rights case. "On consideration whereof, It is now here ordered and adjudged by this Court, that the judgment of the said Circuit Court, in this cause, be, and the same is hereby ordered reversed. And that this cause be and the same is hereby remanded to the said Circuit Court with directions to arrest the judgement."[4]

Blyew and Kennard were to be freed.

The Blyew decision came toward the end of Salmon P. Chase's tenure as chief justice. In March of 1874 he was replaced as chief justice by Morrison Waite, a Midwestern railroad lawyer who had never held a judicial post nor practiced before the Supreme Court. The Courts that sat in the last days of the Chase regime and the first terms of the Waite administration had a profound impact on the fate of African Americans. Their holdings were among the most important ever issued. Although sharply divided on matters of race, Congress managed in the ten years following the end of the Civil War to put in place a substantial body of law intended to provide equal rights for black citizens. Inevitably the meaning and constitutionality of these laws were challenged by forces hostile to the idea of equality. Inevitably, also under Article Three, Sections One and Two of the United States Constitution, it fell to the Supreme Court to rule on the constitutionality and reach of the new legislation.

All of the challenges to the new laws presented cases of first impression. In other words, the Court could only weakly be guided by precedent. The decisions in the first civil rights cases coming before the Court at the end of the Chase regime and the beginning of the Waite years created precedent. They created the legal framework within which issues crucial to black rights were to be adjudicated for decades to come. Those crucial years also saw the Court majority adopt a mode of analysis regarding race and rights that continues to be employed by Court conservatives and that, in this discussion, is termed "formalism." The Blyew holding provides an example of formalism insofar as it derived from a narrow, hyperliteral reading of statutory language which allowed for a conclusion that ignored the underlying unpleasant racial realities the statute was intended to address. As is indicated in the third chapter, the Court's formalist analysis in the first cases coming before it significantly altered the course of race relations in the United States for decades to come, and into the indefinite future.

This book focuses on the Supreme Court and civil rights from the end of the Civil War through *Brown v. Board.* The Court played a decisive role in molding the relationship between race and rights during that ninety-year period and therefore a decisive role in determining what the country was and what it was to become. *Brown* marked a turning point in the meaning and place of race in American society. The holding contributed to the erosion of the moral legitimacy accorded segregation and helped impel the civil rights movement toward the major legislative success of the 1960s, the Civil Rights Act of 1964.

To the extent that an understanding of the past facilitates an understanding of the present, a grasp of the role of the Supreme Court in shaping the dynamics of race in the United States between the end of the Civil War and *Brown*, informs and deepens an understanding of the country's racial odyssey in the post-*Brown*, post-civil rights era.

The Court's formal, legal role in the judicial process is defined by Article 3, Sections 1 and 2 of the Constitution, and make it the final arbiter of the meaning of the language of the Constitution. In practical terms the use and abuse of power under either federal or state law, raising the possibility that a plaintiff's rights under the Constitution have been violated yield appellate jurisdiction to the Supreme Court to decide the matter.

This formal role has made the Court an institution of peculiar and decisive importance in terms of race and rights. The tension between an egalitarian national ethic embodied in the Declaration of Independence and the Constitution and a social dynamic tending toward racial exclusion made the Court a key player in determining the meaning of the language embodying the national ethic and therefore the substance of day-to-day racial realities. The Court's holdings on matters of race are legal pronouncements going to the balance of rights between minorities and the majority. They also have significant political and sociological consequences insofar as they affirm certain values with regard to race and rights and discredit others. They have major consequence with regard to patterns of racial stratification, and, historically, they have shaped the agendas of the civil rights movement and the legislative and executive branches of government.

In this work the Court is examined in historical and social context, the focus being on the reciprocal relationship between it and the larger social and political worlds of which it is a part. The Supreme Court sets its own docket, but the controversies and conflicts that yield the cases it selects to hear are spawned by fissures and contradictions in the political and social systems. Having selected the issues it will address, the Court's holdings affect and reshape the social and political worlds. This book chronicles that reciprocal relationship in terms of race and rights. It examines the manner in which the Supreme Court made the world of race relations in America from the end of the Civil War through the post-World War II days and responded to the cases yielded by the world it had made.

There is no simple or single explanation for the Court's actions over time. A variety of factors come into play, but vary in their importance or centrality from one historical period to another. The picture is complex, but there are patterns. The explanation is not simple, but the facts are amenable to synthesis in an overarching and integrating statement.

The broad framework used to organize the discussion rests on the following five propositions: (1) The role of the Supreme Court as regards race and rights cannot be understood without grasping the centrality of the idea of race in American thought and culture. However, (2) the Court's role in the evolving race story cannot be viewed as a mere reflection of cultural forces, elite wishes, or popular views. (3) The function of the Supreme Court within the framework of the Constitution, the nature of law itself, and the lifetime tenure of justices have yielded a decisive, independent role to it in shaping the course of race relations in the nation. (4) The substantive outcomes yielded by that independence have been a consequence also of the fact that the Court is, in a sociological sense, a small group, and is subject to small group dynamics. In addition, (5) the Court's ongoing role as regards race and rights cannot be understood without perceiving how events were viewed by Afro-Americans as they unfolded. What did *The Civil Rights Cases of 1883* mean to Afro-Americans at that time? What did *Plessy* mean to Afro-Americans at that time? The Supreme Court became an actor largely in response to petitions for redress pressed by Afro-Americans. What drove ongoing faith in the Court such as to set in motion multiple successive circumstances in which the Court had the opportunity anew to define the scope and limits of black freedom?

The balance of this chapter enlarges on these propositions in the interest of clarifying the underlying assumptions and approach. The chapter closes with an outline of the book's organization.

Race, Culture, and the Supreme Court

Fundamental to a grasp of the performance of the Supreme Court in terms of race and rights is an understanding of the idea of race in American culture. In a larger sense the role of the Supreme Court in matters of race cannot be understood without grasping the moral ambiguity attending the founding of the United States. The compromises made in matters of race at the moment of creation yielded a national fate tormented by that ambiguity and yielded to the Supreme Court the impossible task of interpreting the national charter, the Constitution, in such a manner as to reconcile a deep national impulse to exclude on racial grounds with an equally deep, national commitment to inclusive and humanistic values.

The events attending the formation of the new nation spoke of moral contradiction and unhappy compromise. In December of 1775, with the fate of the rebellion in doubt, George Washington wrote to the Continental Congress stating his intention of departing from policy by allowing the enlistment of free blacks to the ranks of those fighting for independence. In closing he indicated: "if this is disapproved by the Congress I will put a stop to it." The Congress did not disapprove.[5]

Within a year Nace Butler, Francis Freeman, Pomp Liberty, and Joel Taburn entered the lists, the number of blacks serving rising eventually to five thousand.[6] In July of 1776, seven months after the Continental Congress had by its silence consented to the enlistment of black troops, Thomas Jefferson submitted draft language for a proposed Declaration of Independence to the men gathered in Philadelphia. That draft contained language condemning slavery as an offense "against human nature itself" and "an assemblage of horror."[7]

In a letter to James Madison, written in 1784, one year after independence had been won, Jefferson commented on the fate of his proposal: "The clause respecting slavery was lost by an individual vote only." Jefferson understood the moral contradiction now made indelibly a part of national identity. "What an incomprehensible machine is man! who can endure toil, famine, stripes, imprisonment, and death itself, in vindication of his own liberty, and the next moment, be deaf to all those motives whose power supported him through his trial, and inflict on his fellow men, a bondage, one hour of which is fraught with more misery than ages of that which he rose in rebellion to oppose."[8]

But Jefferson as a slave holder himself reflected the contradiction and went on, as did the other founding fathers, to ratify a Constitution which explicitly protected slavery in five clauses. Two centuries later the historian David Brion Davis asked, "had the nation begun with a Faustian bargain obligating all future generations to pay the debt?"[9]

The consequences of those early compromises provide the backdrop against which the history of the Court has unfolded. At the inception of the nation, race was made part of national identity. The earliest naturalization laws were written in 1787, 1795, 1798, and 1802 and although varying in detail they all limited the acquisition of citizenship to "freeborn whitemen." Blacks, free or slave, Indians, and all other nonwhites were excluded from possible inclusion in the national family.

Whatever benefits accrued to those among the Founding Fathers who fought to make racial exclusion part of the national charter and national identity, yet other benefits accrued to the waves of European immigrants who came to the nation's shores in the nineteenth and twentieth centuries. In Europe they were "Irish" or "Italian" or "Polish" or "Scots." They might also have been worker or peasant, tradesman or serf, but in the United States they were also "white." Whatever differences of custom or language might have separated them in the old world, whatever tribal hostilities might have set one against the other in Europe, in the new world they were linked in the kinship of race. They were "white" and hence could become part of the national family. However marginal their class status, there were places they could go where no black, rich or poor, could go. Whatever they were, they were not "the other." The idea of race and the reality of racial exclusion were central to acquiring a subjective identity as an "American." They played an important role in the assimilation of diverse immigrant populations into American society.

In the same summer in which slavery was written in to the national charter, the Founding Fathers also composed language that forcefully and eloquently stated that natural law endowed all persons with an inalienable rights. In forbidding titles of nobility and inherited political or ecclesiastical privileges it opened up to the common man the possibility of making of his life what he could. Professor Sylvia Frey indicated the impact of the doctrines advanced by the architects of the new nation:

> The Revolution . . . put a weapon in the hands of the oppressed. It was more than a set of laws. It was a language. Under British rule, the language of both political and social relations was essentially paternalistic. The language of politics assumed the subordination of the people to the King . . . of the People to their rulers. The language of the Republic assumed equality in at least the political if not in all social sides of these relations. The struggles for equality could in the future be fought out in the language of the Republic.[10]

A succession of scholars from DeTouqueville on have grasped the centrality and paradox of the idea of race in American culture. Gunnar Myrdal's classic on the "American Dilemma," published toward the middle of the twentieth century, examined American culture in terms of its strained adaptations to the conflict between deep commitment to egalitarian and humanist values, on the one hand, and its equally deep commitment to racialist doctrines and racial exclusion, on the other. With varying degrees of intensity and with shifts in the weighting of commitment to one side or the other, that conflict has characterized the nation from its inception. It has been the peculiar fate and judicial role of the Supreme Court to work at the intersection of that contradiction, attempting to reconcile the irreconcilable.

According to Professor Paul Finkelman, "The jurisprudence surrounding fugitive slaves was the most divisive constitutional issue in antebellum America."[11] It fell to the Supreme Court to attempt to resolve the contradiction built into the structure and ideology of the nation. To what extent could the federal government limit the spread of slavery? To what extent would federal law support slave states in the return of runaways from free states? The Supreme Court became the arena for resolving the increasingly bitter confrontations over slavery, but as Finkelman indicated, "While settling legal issues, none of (the) cases satisfactorily dealt with the moral and political questions raised when human beings escaped to freedom."[12]

In the last major case on race and rights heard before the onset of the Civil War, a Court majority attempted a final, definitive resolution to the moral dilemma posed by race in the context of a nation otherwise committed to equal rights. The failure of that resolution helped bring on the Civil War. The precise legal issues posed in the *Dred Scott v. Sandford* were technical in nature, turning at the most basic level on whether Dred Scott, suing in federal court for his freedom, was a citizen of the state of Missouri, citizenship being necessary to invoke the jurisdiction of that court. As Finkleman indicated, Chief Justice Roger Taney "wrote a long and complicated opinion in which he attempted to settle, at one stroke, the troubling issue of slavery and the federal territories."[13] The political impact of the case derived both from its substance, declaring unconstitutional the Missouri Compromise, which had sought to limit the spread of slavery, and from the substance and language of the declarations regarding blacks and the moral character of slavery.

Invocation of the jurisdiction of the federal court presupposed citizenship and, hence, Taney and the majority addressed the question of whether that jurisdiction had been properly invoked. "Can a negro, whose ancestors were imported into this country, and sold as slaves, become a member of the political community formed and brought into existence by the Constitution of the United States?" The answer, Taney held, was no.[14]

This conclusion was supported with an elaborate argument using "original intent" as the mode of constitutional analysis. In other words, the Constitution should mean what the Founding Fathers intended it to mean and not what subsequent jurists would like it to mean. This approach allowed the majority to conclude that there was no moral contradiction or dilemma because the Founding Fathers and subsequent generations had, for good reason, never intended that blacks be part of the national family. Taney's attempt to resolve the moral dilemma failed. The holding of *Dred Scott* exacerbated conflict between North and South, and it took a civil war to resolve the issue of slavery.

This book starts at that point. Race has been the most persistent and divisive issue in the life of the Republic. It has always had major consequences for the ways in which social and political life are organized. It has always been an indelible aspect of personal self-identification and has shaped collective views about what the nation is, is becoming, and should be.

Elites, Popular Culture, and the Supreme Court

An argument in support of the proposition that the holdings of the Supreme Court reflect political pressures, elite preferences, and cultural realities has intuitive appeal and a degree of serious, scholarly support. It is necessary, therefore, to briefly discuss the limitations of that approach with regard to race, rights, and the Supreme Court in terms of setting forth the framework employed in this work.

From the time legal realism rose to prominence as a mode of analysis in the first decades of the twentieth century many scholars have recognized that law is imbedded in a social, political, and cultural matrix. Contemporary approaches to legal analysis such as Critical Legal Studies and Critical Race Theory also place law in a larger social network. Clearly, the initial proposition guiding this work regarding the centrality of the idea of race in American culture speaks to the necessity of placing the Court in a larger arena. The central issue is not whether law and the courts are influenced by extralegal factors but the extent to which they are influenced.

The second proposition guiding discussion in this work posits that while the Court is influenced by the larger social environment it is not wholly a creature of that environment. It is not merely an instrument of elite designs or a reflection of political and cultural forces. A brief exposition of a more expansive view of the role of outside influences on the Court followed by a test of that view against the elements of the Court's record as regards race and rights establishes the case for a more balanced and limited position, recognizing that the Court is acted upon but is also a powerful independent actor.

In his book *The Tempting of America*, Robert Bork, former law professor, appellate court judge, solicitor general, and Supreme

Court nominee offered a version of what might be termed the "elite dominance theory." The Court's history can be divided into identifiable eras, Bork stated, and, "in each era the Court responded to the ideology of the class to which the justices felt closest. By observing the values the Court chooses to enforce, it is often possible to discern which classes have achieved dominance at a given time in our history. Dominance . . . refers to the tendency of a class's ideas and values to be accepted by the elites that form opinion. In this century we have seen the Court allied to business interests and the ideology of free enterprise. We have seen that ideology lose its power with the arrival of the New Deal and the effect of that ideological shift on the Supreme Court. The intellectual class has become liberal and that fact has heavily influenced the Court's performance."[15]

Judge Bork stated a type of hypothesis purporting to explain the broad thrust of the Court's holdings over time. As a hypothesis this kind of explanation for the Court's holding is subject to test against the facts of history. The central point here is not whether Judge Bork in particular was right or wrong but whether a particular kind of explanation for the Court's actions is right or wrong. At the immediate factual level so many counterexamples can be adduced that the validity of elite-dominance hypothesis is doubtful. For the sake of discussion let us regard the president and his most important supporters in and out of government as elites.

An historical inquiry relative to race and rights does not support the Bork-type hypothesis. The holdings of the Court under Chief Justice Edward Douglass White ran counter to the sentiments of the segregationist-minded Woodrow Wilson administration. Ironically, White was an exconfederate soldier who had been nominated for chief justice in 1910 by President William Howard Taft as part of a "southern strategy" intended to secure the support of the states of the old confederacy in his unsuccessful bid for reelection. Woodrow Wilson, his successor, promptly proceeded to introduce racial segregation in the federal workplace and to express his hostility to black interests in other ways. He also nominated the rigid segregationist James Clark McReynolds to the bench as soon as an opening materialized.

Among the cases on race and rights coming before the White Court were two that were crucial to the future of blacks. In 1917 the Court took up *Buchanan v. Warley*, a case that is given considerable attention in chapter 5. At issue was the constitutionality of municipal ordinances that divided cities into black zones and white zones. These were, quite simply, apartheid laws and they were proliferating in number across the country. An examination of the case record on *Buchanan v. Warley* indicates that the possibility of explicit racial zoning enjoyed widespread support in political and economic quarters. As with all such statutes, the law passed in Louisville, Kentucky, rested on premises the Supreme Court itself had articulated in *Plessy v. Ferguson* in 1896. Government may make racial distinctions in law where a legitimate governmental interest is advanced. The maintenance of racial peace is a legitimate governmental interest. The separation of the races by law promotes racial peace.

Given the *Plessy* premise, there was no inherent limit to the extent to which segregation could be imposed. The logic of *Plessy* was not inconsistent with a de jure apartheid. The Louisville ordinance was yielded by that logic; hence, Louisville would argue that racial zoning laws were constitutional insofar as they were simply means for accomplishing the legitimate state objective of maintaining racial peace.

A unanimous Supreme Court held that Louisville's statute was unconstitutional despite the fact that it and similar laws in numerous cities enjoyed great support. For reasons that are discussed at length in chapter 5 the Court rested its holding on the assertion that these laws infringed on a constitutionally guaranteed right to contract, rather than on any premise calling into question the fundamental legitimacy of race based laws.[16] But, as is also indicated in chapter 5, it was widely understood at the time by persons of all political persuasions that the holding had enormous implications for the direction of race relations in the country.

In the *Guinn* case, decided two years earlier, also dealt with in chapter 5, the White Court also departed from the expectations and hopes of the Wilson administration. The case had begun to work its way up the appellate ladder during the preceding Taft Administration but did not reach the Supreme Court until after Wilson's election. Under circumstances described in chapter 5 the United States had become a party to the action on behalf of plaintiff's contesting the constitutionality of an Oklahoma law which had the effect of disenfranchising blacks by making access to the ballot contingent upon having had a forebear who would have been eligible to vote. The wording of the law and certain of waiver provisions made it possible for an illiterate European immigrant to vote while excluding black college graduates from the polling place. It fell to Wilson's segregationist-minded administration to argue the case, sentiment being expressed that a loss would not be a tragedy. The Court decision overturning the law on Fifteenth Amendment grounds could in no way be said to reflect elite views. At stake was the access of blacks to the ballot at a time when blacks who could vote were overwhelmingly Republican. Wilson's Democratic Party administration was hostile to blacks on party as well as racial grounds.

At yet an earlier time and from a different political perspective, the Court could also have been said to have failed to reflect the perspective of political elites. Much of the civil rights legislation passed in the years following the end of the Civil War reflected the pragmatic interests of the Republican Party. The 1868 presidential election was the fourth contested by the new party. In 1860 Abraham Lincoln had been elected with barely 40 percent of the vote. Four years later, running while the war was still being fought, he had beaten George McClellan by only a few hundred thousand votes. In 1868 war hero Ulysses Grant had beaten Horace Seymour, a the lackluster Democratic Party candidate, and his rabidly antiblack running mate Frank Blair by four hundred thousand votes. Historians estimate that perhaps four hundred thousand of Grant's votes came from blacks newly able to exercise the franchise. An important, and perhaps decisive portion, of Grant's support had come from freedmen able to exercise the ballot because of a northern military presence in the southern states.

Moved by both principle and self-interest the Republicans in Congress pushed for a constitutional amendment barring denial of the ballot for racial reasons, and for legislation empowering the United States attorneys and the attorney general to undertake criminal prosecution of those who sought for racial reasons to bar black voting. These efforts yielded the Fifteenth Amendment, the Enforcement Acts of 1870 and 1871, and the so-called Klan Act, which, in amended form, was used decades later by J. A. Croson to sue the Richmond city council in a reverse discrimination suit.

The Republican Party, dominant in the executive and legislative branches of government and therefore representative of a measure of both popular opinion and of nonpolitical elite opinion had both a pragmatic and a principled interest in seeing the various constitutional challenges to the Enforcement Act and the Klan Acts mounted by southern forces defeated. In a series of holdings dealt with in chapter 3 the Court disappointed those hopes. The effect of the holdings was to rob the federal government of the capacity to deal legally with Klan and other antiblack terror.

As is indicated in the third chapter, the number of cases prosecuted plunged dramatically following holdings which called into question the constitutionality, reach, and meaning of the Enforcement Acts. Republican efforts to reach a rapprochement with the white south following the deadlock outcome of the 1876 presidential election were generated, in part, by Court holdings making it difficult for the federal government to combat night rider and Klan violence directed at driving blacks from the political arena. As is also indicated in chapter 3, but for Supreme Court emasculation of Justice Department efforts to prosecute night riders, the near tie in the 1876 election might never have occurred.

As these examples suggest, one of the problems with the elite-dominance hypothesis is its assumption of a unified elite. As often as not there is no unified elite point of view, and even if there is the Supreme Court might not follow it. For example, in the Grant era elite opinion was sharply divided on the specifics of race and rights. The Court could not be said to have reflected an elite view because there was no single such view.

By contrast, during the Wilson era there was something close to an elite and popular consensus on the desirability and necessity of racial segregation. At the level of popular culture blacks were objects of derision and ridicule in high art and low. At one end of the spectrum the classic film "Birth of a Nation" released in 1915 was a celebration of the Ku Klux Klan, while at the other end the Florian Slappy series and such shorts as "A Coon in Love" and "The Wooing and Wedding of a Coon" showcased the black as fool. Revisionist history had begun to portray the prewar, slave South in idyllic terms while presenting the reconstruction period as one in which black greed, cupidity, and ignorance had brought ruin to Dixie.

The Kentucky law tested in *Buchanan v. Warley* reflected near universal white acceptance of segregation and its underlying rationale. The nation was ready for laws creating black zones. The Edward Douglass White court, sitting in an era in which the desirability of racial subordination of blacks was taken as self evident, handed down the first decisions in a decade positing limits as to the extent of that subordination. Hence, there is no reasonable reading of the Court's history that lends credence to an elite-dominance hypothesis regarding the Court's holding reflecting or being inspirations of something called an "elite."

An alternative to the elite-dominance interpretive model suggests that the Court's holdings reflect the broad cultural values and norms of a given time, the shared assumptions about what is true and what is not true, and how the world works. A variant on this approach, more amenable to testing as a hypothesis, suggests that the Court is to some degree influenced by public opinion, Thomas R. Marshall took this approach in *Public Opinion and the Supreme Court*.[17]

Although Marshall and others point to weak linkages between the Court's decisions and public opinion, an assessment of the historical record suggests that while the Court's holdings may coincide with public views the Court is not guided by public opinion. Again, as with elite views there has rarely been anything approaching a unified public stance on most of the issues attending race and rights, hence the Court could not be guided by public opinion even if it wanted to. And indeed "public opinion" in the modern, polling sense of the term is a phenomenon that originated during the 1930s with the first fledgling efforts of George Gallup and his organization to devise samples and reliable interview techniques.

In any event the relationship between what the Court does and what the public thinks is a fairly complicated matter. Even though a substantial proportion of the public might subscribe to basic value positions on matters of race there is no clearly formulated or articulated public view on many of the important but technical issues that come before the Court. The 1989 case *Patterson v. McClean* provides an example. At the technical level the case dealt with whether Brenda Patterson, a black woman, could use provisions of the Civil Rights Act of 1866 to pursue redress against a supervisor whom she alleged had harassed her on racial grounds, the relevant clause being one which afforded blacks the same right to contract as enjoyed by whites. In effect, did the language of the Civil Rights Act of 1866 speak only to the matter of the right to form a contract, in the sense of a right not to be denied a job on racial grounds, or did it also provide the basis for a suit under circumstances in which the employer fell short in terms of performance of the contract by tolerating racial harassment of the minority employee.

This was an important but technical question going to the issue of the legal basis on which a minority employee might pursue a claim based on an allegation of a hostile racial environment. Obviously, whatever the public's views as to whether racial remarks on the job constitute levity or harassment it has no view on the applicability of the Civil Rights Act of 1866 as the framework within which legal redress for a claim of harassment might be pursued.[18]

With regard to basic value positions on sensitive issues the Court's holdings appear sometimes to crystallize public opinion rather than reflect it. An analysis of public opinion polls in the years immediately preceding the 1954 *Brown v. Board* decision indicates that there was no expressed public support for school integration prior to that landmark decision. Indeed there was little felt need for racial reform at all. Less than three years before Brown was first argued before the Court less than half the public believed that the federal government should take any steps to curb racial discrimination in employment or intervene to curb lynching.[19] The Court's holding in *Brown* and subsequent cases appears to have provided moral affirmation for integrationist views in addition to substantive legal mandates affecting how people and institutions behaved on a day-to-day basis. Their holdings were also among the factors contributing impetus to the civil rights movement.

In summary, the Court's holdings on race and rights cannot be understood in terms of the influence of elites or as reflective of broad cultural beliefs or public opinion. No view that sees the Court as politically or culturally subordinate can accurately explain the historical record. The Court is an independent actor, better understood in the words of law professor and exponent of Critical Race Theory, Patricia Williams. "There is great power in being able to see the world as one will and then to have that vision enacted."[20]

The Supreme Court as a Small Group

The Supreme Court's functions as defined in the Constitution and the lifetime tenure of the justices allow it to play an independent role in national life. The manner in which that role is played out is, in part, a function of the nature of the Court as a social entity.

The third premise upon which this book rests entails viewing the Court as a small group. Various of the social sciences have made attempts to develop a theoretical understanding of human behavior in small groups. The closed nature of the Supreme Court has not made it a readily available subject for study, yet by the terms of its charter and its rules of operation it is the quintessential small group. An inference as to the actual dynamics of the interaction of the justices and therefore of the interpersonal processes having major consequence for their holdings is yielded by a close study of the available records.

The numerous justices serving on the Court between Joseph Bradley and William Strong, nominated by President Grant in 1869, and Earl Warren, nominated by Dwight Eisenhower in 1953, varied enormously in intellect and personality. At crucial junctures in the evolution of the Court's pronouncements on race and rights these differences became part of the combination of factors having consequence. An understanding of these factors would not be sufficient alone to explain the Court's actions at crucial points in the history of the race struggle, but are important in facilitating an understanding of those actions. An example and the tentative generalization yielded by it will suffice.

In 1872 Chief Justice Salmon Portland Chase died. As is indicated in chapter 3, Chase had risen to national prominence in the fight against slavery and would have been a leading force in both the moral and legal struggle for equal rights in the years after the war, save for a compromise of principle in the pursuit of ambition that destroyed his credibility on matters of race. Chase was replaced by Morrison Waite who had no judicial experience and who had never practiced before the Supreme Court. Among his new colleagues was justice Joseph Bradley, a man of enormous intellectual prowess, predisposed to taking a dim view of those less well endowed. He would later make contemptuous comments regarding the modest gifts of Waite's successor as chief justice, Melville Fuller, but sought in public to ingratiate himself with Fuller and bring Fuller under his influence as he done, successfully, with Waite.

Waite's legal experience lay entirely in the areas of business and commercial law. As the initial pivotal cases dealing with black rights began to come before the Court he admitted a lack of knowledge about the issues and came to lean heavily on Bradley. Later, in another context, he acknowledged Bradley's influence on his thinking. Although the purported author of the 1876 *Reese* and *Cruikshank* holdings, key cases eviscerating post–Civil War laws intended to support black rights, he was not their intellectual sire. His colleagues had sought to lend the holdings the weight of the chief justice's office. As is indicated in chapter 3, his *Cruikshank* holding, undermining federal efforts to protect blacks from mob violence, closely tracked Bradley's circuit court opinion, but he still had to be reminded while drafting the holding to cite relevant precedent cases, and owned up to the fact that he was not used to citing cases.

Bradley was the driving intellectual force behind the Court's key reconstruction era holdings, his influence being yielded by three factors. Under the procedures of the time he sat part of the year as a circuit court judge in the gulf states of the defeated confederacy, the source of many of the key cases. In that role he formulated a legal opinion regarding the issues presented by the pivotal case, *Cruikshank*, before the case reached the Supreme Court. Second, he was a person of great intellectual force and apparent interpersonal charm when the occasion demanded, able to bring his colleagues along on key issues. And third, none of his colleagues, following the death of Salmon Chase, had a career intertwined with the struggle for black rights. In other words, there was no counter weight to Bradley, no one of equal force and conviction able to play the role that Charles Evans Hughes was to play decades later as associate justice and chief justice in winning colleagues to a set of legal doctrines crucial to collapsing the legal underpinnings of state-mandated racial segregation.

Just as the dynamics of the Court as small group play a role in the process whereby holdings are yielded, so also do the underlying views, sentiments, and fears of the justices. It is not entirely possible to separate Bradley's views as Supreme Court justice on the legal issues regarding federalism and the relative balance of power between the federal government and the states in matters of racial redress from his views as citizen on the substantive matter of race. In addition to illuminating his thinking on legal matters Bradley's papers also reflect his private views on matters of race, his views "off stage" as it were. In a letter to fellow judge William Wood, written the same year as the *Reese* decision eroding federal efforts to protect black voting rights, Bradley damned the new federal law prohibiting racial discrimination in public accommodations as imposing "another kind of slavery" on whites. Racial hostility was innate and the law could do nothing to eradicate it: "Does freedom of the black require the slavery of the whites?"[21] Eight years after writing the letter he wrote the Supreme Court opinion declaring the public accommodations law unconstitutional.

Bradley's views, personality, and influence on the Court as regards race and rights are discussed at length in chapter 3, but in his first year on the Court he had plainly and honestly recognized the implication of the majority holding in Blyew and had expressed his views in a dissenting opinion. There was however a deeper, more visceral and negative reaction to Afro-Americans that inescapably became part of his jurisprudence.

Bradley is being used here for illustrative purposes. He illustrates the point but is not, alone, the point. The intertwining of personal views and racial jurisprudence was also a factor with other justices, including, for example, David Brewer, one of the justices in the *Plessy* majority. Many years after *Plessy*, Brewer had occasion to enlarge on his views on race. He observed that most whites viewed blacks as inherently inferior in morals and intellect. In his view, however, it was impossible to determine whether their degraded condition was do to environmental factors or to innate deficiencies. Perhaps in some far distant age they might achieve the same level of civilization as whites. On the other hand, perhaps nature had deprived them of the capacity to rise much above their present debased circumstance. Either way, it was duty of whites to show Christian compassion. Interpersonal abuse of blacks ought to be avoided and support given to those organizations devoted to teaching blacks elementary skills and the rudiments of civilized behavior.[22]

Brewer's fundamental assumptions about race reflected a kind of brutal paternalism. On the one hand, the stern discipline of the lyncher's rope was rejected, but on the other hand the collective degradation of blacks was taken for granted. Christian charity might incline one toward offering a bit of help but surely the law could not, in the words of *Plessy*, compel equal treatment for entities fundamentally unequal.

As a small group the Court is subject potentially to having the interpersonal relations and personality characteristics of the justices play a role in the deliberation process. Clearly, it would be specious to contend that these factors are determinative, but at crucial times, and in crucial ways they may be important. A Bradley, capable and committed but driven by personal visions of racial intrusion, may be able to bring along a majority, less knowledgeable, less committed, whose center of judicial interests lay elsewhere. A Charles Evans Hughes, capable and committed, moved by a vision of racial fairness, was able to bring along a less committed majority, even in a larger social environment committed to racial subordination. A Fred Vinson, lacking in small-group interpersonal skills, confronting the cases that became *Brown v. Board* was unable to move a divided court to a resolution, whereas his successor as chief justice, the more interpersonally skilled Earl Warren, who had never sat a day in his life as a judge anywhere before becoming chief justice, was able to move a potentially divided Court to a consensus on one of the most important issues to come before it in its history.

In short, the view of the Court taken in this book rests, in part, on the assumption that the kinds of analysis brought to bear in the examination of small groups provides insight into the dynamics of the Court. The peculiarities of one member may affect the dynamics of the Court as a whole and the outcomes on cases. The racial views of the arch-segregationist James Clark McReynolds, appointed to the Court in 1914, were certainly closer to the views of the general public than those of Louis Brandeis, the first Jewish member of the Court appointed two years later. McReynolds however was, personally, a very nasty character, interpersonally abusive and insulting. On a nine-person body, with opinion sharply divided on a number of issues, and with the capacity to put together five-vote majority coalitions being very important, McReynolds's interpersonally unpleasant demeanor rendered him less than optimally effective in a number of key race cases that came before the Court during his twenty-seven years on the bench.

Implicit in a view of the Court as a small group in a sociological sense is a view of its history as indeterminant but not capricious. The view of Court's history as indeterminant is close to professor Richard Delgado's articulation regarding "the relative autonomy of law," which "refers to a description of law as connected to but not wholly dependent upon historical, economical and political realities."[23] In the approach taken here the Supreme Court is connected to but not wholly dependent upon historical, economic, or political realities. Analytic approaches that view its holdings as merely reflective of the influence of political or social elites or of the prevailing cultural ethos inadequately account for its decisions in the area of race. In that sense the history of the Court is indeterminant.

On the other hand, neither were the Court's holdings yielded by the influence of "great men." In that sense its history is not capricious. It constitutional role, the lifetime tenure of the justices, and its small size allow for interpersonal factors to influence outcomes, but those outcomes can occur only within certain limits, as determined by the larger social environment and by the canons of legal analysis. Thus, a *Brown* holding could not have occurred in 1914. Neither the social nor the legal foundation existed for it, but on the other hand, it did not have to occur in 1954. As is indicated in chapter 8, at various times a split decision was possible, for or against "separate but equal." An equivocal outcome would have sustained the moral legitimacy of legal segregation with dire consequences for the long-term struggle for black rights. The unanimous decision finally handed down was yielded by what transpired in an interpersonal sense between the Chief Justice Earl Warren and his colleagues.

The history of the Court as regards race and rights is, in part, its history as a small group. The discussion reflects that premise. The discussion also reflects the premise that the history of the Court on race and rights cannot be understood without a grasp of how the actions of the Court in each era were viewed by black and white Americans *at that time*.

The Court as Seen by the Actors

The history of the Court as regards race and rights was emergent and, within limits, unpredictable. Subsequent events were yielded by the way in which people responded to prior events. Understanding the impact of the Court on social institutions, values, and behavior entails understanding what its work meant at the time to the those most immediately affected. Their responses determined what would happen next. In addition to providing a chronicle of events, this work seeks to convey a subjective sense of how events were experienced as they occurred, particularly by blacks.

The sense of how matters were experienced at the time contributes to an understanding of the role and impact of the Court. Two examples will suffice. Although *Plessy v. Ferguson* looms much larger in historical retrospect than the *Civil Rights Cases of 1883*, the *Civil Rights Cases* outcome was immediately experienced by blacks as much more of a horrendous blow and grievous wound than was *Plessy*, and carried considerably more immediate meaning to whites nationally than *Plessy*. The holding in the *Civil Rights Cases* came down in mid-October of 1883 and, in effect, sanctioned the reading of blacks out of civil society by finding the public accommodations provisions of the Civil Rights Act of 1875 to be unconstitutional. The outcry of blacks and their white allies was immediate and pained. Thousands met in Washington to hear Frederick Douglass and others denounce the holding.[24] The *North Carolina Republican* and other black newspapers carried denunciations. White-owned papers, including the *New York Times*, offered mostly approving commentary. Speaking to a mixed audience in an Indiana Baptist Church, future president Benjamin Harrison held out hope that perhaps state legislatures would undo the evil wrought by the Supreme Court. By contrast *Plessy* drew little press attention at the time it was handed down. Days passed before the *New York Times* carried a small notice. No rallies were held to denounce it nor did politicians offer solace to blacks.

Preceding *Plessy* by thirteen years, the *Civil Rights Cases* had greater meaning to blacks and whites living through those times. It was experienced by blacks as a brutal repudiation of their hope for eventual equal treatment and by many whites as a Court-sanctioned affirmation of the impulse to push blacks to the margins of civil life. It was understood by both to mean a final repudiation of the commitment to a equal rights and status implicit in the reconstruction laws. The only serious question remaining was the formal terms of black subordination.

Plessy codified those terms for a generation that had already seen the Court destroy the edifice of legal protection for black rights erected in the first decade after the war. As is indicated in chapter 4, *Plessy* was entered into by its minority plaintiffs not without hope, but defeat of those hopes at the hands of the Court was experienced with a degree of resignation not shown thirteen years earlier in reaction to the *Civil Rights Cases*. Indeed, in the year *Plessy* was handed down Booker T. Washington delivered his famous Atlanta Cotton Exposition speech calling upon blacks to accept exclusion and subordination as realities and to attempt to achieve within the limits imposed by those realities. In effect, he was calling upon blacks to adjust to the kind of world the Court had sanctioned.

The kind of demoralization occasioned by the Court's systematic destruction of reconstruction protection for blacks reflected in the muted response to *Plessy* did not begin to lift until a new generation of blacks came on the political stage around the turn of the century. As is well known, W. E. B. DuBois, Ida B. Wells, Monroe Work, Monroe Trotter, and other blacks of this generation were instrumental in founding the National Association for the Advancement of Colored People in a climate in which its repudiation of the legitimacy of racial segregation and subordination ran counter to conventional wisdom and legal realities.

Numerous organizations pursuing racial justice had come and gone throughout the history of the black struggle in the United States and there was, therefore, nothing inevitable about the survival of the NAACP. The organization received a tremendous boost from the reaction at the time to the outcome of one of the first cases it pressed before the Supreme Court, *Buchanan v. Warley*, looked at from a different angle earlier in this chapter. Legal historians who discuss *Buchanan v. Warley* tend to treat it in nonracial terms as a case dealing primarily with the right to contract. It was viewed at the time by both blacks and whites as a case dealing with race, having significant consequences with regard to relations between the races.

As is indicated in chapter 5, a year after the founding of the NAACP a movement began in Baltimore for the creation by law of black zones and white zones and spread rapidly to other cities. These were apartheid laws which would have restricted blacks *by law* to certain areas. As was also indicated, they derived from the fact that the basic premise on which *Plessy's* separate but equal doctrine rested had no inherent limit with regard to the extent, scope, and degree of racial separation and subordination.

The facts of the case are rather complicated but the 1917 Court decision declaring these kinds of laws to be unconstitutional occasioned as much joy and relief in black communities across the nation as the *Civil Rights Cases* decisions had occasioned grief thirty-four years earlier. As is indicated in chapter 5, the decision gave a boost to the new civil rights organization, affirming its effectiveness and the legitimacy of its strategy.

Cases had meaning to black people at the time that they were decided. Outcomes were either demoralizing or impelled further challenge to racial subordination. An aspect of understanding the history of the Court as regards race and rights entails understanding what the Court's behavior meant at the time to the actors most immediately impacted.

Viewing the Court from the standpoint of blacks also raises fundamental questions about traditional views of judicial stature. One example will suffice. Oliver Wendall Holmes is by traditional consensus the greatest jurist ever to sit on the Court. In his early years on the Court at the turn of the century, however, he put his formidable intellect to work in the service of racial subordination. In his middle years of service he resisted the efforts of Chief Justice and exconfederate soldier Edward Douglass White to put together a majority repudiating the apartheid laws at stake in *Buchanan v. Warley*, possibly threatening at one point to be the lone dissenter. Only in his later years did he seem to be inclined to an interpretation of the Constitution that took into account the grim realities of racial segregation.

Far more important and effective from the standpoint of the black claim to civil rights and equal treatment was Charles Evans Hughes. A celebrated figure in his time, Hughes served on the bench twice and was Holmes's colleague. In contrast to Holmes, Hughes put his considerable intellect to work persuading his colleagues that the Constitution conferred rights on individuals and not groups and that a railroad or a university could not deny access to the individual black on the grounds that overall black demand was not great enough to justify the provision of separate facilities. First articulated by Hughes in 1915 in his first term on the Court, he returned to this doctrine more than twenty years later in the *Gaines* case invalidating Missouri's exclusion of Lloyd Gaines from the state law school and refusal to create a law school for blacks given low demand. The implication of Hughes's formulation was crucial to Thurgood Marshall and the Legal Defense Fund as it pursued the struggle to collapse "separate but equal."

Joseph Bradley also shows up on lists of the most outstanding justices ever to sit on the Court.[25] The unquestioned stature accorded Holmes, Bradley, and some of the other justices who graced the bench between the Reconstruction period and *Brown* highlights the importance of the argument offered by Critical Race Theory: An understanding of law and legal institutions entails taking the perspective of those whose voices are not normally heard. The discussion of the Supreme Court and civil rights undertaken here incorporates the experience and perspective of Afro-Americans and, hence, yields a somewhat different sense of the justices and of the social and political functions of law.

How the Book is Organized

Chapter 2 of this work, "The Meaning of Freedom," focuses on the ten-year period between the end of the Civil War and the presidential election of 1876. The final collapse of the Confederacy came on April 9, 1865, with the surrender of Robert E. Lee and the remnants of the Army of Northern Virginia at Appomattox Court House. It did not follow however, either as a matter of law or in the popular mind that the newly freed slave minority enjoyed the same rights as the white majority. Some commentators advocated resettlement of blacks outside the United States. Others argued that full rights of citizenship and access to the ballot should be afforded selectively, perhaps to blacks who had served in the Union army, and to a few others of demonstrated accomplishment. Only a minority of whites, some of whom were in Congress, urged full and equal rights of citizenship for all blacks. In short, at the end of the

Civil War there was no consensus on what "freedom" meant relative to the nation's black population. Through a set of contingent and extraordinary circumstances, reviewed in the chapter, the views of the egalitarian Congressional minority came to be translated into law.

In their nature the new laws and amendments involved greater federal oversight of state affairs than had been previously viewed as proper. Federal protection of black interests from state abuse implied redefining the relationship between the federal government and the states. It also entailed defining the nature of citizenship. Could federal intervention be sought for any type of race-based disability or abuse or was a black protected only in certain spheres of activity? The language of the new laws masked a deep national ambivalence regarding race and rights. There was sharp and often violent disagreement as to the meaning of "freedom." There was no historical inevitability in terms of how the national ambivalence was to be resolved. The Supreme Court was to play a pivotal role in establishing the direction in which the nation moved.

Chapter 3 examines the six-year span in which the first civil rights cases were to come before the Court. The composition of the Court was new and the cases were without precedent, involving as they did, challenges to recently passed statutes intended to make blacks full and equal citizens of the United States. As previously indicated, protection of the rights of black citizens in the states of the defeated confederacy required greater federal involvement in state affairs than an adherence to the principles of federalism would have traditionally allowed. The Union victory in the war had settled the question as to whether a state could leave the union but had not, in its nature, expanded federal authority relative to matters traditionally left to the states, such as the prosecution of felons in ordinary criminal matters, even if those felons happened to be Klansmen terrorizing freedmen.

At the legal level the Courts holdings on a number of issues posed by the initial civil rights cases established precedent. They established the legal framework within which subsequent issues of race and rights were resolved. At the immediate political level they had the effect of undermining federal prosecution of antiblack terrorists. They also played a role in creating a political climate in which expedience dictated reconciliation with the South on the part of political factions in the Republican Party previously supportive of civil rights efforts. This chapter examines both the dynamics of the Court as it moved to formulate a way of reading the Constitution in relation to issues of race and rights, and discusses the role of black political and social groups in making the Court a forum for the pursuit of rights.

Chapter 4 focuses on the period from the end of Reconstruction and the rise of so-called redemption governments in the South through the turn of the century. The limits that the Court had put on federal efforts to protect black rights and status yielded to the redemptionist governments the opportunity to draft legislation intended to define the place of blacks at the state level. In effect, this legislation addressed the question, If not slavery, what? The Amendments and laws of the first decade after the war had said "full rights of citizenship." In a series of holdings the Supreme Court had eroded the capacity of the new laws to realize that objective. A subsequent series of decisions by the Court affirmed the constitutionality of state laws making distinctions on the basis of race. These holdings reconciled the egalitarian language of the Constitution to the reality of state-mandated racial differentiation by finding such distinctions were rationally related to the legitimate state objective of maintaining racial peace.

The legal premise on which state-mandated segregation rested had no inherent limit, and in the first decades of the twentieth century state and local government in the South and outside the South moved to limit and marginalize black status through ever more encompassing segregationist laws. There was no sphere of public life not subject to racial regulation and when Baltimore in 1910 passed a law creating black zones and white zones the move toward literal apartheid was initiated, there being nothing in the legal logic supporting segregation inconsistent with a pass system relative to blacks being outside their zone at "inappropriate" times. Chapter 5 examines this era. Again, there was no historical inevitability in the Court's holdings in a series of cases that, while not challenging the underlying logic of segregation, had the practical consequence of setting some limits to its expansion. The importance of the holdings of the Edward Douglass White court were recognized at the time by the parties involved, including a new organization called the National Association for the Advancement of Colored People, arguing its first cases before the Court. Again, the political and social context of the Court's action are examined, as is the dynamics of interaction on the Court itself.

Chapter 6 examines what might be termed "the golden age of segregation," the decade of the 1920s. The national consensus on its desirability and the acceptance in jurisprudence of its legal premises was so great that relatively few civil rights cases came before the Court. Attention is given to the cultural and normative assumptions of America in the 1920s insofar as they lent an air of permanency to segregation. Important events were transpiring off stage, so to speak, as the NAACP began to evolve and mature as an organization and as a framework for court-based challenge to legal segregation began to germinate. Attention is given to three cases involving orientals, *Toyota, Ozawaa,* and *Gong Lum* in which the Supreme Court reaffirmed the racial character of national identity; and to the *Nixon* case out of Texas, which turned back another state effort to write racial exclusion into its electoral laws. In his last decade on the Court and past eighty years of age, Oliver Wendall Holmes began to evolve on matters of race, but too late for this otherwise towering figure to have an effect on racial jurisprudence.

Chapter 7 focuses on a series of cases that began to change both the national consensus on segregation and the Supreme Court's interpretation of its own precedents with regard to race and rights. The "Scottsboro Case" was really a series of cases that spanned the decade of the 1930s. National and international protest developed in response to Alabama's efforts to execute six black teenagers on dubious rape charges, signaling the beginning of a change in the political climate within which the Court addressed high-profile race cases. The role of the Court in the 1930s on race cannot be understood apart from grasping the context. The depression and the New Deal wrought change in some fundamental national assumptions regarding the relationship between the federal government and the states. The misery generated by the collapse of the economy created widespread acceptance of the notion that the federal government could and should play an expanded role in shoring up the economy and in protecting working people. The reluctance of the Supreme Court to acknowledge these realities generated controversy and led to the so-called court packing scheme as Franklin Roosevelt sought to get a bench more sympathetic to his policies. The scheme failed but resolution of that crisis yielded an opportunity to Roosevelt to begin to change the composition of Court.

Although made for other reasons, the Roosevelt appointments were also crucial with regard to the reformulation of the law as regards race and rights. Ironically Alabama Senator Hugo Black, the first Roosevelt nominee, was attacked in the press as a former Klansman but had carried on a private correspondence with

NAACP secretary Walter White, showing racial sympathies which, had they been known to his constituents, would probably have led to his defeat at the polls.

Under the leadership of Charles Evans Hughes the Court began to take what Professor Philip Bobbitt would term a "prudential" approach to some of the race cases coming before it, balancing the costs and benefits in the real world of following the rules of segregation. Again, the efforts of black organizations to impact on the justices' frames of reference and the dynamics of interaction among them are examined.

Chapter 8 focuses on the decade and the struggles in and out of court leading up to *Brown*. An evolving set of circumstances began to change the cultural and political environments within which the Court addressed issues of race. Nazism's lethal racism cast a shadow of moral doubt over all espousals of racial superiority. As the cold war developed following the defeat of Hitler, segregation laws and practice placed the United States on the defensive in its contest with the Soviet Union to secure the allegiance of the mostly nonwhite nations coming into existence with the collapse of colonialism. The Court itself began to move away from a kind of formalist approach to racial jurisprudence and to take into account the brutal realities attending social systems defended on *Plessy* grounds. Building on the logic and implications of Hughes's *Gaines* holding, the NAACP began to mount a series of challenges to legal segregation. Initially the issue was framed in terms of a state failure to make separate truly equal, particularly at the level of graduate and professional education. And if, for practical reasons that was not feasible, admit blacks to hitherto closed institutions.

Chapter 9 focuses on the complex of cases which became *Brown*. Although the holding bears the name of the Kansas plaintiffs, the case, posing the more fundamental challenge with regard to the tenacity of segregationist resistance in every form and at all levels, came out of Clarendon County, South Carolina. In the face of the enormity of the issues Chief Justice Fred Vinson wavered, unable to articulate a clear view himself, unable to mobilize his colleagues, likely in the end to have abided a split decision. His replacement, nominated and taking his seat as acting chief justice within a matter of days, Earl Warren had not sat a single day as a judge in any court. An ex-district attorney, attorney general, and sitting governor at the time of his nomination, he had neither judicial experience nor a reputation as an intellectual given to pondering weighty constitutional issues. He brought enormous interpersonal skills to the post, however, along with a clear sense of direction. The issue seemed to him uncomplicated. Brutal realities established the bankrupt nature of a judicial doctrine which had hitherto justified legal segregation in elementary and secondary education.

Chapter 10 examines the legacy of *Brown* in terms of continuity and change. In the immediate aftermath of *Brown* the Court wrestled with school desegregation cases and tenacious resistance to dismantling dual school systems. A new set of issues came before the Court with the passage of the Civil Rights Act of 1964. The Act prohibited discrimination in employment, education, the operation of public accommodations, and in the disbursement of federal monies. Within a few years of its passage it became obvious that a legal bar to overt discrimination left in place the accumulated racial advantages yielded by discrimination.

Chapter 10 also details how a series of policies going under the general heading "affirmative action" came into existence to deal with this reality. The chapter also deals with continuity between the pre-*Brown* and the post-*Brown* Courts in terms of the modes of analysis brought to bear in resolving the challenges posed to the constitutionality of affirmative action policies, and in confronting the ongoing reality of racially segregated school systems.

Specifically, a number of holdings of the Rehnquesit Court are subjected to close scrutiny. Continuity is drawn between the Rehnquist court in the post-*Brown* era and the Bradley-Waite-Fuller Courts in the Reconstruction and post-Reconstruction eras. Formalist analysis characterizes the approach of both to issues of race and rights. Paraphrasing John Marshall Harlan's dissent to Joseph Bradley's majority holding in the *Civil Rights Cases of 1883* striking down the federal law barring discrimination in public accommodations, a kind of ingenious verbalism allows evasion of consideration of the underlying reality of systematic, racial discrimination. As is indicated in the analysis of the Rehnquist Courts' holding in *Croson*, written by Sandra Day O'Connor, formalism is ahistorical. Both the Rehnquist Court and the various Bradley-influenced Courts approach the claims of black plaintiffs as if racial discrimination were a thing of the past, with little or no ongoing impact or consequence. Given that premise, claims for relief became a kind of special pleading, an attempt to acquire an unwarranted advatantage over innocent white citizens.

The premise of this book is that the Court has played a significant role in making the world of race in the United States and, therefore, in the making of the United States. The dynamics of race have been central to the American experience, and the holdings of the Suprme Court have been central to the shaping of that dynamic. The fate of the Ameircan experiment may be determined by the dynamics of race. Chapter 10 focuses on continuity between the past and the future, on the premise that an understanding of the past may yield a greater capacity to shape the future.

Tuesday, November 1, 1864, was an unusually quiet day on the various battlefields. The war was in its third year, but slowly and inexorably the balance was turning in favor of the North. In Maryland voters went to the polls that Tuesday to ratify a state constitution outlawing slavery. It had been one of the anomalies of the war situation that slavery had been legal in some of the states and territories that had not joined the Confederacy in rebellion. Lincoln's Emancipation Proclamation read on January 1, 1863, had freed slaves only in the states then in rebellion. As a state not formally in rebellion Maryland had not been affected by the Emancipation Proclamation and hence had legally retained slavery for almost two years. The vote on November 1st had been very close, some parties believing that the initiative would have failed but for the ballots collected from Maryland servicemen in the Union Army.

On November 3, 1864, the newly freed blacks of Talbot County were gathered together by Philomon T. Hambleton and other now former slave holders for purposes of which later court proceedings made clear. Among the blacks assembled by their former masters was eight-year-old Elizabeth Turner and her mother, both owned by P. T. Hambleton until the vote two days earlier barring slavery in the state. As did the other former masters, Hambleton prevailed upon his erstwhile charges to affix their marks to a document establishing a new relationship. Elizabeth Turner was to be bound over to Hambleton as an apprentice until she was eighteen years of age. Her mother was to be paid ten dollars eight years later and Elizabeth herself fifteen dollars at the end of her apprenticeship ten years later. There was a state law involving the apprenticing of white children requiring authorization of the relationship by a county orphan's court and obliging the master to provide certain benefits for the apprentice, including instruction in reading writing, and arithmetic. The document marked by Elizabeth Turner and her mother held Hambleton to no obligation save the payment of a few dollars many years later.

On April 9, 1866, the Civil Rights Act of 1866 was passed and shortly thereafter suit was brought against Philoman T. Hambleton by Elizabeth Turner's mother who had sought the return of her daughter, and the case was heard by Supreme Court Justice Salmon P. Chase sitting as a circuit court judge. Hambleton had been advised at the time that the new law was passed that it did not affect him, that he had a valid contract binding Elizabeth Turner to his service. As the case was joined and argument invited he refused, despite Chase's urging, to appear and submit himself to the jurisdiction of the Court. Nevertheless, on October 13, 1867, Chase handed down his opinion. The recently ratified Thirteenth Amendment barred involuntary servitude. Without question, "The alleged apprenticeship in the present case is involuntary servitude, within the meaning of the words in the amendment."

In addition, the new Civil Rights Act assured "to all citizens without regard to race or color, full and equal benefit of all laws and proceedings for the security of persons and property as is enjoyed by white citizens."[26]

The case went no further. Elizabeth Turner and all similarly bound "apprentices" were no longer bound.

Just over a year later John Blyew and George Kennard set out for Laura Foster's cabin, setting in motion the events which were to bring another test of the Civil Rights Act of 1866 and provide the Supreme Court with its first opportunity to define the meaning of freedom for blacks in the new United States.

Chapter 2

◁◇▷

The Meaning of Freedom

On Wednesday, February 1, 1865, General William Tecumsah Sherman began his long-awaited invasion of South Carolina. Union troops of the 15th and 17th Corps, veterans of the long and destructive march through Georgia, moved northward from Savannah in a drive toward Columbia, South Carolina, barely stalled by the resistance of the rebel forces burning bridges and felling trees across the roads in a futile attempt to slow the Northern onslaught.

To the north, Ulysses S. Grant's troops moved into position for the final assault on Richmond, the remnants of Robert E. Lee's Army of Northern Virginia being all that stood between Grant and the rebel capital. Confederate President Jefferson Davis, acknowledging that the situation was desperate, accepted the resignation of his Secretary of War James Haddon, and sent a message to veteran commander P. T. Beauregard to rally the remaining rebel forces in the lower South for the coming decisive battles. On the same day, far from the front, Illinois became the first state to ratify the Thirteenth Amendment, abolishing slavery. Other state legislatures followed in quick succession, eight having voted ratification by the time Sherman's army reached the shattered outskirts of Columbia, South Carolina on February 17th.[1]

In the year and a half since Gettysburg a shadow had fallen across Confederate fortunes. In that distant earlier summer of 1863 the Confederacy had reached its high tide. Union armies had crumpled at Fredricksburg. Lee and his Army of Northern Virginia had taken the war into the North, invading Pennsylvania, causing panic as the roads filled with civilians fleeing before the rebel tide. A victory on Northern soil—a massive decisive victory—might bring recognition by a European power, transforming the armed upstarts into a nation among nations.

In the three days of Gettysburg more than eight thousand rebel troops died. The seventeen-mile-long wagon train carrying Lee's broken army back to Virginia also carried the final hope of a southern victory on the battle field. The only remaining chance for survival lay in prolonging the struggle, battle to battle, hoping to break the will of the north to continue to fight. But Abraham Lincoln's defeat of his accommodation-minded opponent, George Brinton McClelland, in the presidential election of November 1864 ended that dream.

Thus, as spring came in 1865 and the willows bloomed in Richmond, the Confederacy was dying. As Sherman's troops entered Columbia and Grant's army advanced on Richmond the fate of the Confederacy was no longer in doubt. One of the two great issues of the war was about to be settled. The union was indivisible, states could not secede. Federalism allowed for a high degree of state autonomy, but only within the framework of a single nation state. The other great issue had not been settled, save only in one sense. Involuntary servitude—slavery—was to be abolished by constitutional amendment, but even that had been a matter of dispute. It had taken months to achieve the necessary votes in Congress in support of an amendment to abolish human bondage once and for all.

Passed by the Senate on April 8, 1864, the proposed Thirteenth Amendment to the Constitution would have abolished involuntary servitude and given Congress the power to enforce its terms by appropriate legislation. Two months later the House of Representatives failed to provide the two-thirds vote necessary to send the Amendment on to the states for ratification. Made the subject of a renewed appeal by President Lincoln in his annual message to Congress on December 6, 1864, the new amendment finally gained House approval on January 31, 1865.

Passage of the Thirteenth Amendment by Congress and its move toward ratification by the states reflected neither widespread belief in equal rights for black people nor repudiation of the view that they were an alien and inferior group. Joined by some Republicans, the Democratic Party minority in the House of Representatives had fought bitterly against Congressional approval. New York Democrat Fernando Wood had denounced it as "an imperious dogma . . . opposed to the fundamental aims and ends of the Constitution,"[2] while Pennsylvania Republican, William Kelley, had refused to deny the moral legitimacy of slavery, "All who know anything of the negro character know this to be true. Sudden freedom to the negro, without the capacity to appreciate and improve it, has proved not a blessing but a curse."[3]

The view that slavery was morally legitimate led Kelley to demand compensation for slave owners, were their "property" to be taken from them. "If the public good really demands that the slaveowners of the South should surrender their slave property, is there any principle of constitutional freedom or of public justice that justifies the demand for that surrender without making adequate compensation?"[4]

Although the Thirteenth Amendment abolished slavery it did not follow either as a matter of law or in the minds of many of its supporters that black people therefore enjoyed the same political, civil, and social rights as the majority white population. None of the Northern states provided free blacks with legal protection against racial discrimination, and in the wake of the war only Massachusetts moved to do so by adopting a law in May of 1865 prohibiting color discrimination in inns, parks, and other public accommodations.

Final ratification of the Thirteenth Amendment had not yet occurred when Robert E. Lee sent word to Jefferson Davis in Richmond on Sunday morning April 9, 1865, that the front could no longer be held. Within a week Davis was in flight, Richmond was in flames, and Lee had surrendered to Grant at Appomattox Courthouse. By the time New Hampshire voted ratification on July 1, 1865, Jefferson Davis was in the military prison at Fort Monroe, Virginia, and the war was over.

The collapse of the Confederacy and the freeing of more than three million blacks sharpened the debate regarding their legal status and political fate. There had never been a consensus in the North with regard to black rights nor did victory yield widespread support for the belief that blacks should enjoy the same rights as whites. Indeed, there had been fear expressed that the practical consequence of the Emancipation Proclamation of January 1, 1863, freeing slaves in the states still in rebellion would be that "the whole of the Northern States would be overrun by negroes from the South." To avoid this possible "calamity" Congress had appropriated six hundred thousand dollars to transport blacks "to the West Indies or to any other place, so long as it was beyond the borders of this country." And indeed one boatload of blacks was sent from Fort Monroe to Haiti.[5]

In the months following the defeat of the rebels there was substantial agreement that slavery was dead, but little accord on the meaning of freedom in terms of the rights of the newly freed population. Only a minority of whites subscribed to the notion that blacks and whites should have the *same* rights, the majority, North and South, repudiated such an idea. Some rejected the notion as ridiculous on its face given the presumed racial inferiority of blacks, others doubted that Congress had the power under the constitution to bring about legal equality between the races, even if such a situation was desirable. In other words, two powerful ideas—racism and federalism—intersected to obscure the meaning of freedom in terms of the newly freed population.

It is a truism in law that not every wrong has a legal remedy. It did not follow in the months after the war ended that the denial of the ballot to blacks, their exclusion from places of public accommodation, or their restriction to the margins of the economy were wrongs yielding a legal basis for redress. The myriad strictures placed on black status and life chances were objectionable from the standpoint of blacks and their reform-minded allies, but they were neither illegal nor unconstitutional.

Redress from civil wrongs requires the existence of statutorily conferred rights, the enactment of a body of law affirming that the aggrieved party has a legally cognizable right. The exact contours of those rights and, indeed, the constitutional status of such laws themselves is a function of court interpretation, and ultimately of the United States Supreme Court.

As the guns of April fell silent, blacks did not have legal rights; hence, the struggle over the meaning of freedom was joined early on after the end of the war. Despite a political and social climate that was only intermittently hospitable, the decade following the end of the Civil War witnessed a remarkable body of legislation being put into place, including the Civil Rights Act of 1866, the Fourteenth Amendment, the Fifteenth Amendment, the anti-Klan Enforcement Acts, and the Civil Rights Act of 1875. Save for the Civil Rights Act of 1875, parts of which were found unconstitutional by the Supreme Court in 1883, this legislation provided the constitutional framework for the decades long black resistance to caste-like subordination and is, along with the Civil Rights Act of

1964, the principal legislative vehicle for the continuing black struggle at the end of the twentieth century.

This chapter examines the processes by which this body of legislation came into existence, the statutes providing the framework within which the Supreme Court addressed and continues to address issues of black rights. An understanding of the political struggles and social dynamics yielding this body of law is a necessary backdrop to understanding how different courts and different justices dealt with the issue of race and rights.

That the laws came into existence at all is remarkable given the absence of widespread support for the idea of black equality. Hence, a review of the genesis of this remarkable body of legislation is, perforce, a discussion of political struggle between factions having fundamentally different visions of the place of blacks in American society, the Supreme Court coming early to determine which vision was to be honored.

Crucial to an understanding of how the status of blacks evolved in the period after the war, and of how "civil rights" came to be defined by the law and the Supreme Court, is an understanding of the intellectual climate within which the struggle over black fate took place. What beliefs did a majority of the white citizenry hold? What "truths" were taken as self-evident? What body of law, if any, would be put in place redefining black status? What balance would those laws strike between racial reform and federalist principles?

Racism and a belief in the principles of federalism were significant parts of the mental, emotional, and political environment within which the struggle to define freedom unfolded. A grasp of the subjective meaning of each in the context of the times is crucial to understanding how the fundamental civil rights laws addressed by the Supreme Court evolved, including their vast goals with regard to transformation of the meaning of race in the United States and their significant limitations and compromises.

A feel for the meaning of race and federalism at the end of the war can be facilitated by stepping back a decade or so before the war's onset in order to grasp what they meant as the struggle approached. Slavery rested, in part, on certain widely held assumptions about race. While many of those who entertained notions of black inferiority held back from the actual ownership of slaves, people who chose to own and trade in human property were not held in disrepute. An incident widely reported at the time speaks to the norms and outlook regarding race as the war approached.

Race and the Meaning of Freedom

Early in 1853, shortly after the inauguration of a new administration in Washington, D.C., the vice president's barber, a slave named Jackson, escaped. A native of Alabama, a plantation owner and a slave holder, the vice president, William Rufus DeVane King, had brought Jackson to Washington with him, but within days Jackson bolted for freedom. The details attending the pursuit and recapture of the vice president's slave reflect the meaning of race in the United States for the people who fought the Civil War and made policy in its aftermath.

Jackson fled to Ohio, a nonslave state, and sought to lose himself among Cincinnati's population of free blacks. Neither Ohio nor any other nonslave states provided equal rights for free blacks. Ohio denied the vote to its citizens of color and provided taxpayer-supported schools for white children but not black, but from the perspective of the fugitive it was at least a state in which he was not chattel.

The momentary ambivalence regarding slavery which had characterized the generation that had fought and won freedom from England had hardened by Vice President King's generation into a firm devotion to slavery, supported by a fervent belief in the inferiority of people of African descent. Antiblack ideology, advanced initially to mask self-interest, had come to be championed as objective truth. In the decade preceding the war, supporters of the "peculiar institution" put pen to paper in considerable numbers in its defense. Blacks were descendants of Ham, cursed by God for all time to atone by servitude for Ham's sin of dishonoring his father. Aristotle and other fountains of classical learning regarded slavery as natural and as reflective of differences in the quality of human stock. And the new sciences of ethnography and anthropology suggested that black people were mired in the swamp of barbarism, perhaps deprived by nature of the capacity to develop a higher civilization.

The laws and social restrictions reflected popular sentiment. Blacks in general were the objects of popular contempt and animus. Free blacks were constrained to the margins of society politically, economically, and socially, neither slave nor free. It was neither surprising or unusual therefore that Jackson's pursuers ignored even the minimal due process considerations which attended the apprehension of possible runaway slaves.

Having tracked Jackson to Cincinnati the vice president's

agent resolved to seize him without obtaining a writ as was required by law. A band of armed ruffians was hired and a ferry boat chartered to carry the fugitive across the river to a slave state, Kentucky. At about noon on the appointed day Jackson was seized by the gang and dragged through the streets toward the wharf and the waiting ferry, putting up a fierce struggle and calling for help along the way. A contemporary report indicated that local peace officers "who were generally on the side of the slave holders remained out of sight." An attempt by Thomas Franklin, a Quaker, to affect a rescue failed and the hapless Jackson was bundled aboard the ferry and taken across the river back to slave soil.

Slavery was a southern phenomenon, but the sentiment which abetted the recapture of the vice president's slave animated much of northern behavior with regard to race. There was no necessary desire to see slavery spread but, on the other hand, in the view of many in the North, blacks were a despised group, made unfit by nature and history for civil society. Daily occurrences reflected this reality. At about the time that Jackson was in flight from the vice president's agents, Prudence Crandall, a Connecticut woman of progressive sympathies, was fined by the town of Canterbury for opening her school to black children as well as white and when she remonstrated with the town's authorities was threatened with the lash.[7]

In Canaan, New Hampshire, at one end of the continent, white citizens had demolished and then burned an academy that had admitted three black students, while in Sacramento and San Francisco, at the other end, protests were lodged against admitting black children to white schools or providing public dollars for the support of black schools. In New York City Charles Ray, president of the Society for the Promotion of Education Among Colored Children, sought redress from circumstances under which forty times as much was spent in taxpayer dollars per pupil for students attending white schools as was spent for those in the segregated schools black children were compelled to attend.[8]

Iowa and Indiana barred blacks from permanent residence within their borders, while other states required free blacks to post a substantial bond upon entry. Most states denied the vote to free blacks and many barred them from certain occupations or professions or placed special disabilities upon them. In Maryland, for example, any black wishing to become a retail shopkeeper had to produce upon demand a certificate from the local justice of the peace or "three respectable persons residing in the neighborhood of said Negro, of the County in which such Negro resided (affirming) that he or they have reason to believe and does believe that such Free Negro or Mulatto came honestly and bona fide into possession of such article offered for sale."[9]

Slavery and the racial marginalization of the North were more than technical legal arrangements. They were inextricably bound up with notions of race, and ideas about race were an integral part of the nation's definition of self and of the definition of "self" of every white citizen in the nation. The nation and its citizens defined what they were by identifying what they were not. Culture was a part of personality. Save for a small group of abolitionists and Quakers, whites rejected the idea of racial equality, but many also rejected the legitimacy of slavery. The end of slavery as a result of the war did not yield commitment to black freedom, but, instead, posed the question as to what freedom was to mean for the newly freed population. The answer to that question was inextricably bound up with issues of federalism.

Federalism and the Meaning of Freedom

The war did not settle the issue of the power of the federal government relative to that of the states other than to establish that states could not withdraw from the union. Federalism as an idea and a practice had been central to the organization of the new nation. An incapacity to resolve different conceptions of federalism had played a role in the onset of the Civil War. As the new nation expanded, North and South clashed as to whether slavery would be allowed in newly admitted states. A series of failed compromises, culminating in the 1860 election of Abraham Lincoln with only 39 percent of the vote in a four-way contest, triggered southern secession.

The political theory undergirding the position of the Confederacy posited that the states were sovereign entities, which had voluntarily surrendered a portion of their sovereignty to a central government. Hence they could, if they so chose, take back that voluntarily ceded sovereignty and withdraw from the union. The defeat of the Confederacy redefined the federalist issue rather than removing it from the national agenda. And, indeed, in the context of the question of the meaning of freedom in the aftermath of the war, federalism became a central issue.

As the war came to an end, competing conceptions of federalism came to be implicated in the bitter struggle that developed over black suffrage and black rights. It was strongly believed in some quarters in the North that black suffrage was necessary in the states of the beaten confederacy in order to prevent the old planter elite from simply again assuming power. On the other hand, the determination of criteria of voter eligibility had always been a state prerogative, free from federal oversight. Hence, under what circumstances could the federal government lawfully intervene in this ancient area of "states' rights"?

Within weeks of the end of the war the *New York Times* called for black suffrage in the old South to sustain the fruits of victory, but at the same time shrank back from the use of federal power to establish criteria of voter eligibility at the state level. "Hitherto the National Government has never claimed any such power. . . . Some Northern States exclude negro voters altogether—some require a property qualification, while others admit them on the same terms as whites. If the national government asserts control over this whole question, we must be prepared to see that control exercised everywhere."[10]

The racial idea and the issue of federalism were inextricably intertwined as the war ended. If southern states moved to restrict black rights in areas which had traditionally been matters of state prerogative, on what legal basis and to what extent could the federal government intervene such as to limit the scope of state action? Even though prosecution of the war had expanded the powers of the federal government, it was in 1865 a much more limited enterprise than it was to be a century later. The prospect of expanded federal involvement in affairs traditionally left to the states was decried in many quarters in the name of federalism.

The *New York Times* reflected widespread moderate sentiment when it attacked Wendell Phillips's, December 22, 1863, speech calling for an expanded federal role in guaranteeing the rights of blacks after the war. "He would not content himself with compelling every State to make an end of Slavery forthwith, but would also force them to clear their statute books of every distinction between the black man and the white. If Maine law does not allow black men upon juries, the Federal arm must force it; . . . So, too, must the Federal arm force New York to abolish all of her property limitations upon the elective franchise possessed by black men; Ohio to strike down every bar against the election of black men to any and all offices; Illinois to abrogate her statutes against black immigration into her borders. . . . In other words, every State loyal and disloyal, is to be deprived of all power to regulate its own vital concerns."[11]

Indeed, some of the older actors in the unfolding post-Civil War drama had personal memory of James Madison and Thomas Jefferson, revered as members of the revolutionary generation, vigorously asserting the right of states to resist over-reaching federal legislation. In response to Congress's Alien and Sedition Act under which local newspaper editors espousing "dangerous ideologies" had been prosecuted, James Madison had drafted a resolution for the state of Virginia asserting that states had a right and a duty to interpose their own authority where federal law exceeded the limited powers granted the federal government under the Constitution. Thomas Jefferson drafted a resolution for Kentucky averring that states had the right to "nullify" unauthorized federal acts.[12]

Both racism and federalism were factors in bringing on the war in that the substantive issue over which the southern states claimed a right to voluntarily withdraw from the union was the power of the federal government to limit the expansion of slavery. Lee's surrender at Appomattox Court House merely yielded the old struggle in different terms. As the war ended the nation had no clear or coherent idea of what freedom was to mean for blacks, and was committed to a conception of federalism which left the fate of blacks largely to the vagaries of local sentiments, interests, and biases.

There was no body of law either defining or protecting black rights. Indeed, there was no body of law that defined the situation at all. The last major Supreme Court pronouncement on race and rights, the *Dred Scott* decision, had averred that as a matter of constitutional interpretation blacks were not citizens of the United States. Less than a year after the war ended, a Georgia correspondent for the *Chicago Tribune* articulated the elusive quality of the "freedom" won by the former slave population, saying of the black:

> He has not got his freedom yet and isn't likely to get it right away. Why, he can't even live without the consent of the white man! He has no land—he can make no crops except the white man gives him a chance. He hasn't any timber—he can't even get a stick of wood without leave from the white man. We crowd him into the fewest possible employments, and then he can scarcely get work anywhere but in the rice fields and cotton plantations of a white man who has owned him and given up slavery only at the point of bayonet . . . he can't

get a pail of water from a well without asking a white man for the privilege. He can hardly breathe, and he certainly can't live in a house, unless a white man gives his consent. What kind of freedom is that?[13]

Clearly this situation could not persist. Opinion makers and the politically powerful had different and conflicting views as to what should be done and how "freedom" should be defined. Some saw it as a condition just short of slavery, others as the enjoyment of full and equal rights.

The Meaning of Freedom: The Nation Struggles to Define Itself

The war had been over less than a week when Andrew Johnson succeeded the assassinated Abraham Lincoln. Lincoln had not left his successor or others any clear sense of his own views on what freedom meant in practical day-to-day terms for the millions of freed slaves or for the hundreds of thousands of free blacks who had served in the union army but who were, in most northern states, still denied the ballot and made subordinate to whites in civic and social affairs. Lincoln's views concerning race were subtle and complicated and probably evolving at the time of his death.

He had allowed in the Lincoln-Douglas debates that blacks were, perhaps, not his equal "in moral or intellectual endowment" and had, from time to time, entertained ideas about black resettlement in Central America or the Caribbean. In August of 1862 he had met in the White House with four prominent blacks to encourage migration to Central America, condemning slavery but holding that blacks and whites could never live together in harmony. His remarks were carried widely in the northern press and drew denunciation from black leaders, including Frederick Douglass who called him, "a genuine representative of American prejudice and Negro hatred."[14]

He regarded slavery as the great nightmare threatening the American dream but in his first inaugural address sought to dissuade the southern states from seceding by giving assurances that he would not fight the Crittendon proposal to add an amendment to the Constitution barring the federal government from interfering with the domestic institutions of the states, including slavery. Less than a month later the South seceded in any event, bringing on the great conflagration.

He had been brought reluctantly to issue the Emancipation Proclamation, but by the end of the war appeared to entertain the idea that the vote might be extended to blacks who were "very intelligent and those who serve our cause as soldiers."[15] In December of 1863, just weeks after having delivered the address at Gettysburg commemorating the thousands who had died in the name of freedom, he indicated a willingness to accommodate something short of freedom for freed slaves. "Any provision which may be adopted by any (postwar Southern state government) in relation to the freed people . . . which shall recognize and declare their permanent freedom, provide for their education, and which may yet be consistent, as a temporary arrangement, with their present condition as a laboring, and homeless class, will not be objected to by the national Executive." In other words, rebel states readmitted to the Union might be allowed to hold their former slaves in some form of mandatory "apprenticeship."[16]

As the bloody war ground on he came to recognize the military importance of recruiting blacks into the Union Army, and eventually recognized their valor. He began to develop a close relationship with Frederick Douglass and became the first president to have blacks in the White House as guests, and although it is possible to discern evolution in Lincoln's thinking on matters of race, at the time of his death there was not a clear sense of policy direction or a coherently articulated positive view of black rights to which his successor might be held.

Andrew Johnson, a blunt-spoken man with a hard and humorless face, brought a clear political agenda to the office intertwined with a distinct view of the newly freed population. Born poor, he was a self-made man driven by class envy and resentment. At the political level he sought to break the power of the old, southern planter class and secure the loyalty of the white laboring classes and poor farmers. His class resentments were intertwined with his loathing for blacks. He viewed Afro-Americans as an inherently inferior race who would, if given the ballot, be easily manipulated by their former masters, and whose enfranchisement would, in any event, inflame the mass of working and poor whites. For Johnson the war had been about class revenge rather than ending human bondage.

Andrew Johnson's presidency represented the peculiar interaction of personal biography with national history. Who he was had fateful consequences for what the nation became with regard to race and rights. Unlike Lincoln, he seemed unable to grow and evolve in response to new experiences and new challenges. There seemed to be a core of insecurity in him which made it impossible for him to admit error or redirect his efforts in response to criticism. His private demons robbed him of the degree of flexibility necessary to navigate in the turbulent, uncharted waters of the postwar years even though his political views were potentially not without widespread support.

Johnson was not an individual crank or bigot. He represented a school of thought and a sector of the political arena. Indeed, it was that fact which accounted for his having been placed on the national ticket. Dissatisfaction with Lincoln's conduct of the war was widespread as the Republican Party convened in Baltimore for its nominating convention in June of 1864. As had been the case with the two previous Republican conventions, participation was not limited to party loyalists. Democrats standing behind Lincoln were urged to attend and take part.

Lincoln secured renomination on the first ballot but then threw the convention open to select his vice presidential running mate after his first choice, Ben Butler, refused a place on the ticket. Butler, a fierce advocate of black rights during and after the war had indicated he would take the spot only if Lincoln could guarantee he would die in office within three months. Johnson, a Democrat, a former slave owner and military governor of Tennessee emerged as an early favorite once the decision was passed to the convention. He secured the nomination after states that had supported other candidates moved to his colors following the first ballot.

Drunk at his swearing in on March 4, 1865, Johnson delivered a rambling address reflective of his class resentments. He was a man of the people. He had risen from the soil. The powdered, puffed, and powerful need not think themselves better than the common man. Five weeks later he became president.

In the months preceding the collapse of the Confederacy, thought had turned in various quarters to the particulars of postwar policy relative to the defeated South. Conservative democrats favored withdrawing the Emancipation Proclamation, the granting of amnesty to confederates, and the restoration of their right to participate in the political process. More moderate democrats and a spectrum of republicans insisted on the abolition of slavery and the assumption of leadership by men who had remained loyal to the Union.

A small faction within the Republican Party, numbering former abolitionists in its ranks, favored dealing with the defeated states as a set of conquered provinces. There would be insistence on equal rights irrespective of race. Reintegration into the union would be conditioned on the capacity of the new leadership of the South, potentially biracial, to put in place the laws and institutions necessary to sustaining a free and open society. Champions of this view had little faith in the potential of the White House to push for radical change in the South. They looked for and anticipated the need for strong Congressional leadership. A minority within Republican ranks looked for the extension of the ballot to blacks both as a measure to prevent the reassertion of planter power and as a moral necessity.

Johnson's broad views were reflective of those of members of the Democratic Party who utterly rejected the notion of black equality. In Johnson's view blacks would never get the vote given their presumed incapacities and, in the short run, moderate perspectives were closer to Johnson than to the Congressional progressives. The *New York Times* in an editorial held out extension of the franchise as a goal but denied its immediate practicability, observing that "we require of foreigners who come to our shores some years of instruction . . . before they are admitted to (suffrage). The same reasons which make this wise, would also require a similar probation from those who have but just escaped from the ignorance and degradation of slavery."[17]

Johnson favored a policy of executive leadership involving the appointment of loyalists to positions of power in the defeated states, men like himself. His antiblack views promised tenacious resistance to possible legislative attempts to realize equality, the attack focusing both on the presumed destructive social consequences of black equality and on the incapacity of the federal government under the constitution and the tenets of federalism to enforce an equality-centered legislative agenda. Believing himself on firm ground and that the public was behind him, he moved early on to assert his leadership.

The Failure of the Johnson Governments

On Thursday, June 13, 1865, President Andrew Johnson appointed William L. Sharkey governor of Mississippi, charged with calling a convention of citizens who had been loyal to the union to write a new state constitution and form a new state government. Within a week provisional governors were also appointed in Georgia, Texas, and Alabama. Johnson was seeking to empower a class of white yeomen whom he viewed as having been subordinate to a planter aristocracy in the prewar south. Free or slaves, blacks were, in his view, fodder for the old aristocracy: docile chattel before the war, dependent serfs after. Either way, the aristocracy's status rested on black foundations. From the Johnson perspective the South was a "white man's country," by which he meant white farmers and working men. When visited by a black delegation in February of 1866 he suggested that black emigration to another county might be a solution to the country's race problems.

Whatever Johnson's hopes or aspirations with regard to the empowerment of a white yeomanry and the place of blacks in the new order, the men who actually assumed office in his new, reconstruction governments had their own ideas about the road to southern recovery and the role of blacks in achieving that recovery. As the Confederacy collapsed, many whites, even those who had opposed secession, came to fear that southern recovery and prosperity was not possible except by maintaining control over black labor, the emigration of whites from other parts of the country being feared as threatening the displacement of southern whites from the land and from positions of political dominance.

As the Louisiana legislature convened in the fall of 1865, commentator Benjamin Flanders predicted, "There whole thought and time will be given to plans for getting things back as nearly to slavery as possible."[18] Mississippi and South Carolina preceded Louisiana, however, in passing legislation intended to control black labor by enacting the first of what came to be known as "Black Codes" in the fall of 1865. Legislation of this type, eventually widespread in the South, imposed a number of specific constraints on blacks in economic, civic, and social affairs. In effect, the state became an instrument for sustaining the kind of domination over black life otherwise disallowed by the banning of slavery.

The thrust and intentions of the former overseers was grasped at the time by their former chattel. The December 30, 1865, edition of *The Colored American* newspaper decried the newly enacted Georgia statute binding black workers to white masters by making it a crime for anyone to entice a laborer to leave his boss for another job. The January 6, 1866, edition commented on the motive behind the newly enacted Alabama labor law. "It is hoped and expected that . . . they will be enabled to . . . make the present or future system of labor approximate the old . . . as nearly as possible."[19]

South Carolina law barred blacks from any occupation other

than farmer or servant except by paying a large fee. Mississippi imposed a fine on any party offering employment to a black who was already employed. Under Florida law a black who broke an employment contract could be whipped, pilloried, or sold to the highest bidder for up to one year's labor. By contrast, a white employee who broke a labor contract was subject to a civil suit for damages. The definition of "vagrant" was expansive in many of the codes allowing for the seizure of blacks and their delivery as labor to whites who paid their fines.[20]

The objective of the black codes, as articulated by proponents, was to regain control over black labor and to reassert the primacy of racial status. The Georgia correspondent to the *Chicago Tribune* captured this aim, recounting the remarks of a confederate army veteran regarding the Johnson legislature convening in the state of Georgia.

> I know there will be private talk this session, even if there isn't an open effort to make the penal code take (the black) back into the condition of slavery. It will be called "involuntary servitude for the punishment of crime," but it won't differ much from slavery. . . . I know men . . . who believe in making the breaking of a contract a crime for which (a) nigger may be sold . . . three fourths of the counties in the State would vote for such a penal code as would practically reduce half the negroes to slavery in less than a year.[21]

C. G. Memminger, former Secretary of the Treasury for the Confederacy, articulated a rationale for the codes from a Southern point of view, arguing that "the natural indolence of the African race" required some form of restrictive indentureship in order to secure their labor for their own good and for the good of whites.[22]

The policies pursued by the Johnson Reconstruction governments transformed the clash of views into a political struggle that set Congress on the road to passing the nation's first Civil Rights Bill. The struggle also produced the Fourteenth Amendment, the actions of the Johnson governments giving that amendment its particular thrust and focus.

Events moved rapidly. Criticism of Johnson's governments began to mount even as he made additional appointments. Initially Johnson enjoyed the upper hand in his struggle with the proponents of full and equal rights for blacks. Efforts to repudiate his governments and to commit Congress to the ballot for the black man proved unsuccessful. Even John Andrews, a former governor of

Massachusetts who had played a key role in breaking down white resistance to the recruitment of blacks for military service during the war, felt that Southern leaders ought to be given the benefit of the doubt with regard to their intentions toward blacks.

But, in the fall of 1865, Northern dead and wounded were still being returned from the battlefield. In November of 1865 Captain Henry Wirtz, commandant of the Confederate prison at Andersonville where thousands of union captured had died, was executed for war crimes. From the Northern perspective the black codes repudiated the meaning of victory. Although there was no widespread Northern sentiment in favor of social equality, there was consensus on the repudiation of slavery. The black codes seemed to allow the South to win victories in the halls of state legislatures that it had not been able to win on the battlefield.

The initial impetus to provide a definition in federal law of the meaning of freedom came from a small group in Congress referred to even at the time as "radical Republicans." During the war they had been critical of Lincoln for not articulating black freedom as a central cause of the struggle sooner and more forcefully. In the aftermath of the war they pushed an agenda of full racial equality. Their radicalism consisted of an insistence on full legal and social equality for blacks.

Without question they were committed to a notion of black rights that placed them outside of what was at that time the mainstream. Events, and the strategic blunders of more conservative, antiblack elements allowed this small group to mobilize sufficient Congressional sentiment to lay an enduring and essential legislative foundation for black rights.

Among these key figures, perhaps the most important, were Thaddeus Stevens and Charles Sumner. Handicapped with a clubfoot, which some said made him sympathetic to others crippled by accidents of birth, Stevens was a bitter foe of white supremacy. As a congressman he had introduced a bill in 1836 to abolish slavery and the slave trade in the District of Columbia. In 1839 he had refused to sign the Pennsylvania Constitution, which limited the ballot to white men, and in 1851 he had lost his seat in Congress over his defense of fugitive slaves. Reelected in 1858, he served during the war as chairman of the powerful House Ways and Means Committee, a body crucial to securing the financial means to prosecute the war. In the turbulent aftermath of the war the national conscience and Stevens's vision were to temporarily coalesce to yield the Fourteenth Amendment.

Stevens's counterpart in the senate was Charles Sumner. Not as effective a legislator as Stevens, Sumner nevertheless articulated an uncompromising position with regard to black rights, extending the conception beyond the political realm to embrace notions of equal access to places of public accommodations, a position not taken by many people otherwise committed to racial reform. Joined by a minority of other members of the House and Senate, Stevens and Sumner defined black freedom in terms not shared by many of their colleagues or by much of the white citizenry. Yet, remarkably, within a decade their views gained legislative reality and were incorporated into the Constitution, forming the touchstone for the struggle for equal rights.

The majority in Congress was comprised of so-called moderate Republicans, led by Lyman Trumbull of Connecticut. They believed in an indissoluble union and they repudiated slavery. They reflected the view that blacks were due civil equality short of suffrage, but most came from states which were nonslave but which made distinctions in law based on race. Of the states which ratified the Thirteenth Amendment, eighteen criminalized sexual relations between blacks and whites, while ten denied blacks the ballot. The ratification of an amendment abolishing slavery was not seen as inconsistent with the use of state power to otherwise regulate social and political life in terms of racial identity. The wide divisions in Congress and the incipient split between the White House and Congress reflected the absence of consensus on the meaning of freedom. For some it meant the mere absence of slavery, for others it meant equal rights for black and white. For many it translated into vague notions of "doing the right thing," the *New York Times* editorializing in August of 1865 that blacks should "be protected by constitutional safeguards against injustice and oppression."[23]

As fall turned to winter and the black codes that proliferated the contours of those "constitutional safeguards" began to emerge. Legal meaning began to be attached to black "freedom."

The Coming of "Civil Rights"

In December 1865, eight months after the end of the war and six months after Johnson had appointed the governor of Mississippi, Lyman Trumbull, moderate Republican congressman from Connecticut, introduced the nation's first civil rights bill, the immediate impetus being the passage of the black codes in the states of the former confederacy. Even in moderate Republican circles the codes were seen as repudiating one of the two great outcomes of the war—the destruction of slavery. For the first time in the nation's history Congress began to debate the kinds of racial distinctions that could be made in law among free people.

In its particulars the proposed bill offered four major provisions. It declared that all persons born in the United states are (with some designated exceptions) citizens of the United States. This clause anticipated an argument of the pro-code forces that blacks were not citizens under the Constitution, as indeed had been declared in *Dred Scott* less than a decade earlier, and that they were not therefore beneficiaries of the legal rights otherwise enjoyed by citizens. Indeed, such had been the assertion of the Mississippi governor to the legislature in the fall of 1865. "The Negro is free whether we like it or not . . . to be free, however, does not make him a citizen, or entitle him to social or political equality with the white man."[24]

Citizenship was itself a contested matter. Yet without citizenship the legal basis for securing other rights for blacks was in doubt. The *New York Times* in an April, 1866, editorial, concurrent with the debates on black rights and new laws, reflected the view of those who argued that conferring citizenship on black by virtue of their birth in the United States constituted a kind of antiwhite discrimination, opining that, "The one is required to undergo a five years' probation, and to produce testimony as to his fitness for citizenship; the other is to be deemed a citizen by reason of his birth, although all the conditions that surrounded him, from then till now, have tended to unfit him for the immediate discharge of the higher duties of citizenship."[25]

The bill also identified specific rights, which could not be denied or constrained for reasons of race, specifying the right to make and enforce contracts, the right to hold property, the right to be secure in one's person and to not be subjected to peculiar race-based punishments. The third section made it a crime to deny anyone enjoyment of any of these specified rights because of race or color, or "under color of . . . law," while the last section gave jurisdiction to federal courts to try cases arising under the bill.

The language of the statute was addressed specifically to the evils advanced by the black codes. Whereas the codes sought to impose a kind of serfdom on black labor, the act sought to confer on the black worker the same right to bargain and contract freely in exchange for his services as enjoyed by the white worker. Whereas the codes singled out blacks for peculiar punishments intended to facilitate binding them over to white overseers as chattel workers, the act forbade racially targeted punishments. And whereas the agents of the state, the sheriffs and other agents of law enforcement, had been the instruments through which the designs of the black codes were accomplished, the act forbade the state's servants from denying any person their specified rights under color of law.

Considerable testimony before Congress detailing antiblack terror and oppression in the southern states seem to speak clearly to the question of whether they could be left to manage their own affairs without federal intervention; hence moderate Republicans assumed, incorrectly, that Johnson would support the new bill. The Johnson message to Congress accompanying his veto of the Civil Rights Bill offered arguments that echo down to the end of the twentieth century. He raised the specter of "big government," arguing that the measure represented an unprecedented intrusion of the Federal Government into local affairs. In addition, he asserted, the bill discriminated against whites: "The distinction of race and color is by the bill made to operate in favor of the colored and against the white race." The Johnson perspective reverberates down through the decades in terms of a mode of critique of civil rights legislation—any legal constraint on whites in terms of the privileges ordinarily enjoyed vis-a-vis blacks or the power ordinarily held over black life being deemed to be antiwhite discrimination.

On April 6, 1866, for the first time in American history, the Senate by a margin of 33 to 15 and the House by 122 to 41 passed a major piece of legislation over a presidential veto. The Civil Rights Act of 1866 thereby became the first federal civil rights law on the books.[26] And within months a Justice of the United States Supreme Court was called upon to construe the law and rule on its meaning. The law was without precedent and the nation was deeply divided. Even persons of good will as regards the status of African Americans understood that some of its provisions might run afoul of the Constitution, while champions of the old order looked for its repudiation in the Court. Within a year of the end of the war the Court was beginning to assume its historic role as regards race and civil rights. Its holdings could confer moral legitimacy, legal affirmation, and political impetus on movements supportive of black interests or on movements deeply hostile to those interests.

Approximately three weeks after passage of the act, white burglars entered the home of Nancy Talbot, a black woman living in Nelson County, Kentucky. Their subsequent indictment set forth their transgression in the formal language of the time: "On the 1st day of May, 1866 . . . at the hour of eleven of the clock in the night . . . (the defendants) feloniously and burglariously did break and enter the dwelling house . . . of Nancy Talbot, a citizen of the United States of the African race . . . denied the right to testify against said defendants in the courts of the state of Kentucky . . . with the intent the goods and chattels, moneys and property of the said Nancy Talbot . . . to steal, take, and carry away, contrary to the statute . . . and against the peace and dignity of the United States."

Under the new Civil Rights Act the case was shifted to federal court, given Kentucky law which barred black testimony being received against a white defendant. Rhodes and his companions were convicted, but appealed their convictions, arguing for an interpretation of the law that would have rendered it impotent. Under the practice of the time individual justices of the Supreme Court sat during part of the year in designated circuits hearing appeals and handing down decisions. The appeal in Nancy Talbot's case came before Supreme Court Justice Noah Swayne sitting as a circuit court judge. A Lincoln appointee and the son of antislave Quaker parents, Swayne had been involved in cases defending runaway slaves before ascending to the bench. His wife of thirty years, Sarah Wager, had freed her slaves at his urging at the time of their marriage.

Rhodes and his accomplices advanced the argument to be offered by Blyew and Kennard a few years later. The law conferred federal jurisdiction in "all causes, civil and criminal" affecting persons unable to enforce their rights in local courts. In a criminal proceeding, Rhodes argued, the only parties affected are the prosecution and the defendant, in that one prevails and the other does not. The victim may be the subject matter of the proceedings, but is not affected by those proceedings. Whatever has happened to the victim has happened and could not be undone by the outcome of the proceedings against the accused. The murder victim is still dead. The stolen goods are still missing. Nancy Talbot was not affected by the proceedings and, hence, the case should have been tried in a Kentucky state court rather than federal court.

Swayne quickly disposed of this argument, adopting legislative intent as his mode of analysis. The language has to be interpreted in terms of the objectives the legislature had in mind in writing the statute in the first place. The practical meaning of the reading Rhodes gave to the statutory language would have been to limit federal removal to circumstances in which there was a black defendant. Surely, he concluded, Congress had different and larger objectives in mind. Rhodes's construal of the statute would "produce the opposite of those intended" by Congress in that a Nancy Talbot would be left with no means of legal redress save in a Kentucky state court, where her testimony as a black would have been barred in any proceeding against the white perpetrators.[27]

Swayne's holding was the first by a justice of the Supreme Court addressing the status of a civil rights statute. It was to be several years before the full Court heard a civil rights case, but the Swayne holding affirming the constitutionality of the Civil Rights Act of 1866 supported efforts in Congress to move further in the creation of a legal framework for the achievement of black rights. In a tense and turbulent time when resistance to a change in the old order intensified, the Swayne holding affirmed the legitimacy of reformist efforts and accommodated an impetus to an even more radical effort to put a legal foundation for equal rights in place.

The Fourteenth Amendment and "Equal Rights"

Johnson's veto of the Civil Rights Act lent credibility to the claims of the radicals regarding the need to avoid losing after the war a goodly measure of what had been won in the war by acquiescing in the reimposition of slavelike domination by Johnson's reconstruction governments. Thereafter, matters moved swiftly. A consensus developed among the Republicans on the need to protect black rights via a constitutional amendment which would place those rights beyond the hostility of presidents or the shifting moods of Congress.

The Joint Committee on Reconstruction had already been at work on a possible constitutional amendment, but there was little agreement as to the rights to be protected. Implicated in the language of the proposed amendment as it was debated were distinctions which were to be decisive with regard to the framework within which the Supreme Court decided on matters of race and rights. In December, 1863, Wendell Phillips, a leader in the radical wing of the Republican Party, had given a speech in New York City in which he had asserted: "The nation owes the Negro after . . . a war, in which he has nobly joined, not technical freedom, but substantial protection in all of his rights. . . . I would have an amendment to the Constitution providing that no state shall make any distinction in civil rights and privileges among the . . . citizens residing within its limits . . . on account of race, color, or descent."[28]

The advocacy of a colorblind Constitution by this wing of the party was undoubtably shaped by the Roberts case in Massachusetts in which radical stalwart Charles Sumner had been involved. In 1849, four-year-old Sarah Roberts had been denied admission to the elementary school nearest her home solely on the grounds of race and had been directed, instead, to one of two schools maintained exclusively for black children. Her father brought suit against the city of Boston on the grounds that the assignment of children to schools by race violated the guarantee in the constitution of the state of Massachusetts of legal equality for those residing within the state. Robert Morris, one of the first black attorneys in the United States, and Charles Sumner represented the plaintiffs.

In resolving the case, Lemuel Shaw, chief justice of the Massachusetts court held that a constitutional guarantee of equality did not mandate identical treatment. Legal equality did not require that "everyone be treated identically but that like be treated alike within a reasonable system of classification." Racial distinctions in law were both "reasonable" and justifiable, according to Shaw, and did not necessarily yield a conclusion that blacks were being subjected to unequal treatment.

The implication of the Shaw holding was not lost on Sumner and other radicals more than a decade later as events placed before them the possibility of amending the Constitution in support of racial justice. A guarantee of equality, not otherwise barring considerations of race, did not necessarily deprive the states of the right to segregate by race. Thus, as Congress moved to consider the legal protection of black rights in the context of the unfolding dispute with the executive, Thaddeus Steven introduced a new amendment reflecting the spirit and thrust of Phillips's proposal. The new amendment would mandate that in all national and state laws "no discrimination shall be made on account of race and color." The next day, moderate Ohio Congressman John Bingham offered an alternative calling merely for an amendment securing to "all persons in every State of the Union equal protection in their rights."[29]

As events and the debate unfolded, the Republicans were confronted with a practical problem that made both alternatives attractive but, in the end, only one of them politically feasible. The radical alternative of Constitutionally mandated colorblind state laws had appeal. But, on the other hand, only five northern states allowed blacks to vote, and in the fall elections of 1865, held a few months before Congress had convened, Connecticut, Minnesota, and Wisconsin white voters had rejected propositions that would have extended the ballot to blacks. There was little reason to believe that an amendment mandating colorblind law and ensuring the black ballot would be ratified by a sufficient number of states and, in addition, might lead to a backlash of white voters against the Republican Party. Hence, the Bingham-type amendment, affirming a broad commitment to "equality" without necessarily impacting on traditional northern patterns of segregation and discrimination had a certain appeal.

In the Spring of 1866 events moved with increasing speed. On March 27, President Johnson vetoed the Civil Rights Act. On April 6th, Congress overrode his veto. And in June, 1866, propelled partially by Johnson's intransigence, the Fourteenth Amendment was passed and moved on to the states for ratification. In its final version the amendment reflected the Bingham approach. It contained five clauses, the first and fifth of which came to be pivotal in Supreme Court history and the litigation of black rights. The first clause reiterated the citizenship status of all persons born in the United States. It also prohibited states from making any laws that (a) abridged the "privileges and immunities" of national citizenship, (b) denied any person life, liberty, or property without due process of law, or (c) denied any person the equal protection of the law. The fifth clause gave Congress the power to enact legislation enforcing the other provisions of the amendment.

The language of the amendment avoided the explicit colorblind mandate of the original radical proposal and honored the federalist principle by leaving it to the states to protect its black citizens, providing a claim for citizen redress only if the state failed in some way to provide "equal protection of the laws" or denied life, liberty, or property without "due process of law." It was to fall to the Supreme Court very soon to begin to interpret this language. What were the "privileges and immunities of citizenship" relative to blacks? To what extent could a statute explicitly differentiate by race without violating the language of the equal protection clause?

The practical meaning of the difference between the language of the initial Stevens proposal and the subsequent Bingham language actually adopted had enormous consequences. The original language would have made unconstitutional the array and panoply of race-based laws that structured segregation and would also, in the contemporary era, deny constitutional legitimacy to any affirmative action statute or ordinance making distinctions based on race.

At the same time the ambiguous language yielded an enlarged role to the Supreme Court in defining the place of race in American life. The immediately political virtue of the Fourteenth Amendment was that it affirmed majority sentiment with regard to the desirability of blacks having equal rights without being clear as to what those rights were. The long run consequence was to cede to the Court an enormous and perhaps decisive role in determining what freedom for African Americans was to really mean in the ensuing decades and century.

Coming of "Voting Rights"

In the fall of 1866, fifteen months after the end of the war, the political and social situation in the nation was becoming increasingly polarized. In the end President Johnson's views really were closer to those of the Democrats than the Republicans on whose ticket he had been elected vice president. He was fueled by class resentment of the old plantation elite and contempt for slaves on whose backs the elites erected their Valhalla, but had no objections otherwise to a social system based on racial hierarchy. He had not articulated a clear view of how society ought to be organized in the postslavery era, but his support of the governments responsible for the black codes indicated a willingness to accommodate a kind of legal serfdom for the newly freed black population.

On the other hand, the North had bled as no other society before it had. In the four years of the carnage more than 360,000 men had died in the union cause from battle-related deaths and disease. By contrast there had been fewer than 5,000 battle deaths in the revolutionary war, fewer than 3,000 in the War of 1812, and less than 15,000 deaths from all causes in the Mexican War of 1846 to 1848. And although preservation of the nation had initially been at the heart of the union cause, by 1863 emancipation of the slaves had also come to the fore and became the moral centerpiece in the struggle against the South. Hence, as the schism between Johnson and Congress deepened, the president appeared to be turning the reigns of government in the defeated states over to men whose loyalty to the North had been weak or doubtful during the great struggle and who were now proceeding to use their power to restore racial bondage under the guise of civil law.

Antiblack rioting in Memphis and New Orleans in the fall of 1866 by elements sympathetic to the old order, combined with the

refusal of ten of the states of the old confederacy to ratify the Fourteenth Amendment led to a sweeping Republican victory in the
1866 congressional elections.[30] In 1867 the Republican-dominated
Congress took control of reconstruction from the president via the
passage of Reconstruction Acts dividing the South into five military districts. The commanders of these districts were empowered
to oversee the writing of new state constitutions mandating, among
other things, black suffrage and ratification of the Fourteenth
Amendment. Johnson vetoes were overridden on March 2 and
March 23, 1867.

Pragmatic considerations along with the humanist objectives
of the radicals had brought a majority of the congressional Republicans around to the support of black suffrage for the defeated South,
even though there were northern states that denied blacks the ballot. Access to the polling place was viewed as an alternative to perpetual military occupation. With the vote the black could protect
himself. The role of the military was to ensure access, given the
revolutionary nature of the change and the deep resistance in some
quarters to the idea of black exercise of the franchise. Radical Senator Richard Yates articulated the long-range objectives with regard
to enfranchisement: "The ballot will finish the negro question: it
will settle everything connected with this question. . . . Sir, the ballot is the freedman"s Moses."

Surviving impeachment and removal from office by one vote
in the spring of 1868, Johnson sought unsuccessfully in his remaining days as president to mobilize sentiment in the country for a
new, anti-Reconstruction political alignment. The Republicans
selected war hero Ulysses S. Grant, while the Democrats put up
colorless New York governor Horace Seymour, but nominated as
vice president Frank Blair, an ex-aide to war hero Phil Sheridan and
a rabid racist. His extraordinary campaign reflected the deep
national divisions over the meaning of freedom for the former
bondsmen. Calling for an end to Reconstruction on federalist and
racist grounds, he declared that "Whole states and communities of
people of our own race have been attained, convicted, condemned,
and deprived of their rights as citizens . . . by Congressional enactment. . . . The same usurping authority has substituted as electors
in the place of men of our own race . . . a host of ignorant negroes,
who are supported in idleness with the public money, and combined together to strip the white race of their birthright."[31]

Blair railed against blacks as a "semi-barbarous race" avid to
"subject white women to (their) unbridled lust." He claimed that

the fate of blacks was best left in the hands of their former masters and raised the specter of another war to put things aright again. His wild and extraordinary fulminations perhaps also played a role in the murders that generated the first civil rights case ever heard by the Supreme Court as a whole, the *United States v. Blyew.*

Urged on by the inflammatory rhetoric of Frank Blair, exrebels, along with northern copperhead allies had seen a chance of gaining the White House and reversing reconstruction policy. As election day had approached, the fury of antiblack terror had increased. For example, in Louisiana, as later testimony before Congress would reveal, more than two thousand people had been killed or injured in the weeks leading up to the election. The impact of the terror had been most evident and remarkable in Saint Landry Parish. In the spring of 1868 there had been 1,071 more registered Republicans than Democrats, but in the fall election the Democratic ticket of Seymour and Blair had gotten 4,787 votes while Grant had gotten none.[32]

In the ensuing election Grant won by a wide electoral vote, 214 to 80, but by a much narrower popular vote, three million to Seymour's two million seven hundred thousand. Historians estimate the black vote for Grant as variously between three hundred thousand and seven hundred thousand. Whatever the correct figure, it was clear to the Republicans at the time that without the newly enfranchised black vote generated by Reconstruction policy Grant's election might have been a chancier matter.[33]

The pragmatic perception among Republicans of the importance to them of the black vote, along with the persistent idealism of the radicals, led to serious consideration of yet another constitutional amendment aimed at protecting black access to the ballot. The proposed Fifteenth Amendment was yielded by the political fears, calculations, intrigues, and idealistic aspirations attending the outcome of the 1868 presidential election but became a bulwark in the long-term struggle for black rights. The Voting Rights Act passed by Congress in 1968 was intended to realize the objectives of the Fifteenth Amendment. The numerous contemporary court decisions ordering the redrawing of district lines such as to facilitate minority involvement in the political process derive their authority ultimately from the Fifteenth Amendment.

At the pragmatic level the black vote had proven to be crucial to Republican presidential success. In 1868 the Republican Party was still a comparative newcomer on the political stage, much more recently organized than the Democratic Party. It had contested four presidential elections, 1856, 1860, 1864, and 1868. In 1856, 1860, and 1864 it had, for various reasons, received less than half the white vote. In 1868, running a war hero at the head of its ticket, it had still failed to achieve a commanding white majority of the popular vote. Its vigor could by no means be taken for granted. The bitter 1868 presidential campaign crystallized the importance, from a Republican perspective, of sustaining black access to the ballot box.

Both the moderates and the radicals agreed that a constitutional amendment was needed to protect black access to the polls no matter who occupied the White House or which party dominated Congress. Hence, after much debate, the Fifteenth Amendment was passed on February 26, 1869, declaring that "the right of citizens of the United States to vote shall not be denied or abridged . . . on account of race, color, or previous condition of servitude." Not surprisingly, Grant expressed support for the amendment, and on March 30, 1870, the ratification process was completed, making the amendment part of the Constitution. Events had again conspired to link moderate Republican interests to the ideals and aspirations of the radicals. Only a few years earlier a proposed amendment guaranteeing black access to the ballot would have been viewed as preposterous. Indeed, into 1868 only eight Northern states had afforded the vote to blacks.

The Enforcement Acts of 1870 and 1871

Neither the moderates nor the radicals were so naive as to believe that the terms of even a constitutional amendment would be honored by those forces resisting the idea and the reality of black equality. From the end of the war onward the terror directed at blacks in the states of the former Confederacy had been relentless and had been waged on many fronts. In Congress, Democrats invoked federalist principles regarding state's rights and base beliefs concerning racial inferiority in the fight against the Civil Rights Act of 1866 and the new amendments, but in the towns and villages, in the hollows and backwoods country, raw terror was the instrument of resistance to change in the racial order. A petition "To the senate and house of representatives assembled" from blacks in Kentucky asking their help set forth more than a hundred acts of terror between November 1867 and April 1871, including the lynching of Samuel Davis and William Pierce, William and John

Gibson, F. H. Montfort, William Glassgow, and others, the burning of "colored school houses" in Breckenridge and in Christian County, and numerous instances of whippings, burnings, and beatings. The climate of terror found in Kentucky characterized the entire south.[34]

In the beginning terror was anonymous, the work of masked riders striking in the night. By the time Congress assembled to debate the voting rights amendment terror had assumed a face and a name. The Ku Klux Klan had grown out of a meeting of six Confederate veterans in the law office of Thomas M. Jones in Pulaski, Tennessee, in May or June 1866. All were educated men by the standards of the time and were familiar with various kinds of rituals and secret oaths connected with college fraternities. These rituals and rites were adapted to use in their new organization. Within a year members of the growing organization were abroad in the countryside at night, hooded and robed, and striking at blacks whose initiatives or ambitions were seen as threatening to the traditional racial hierarchy.

Made up largely of Confederate war veterans, former Confederate General Nathan Bedford Forrest was one of its first leaders. Forrest's grip on the Confederate imagination derived, in part, from his role in the events that had transpired at Fort Pillow in the third year of the war. On April 12, 1864, Forrest's Confederate cavalry, 1500 strong, attacked Fort Pillow in Tennessee, defended by just over 500 Union troops under the command of Major William F. Bradford, about half of his force being made up of black soldiers. After his outnumbered garrison had beaten back the initial assaults, Bradford signaled that he was willing to suspend fire for purposes of negotiation. While the negotiations were in progress and while the two sides were, presumably, standing down in place, Forrest moved troops to a vantage point not otherwise attainable. Upon discovering the covert Confederate movements, Bradford broke off the talks and the fighting resumed. The fort was overrun and taken and the black troops massacred. In his dispatch announcing the fall of Pillow, Forrest had written: "We busted the Fort at ninerclock and skatered the nigers. The men is still cillanem in the woods."

Whatever Forrest was as a person, the Forrest myth contained all of the elements that were to echo down through the years in defense of the South and the Southern way of life: the romantic cavalier, willing to sacrifice all for a noble but lost cause, driven in defeat to organize clandestinely to protect what was left of honor, virtue, and civilization against the weight of a brutish and untamed race, set loose by venal or ignorant Northerners to prey on an innocent South.[35]

The terror struck with fury at black political involvement. In South Carolina Jackson Surratt and Alfred Richardson were among the victims of beatings for voting with the Republicans, while James Martin and B. F. Randolph had been killed. In Georgia Scipio Eager was whipped and his brother killed for voting Republican after being told not to by Klansmen. In Mississippi, Abraham Wamble, a black minister was shot by Klansmen after appearing at political rallies, while Charles Hendricks, also politically active, barely survived being shot in the abdomen. Some blacks sought safety in publicly renouncing allegiance to the Republican Party. Thus, a local paper reported that "Anthony Thurster, the negro preacher who was so severely whipped by a party of disguised men . . . asks that we announce to his white friends that from this time forward he will prove himself a better man; will never again make a political speech, deliver a sermon, or vote a Republican ticket.[36]

Inevitably, amendments ended with language to the effect that Congress could implement their terms via appropriate legislation. Hence, in the early days of the Grant Administration, Congress moved to develop the means of enforcing the terms of the Fifteenth Amendment by passage of new legislation directed at local sheriffs, deputies, and other state officials involved in intimidating and terrorizing black voters. By the end of March, 1870, a sufficient number of states had ratified the Fifteenth Amendment as to allow it to become part of the Constitution. Two months later Congress passed a law intended to put federal law-enforcement muscle behind the new Amendment.

The Enforcement Act of 1870 criminalized official and private interference with voting or registering to vote. It also criminalized the acts of private individuals interfering with another persons' "free exercise . . . of any right or privilege granted or secured . . . by the Constitution." It allowed, further, for prosecution in federal court for state law crimes committed while in the course of blocking another person from voting or otherwise denying them the enjoyment of a constitutionally secured right.

The debate preceding passage was bitter. And passage of the act was highly controversial even in circles otherwise sensitive to the need to protect black rights. One of the objectives of the new law was to facilitate federal prosecution of private individuals who committed criminal acts for racial motives where state officials failed to act. The bitter objection raised to the law was that it violated the principle of federalism by giving Washington power over matters previously within the sole jurisdiction of the states. The language of the Fifteenth and Fourteenth Amendments allowed Congress to speak to possible malfeasance by state government and its agents, it was argued, but did not give it the power to punish the misdeeds of ordinary felons, whatever motives the felons might have had for their transgressions. The proposed statutes were "unconstitutional . . . as they deal with *individuals* and not *states*," argued Eugene Casserly, senator from California in a losing cause. "This is the rock which is to wreck these scoundrel bills." In answer, John Poole, Senator from North Carolina, elected by a reconstruction legislature, contended that the state might violate the freedman's right to vote by direct action or by inaction. The failure of local officials to curb violence by private parties constituted state complicity in the violation of the freedman's rights, thereby triggering federal authority to intervene and move against private perpetrators of racial violence.[37]

Within a year Congress moved to strengthen the Enforcement Act with the Klan Act of 1871, which sought to strike directly at the hooded empire by prohibiting two or more persons from obstructing law enforcement via the use of force, intimidation, or threat. The law also proscribed threats against public officials, and against witnesses or jurors in court proceedings, and prohibited acts of coercion intended to deny citizens "due and equal protection of the law." Where local authority proved unwilling to prevent racial violence or unwilling to undertake the task, the president was authorized to suspend habeas corpus and use the military to restore and maintain order.[38]

The impact of the Supreme Court decisions in *Reese* and other cases on race and rights to be dealt with in the next chapter has to be understood in terms of the results of the extremely effective prosecutions brought under the Enforcement Acts during a brief period of vigorous effort. The law proved to be an effective instrument for breaking up the Klan and reducing the volume of terror. The effect of Supreme Court decisions invalidating key parts of the statutes was to emasculate any federal effort to curb Klan violence and political intimidation. The deadlocked presidential election of 1876, resulting in a removal of federal troops from the old South, was substantially a consequence of a renewed Southern capacity to intimidate black voters as a result of Supreme Court evisceration of key parts of the Enforcement Acts.

The initial move to enforce the Klan Act came in South Carolina. Given the complicity of local law enforcement in Klan terror, The state's governor asked the president to exercise his authority under the law to send in federal troops to restore order. In the spring of 1871, units of the Seventh Cavalry—later, under George Armstrong Custer, to have an encounter with Sitting Bull and the Souix Nation at the Little Big Horn—were shifted from the western plains to South Carolina to tame the Ku Klux Klan.

Under Amos Ackerman, United States Attorney General, and Benjamin Bristow, Solicitor General, the recently constituted Justice Department moved vigorously against the Klan. In Mississippi nearly seven hundred Klansmen were prosecuted, and in North Carolina hundreds were indicted. In South Carolina troops were used to restore order, with mass arrests of Klansmen occurring. Some of the accused went to prison, some agreed to testify against leaders in return for more lenient sentencing, many were put on probation. Despite widespread support for the Klan among Southern whites, within a year vigorous enforcement of the law had brought about a decline in Klan violence.[39]

The will of the Grant administration to continue the fight aside, the Supreme Court was to have the decisive voice as to whether it would be legally possible to sustain the effort to secure black access to the ballot and freedom from local violence. As is indicated in the next chapter, it can be argued that the Enforcement Acts were intermittently effective instruments in fighting the Klan and sustaining black access to the ballot box. More than three thousand cases were brought under the acts within a five-year period, and there were hundreds of convictions. Successful convictions did seem to bring an abatement of antiblack violence. Major decisions of the Supreme Court handed down at a time when the acts were serving as effective instruments of prosecution undermined them, and in doing so contributed significantly to the dynamic that defeated efforts to define freedom in other than restrictive terms.

The Civil Rights Act of 1875

Despite a schism in the Republican ranks, Grant survived the 1872 presidential election, only to see his problems mount as corruption in his administration and the collapse of the economy threatened the party's fortunes in the midterm 1874 congressional elections. Many of the radicals had passed from the scene. A new generation was assuming power in Washington, consumed by issues other than the status of the South and the relationship between race and rights. Indeed, in a legal sense it appeared that the bulk of the work had been done and the laws and necessary amendments put in place. The impetus for the last piece of legislation aimed at achieving equal rights came from the last remaining lion among the radicals.

In March, 1874, Charles Sumner lay dying. At his deathbed stood Frederick Douglas and other prominent blacks as well as some of his Congressional colleagues. As the end neared he whispered to those closest to him to "take care of the civil rights bill—my civil rights bill—don't let it fail." Sumner had introduced the first version of his bill in 1870 and in various altered versions thereafter, but by the time of his death in 1874 it had still not been passed by Congress.

As first introduced, the bill prohibited discrimination in railroads, steamboats, public conveyances, hotels, restaurants, theaters, public schools, church organizations, and cemeteries. To the extent that a definition of "freedom" had begun to be formulated in law in the post–Civil War statutes it revolved around the right to political participation and around a rough idea of equality before the law. The Sumner civil rights law spoke to a more sweeping conception of freedom, defining it not only in terms of the right to participate in the political process and to be safe from racial violence but also in terms of the right to be free of gratuitous racial insult as one went about one's daily business.[40]

In support of the statute, Sumner had over the years solicited and put before Congress voluminous black testimony regarding "freedom" as they experienced it. Witnesses spoke of sustained racial affronts and gratuitous abuse in the pursuit of everyday business—walking the streets and roads, entering stores, seeking out a commercial pastime. The common occasions of everyday public life, taken for granted by whites, became a time of trial for blacks. Surely, Sumner argued before his congressional colleagues, freedom meant also the right to go about one's daily affairs without being subjected to abuse and exclusion as a lower caste.

Opponents of the proposed new civil rights bill argued that it moved into new territory. Whereas the civil rights amendments and laws spoke to the actions of state governments and officials and to the criminal acts of individuals, the proposed new law sought to regulate the noncriminal behavior of private citizens relative to whom they would serve in their businesses. There was no precedent for such a law nor was it clear that the Constitution gave Congress the power to reach the conduct of business people with regard to their choice of customers. Yet the Sumner bill spoke to a conception of freedom beyond the political and beyond protection against race violence. Freedom meant being free eventually of the stigma of caste.

Sumner accomplished in death what he could not accomplish in life. In 1875 as a memorial to him Congress finally passed a version of his civil rights bill, although this final act of homage was clouded. The Republicans had suffered major reverses in the fall elections of 1874 due to the collapse of the national economy and charges of corruption in the White House. President Grant later expressed belief that voter opposition to the specter of social equality raised by the proposed civil rights bill had also contributed to the party debacle.

When both houses of Congress met in January, 1875, a heated debate took place over the meaning of freedom for the black population a decade after the end of the Civil War. Surviving radicals Ben Butler and Levi Morton maneuvered to pass this new civil rights bill in the days that remained of Republican control of both houses. Earlier versions of the bill offered by Sumner had mandated public school integration, but fighting to hold their coalition together, the radicals dropped that provision and managed to defeat an amendment allowing racial separation as long as the service available were equal.

As finally passed, the Civil Rights Act of 1875 prohibited discrimination on racial grounds in the operation of inns, public conveyances on land or water, theaters, and other places of public amusement. An aggrieved party could seek redress in federal court in the form of monitary damages; the guilty party also ran the risk of conviction for a misdemeanor with an accompanying fine and possible jail time.

By 1875 the Supreme Court had already begun to speak on the matter of civil rights. Their pronouncements and their effects are examined in the next chapter. Eighty-two years would pass before enactment of another civil rights bill.

Summary

In the ten-year period between 1866 and 1875, a bedrock of legislation was put in place to secure black rights. A shifting combination of idealists, former abolitionists, and political pragmatists provided the necessary votes in Congress. In the nation at large, with the exception of major areas of the old Confederacy, there was consensus on the repudiation of slavery and of the servitude imposed on the newly freed population by the Black Codes. Beyond that there was little consensus on the meaning of freedom. At the time that the Reconstruction Act gave union commanders the right to oversee the registration of black voters in the states of the defeated South, sixteen out of twenty-six Northern and border states did not allow black suffrage. Although the first laws mandating segregation in public accommodations were passed in Florida in 1865, many areas in the victorious North discriminated against blacks in public accommodations as a matter of custom. Continually on the floor of Congress the moderate supporters of legislation promoting political empowerment and equal protection of the law stressed their abhorrence of social equality, their repudiation of the idea that whites would have to mingle with blacks in social settings—inns, theaters, hotels—if they did not want to.

Despite the absence of consensus on the meaning of freedom, the legislation yielded in the ten years following the end of the war provided a foundation for black rights. Despite the ambivalence, hesitance, doubts, and compromises, the decade yielded the Civil Rights Act of 1866, the Fourteenth Amendment, the Fifteenth Amendment, the Enforcement Act of 1870, the Klan Act of 1871, and the Civil Rights Act of 1875. It is not clear that additional laws would have been necessary nor what those laws would have spoken to. The laws on the books spoke to political rights, personal safety, equal rights before the law, and a right to be free from caste exclusion in pursuit of one's daily affairs. It was a comprehensive and impressive body of law, which eventually transformed American society and which in the late twentieth century provides the legal foundation for the pursuit of equal rights across a spectrum of areas of conduct and for different categories of persons.

There is no inevitability in history. It was not inevitable that a body of law would be put in place intended to secure black rights. Every "today" is pregnant with many future "tomorrows." The recounting of the shifting events and unforeseeable outcomes of that first decade after the war indicate that this is so. Nor was there any inevitability that events would take the turn that they did in the second decade after the war. It was by no means inevitable that black rights would be sacrificed. The decisions of the United States Supreme Court played a major role in pushing events in the direction they subsequently took. As is indicated in the next chapter, a case can be made for the proposition that the electoral outcome in the presidential election of 1876, which yielded that the compromise of 1876, resulting in the removal of federal troops from the south, was itself yielded by prior Supreme Court decisions that had emasculated the federal capacity to protect black access to the ballot box.

In the next chapters we will turn to the role of successive Supreme Courts in defining and redefining the meaning of freedom. The Court shaped events rather than merely reflecting them. The discussion of their role in civil rights is a discussion of how they made America. In 1865, a few weeks after the end of the war, C. G. Memminger, former Confederate secretary of the treasury, wrote regarding blacks that "The country . . . seems prepared to assign this race an inferior condition; but the precise nature of that condition is yet defined."[41]

Memminger was premature in his assertion. The nation was prepared to struggle with the meaning of freedom and was able to enact a set of laws and ratify a set of constitutional amendments which defined legal freedom in terms more expansive than any save abolitionists and blacks had conceived of when the guns fell silent on April 9, 1865, at Appomattox Courthouse. There was no national consensus on the meaning of actual freedom however. Shifting coalitions of political factions, commercial interests, and ideological blocs yielded a situation pregnant with many possibilities. It was to fall to the Supreme Court to play midwife to the nation's future as it to began to provide a precise definition of the meaning of the new freedom.

Chapter 3

The First Cases

I n the fall of 1876, Judge William B. Wood wrote to Supreme
Court Justice Joseph Bradley asking his thoughts about the
recently passed Civil Rights Act of 1875 containing, among
other things, a public accommodations clause prohibiting racial
discrimination in access to such places as inns, theaters, hotels, and
restaurants upon pain of civil and criminal penalties. Justice
Bradley drafted a response to Judge Wood, but also recorded his
thoughts on race in general in a background memo. The private
memo provides a rare and valuable opportunity to see a Supreme
Court justice off stage, so to speak. Bradley is regarded, in historical perspective, as having been an intellectually acute and influential member of the Court, and he played a particularly crucial role
with regard to the pivotal first cases coming before the Court determining the reach and meaning of the new laws. Yet at the same
time his holdings on race and rights must have been informed by
his most basic feelings about race as well as by the issues and facts
in the cases before him.

The implicit assumption of conventional examinations of
judicial behavior is that a justice comes to the issues presented by
a case prepared to be guided in whatever direction the dispassionate application of a set of accepted rules of legal analysis lead, differences between justices being yielded by the use of different but
nevertheless accepted and accessible rules of analysis. The Bradley
memo raises questions about Bradley and about the broader ques-

tion of the extent to which a justice's most basic feelings about race have a crucial, albeit unconscious impact, on his position regarding the issues presented by a case.

Seven years before *The Civil Rights Cases of 1883* brought the issue before the Court, Bradley recorded his thoughts on the public accommodations provision in the statute.

> Surely Congress cannot guarantee to the colored people admission to every place of gathering and amusement. To deprive white people of the right of choosing their own company would be to intrude another kind of slavery. The Civil Rights Bill (of 1866) has already guaranteed to the blacks the right of buying, selling and holding property, and of equal protection of the law. Are not these the essentials of freedom? Surely a white lady cannot be enforced by Congressional enactment to admit colored persons to her ball or assembly or dinner party? . . . what are essentials to the enjoyment of citizenship? Is the white man's theater such an essential, if the colored person is free to have his own theater? Is the white man's carriage or railroad car such an essential, if he can have his own hotel and public accommodations?
>
> It can never be endured that the white shall be compelled to lodge and eat and sit with the negro. The latter can have his freedom and all legal and essential privileges without that. The antipathy of races cannot be crushed and annihilated by legal enactment. The constitutional amendments were never intended to aim at such an impossibility . . . does freedom of the black require the slavery of the whites? An enforced fellowship would be that.[1]

The memo is remarkable in several respects. It revealed mental territory beyond the realm of law. It reflected background assumptions regarding "innate" racial antipathy, which Bradley brought to the analysis of those first crucial cases defining the meaning of the Civil War amendments. It spoke to his frame of mind as the facts began to unfold which would bring constitutional challenge to the public accommodations law before the Court in *The Civil Rights Cases of 1883*, the holding of that case along with the holding of *Plessy v. Ferguson* being decisive in fixing the meaning of freedom for blacks for half a century.

As an attorney Bradley had been schooled to read the language of statutes in a precise manner. His business as a jurist was to understand what words meant. There was no language in the public accommodations provisions of the Civil Rights Act of 1875 suggesting that white ladies would be compelled to admit blacks to their ballrooms. The specter Bradley raised was yielded by his haunted imagination rather than the words of the statute in front of him. These spectral imaginings would have been of clinical interest had Bradley been an average citizen, they were to have weighty consequences for blacks given that he was an admired and influential associate justice of the Supreme Court.

This chapter focuses on and attempts to explain the Court's reaction to the first cases coming before it testing the meaning and reach of the new amendments and laws intended to secure black rights. The Court's holdings in these cases had enormous immediate consequences for the black population and for the political process, particularly the 1876 presidential election. They also became precedent holdings in terms of which later cases involving race and rights were decided.

A New Court Forms

On March 14, 1870, William Strong was sworn in as an associate justice of the Supreme Court, followed a week later by Joseph P. Bradley, stabilizing the size of the Court at nine. In previous years the number of justices had fluctuated in response to political considerations. The Judiciary Act of 1866 had reduced the number of seats from ten to seven, the intent and practical effect being to deny Andrew Johnson the opportunity of making any nominations. Following the election of Ulysses S. Grant in 1868, the Judiciary Act of 1869 raised the number to nine, and with the departures of James Wayne and Roger Grier the new president was given the opportunity of naming two new justices.

The selection of Supreme Court nominees has always been influenced by the immediate political issues facing a president. Thus it was for Grant and his party. But it was also true that the Republican Party had multiple interests in the years immediately following the war. The irony and tragedy with regard to Grant's appointments lay in the fact that they served the immediate interests of the party while undermining the party's long-term interest in sustaining black security and black voting rights.

The politics of race and emancipation had driven debate during the presidential election, but by the time Grant assumed office a more serious problem loomed before him. In the weeks immediately after the outbreak of hostilities in 1861, belief had been widespread in the North that the war would be over quickly. The Union defeat at Bull Run dispelled that fantasy, thereby facing Lincoln with the unhappy prospect of making demands on a demoralized population for financial support of an open-ended struggle with the South. Contemporary comment indicated that "there was widespread opposition among the strongest advocates of the war, to all measures which would at an early stage render the contest, pecuniarily oppressive, and hence make it unpopular."[2]

In the dark days after the loss at Bull Run, the administration was faced with multiple challenges: sustaining civilian morale, encouraging enlistment in the ranks, and finding the money to finance the war. Among a variety of measures intended to meet the fiscal challenge, Congress authorized the issuance of paper money, making the new currency "legal tender" for the payment of all public and private debts. The law allowed Washington to finance the war with new greenbacks of its own issuance.

The substitution of paper for metal was a matter of enormous concern to contractors who supplied war materials, expecting to be paid in gold, but who were forced instead to take paper currency of uncertain value. The immediate concern of the Grant administration related to the possibility that the Supreme Court might repudiate the use of greenbacks to pay off debts incurred before the law had been passed. And indeed in the case of *Hepburn v. Griswald*, much to the chagrin of the Grant administration, the seven-member Court appeared to have done precisely that. If the decision were to be sustained following reargument before a fully staffed Court, dark days and a heavy burden loomed for the United States treasury. Grant sought nominees who would see things the government's way on the legal tender issue and, indeed, in their first term on the bench Strong and Bradley formed part of a majority on a divided court ruling that greenbacks were legal tender for all purposes.

The Grant administration and the Republican Party also had a stake in the looming court challenges to the constitutionality of federal efforts to intervene on behalf of blacks in matters which had traditionally been left to the states, but concern with Strong and Bradley's soundness on the legal tender issue obscured consideration of their views and probable tendencies on the equally fundamental issue of race and rights.

The views and holdings of the two new justices were to have

an enormous impact on black fate and fortunes. Bradley, in particular, in his twenty-two years on the bench was to play a major role in formulating the definition of freedom. He was instrumental in shaping a mode of constitutional interpretation that reconciled the egalitarian language of the reconstruction amendments to the harsh realities of an evolving caste system. The short-run benefit of two sound votes on the legal tender issue were obtained at a cost unforeseen by the Republicans in terms of their stake in racial equity. The dearest price however was to be paid by Afro-Americans.

Bradley and Strong joined a Court for which the underlying issues of the war—race and federalism—had been the defining issues of their generation. More than a century later the experience of the Vietnam War and positions taken on the role of the United States in that struggle were to define a political generation. To an even greater extent the Civil War defined political generations well into the twentieth century. The subjective meaning of the Civil War experience for the jurisprudence of the men sitting on the bench as the first civil rights cases worked their way up to the Court is of more than theoretical importance.

To a great extent the Court to which Strong and Bradley ascended helped make America. It was the first court to grapple with issues related to the meaning of "freedom" and "civil rights" for a free black population. In the absence of a national consensus the Court was peculiarly poised to give impetus to one side or the other by virtue of its mandate to state what the Constitution might allow in terms of federal intervention to protect blacks and redefine their status. Fundamental to an understanding of their jurisprudence relative to the new issues of race and rights is an understanding of how they related to the underlying issues in the defining event of their generation—the Civil War.

There were two men on the Court whose personal biographies spoke to a deep concern with black rights and who might have been expected to lead in any struggle to redefine federalism in such a way as to accommodate an expanded federal role in the protection of black rights. But as the first cases began to work their way up through the system toward the Supreme Court, the figure who would have been expected to be the leading voice for a jurisprudence of racial reform was deeply compromised.

The Court to which Bradley and Strong ascended was presided over by Chief Justice Salmon Portland Chase, once a towering figure on the political landscape, a former governor, senator, and Secretary of the Treasury during the war. Upon meeting Chase for the first time in 1861, Lincoln himself had said, he "is about 150 to any other man's one hundred."[3] Other commentators remarked that he "looked as you would wish a statesman to look."[4] But by 1870 he was a hollow figure, bereft of meaning and purpose in his life and bereft of dignity or the respect of his colleagues. Neither the calculations of ambition nor the bedrock of principle provided a framework for his thinking with regard to the new issues coming before the Court. Chase's personal biography, his betrayal of "the better angels of his nature," foreshadowed the trajectory to be taken by the Republican Party itself on matters of race, rights, and power.

Two years before the new justices took their seats Chase had been tempted by king makers with visions of a presidential nomination, obtainable only if he repudiated the principles of racial equity that he had championed all his adult life. Indeed, had Chase not been an early and forceful spokesman for black rights he might never have been on the national stage to begin with. As a young attorney he had championed the cause of Matilda, a black child who had escaped from her slave master and sought refuge in the home of an Ohio abolitionist. Later he gained national prominence defending Peter Van Zandt, accused of violating the Fugitive Slave Act by helping a number of blacks escape bondage. In 1860 he sought the Republican presidential nomination, receiving strong support from antislavery elements within the party. Drawing on his talents, Lincoln had made him secretary of the treasury, charged with finding a way of paying for the increasingly cataclysmic struggle with the South. But also sensing a rival for the oval office, Lincoln appointed him to the Court in 1864.

Although he had flirted with colonization schemes at an early point in his life he had more consistently been a vigorous advocate of black rights, constantly seeking to enlarge the sphere within which blacks were guaranteed fair treatment under the law. Within the cabinet he had been a vigorous spokesman for racial justice and had pressed Lincoln to seek nationwide emancipation by Constitutional amendment. In April, 1865, barely two weeks after the war's end, the *Black Republican* newspaper carried an account of his presiding over a meeting of the National Freedman's Association, calling for greater aid for the recently emancipated population.[5] Later he sought to convince Andrew Johnson that the Thirteenth Amendment incorporated the Bill of Rights and that the Constitution could be read to bar private as well as official acts of racial discrimination.

As the 1868 election approached, Chase saw the names of what he must have regarded as lesser men advanced as serious candidates for the presidency. He was also a man now past sixty for whom the crown, if were to be worn, must be worn soon. Whatever Chase's moral stature as a defender of runaway slaves, whatever his accomplishments as cabinet officer and chief justice of the Supreme Court, Ulysses S. Grant's glamour as conqueror of the South and savior of the union made him a more attractive nominee to the majority of Republicans.

As the cold wind of political reality dimmed the candle of his political ambitions Chase succumbed to the blandishments of operatives within the Democratic Party who dangled before him the possibility of that party's nomination. He had but to express appreciation of the South's predicament, profess an understanding of that region's struggle to find a proper place for a barbarous African horde, unfit by nature for the demands of a civilized society.

A colleague on the Court had commented that it was unfortunate that, upon accepting the chief justiceship, Chase "did not give up entirely his ambition for the Presidency (which) amounted to a passion." And in the summer of 1868 pursuit of that passion was to consume whatever sense of moral purpose had hitherto guided his public life, and also destroy his capacity to lead the Court when the first great cases involving the meaning of black freedom under the Constitution came before the justices.

Late in June, 1868, leaders of a faction within the Democratic Party were in touch with Chase by letter: "If you are not nominated, Grant will probably be elected, and the South Africanized or the negro destroyed." Early in July Chase let it be known that he believed that the South should be left to solve its own problems free from federal intervention: "the practical disposition of the question of suffrage, as well as all other domestic questions, is for the People of the States themselves, not for outsiders." Shortly thereafter the *New York Herald* newspaper carried as its lead editorial, "Universal Nigger Suffrage—The Great Issue of the Campaign," and went on to opine that "if Mr. Chase becomes the candidate . . . he will recognize it as the issue and sustain the constitution and the legitimate right of the States as the true law. We can announce from the best authority that he will do this."[6]

The Chase faction failed to prevail. The Democratic nomination went to Horace Seymour, leaving Chase's integrity in the wreckage of their failure. A student of his career remarked that "it had been Chase's peculiar distinction that he seemed always to take his stand on the highest moral ground—from which his admirers were convinced he could never be moved." In May, 1868, he had himself written, "I believe I could refuse the throne of the world if it were offered me at the price of abandoning the cause of equal rights and equal justice for all men. Indeed, 'what would it profit a man to gain the whole world and lose his own soul?'"⁷ Yet within a month he had declared himself prepared to turn black fate over to Southern mercies if the crown could be fitted to his head. And when the crown was snatched away he stood bereft of dignity, honor, and whatever ability he might have had to lead the Court in the fight to accommodate strong federal intervention on behalf of black rights to traditional, and often racially motivated, defenses of federalism.

Chase's loss of credibility left only one justice on the Court whose personal involvement in the moral struggle against slavery and for the rights of blacks translated into a judicial philosophy appreciative of what "states rights" meant in human terms for black citizens. Noah Swayne, Lincoln's first nominee to the Court in 1862, had shown a lifelong commitment to black rights. The son of antislavery Quakers, he became involved in defending runaway slaves as an aspect of his legal practice. Once a Democrat, he switched to the Republican Party in the 1850s as the issue of slavery began to tear the nation apart. From his seat on the Court he had lobbied hard for passage of the Fifteenth Amendment, guaranteeing black voting rights. As indicated in the previous chapter, he had handed down the first ruling ever on a civil rights law, upholding the constitutionality of the provision of the Civil Rights Act of 1866, which had permitted the shifting of the prosecution of the white burglars of Nancy Turner's home to federal court, given that Kentucky law barred her from testifying against them in state court.

Chase's moral collapse and retirement from the court in 1873 and Swayne's modest gifts ceded intellectual leadership of the court on matters of race and rights to Joseph Bradley. Historians refer to the Court of that period as "the Waite Court," after Morrison Waite who succeeded Salmon Chase as chief justice, but in the pivotal cases going to the reach and meaning of the reformist amendments and laws of the postwar period it was really the "Bradley Court."

Bradley was the driving intellectual force behind the court's holdings in *Cruikshank* and *Reese*, pioneer cases having decisive consequences with regard to the definition of freedom for blacks. In the cases coming before the court testing the reach of the new amendments and the meaning of freedom, Bradley's was the dominant intellect. Although Morrison Waite wrote the holdings of both *Cruikshank* and *Reese,* the chief justice "often relied upon Bradley as his intellectual superior, and apparently worked well in that relationship."[7] Students of the Court have indicated that only Stephen Field and Samuel Miller could compete with Bradley intellectually, but "Bradley was a better lawyer than either of them."[8]

The mode of analysis formulated by Bradley in the pioneer cases involving the post–Civil War civil rights laws remain more than a century later the preferred mode employed by justices generally unsympathetic to the laws passed in the wake of the civil rights movement of the 1960s. This mode of analysis can be termed "formalism." It involves an exceedingly narrow construction of statutory language, words being given such a constricted meaning that a progressive statute is divorced from the untidy abuses it was meant to correct. Justice John Marshall Harlan, Kentuckian and ex-slave holder captured the essence of formalism in his dissent from Bradley's majority holding in the *Civil Rights Cases of 1883* declaring the public accommodations sections of the Civil Rights Act of 1875 unconstitutional. "The opinion in these cases proceeds . . . on grounds entirely too narrow and artificial. The substance and spirit of the recent amendments . . . have been sacrificed by a subtle and ingenious verbal criticism."[9]

By all accounts Bradley was a man possessed of sharp intellect, but it was an intelligence that functioned within the framework of the most conventional conservative assumptions and pieties of his day. There is hardly a word or thought in his holdings on race derived from assumptions outside the boundaries of the conventional wisdom of the most staid sectors of society. But within those limits he was an acute thinker. In this respect, his nearest equivalent among more recent justices would be William Rehnquist.

It would be idle and simplistic to posit obvious relationships between a justice's personality and his jurisprudence, but students of the Supreme Court have suggested that "An examination of the personalities of judges is a useful approach in understanding aspects of judicial behavior."[10] And, indeed, there are grounds for viewing certain deeply imbedded traits of Bradley's personality as coextensive with the world view reflected in his jurisprudence. He was a man obsessed by the need for order, biographers recounting that "order was the key to Bradley's day." In an 1882 letter he recounted in precise detail the sequence of his day: "I don't rise till 7 . . . and at (7:30) go into my study . . . and put a pot of coffee on the gas, and when hot—fill a large cup having cream and sugar in it—and drink it." He also recorded the seating arrangement of every dinner party he attended.[11] His concern for detail and order extended to the mode in which he involved himself in religion in that he expended enormous effort in attempting to determine the precise dimensions of Noah's ark and the exact year and date of the crucifiction. Clearly, he found psychological comfort and emotional safety in precise order and strict predictability.[12]

His obsession with order and exactitude and the notion that everything should be in its proper place extended to his view of the social order. Adherents of different religions, women, racial groups—all had a proper place in the social hierarchy. In his youth he had expressed the view that Catholics were untrustworthy and allowed as how he could never vote for a Roman Catholic, these views perhaps accounting for an inquiry from the National Anti-Papal League years later as to whether he would accept honorary membership in the organization. He allowed that his position on the bench precluded him from doing so.[13]

His concurrent opinion in the celebrated case involving Myra Bradwell reflected his view of the proper place of women in the social order. *Bradwell v. Illinois* began in 1869 with the Illinois Bar Association denying Myra Bradwell a license to practice law on the grounds that she was a woman. There had been no question as to her qualifications: the sole issue was her gender. Bradwell contested the matter, arguing that the language in the Fourteenth Amendment prohibited states and their agents, including bar associations, from denying their residents the "privileges and immunities" of citizenship. In other words, no state could deny a resident a right he or she enjoyed by virtue of being a citizen of the United States. By 1873 the matter reached the United States Supreme Court, a majority of the Court siding with Illinois in not finding the right to practice law to be one of the "privileges and immunities" guaranteed by the new amendment.

Not leaving well enough alone, Bradley wrote a concurrent opinion going beyond the particulars of the law, issues of federalism, and the meaning of the Fourteenth Amendment. The state could properly refuse to license women to practice law because, "The paramount destiny and mission of woman is to fulfill the noble and benign office of wife and mother. (This) is the law of the creator." And although he believed in the "human movement for the advancement of women . . . they should not aspire to professions such as law for which their . . . proper tendency and delicacy" made them unfit.[14]

His judicial comment on gender reflected sentiments expressed in private correspondence. Nine years earlier he had written to his daughter complimenting her on her graceful use of the language in her letters to him. Skill in the use of the mother tongue "is one of the most fortunate of gifts . . . a man who has it can make his way in the world anywhere. A woman who has it is a fit companion and help mate for man."[15] In a similar manner, his privately expressed sentiments regarding race would later be reflected in his public and judicial holdings on civil rights.

Bradley was most comfortable in a world of order, precision, and predictability. To the extent that he could, he arranged the circumstances of his daily life such as to yield order and fixed predictability. He became furious when forced to depart from his schedule. A biographer recounts that he once missed a train because his wife insisted that he wear a new pair of trousers. He returned home, seized a pen knife, and slashed up the trousers, muttering, "You'll never compel me to miss another train."[16]

The rigidity and inflexibility in his approach to life translated into an expectation that everything happen precisely as he should desire, that life hold no surprises nor pose any need for adaptation to the unexpected or the unknown. His voluminous correspondence reflects no grasp of this tendency, no insight into self, as he recounts incident after incident of a visceral intolerance for ambiguity and the unexpected. In an 1871 letter to his daughter he told of being in Savannah, Georgia, and boarding a horse drawn trolley to go to church. "I requested the driver to put me down at Broad Street (in which the best Presbyterian preaching was to be had); but the stupid fool (who makes me mad every time I think of him since) put me out at Broughton Street, which had nothing but an Episcopal Church in it. . . . This accident had such an effect on my temper, that I have not made an attempt to go to church since."[17]

The postwar laws and amendments represented, above all else, a breach of order. They sought to alter the relationship between the races. They spoke to revolutionary changes in the relationship between the states and the federal government. Under the best of circumstances, and had there been universal acceptance of their premises and objectives, the nation would still have had a prolonged period of confusion and uncertainty as to the rights and duties of its citizens and the authority of the various levels of government.

For the obsessive personality the proposed, law-driven changes, were probably viscerally unsettling. For the obsessive personality with judicial responsibilities the massive social transformations promised by the new statutes, the mammoth departures from order, were probably intellectually as well as emotionally repugnant. For the gifted obsessive with judicial responsibilities, the ambiguities of statutory language yielded the possibility of formulating intricately reasoned, finely honed arguments resolving those ambiguities in favor of meanings supportive of an already understood system of racial hierarchy rather than an unknown world of racial reorganization.

The remainder of the Court in 1870 embraced men who had been in favor of preserving the Union, but who had not necessarily been opposed to slavery or supportive of black rights. None had been involved personally or professionally in the struggle against slavery and none had championed the postwar Amendments. Political expediency and the pressures of immediate political concerns had led to their appointments, their views on the looming matters of race, rights, and the Constitution being neither known nor regarded as important in relation to whatever immediate political objective the nominating president—Lincoln or Grant—was seeking to achieve.

William Strong joined the Court at the same time as Bradley. His legal expertise was in the areas of patent and business law, there being no record of his having championed the cause of runaway slaves or expressing deeply held views on race and rights. His judicial conduct was affected by deeply conservative social views however. Even while on the bench he repeatedly expressed concern about the corrupting influence of secular values on American society and, for a period, headed the National Reform Association, a group that sought to amend the Constitution to establish the "Lord Jesus Christ as governor among nations, and His revealed will . . . as supreme authority."[18]

David Davis, a vigorous political operative in the affairs of the Republican Party, had been Lincoln's campaign manager in 1860 and continued to be absorbed in party business following his nomination to the Court. He brought neither zeal nor a history of involvement to issues of race and rights. Stephen Field, a wild and colorful figure, had been a pro-union Democrat. Twice disbarred while practicing law in California he had been nominated to the Court by Lincoln during the war in the belief that he would support the federal government against challenges to its expanded authority. Later he became the first and only justice to be arrested while serving on the Supreme Court, being taken into custody following the shooting of the male companion of a woman against whom he had delivered a judgment.

Nathan Clifford had been on the bench for years, having been nominated by James Buchanan in 1857. He was plainly sympathetic to the Democratic Party and was, hence, by implication, hostile to the reconstruction reforms. Becoming increasingly infirm from 1880 onward, he attempted to hang on in office until a Democrat won the White House and could name his successor. Samuel Miller had also been appointed by Lincoln during the war. He had grown up in Kentucky and had left, in part, because of his distaste for slavery, settling in Iowa, then on the frontier. He had favored the gradual abolition of slavery, but as the Court convened in the fall of 1870 had no known views on the bitter struggle over race and rights evolving in the South.

Collectively, these men constituted a judicial generation charged with writing the first chapter on the meaning of race and rights under the Constitution in the post–Civil War era. Their holdings would become the precedent decisions to which future courts looked in accessing black claims to equal rights. As they met in the fall of 1872, the slate on which they were to write was still largely blank.

1872: The Delicate Balance

As the nine justices took their seats on the opening day of Court in the fall of 1872, the country's future as regards race relations was yet to be written. On the one hand, prevailing notions of federalism yielded broad powers to the states to determine the rights of citizens, but on the other, the North's victory in the war and the postwar amendments had constrained the states to afford all of their citizens "the equal protection of the laws" and to refrain from depriving them of life, liberty, or property without due process of law.

These were new and, indeed, even revolutionary ideas with regard to race. They completely overturned prewar notions concerning the legal meaning of race and the power of the states to allocate rights among citizens based on color. Yet it was not clear what the grand and noble language meant on the ground. The new amendments had extended constitutional rights of some sort to black citizens and had constrained the states in some manner not yet clear.

Whatever "freedom" meant was to be determined by the Supreme Court. Collectively they would refine the meaning of freedom and speak to the protection available to blacks: What did it mean to be a black "citizen" of the United States? To what extent would federal courts be available to blacks denied justice in state courts? Had Congress exceeded its powers under the Constitution in attempting to punish Klan and night rider terror? Were these merely acts of local lawlessness best left to local authorities? Was there a constitutional basis for federal intervention? Did the Fourteenth Amendment bar the states from making any race-based distinctions in law?

Popular sentiment was neither uniform nor clear in the fall of 1872. Charles Sumner's ideal of a racially integrated, colorblind society had never been a majority sentiment. But on the other hand, the civil rights amendments had become part of the Constitution only because a sufficient number of popularly elected state legislatures had ratified them, fully knowing that they expanded the rights of blacks and expanded the power of the federal government to hold the states accountable for honoring those rights. Contemporary and respected journals of opinion reflected the deep ambivalence of the better educated classes on matters of race. On the one hand, Blacks were seen as deeply flawed specimens of humankind, cheated by nature of the potential for higher intellectual achievement; but, on the other hand, efforts to uplift the race via training and education were applauded. Indeed, the ambivalence could be found within the pages of the same publication. In the summer of 1872, *Nation* magazine carried an article by a correspondent who had been conducted on a tour of a plantation by its owner, Mr. B. The correspondent recounted his reaction to the black field hands.

> In appearance these negroes are simply brutish—the word is not too strong. The projection of lip and flatness of nose struck me as remarkable even for the negro, and I called attention to this fact while riding with Mr. B. Stopping a passing negro he called him up close to the carriage, and taking a knife from his pocket, applied one end of the handle to the tip of his nose, endeavoring at the same time with the other end to touch his chin. But the projection of the lips was too great: the end of the knife-handle stood out an inch or more from the chin. . . . "Now," said Mr. B., "if I were selecting a negro and wished a common field hand, all muscle and no brain, I should choose just such a man, while if I wanted intelligence

I would bring my knife into play, the straightness of nose and thinness of lips being indicative in a direct ratio of the desired quality."[19]

But shortly thereafter the *Nation* lauded efforts to extend education to the newly freed population, opining that, "It required no keen eye to see . . . that one half of the Southern problem would be solved when a class of skilled laborers should be created . . . and further than this, to perceive that for the present such a class could be drawn . . . only from the superabundant colored population."[20] The newly created Hampton Institute was seen as an instrument of this regional redemption. "The success of the school which is now beyond doubt, has been marked by . . . distinctive features. . . . The first notable fact in the history of this experiment has been the eagerness of the blacks themselves to take advantage of the opportunity afforded them, and their appreciation of the value of education, for the sake of which they are willing to make real and great sacrifices."[21] The "better class" of Northern and Southern politicians and philanthropists were called upon to support such efforts to raise up the race.

Many futures were possible in the fall of 1872 as the Court opened its term in the basement of the old Capital Building. At the same time that Mr. B. sought to convince visitors that blacks were a primitive life form, somewhere between apes and true human beings, ex-rebel fire brand, Robert W. Hughes served on the Board of Trustees of Hampton Institute, committed to a vision of racial uplift informed by a deep paternalism, a taken-for-granted view that blacks, collectively, lagged in the refinements, knowledge, and qualities required for responsible participation in a democratic society. This vision did not entertain the notion of blacks as full and equal members of the national family, but held out the hope that they might come to participate in a more productive way in the national enterprise at some point in the future. In more concrete terms, this version of the elite vision eschewed immediate interpersonal abuse of blacks or wanton violence in the service of restoration of total white supremacy.

In addition, by the fall of 1872, the law had been put to use in the pursuit of racial justice. More than one thousand indictments had been brought against Klansmen and night riders under provisions of the Enforcement Acts. And in the classic pattern of felons apprehended, Klansmen had begun to testify against each other in the quest for lighter sentences.

The underlying theory of the Civil War amendments and the new laws was broadly accepted by the federal judges before whom night riders were hauled. Traditionally, prosecution for assault, murder, arson, burglary, and the other malefactions in which night riders had engaged had been the responsibility of local law enforcement and local courts rather than the federal government. The Enforcement Acts rested on a theory of "national citizenship." Their constitutionality derived from the premise that the new amendments vested broad rights in blacks by virtue of their being citizens of the United States. The states were barred from treating black citizens differently than white under the "equal protection clause" of the Fourteenth Amendment, while the Fifteenth Amendment prohibited states and their agents from using race as a basis for denying access to the ballot box. Presumably, state inaction in the face of private violence against blacks seeking to vote or enjoy other rights, or tacit complicity in the perpetration of such violence, was sufficient to yield federal jurisdiction and prosecution of the felons acting as private individuals under the terms of the Enforcement Acts.

The Supreme Court had not yet pronounced on this premise, but in the two years following their passage, the Enforcement Acts had proven to be effective instruments in curbing Klan power. United States Attorney G. Wiley Wells had taken the lead, securing the indictment of almost 200 Mississippi Klansmen under the 1870 Enforcement Act. From late 1871 onward into 1872, mass arrests were carried out in South Carolina, some of the suspects escaping before apprehension.[22]

In the subsequent trials even the defense appeared to be shaken by the evidence establishing the extent and depravity of the terror campaign against blacks. Convictions and guilty pleas yielded jail time for a number of the accused. Successful North Carolina prosecutions were overseen by Attorney General Amos Akerman, erstwhile supporter of the Confederacy, now viewed as a turncoat and himself the target of Klan threats. The hooded empire never completely disappeared but the hundreds of cases brought against them under the acts made the 1872 election the most peaceful of the Reconstruction era.[23]

Irrespective of the absence of a national vision of racial equity, by 1870 certain concrete realities had emerged. The Reconstruction Act of 1867 had authorized a federal military presence in the South. The Fifteenth Amendment and the power to strike at Klan terror yielded by the Enforcement Act contributed to sustained black political participation and office holding. There were blacks in the Congress which met during Bradley and Strong's first year on the bench. All were Republicans and the Republican Party enjoyed office at all levels in the states of the former confederacy due to black electoral support.

As Grant was sworn in for a second term in March, 1873, a delicate and unstable balance existed in the country concerning matters of race and rights. In limited quarters there was still a strong strain of idealism and an inclusive vision of the national community. Most of the white population outside the South was not deeply invested in matters of race. Elite thinking about social organization was increasingly influenced by the such commentators as Herbert Spencer who explained class differences in terms of supposed innate differences of ability and character as between rich and poor. An ungenerous view of the white poor was not likely to accommodate a generous view of blacks. Nevertheless some sectors of the white elite class brought a strong strain of paternalism to the issue of race, yielding financial support for various kinds of programs and efforts to improve black education and enhance work skills.[24]

But there was also an explicit, antiblack ideology, more prevalent in the South than elsewhere, but found, nevertheless, in all parts of the country. This ideology asserted the inherent inferiority of blacks, citing the corruption of some Reconstruction governments as proof of that assertion. Where antiblack fever escalated to antiblack terror, prevailing constitutional theory provided a basis for the assumption of federal jurisdiction in pursuing the wrongdoers. But on the other hand, Democrats and conservatives argued that the new amendments did not give Congress the power to pass laws giving the federal government jurisdiction over criminal matters traditionally left to the states, including the criminal behavior of whites acting as individuals, even where the intent was to deprive a black of a constitutional right.

The stakes were very high and the issue was more than theoretical. If conservative theory prevailed the prosecution of the night rider would be left to local authorities. His friends and neighbors. If the reformers' theory prevailed, the potential for effective federal action against night rider terror would continue to be a reality. The law appeared to have been an effective instrument in confronting Klan terror and sustaining black assess to the ballot box and, indeed, continued to be a club wielded against the Klan even after the 1872 election. More than two thousand cases were brought under the Enforcement Acts in 1873 and 1874. Then the number fell off steeply as the lower courts and the country awaited the Supreme Court's pronouncement on the new laws. In 1873 the Supreme Court began to speak to the matter, and in speaking played a decisive role in shifting the delicate national balance. The balance of this chapter examines the Court, race, and rights in terms of three decisive cases—*Slaughterhouse, Cruikshank,* and *Reese.*

The Slaughter House Case and the Irony of History

As history in the irony of its unfolding would have it, the first case in which the Supreme Court was called upon to construe the language of the Fourteenth Amendment did not involve the rights of blacks at all, but rose instead out of the miasma of corrupt Louisiana politics. At stake at the factual level was the fate of an association of independent butchers in New Orleans who had challenged a new state law on grounds that it denied them a right to make a living by conferring a monopoly on a small group of insiders with regard to the slaughtering of live stock. In a legal sense the constitutionality of the Louisiana law was at stake. The Butchers argued that the legislature's action in passing the law constituted state action abridging their "privileges and immunities" and was therefore unconstitutional under the language of the newly ratified Fourteenth Amendment. In a more profound legal sense the new amendment's potential for what some termed "revolutionary change in American federalism" was the issue. To what extent did the new amendment limit a state's power over its citizens? Blacks were not involved in the sordid facts of *Slaughter Houses* but, by implication, the issue was a key to black fate. To what extent did the new amendment curb the state's power to sort out citizens for special treatment, including possibly on the basis of race?

The *Slaughterhouse* cases began in New Orleans in 1869 with a series of corrupt acts in pursuit of a legitimate objective. As a better understanding of sanitation and the causes of epidemic spread, New Orleans, like other cities took steps to regulate the location of slaughterhouses such that they would not pollute rivers and streams from which drinking water was drawn. Public health concerns had already lead the legislatures in New York, Massachusetts, and California to enact legislation yielding a measure of public oversight relative to the operation of slaughterhouses. In Louisiana however the legislature's exertions on behalf of the public were significantly influenced by a collection of con men, scoundrels, and insiders led by one Durbridge. More than $60,000 in bribe money had been spread around, leading in March, 1869, to the passage of a bill called "An Act to Protect the Health of the City of New Orleans." This inspired piece of legislation created the Crescent City Live Stock Landing and Slaughterhouse Company and yielded to this entity a twenty-five-year monopoly with regard to the operation of stockyards and slaughterhouses for the city of New Orleans. It was discovered later that the powerful and the influential, ranging from the governor to people connected with the local newspapers, had been given stock in this potentially lucrative legal monopoly.

Even before the law could take effect, two centers of opposition developed. One group, the Butcher's Benevolent Association, was comprised of about four hundred small, independent butchers; the other, The Live Stock Dealers' and Butcher's Association, was made up of livestock dealers not sufficiently well placed as to have been in on the initial scheme. A veritable blizzard of suits and countersuits ensued, first at the state level, and then spilling over into federal court, as the various contenders sought relief under the Constitution. Eventually Crescent City bought off the Live Stock Dealers Association by placing several of its members on Crescent City's Board of Directors and by otherwise giving them a share in the spoils.

The butchers remained outside the tent, however, and their cases began to move up through the federal system toward the Supreme Court. Early on the butchers retained John A. Campbell to represent them and it was Campbell's genius that led to the formulation of the butchers' grievances in terms of an amendment newly added to the Constitution for the purpose of securing the rights of blacks. Campbell had been an associate justice of the Supreme Court from 1853 to 1861, resigning his seat to join the ranks of the Confederacy. And thus, as history would have it, the former Supreme Court justice who had risked death on the battlefield in defense of slavery drew on the amendments intended to protect former slaves in devising a Constitutional argument on behalf of the beleaguered butchers.

The blizzard of suits and countersuits had coalesced into three cases as the matter came before the Supreme Court. The butchers challenged the constitutionality of the law and hence the monopoly it had conferred on the Crescent City Gang. The second case had been instituted by the attorney general of Louisiana to protect the gang in enjoyment of its privileges by enjoining the butchers and others from competing with Crescent City within the domain the state had carved out for it. The third suit had been initiated by Crescent City itself to restrain the butchers and others from setting up a similar business within its fiefdom.

Appearing before the Court in February of 1873 in support of the butchers' challenge to the constitutionality of "An Act to Protect the Health of the City of New Orleans," Campbell offered four arguments, contending that it offended the Thirteenth Amendment by imposing a condition of involuntary servitude upon the butchers insofar as they would be constrained to pursue their living within the confines of Crescent City's monopoly. The act was also alleged to offend the privileges and immunities clause of the Fourteenth Amendment by abridging the butchers' rights as citizens of the United States to pursue an honest living in an open marketplace, and was alleged to do violence to the Equal Protection clause by conferring an unfair and unearned legal entitlement on a favored group. Finally, Campbell contended that the act deprived the butchers of their property without due process of law, contrary to Section One of the Fourteenth Amendment.

Winter cold had given way to the promise of spring as the Court prepared to hand down its decision in *Slaughterhouse* in April, 1873. All of the justices understood that their holdings would have more than a little to do with the terms in which the race struggle was to be carried on. Reflective of this sense of the magnitude of the case was Stephen Fields's statement in his dissenting opinion: "No questions so far reaching and pervading in their consequences, so profoundly interesting to the people of this country, and so important in their bearings upon the relations of the United States and of the several states to each other, and to the citizens of the states and the United States, have been before this court during the official life of any of its present members."[25]

Though not implicated in the sordid facts of *Slaughterhouse*, black fate was hostage to the alternatives the Court felt it had before it. Were the law to be found unconstitutional, the powers of the states relative to the pursuit of measures reasonably addressing matters of public health and safety would be compromised. By implication, the state's power to limit black rights would also be compromised. But, on the other hand, were the law to be found constitutional, the state's power to order, structure, regulate, and limit the daily lives of its citizens would be expanded, with the possible use of that power to shrink the domain of black freedom.

The Court divided five to four on the constitutionality of the Louisiana law, the majority rejecting the claims of the butchers. They understood that their holdings had implications for the ongoing struggle over race and tried to accommodate the broad objectives of the reform amendments to a defense of federalism and states' rights. The results were a disaster for a jurisprudence of racial reform.

Samuel Miller began the majority holding with a long and detailed review of the genesis of the post–Civil War amendments and did not shy away from a candid recital of the violence and racial abuse the Amendments were intended to address. Indeed, "the protection of the freeman and citizen from the oppression of those who had formerly exercised unlimited dominion over him" lay at the foundation of new amendments, "and without which none of them would even have been suggested." And even though the amendments were addressed to racial reform, the general language suggested that relief might be sought on other than racial grounds.[26]

At that point the pivotal discussion occured. Surely Congress intended to protect the rights of blacks and others from the depredations of state governments, but what was the scope of that protection? "Was it the purpose of the 14th Amendment, by the simple declaration that no State should make or enforce any law which shall abridge the privileges and immunities of citizens of the United States, to transfer the security and protection of all civil rights . . . from the States to the Federal Government? And where it is declared that Congress shall have the power to enforce that article, was it intended to bring within the power of Congress the entire domain of civil rights heretofore belonging exclusively to the States?"[27]

In other words, when Congress passed the proposed amendments, which it thought addressed the abuse of blacks, did it intend to assume oversight of all state acts impacting on any putatively aggrieved group? Did it intend to abandon accepted principles of federalism? The majority answered its own question: "We are convinced that no such results were intended by the Congress which proposed these Amendments, nor by the Legislatures of the States, which ratified them."[28]

What then did the language mean? How was the domain of authority of the states to be determined? How was a state legislature to know whether its acts were consistent with the Constitution or violative of its language and objectives? In moving to answer those questions Miller articulated a doctrine of "dual citizenship." An individual can be a citizen of the United States and also a citizen of a particular state. National citizenship was a function of birth in the United States or of naturalization, while state citizenship was a function of residence in the particular state. Each type of citizenship carried with it certain rights and privileges. National citizenship, for example, yielded the right to travel freely among the states, while state citizenship, generally a function of length of residence, yielded the right to participate in state elections.

According to the *Slaughterhouse* majority, the language of the Fourteenth Amendment prohibited the states from abridging the privileges and immunities of "national citizenship." And although there was no definitive list of such privileges and immunities commended to the special care of the federal government by the Fourteenth Amendment, examples included the right to demand protection when on the high seas or within foreign jurisdictions, the right to use the navigable waters of the United States, and the right to acquire state citizenship by residence.

The language of the Fourteenth Amendment did not deprive the states of the right to legislate and regulate in those areas traditionally under state authority. To interpret the Fourteenth Amendment otherwise, the majority declared, "would constitute this court a perpetual censor upon all legislation of the States, on the civil rights of their own citizens, with the authority to nullify such as it did not approve." It followed, the majority concluded, that "the rights claimed by these plaintiffs . . . even if they exist, are not privileges and immunities of citizenship of the United States within the meaning of the clause of the Fourteenth Amendment under consideration."[29]

The holding was hailed in many quarters at the time as a triumph of judicial statesmanship. The *Nation* lauded the Court for upholding federalism and avoiding "the monstrous conclusion" urged on it by Campbell and the butchers.[30] But there were other more ominous implications. If the new amendments did not yield constitutional authority for federal intrusion into domains traditionally under state sway, was federal involvement in the prosecution of private individuals for criminal acts constitutionally legitimate, even if those acts involved the victimization of blacks attempting to vote? Indeed, if "national citizenship" embraced only the few esoteric areas cited by Miller, were the states not free to deal with people within their borders pretty much as they saw fit? The implications of these questions were soon to be felt in the courthouses, highways, and hollows of the South. As *Slaughter-house* was being handed down, events were unfolding that were to yield the Supreme Court's answer to the federalist and civil rights issues posed by the decision.

The Grant Parish Massacre

The Red River flows southeast through Louisiana, joining the Mississippi about 125 miles north of New Orleans. In 1873 river boats making the long trip from Shreveport down to New Orleans stopped at the little towns clustered along the bank. In the early evening of Sunday, April 13, the boat headed downriver docked at the town of Colfax, the county seat of Grant Parish. Hordes of armed white men lined the river bank, behind them smoke could be seen rising from the charred remains of the courthouse. According to one witness, "the horrible smell of burning flesh" hung in the air. And everywhere, along the bank, floating in the water, in the fields, were the bodies of dead black men. Excited and incoherent accounts of the events were conveyed. There had been a struggle of some sort. Hordes of blacks had been killed and those who had escaped were being pursued. One white man had been killed, two had been wounded—Sidney Harris and J. W. Hadnot.

Late in the evening as the steamer resumed the trip downriver, away from the corpses, the smoke, and the reeking odors, it carried the two wounded whites, taking them down to Alexandria for medical treatment. From Alexandria the boat moved on to New Orleans, docking there on Tuesday, April 15, bringing to a stunned nation news of the apocalypse that had occurred on Easter Sunday upriver in Grant Parish.

The news swept the nation. On Wednesday, April 16, the New Orleans *Republican* reported "Horrible Massacre. Many Colored Men Killed. A Few White Men Wounded." The *New Orleans Times* declared "War at Last!" Newspapers and journals nationwide featured the story, and eventually it was picked up by papers in Europe. Although most publications denounced the occurrence as an infamous and bestial exercise in blood-letting a considerable body of printed opinion saw the killings as an unfortunate but necessary response to prolonged and extreme black provocation.[31] In the end, the Supreme Court was to speak to the matter of whether those charged with complicity in the Grant Parish massacre had committed an act punishable under any post–Civil War amendment or law. Their answer was to carry enormous implications for the immediate fate of blacks.

The apocalypse at Colfax had grown out of the ongoing struggle for political control of the South. Local white sentiment strongly supported the Democratic Party and a vision of the racial order which subordinated blacks to white domination. In pursuit of this vision, white factions had resorted to violence. Politically active or ambitious blacks and their white allies had been killed, homes burned, people driven from their communities. Black sentiment strongly supported the Republican Party, and with black support the Republicans were able to gain and hold state office even though enjoying only meager support from white voters.

The divisions were deep and bitter. Men who had fought to maintain slavery now saw former bondsman owning land, participating in the political process and holding office. Former slaves saw erstwhile masters seek to use the political process and terror to restore a goodly measure of their past sway over black life. Hence, the election in the fall of 1872 in Louisiana was a charged and bitter affair which set in motion the events that led to Grant Parish. Amid charge and countercharge with regard to vote fraud and intimidation, John McEnery, favored by the Democrats, and William Pitt Kellogg, a Republican and transplanted Northerner, claimed to have won the governor's race. At stake also was the tenure of a large number of patronage office holders, including a number of local sheriffs. Amid increasing disorder, a local judge directed the United States marshal to seize the building in which the legislature met and to hold it in support of the elements backing Kellogg. As the dispute dragged on and became increasingly bitter, claimants to local offices began to take action on their own. Thus, late in March, 1873, Columbus C. Nash declared himself to be the rightful sheriff of Grant Parish only to have his claim challenged by Dan Shaw, a black Republican.

Accounts differ as to what transpired in the two weeks between the time Shaw challenged Nash's claim and the time the riverboat docked at Colfax, bloated bodies bumping up against its sides. Testimony offered in the trials following the massacre established that Shaw and a number of blacks had occupied the courthouse and refused demands that they leave. On April 13, Easter Sunday morning, Nash and a large number of armed white men surrounded the court house. When the blacks inside refused demands to vacate, the torch was put to the building. Some of the occupiers died in the flames while others were shot as they fled the burning building. Those who managed to burst through the armed cordon of Nash supporters were hunted down and killed.

Three days later federal troops arrived. Most of the mob had fled, only nine men being arrested and held for proceedings under the terms of the new amendments and laws that had been passed to secure the rights of blacks as citizens. Varying figures were given as to the number of blacks killed, from a low of 60 to a high of over 250. Those who were later to celebrate the event with a plaque on the cite of the killings honoring Nash and his followers fixed the number at 150.

On June 16, 1873, the grand jury empaneled for the spring term of the Federal Circuit Court for Louisiana was presented with an indictment drawn up by James R. Beckwith, United States Attorney for that district. Columbus C. Nash, Wllliam Cruikshank, and a number of other parties were to be charged with violating Sections Six and Seven of the Enforcement Act of 1870. The act had proven an effective instrument for breaking the back of the Klan, but none of the convictions secured under its terms had reached the Supreme Court on appeal. The carnage at Colfax promised to be the first test before the Supreme Court of the constitutionality of those provisions of the Enforcement Act yielding federal jurisdiction in criminal matters.

Ordinarily, murder, assault, and similar crimes were left to the ministrations of local law enforcement. There was little to suggest, however, that local law enforcement had the will to track down and prosecute night riders and White League terrorists, particularly in view of the fact that the face behind the mask might be a brother, cousin, son, or neighbor. Yet the negligence, indifference, or complicity of local law enforcement did not, by itself, yield federal jurisdiction. A key objective of the Enforcement Acts was to provide a legal basis for federal intervention where local law enforcement failed to protect black rights.

Beckwith, the United States Attorney, and others leading the fight to use law as an instrument to counter antiblack terror, believed that the Fourteenth and Fifteenth Amendments gave Congress the power to address criminal behavior at the state level. The Fourteenth Amendment averred in its first sentence that, "All persons born or naturalized in the United States . . . are citizens of the United States and of the state wherein they reside." As citizens, blacks were due those rights and privileges attaching to citizenship, including the right to participate in the political process free from race-motivated terror occurring in a context of state indifference or tacit complicity. That indifference or tacit complicity might also constitute an affront to the Fifteenth Amendment bar to state interference with the right to vote. The final clause of both the Fourteenth and the Fifteenth Amendments gave Congress the power to realize their objectives via the passage of "appropriate legislation." The Enforcement Acts were intended to be "appropriate legislation."

Murder had taken place at Colfax. The felons had not been impelled to fury by the outcome of a sporting event. They had disputed the right of the victims to participate in the political process. Under the government's theory they had infringed on rights protected by the Fourteenth and Fifteenth Amendments, which the government was sworn to protect under the terms of the Enforcement Act. Hence, federal jurisdiction was in order. Columbus C. Nash and his associates would confront their fate not before other worthies drawn from Grant Parish but in federal court before a jury panel drawn from a wider venue.

The indictment was complex and contained a number of counts, but amounted, essentially, to charges of conspiracy under Section Six of the Enforcement Act and of homicide under Section Seven. Under Section Six, Nash and his codefendants were accused of banding together and conspiring to deny two specific victims, Levi Nelson and Alexander Tillman, of their right to peacefully assemble, bear arms, and vote without suffering fear of bodily harm or reprisal. In addition, there were more broadly stated counts accusing the defendants of conspiring to deprive Nelson and Tillman of "rights and privileges secured under the Constitution," of their immunities as citizens, and of their enjoyment of the same rights and privileges as whites.[32]

Under Section Seven the District Attorney reasoned that Nelson and Tillman had been murdered while in the exercise of political rights guaranteed to them under the Constitution. While murder itself was not a federal crime, the circumstances of these murders brought Section Seven into play. They had been committed for the purpose of denying the victims participation in the political process Hence, each man in the dock faced two counts of homicide.[33] Some of the counts in the indictment specified racial animus as the motive for the conspiracy and the lethal acts yielded by it. Others did not—the implication being that the racial hatred cited as the motive for one act must, obviously and necessarily, have been the motive for a related act.

The trial of Nash and eight codefendants started on February 23, 1874, and lasted until mid-March, the Court meeting six days a week. On March 16, the jury brought in a verdict. One man was acquitted, while as to the others the jury was unable to agree. On May 8, the retrial of the remaining eight defendants commenced. A transaction set in motion following the impaneling of the jury but before testimony was taken was eventually to have grave immediate consequences for blacks and ominous long-range implications for the fate of the new reform laws. Under the practice of the time, each Supreme Court justice was assigned a circuit to which he repaired for several months of the year, sitting as a jurist and entertaining appeals. Hence, as the second trial of the Colfax accused began, William Woods sat as the presiding judge, but sitting with him was Supreme Court justice Joseph Bradley. The Supreme Court spring term had ended May 4, whereupon Bradley had left Washington to pursue his responsibilities as a circuit court judge, a task which would occupy most of May and June and which would take him to New Orleans and Galveston and a number of stops in between.

Thus, on the Monday morning, May 18, Bradley found himself in New Orleans sitting with Judge Wood as Columbus C. Nash and his fellow defendants stood in the dock. Before the first witness could be called, counsel for the defense made a motion to strike all charges against them save those having to do specifically with interference with voting. Bradley pondered the matter overnight then indicated the next morning that he would reserve judgment on the question. If Nash and the others were convicted he would treat it as a motion to set aside the judgment. If they were not convicted the matter would be moot anyway. He remained in New Orleans the rest of the week hearing other cases before departing for Galveston and Austin.

On Sunday, June 6, he took the train from Austin to Washington, arriving on Wednesday, June 10, the day the jury came back with a verdict convicting William Cruikshank, J. W. Hadnot, and a third defendant of sixteen counts of conspiracy, while acquitting them of the murder charges. The other five defendants were acquitted on all counts. The jury had been persuaded that Cruikshank, Hadnot, and their companion had banded together for illicit purposes, but had not been convinced that they were personally responsible for the deaths of the victims. Nevertheless they faced up to ten years in prison and a heavy fine. Bradley undertook examination of the defense counsel motion in anticipation of an appeal to set aside the verdict.

Three weeks elapsed between the day the Cruikshank jury came back with guilty verdicts and Wednesday, July 1, the day Bradley's completed opinion went to the printers. Two days later, Friday, July 3, he sent copies to his fellow justices, to opposing counsel, to various law journals, including Myra Bradwell's *Chicago Legal News*, and, most importantly, to district judges in the South who were in need of guidance as to how to interpret and apply the terms of the Enforcement Acts relative to black rights, pending review by the full Supreme Court.

Bradley offered three overlapping grounds for finding against every count in the indictment: Congressional overreaching, failure to state race as the motive for the evil acts, and vagueness with regard to the alleged misdeeds. Section six of the Enforcement Act criminalized conspiracies to deprive citizens of rights guaranteed to them under the Constitution. The Grant Parish indictment cited curtailment of the right to peacefully assemble and the right to bear arms as among the objects of the conspirators. The Fourteenth Amendment placed a bar on state action, but did not speak to the bad acts of individuals acting in a private capacity relative to the specified offenses. The maintenance of public order was a matter of state law, and there was nothing in the Constitution or the new amendments that gave Congress authority over matters traditionally left to state law enforcement. If the United States attorneys were interpreting the language of the Enforcement Act such as to yield federal jurisdiction for ordinary criminality, they were in error. If that is what the language meant, Section Six was unconstitutional: "There can be no constitutional legislation of Congress for directly enforcing the privileges and immunities of citizens of the United States . . . where the only Constitutional guarantee of such privileges and immunities is, that no state shall pass any law to abridge them."

Bradley allowed as how the Thirteenth Amendment prohibition on slavery and the Fifteenth Amendment repudiation of race as a bar to voting might have given Congress the power to reach the evil deeds of private parties seeking to enslave or to bar access to the ballot box. But, he held, an indictment had to recite race as the motive for the felonious act. The sixth count in the indictment had charged Cruikshank and his cofelons with conspiring to deprive the victims "of the right and privilege to vote in any election thereafter to be held," but was, nevertheless, deficient because "It should, at least, have shown that the conspiracy was entered into to deprive the injured persons of their right to vote by reason of their race."[34]

Other counts were also deemed deficient in the absence of a speci-fication of racial bias as the motive force behind the conspiracy and the consequent murders.

But those counts that did recite race as the motive for the crimes were found to be deficient on yet other grounds. Counts four and five charged Cruikshank and his compatriots with conspiring to deprive the murdered men of "rights and privileges, immunities and protections secured to them as citizens of the United States" and of denying them the "equal benefit of all laws" enjoyed by white people. These charges were too vague, according to Bradley: "there should be specification of the laws whose benefits were denied."

Other counts where race was mentioned as a motive were also struck down as defective for their "vagueness and generality." The logic of the holding suggests that, had the counts alleging racial bias as a motive for the crimes been more specific, they would have been found wanting in terms of congressional overreaching relative to the bad acts of private parties. Indeed, the attorneys for the accused had petitioned Bradley to dismiss all counts save those having to do with voting, thereby conceding their validity, without doubt, not anticipating the windfall to come their way.[35] Willaim Cruikshank and his companions had been improperly convicted. The facts were not in dispute. It was a matter of law. And, accord-ing to Justice Bradley, the law had misused them.

On October 7, 1874, United States attorney J. R. Beckwith wrote to his boss, the attorney general indicating, "The armed White league organizations in the South from which the most grave and serious danger and consequences may be apprehended sprung into life or received their vitality from the action of Justice Bradley in (the *Cruikshank* case)."[36] Klan indictments had numbered more than a thousand in 1873 but had declined sharply in number given the clouded status of the laws under which they had been brought. The curbing of Klan terror had consequences with regard to the political process. The inability to curb terror could also be expected to have consequences.

Although his opinion constituted his first official pronounce-ment on the Enforcement Acts, unbeknownst to Beckwith and other champions of the law, Bradley had already unburdened him-self unofficially and in private. Following bloody antiblack rioting in Alabama in 1870, Judge William Wood had sought Bradley's opinion as to whether the killings constituted an offense under Sec-tion Six of the Enforcement Act. Bradley replied in writing indicating that as an abstract matter an attack by private parties upon persons seeking to exercise a constitutionally guaranteed right might be actionable under the new law. At a later point, however, he allowed as how considerations of race might change the abstract equation: "The views expressed in the foregoing letters were much modified by subsequent reflection so far as relates to the power of Congress for enforcing equality between the races."[37] In other words, as is indicated in chapter 4, a kind of "racial exceptionalism" underlay his judicial formulations. The power of Congress under the Constitution was a function of the race of the beneficiaries.

As worldly men attuned to the nuisances of public life, the other members of the Court must have been aware of the real-life implications of the decision they would be asked to review. The law had served as an effective instrument for the prosecution of night riders and terrorists. Now one among their number, for reasons they would be asked to explore, had said that the law that allowed those prosecutions could not be sustained. The night rider and the cross burner had received renewed hope as a result of that decision and set about to threaten, burn, and kill with renewed energy.

The appeal from the convictions eventually reached the United States Supreme Court, oral argument being heard on March 30, 31, and April 1, 1875. The record does not indicate that William Cruikshank or his companions were men of means yet the defense team numbered in its ranks John A. Campbell, architect of the butchers' *Slaughterhouse* argument and former member of the Supreme Court, and David Dudley Field, brother of then sitting Justice Stephen Field. Money raised from Klan sympathizers had paid for expensive legal talent in earlier Enforcement Act prosecutions in Mississippi and South Carolina and probably also paid for the lawyers defending Cruikshank and his codefendants. Whatever the case meant to the men facing jail, it also meant a great deal to parties supporting their cause in the hope of seeing the law undermined.

In the fall of 1875, views began to crystallize. Joseph Bradley had provided the basic framework for a position and an opposing view, if it emerged, would have to challenge his premises and his argument. Pre–Civil War holdover Nathan Clifford was sympathetic to the Democrats and unlikely to offer an argument for extended federal authority in the interest of protecting black rights. Neither Stephan Field nor William Strong had a prewar history of commitment to racial reform and had not demonstrated a consistent interest in their tenure on the Court. Indifference to black concerns and a commitment to federalist principles might incline them to affirm Bradley's approach. David Davis had been involved in the formation of the Republican Party but was primarily a political operative rather than an ideologue. He would eventually leave the Court and return to politics. Samuel Miller had been strongly opposed to slavery prior to the war but that view did not necessarily translate into an expansive view of black rights postemancipation. The composition of the Court did not suggest that there was either the intellect or the will to resist the Bradley formulation and emasculation.

As the political meaning and implication of the holding grew with the approaching presidential election it was agreed that the holding should carry the weighty imprimatur of the office of the chief justice. The Louisiana case, along with *Reese* out of Kentucky, were of vast importance and great public interest. New to the Court, Chief Justice Morrison Waite was not held in the highest esteem by his colleagues. It was the office rather than the man to whom they turned. He had no judicial experience nor had he ever practiced before the Supreme Court. His legal experience lay entirely in the areas of commercial and business law. His one notable venture into public life prior to coming to the Court had been as a member of a commission that had negotiated the receipt of money damages from England for allowing confederate ships to be overhauled, take on provisions, and sail from British ports during the Civil War. This experience brought him to the attention of President Grant. Upon the death of Salmon Chase he became the president's choice after three other possibilities failed to materialize.

Upon his nomination Stephan Field had commented, "He is a new man who would not have been thought of by any person except President Grant. How much of a lawyer he is remains to be seen."[38] Samuel Miller moved to answer that question soon after Waite was sworn in, the tone being patronizing: "He is pleasant, a good presiding officer, mediocre, with a fair amount of professional training."[39]

Whereas Miller and some of the other justices were undisguised in their patronizing view of Waite, Bradley exercised great charm in dealing with the chief justice, leading one biographer to indicate that "Waite, particularly in his early years on the Court, often wisely relied on Justice Bradley."[40] One consequence of

Waite's intellectual dependence on Bradley with regard to race and rights was that there was no counterweight to Bradley. Bringing neither great national stature nor unusual distinction to the post of chief justice, Waite appears to have been patronized or merely tolerated by some of his colleagues in his early days on the Court. The interpersonal comfort Bradley provided perhaps also facilitated Bradley's assumption of intellectual dominance over the Midwestern newcomer.

Although he was incapable of providing leadership to the Court on matters of race and rights or of challenging Bradley's emasculation of the Enforcement Act, he brought a more complicated view to race issues than his more gifted colleague. Bradley's correspondence suggests that his judicial formulations on race and rights masked a visceral antiblack impulse. Waite, on the other hand, brought a different sensibility to matters of race. He abhorred the violence and terror directed at blacks but looked to the "better elements" among whites to constrain the night riders and cross burners. He regarded blacks as a benighted race, but felt that they might eventually pull themselves up through education. To that end he became an officer in the Slater Fund providing support for blacks pursuing education, including the young W. E. B. DuBois.[41] It is not clear that Bradley ever considered what the judicial or Congressional response should be if local authorities consistently failed to curb violence against blacks seeking to exercise constitutional rights, or indeed if local authorities were implicated in the violence. Waite, on the other hand, entertained the notion that the interests of the South and the nation would be best served if the better classes among whites were given the opportunity to restrain, and even punish, the excesses of the worst elements.

Even though he had Bradley's opinion, Waite faltered. When shown a draft of the *Cruikshank* holding at the Saturday conference two days before the opinion was to be released, Samuel Miller drew Waite's attention to his failure to mention the *Slaughterhouse* distinction regarding national and state citizenship as one of the factors in overturning the convictions. The next day Waite sent a note to Miller thanking him for drawing his attention to the omission and allowing as how he was not used to citing cases.[42]

Finally, on March 27, 1876, almost three years after the downriver steamer had put into Colfax, the United States Supreme Court spoke to the matter of whether violence had been done to the constitutional rights of any of the black men seen floating dead in the river or sprawled in the fields that Easter Sunday evening. The holding tracked Bradley's earlier opinion. He began with a statement of general principles, citing *Slaughter House* for the proposition that "The same person may be at the same time a citizen of the United States and a citizen of a State." Congress was empowered to protect only those rights which were attributes of national citizenship, and only from certain kinds of abuse. It could not abridge these rights itself nor, under the post–Civil War amendments, could the states abridge them.

This slightly reworked version of the Bradley holding articulation of general principles was then applied to the Grant Parish facts with the same outcome. Congress was itself restrained under the First and Second Amendments from abridging the right to peacefully assemble or bear arms but had no authority under any clause or language found in the Constitution to punish other parties who might abuse a citizen seeking to exercise those rights. The Fourteenth Amendment gave Congress the power to prohibit state denial of life, liberty, or property without due process of law, but the Colfax murders had been the work of private parties, not the state of Louisiana. If Cruikshank and his fellows had harmed the blacks it was not in terms of any "right granted or secured by the Constitution." At best the charges alleged "nothing more than a conspiracy to commit a breach of the peace within the state," meaning that the matter should have been left for adjudication within the Court system of Louisiana.

Waite then tracked and elaborated on Bradley's formalist argument. Even had the constitutionality of Sections Six and Seven of the Enforcement Act not been suspect, some of the counts in the indictments brought against William Cruikshank and his codefendants were defective insofar as they did not allege racial bias as a motive for the killings. In other words, even if it were assumed that Congress had the power to criminalize the abuse of blacks seeking to exercise various rights and prerogatives found in the Constitution, a necessary element of any indictment would be the assertion that the abuse had racial motives. A violation of the right to peacefully assemble was not per se violation of a constitutional right. It depended on why people were assembling and the motive for the violation. And with an unembarrassed literalism Waite restated Bradley's conclusion with regard to the absence of mention of race in some of the counts: "We may suspect that race was the cause of the hostility; but it is not so averred. . . . Everything essential must be charged positively, and not inferentially. The defect here is not in form, but in substance."[43]

The argument reflected the underlying mood and inclination of the Court apart from the subtleties and intricacies of legal argument. It reflected a predisposition beyond law for which legal argument was merely a rationalization. The matter would have been of substance had failure to mention race in some of the counts prejudiced the accused in their capacity to defend, but contemporaneous accounts of the events do not suggest that it ever occurred to anyone at the time that anything other than race had animated the attack on the deceased. Indeed, supporters of the accused celebrated their racial motives, the *Shreveport Times* describing the massacre as "the summary and wholesome lesson the negroes have been taught in Grant Parish . . . by the white men of Grant."[44]

Without doubt, the formalist element in the holding was also read at the time as having less to do with the particulars of drafting indictments than with the inclination of the Court on matters of race and rights. Certain counts in the indictment had not mentioned race and were, thereby, found to be defective. Other counts did mention race and were found to be defective on other grounds. And, at the heart of the matter, Sections Six and Seven of the Enforcement Act were held to be defective insofar as they targeted private individuals rather than the state for bad acts not entailing denial of any constitutionally protected right. Congress had already moved to redraft the language of the Enforcement Act, but the holding suggested language might not be the issue.

The convictions of William Cruikshank, W. D. Hadnot, and their companion were reversed.

Several years later a marker was placed on the grounds of the Grant Parish Courthouse bearing the inscription: "On this site occurred the Colfax Riot in which three white men and 150 negroes were slain. This event on April 13, 1873 marked the end of carpetbag misrule in the South."[45]

Hiram Reese and William Garner

On the same day that William Cruikshank learned whether he would go to prison, Hiram Reese learned his fate relative to alleged misdeeds three years earlier. Reese had neither killed nor assaulted William Garner, rather he was charged with using official chicanery to deny Garner the opportunity to vote because he was, in the words of the indictment, a person of "African descent." Whereas *Cruikshank* spoke to whether the Enforcement Act could be used to curb violence against blacks seeking political power, *Reese* dealt with the use of the law to curb official fraud as an mechanism for denying blacks the opportunity to vote. The twin holdings spoke in a definitive way to the meaning of freedom. The circumstances yielding *Reese* began in Kentucky at about the time that the Grant Parish apocalypse was unfolding. Whereas the states of the old Confederacy had resorted to violence to sustain white supremacy, the masked strategy at issue in *Reese* reflected Kentucky's more subtle and complex approach to perpetuating racial dominance. Kentucky had been the last state in the union in which slavery remained legal, the war having been over eight months before human bondage was finally abolished. Unlike other slave states, Kentucky had remained loyal during the war and thus had escaped the reach of the Emancipation Proclamation, issued in January, 1863, freeing slaves in the states still in rebellion. The other border states, Maryland, Missouri, and Tennessee, moved on their own to abolish slavery, while the Kentucky state legislation refused to act. Hence it was not until the Thirteenth Amendment was ratified and became part of the Constitution that slavery in Kentucky finally ended.

Just over sixty thousand Kentuckians served in the Union army while thirty thousand entered the lists on the Confederate side. Even though the state remained loyal, pro-Union white sentiment was neither opposed to slavery nor supportive of black rights. Black testimony was not allowed in the courts of the state until 1874 and black suffrage did not become a legal possibility until the ratification of the Fifteenth Amendment in 1870, the Kentucky legislature being among those refusing to vote approval. In the same year that the new amendment barring the states from denying the right to vote "on account of race, color, or previous condition of servitude," the Kentucky legislature moved to defeat it. A law was passed on March 3, 1870, allowing the city of Lexington to amend its charter to require payment of a tax or fee, in addition to other requirements, in order to be allowed to vote, this tax to be paid by the 15th of January in an election year.[46] The implementation of this law in a city in which the black population outnumbered the white population set in motion the circumstances yielding *Reese*.

On January 30, 1873, William Garner, "a free male citizen of the United States of America and of the State of Kentucky, of African descent," presented himself at his polling place in the third ward in Lexington to vote in the city council election. Garner had been a resident of the state for more than two years, of the city for more than a year, and of the ward for more than sixty days and thus satisfied all of the residency requirements. William Farnough, Hiram Reese, and Matthew Faushee were "lawful Inspectors . . . charged by law with the duty of receiving, counting, certifying, registering, and giving effect to the vote at the election."[47]

According to the subsequent indictment, Farnough "consented to receive, count, register and give effect to the vote of said William Garner," but was overruled by Reese and Faushee who demanded proof from Garner that he had paid the $1.50 capitation. The indictment also recited that on January 15, pursuant to the requirements of the Kentucky law, Garner had sought to pay the capitation tax "in order that he might become qualified to vote" but that James F. Robinson, the city's tax collector had "wrongfully refused on account of his race and color, to give said William Garner any opportunity to pay said capitation tax . . . having . . . given to citizens of the United States of the white race, an opportunity to pay capitation taxes . . . in order that they might become qualified to vote."[48] And at the polling place Garner offered an affidavit indicating that he had sought to pay the tax and had been refused, but was again denied the opportunity to cast a ballot. Suit was filed against Reese and his companions shortly thereafter, alleging violation of provisions of the Enforcement Act of 1870.

The context within which the Supreme Court was to determine whether the language of the Enforcement Act held Reese accountable was one in which the true motive for the tax law was barely disguised. Fairman reported a contemporary newspaper account, "The city elections passed off quietly. . . . The negro population largely outnumbers the whites, but a provision of the city charter requiring the payment of a capitation tax as a prerequisite to the right to suffrage disenfranchised about two-thirds of the negro vote and left the Democrats an easy victory. The result secures the management of city affairs to the whites for the next three years."[49]

In the ensuing indictments the election officials were charged with violating Sections Three and Four of the Enforcement Act of 1870. Section three spoke to circumstances in which a citizen's offer to meet a requirement of voting was wrongfully denied. The citizen was allowed to present an affidavit affirming the attempt and capacity to meet the requirement and the wrongful denial. The election official's refusal to allow the citizen to vote upon presentation of the affidavit constituted a misdemeanor. The facts attending Garner's complaint appeared to fit within the four corners of

Section Three. Section Four criminalized the obstruction of citizens in their efforts to vote, either by individuals or combinations of individuals acting as conspirators.

Following conviction Reese appealed to the circuit court in Kentucky and, following a split at that level in terms of whether to uphold or overturn the convictions, the case went to the United States Supreme Court. The importance of *Reese* was reflected in the fact that more than forty cases were being held in abeyance pending the Court's decision relative to William Garner's claim of having been kept from the polling booth in defiance of federal law.[50]

Attorneys for Reese and his codefendants argued that Section Three of the Enforcement Act was defective insofar as it failed to require the allegation of racial bias as the reason not being allowed to qualify to vote, thereby transforming any type of election chicanery into a possible federal offense in violation of the principles of federalism and in access of any power available to Congress under the Constitution. Section Four was alleged to have the same defect.

In its brief the government argued that the power of Congress to address factual circumstances of the sort attending the denial of William Garner's opportunity to vote derived from the Fifteenth Amendment. States and their agents were barred from denying the right to vote based on race or color. The amendment allowed Congress to realize its objectives through appropriate legislation. The Enforcement Act and the sections at issue constituted appropriate legislation.

In November of 1875 a series of Saturday meetings yielded a consensus on *Reese*. The indictments should be dismissed. Again, there is some evidence that the deliberations were strongly influenced by Bradley. Fairman recounts Bradley's notes analyzing the case prior to the November conferences. His position reflected the premises of the defense argument. Read in an expansive manner Section Three might compel an election official, upon penalty of a criminal sanction, to allow an otherwise unqualified individual to vote on the basis of an affidavit alleging something other than racial abuse. Congress had no power to compel such an outcome. Therefore Section Three was unconstitutional. Section Four was similarly defective.

Nathan Clifford was assigned the task of writing the opinion for the majority but came back with a draft which was deemed unsatisfactory. A holdover from prewar days and a Democrat unsympathetic to racial reform, Clifford focused on alleged technical failings in the language of the indictment. It had not been alleged that whites had been allowed to pay the head tax whereas Garner, the black man, had not, nor that whites who had not paid the tax had been allowed to vote upon submission of an affidavit whereas Garner had not. And finally, the indictment did not establish that the only reason Garner had not been permitted to vote was race. The practical consequence of Clifford's draft would have been to leave intact and constitutionally unblemished the offending sections of the Enforcement Act, while requiring more precise and formulaic pleading to establish race victimization.

Clifford's colleagues in the majority were not happy. Coming to the conclusion that the issues were of great importance and that the chief justice should speak for the Court, Morrison Waite undertook to author the majority holding himself, laboring on the task through the winter months into the new year.

The majority holding was handed down on March 27, 1876. A companion to the *Cruikshank* holding, was brief and direct: Although Congress could enforce the Fifteenth Amendment's prohibition on race discrimination in access to the ballot box via "appropriate legislation," Sections Three and Four of the Enforcement Act were fatally defective. The Fifteenth Amendment limited Congress to punishing discrimination based on race, whereas the literal language of Sections Three and Four posited punishment for the wrongful acts of election officials against "citizens." Insofar as a white official could be indicted for wrongful acts against a potential white voter under a literal reading of the law, Congress had intruded itself into an area for which it had no constitutional authorization given the objectives and limits of the Fifteenth Amendment. Hence, the indictments should be dismissed because the statutes which had yielded them were unconstitutional.

In the end however, as is reflected in Ward Hunt's dissenting opinion, it was a matter of a mode of analysis yielding the most restrictive and emasculating conclusion with regard to the curative potential of statutory language. The Court had been asked to undertake the task of statutory interpretation, a task not uncommon in the cases coming before it. How should the language of a statute be construed?. What is the most reasonable interpretation of the language relative to the intent of the legislature? Writing in dissent, Hunt made the obvious point with regard to statutory interpretation. The term *citizen* in Sections Three and Four had to be read in conjunction with the specific references to prohibitions on "race" discrimination in Sections One and Two. Obviously, "citizens" in

the latter two sections meant persons of African descent. By implication Hunt was saying that any other reading with regard to fan-
ciful possibilities attending unlikely occurrences was at variance
with the known intent of Congress and therefore, the only reasonable reading of the language. And in the end he addressed the deter-
rent value of the law and the damaging impact of the Court's decision: "The arrest, conviction, and sentence to imprisonment of one
inspector who refused the vote to a person of African descent on
account of his race, would more effectually secure the right of the
voter than would any number of civil suits in the state courts, prosecuted by timid, ignorant, and penniless parties against those possessing the wealth, the influence and the sentiment of the community."[51]

The impact of *Cruikshank* and *Reese* was immediate, practical, and devastating. The 1876 presidential election was months
away. Along with the defeat of a new enforcement bill in 1875,
Cruikshank and *Reese* contributed to the demoralization of Southern Republicans. In practical terms the Court had eroded the legal
basis for an effective federal presence in the South under circumstances in which state and local authorities could not be expected
to protect blacks against Klan and mob terror. In 1873 there had
been more than twelve hundred cases brought in the Southern
states under the Enforcement Acts, and in 1874 almost one thousand. In 1875 as the decisions in *Reese* and *Cruikshank* were
awaited and as White League terror increased, the number fell to
just over two hundred.[52] In *Cruikshank* and *Reese* the Supreme
Court disarmed one of the sides in the struggle to maintain black
access to the ballot, thereby bringing on the most serious electoral
crisis ever to confront the nation.

The Fifth Justice and the End of Reconstruction

About 3:00 A.M., Sunday morning, November 5, two days
before the presidential election and eight months after the Supreme
Court had handed down its decisions in *Cruikshank* and *Reese*, a
number of men converged on Henry Pinkston's cabin in rural Que-
chita County, Louisiana. Testimony offered later regarding the
events that were about to transpire averred that Pinkston was "a
respectable colored man . . . known in the parish as a steadfast and
somewhat demonstrative Republican."

On Saturday, November 4, the last full day of his life, he had held a series of meetings with local blacks concerning the election, only a few days away. Returning home later that night to his wife Eliza and their child he "went to bed . . . not fearing or apprehending any danger." Hours later a loud and insistent banging on the door awakened Pinkston and Eliza, the blows punctuated by cries that he come out and join his "Yankee friends."

The terrified couple refused entry to the night visitors only to see the door broken down and a number of armed white men enter. Cursing Pinkston for voting they dragged him from his bed and shot him a number of times. Eliza, screaming was sent sprawling to the floor by a pistol blow to the head. She was struck repeatedly, slashed with a knife, then shot and left for dead. Seeing that Pinkston was still alive, the assailants dragged him outside and finished the job, firing several more shots into his body. There was one more task to complete. Reentering the cabin, they found the baby on the floor next to the bleeding mother. They cut the baby's throat from ear to ear, threw the body into a nearby pond, then headed back into the night.

According to contemporaneous accounts, "there were 2,107 republican voters in the parish where Henry Pinkston lived, but only 781 went to the polls on election day."

The full story of what transpired would have vanished into the night had not Elizabeth Pinkston survived the attack and testified later at a hearing investigating the terror and intimidation that attended the election. As recounted at the time, "The appearance of the poor woman Elizabeth Pinkston created a marked sensation. She was unable to walk and had to be carried into the meeting room. Her entire body was covered with cuts and wounds. There was a terrible gash across her face. She has three deep wounds in the breast, and the muscles about the joint of her heel have been cut, so her foot hangs limp and useless. She was very weak and fainted while she was being examined. Still she gave her testimony in a clear and straightforward way that carried conviction to the mind of every impartial hearer."[53]

The board's charge was to determine whether fraud or violence had influenced the outcome of the election. Given the reasoning of the Supreme Court in *Cruikshank* and *Reese* the prosecution of Billy Parks, Frank Durham, Buck Baker, and the other assailants fell to local law enforcement. And if there was no local effort, no other legal recourse existed. The assault on Henry and Eliza Pinkston was part of a larger campaign mounted in the weeks leading up to the election. It would be idle to contend that but for

Reese and *Cruikshank* violence would not have occurred, but the consequence of the twin holdings was to deny United States attorneys the capacity to use the law as an instrument to stem the fury.

The Southern struggle against black suffrage had been fiercely waged and was now nearly won. Resistance to blacks voting had been the proximate cause of the conflicts in both *Reese* and *Cruikshank*. The effect of the Court's decisions in these cases had been to make efforts to sustain black access to the ballot not only ineffective but illegitimate. In effect, the Court cast the Cruikshanks and the Hiram Reeses as victims of congressional overreaching. These decisions contributed significantly to the electoral crisis of 1876 and to the formal end of Reconstruction.

The presidential election was eight months away at the time the Court handed down *Cruikshank* and *Reese* and those decisions almost immediately effected the course of political events. In Louisiana an emboldened White League steadily escalated terror against the Henry Pinkston's as the Court raised doubts regarding the constitutionality of federal efforts to protect blacks, save where the abuse was clearly at the hands of agents of the state acting on behalf of the state. The successful prosecutions of 1871 and 1872 under the Enforcement Acts had eroded the power of the Klan and the rifle clubs and the night riders. But as the Court's holdings began to undermine the statutory basis for federal prosecution, antiblack terror became more ferocious.

In 1873 the Grant administration reduced funding for civil rights enforcement. Even had this not occurred, doubts as to the legitimacy of federal intervention as yielded by *Slaughterhouse* and confirmed by *Cruikshank* and *Reese* would have made it difficult to successfully prosecute. The thrust of those holdings had been to affirm state primacy in law enforcement save where the transgressions were state acts. The practical effect was to turn the protection of blacks over to the attention of local sheriffs. The political consequence threatened an essential base of Republican support in the South with possible dire consequences for the party at the national level.

And indeed, as the Southern base was being undermined, a confluence of other factors began to threaten the party's fortunes in other parts of the country. In 1873 the economy collapsed, setting in motion a cycle of social breakdown and class conflict not equaled until the worst days of the depression of the 1930s six decades later. One quarter of the workforce of New York City was believed to be unemployed. Hordes of homeless men and their families took to the road looking for work. Labor violence gripped the country, ranging from textile worker strikes in the east to bitter warfare in the coal fields of Pennsylvania, pitting the "Molly Maguires" against management

As the contraction became more severe in the winter of 1873–1874 and more and more businesses shut down throwing yet thousands more workers out into the street, demonstrations were held demanding government-backed public works programs to ease the suffering. The ideology of the educated and professional classes was not hospitable to a view of government as an agent for the economically displaced, however. Indeed, even the fledgling and somewhat reform-minded American Social Science Association condemned private charity for the unemployed on the grounds that generous help would discourage them from taking work at whatever wages were offered.

The immediate political consequence of the economic catastrophe was Republican loss of the House of Representatives in the 1874 elections. This made it difficult to respond legislatively to the implications of *Slaughterhouse* or Bradley's early casting of the *Cruikshank* decision emasculating provisions of the Enforcement Act. The last act of the rump session of Congress meeting after the Republican debacle was passage of the Civil Rights Act of 1875, with its public accommodations provisions. Benjamin Butler and other congressional radicals understood that the rump session provided the last opportunity in the foreseeable future to advance the civil rights agenda legislatively but, probably did not anticipate that eighty-two years would pass before another civil rights measure became law. The growing threat to their electoral base in the South, inspired in part by the Supreme Court's perceived tilt against the protection of black rights, exposed the Republicans to the risk of losing the Senate and possibly even the White House in 1876.

The mathematics of the electoral process also posed ominous prospects. One hundred and eighty-five electoral votes would be needed to win the presidency. White terror had played a role in restoring eight of the eleven states of the old Confederacy to Democratic Party hands with the prospect that the Democratic nominee would also carry those states in the fall election. Only Louisiana, South Carolina, and Florida remained in Republican hands with Republican governors. But the prospects of the party's presidential candidate in those states in the fall election hinged on black access to the polls.

The perceived sympathies of the Supreme Court and the

Court's holdings had compromised the possibility of effective action against the White Leagues and night riders, and the compromised legitimacy of the Grant administration due to scandal and the collapse of the economy denied it the legal and moral authority to intervene on behalf of black rights. Yet the electoral fate of the party depended upon blacks being able to exercise their political rights.

The resulting paralysis yielded a circumstance in which the outcome of the 1876 presidential election was significantly effected by the terror visited upon blacks seeking to vote in the states of the old Confederacy. *Cruikshank* had deprived Washington of the authority to bring charges against agents of antiblack terror. Hence, the weeks leading up November 7, 1876, election day, were marked by a sustained campaign of violence directed at driving blacks away from the polls, Henry and Eliza Pinkston being among the victims.

Election day, Tuesday, November 7, yielded the fruits of the terror campaign. On the morning of November 8, some newspapers proclaimed Tilden the winner, others hailed a Hayes victory. Hayes himself recorded in his diary that the"election has resulted in the defeat of the Republicans after a very close contest." In the next few days however it became clear that neither candidate could claim victory. Samuel Tilden, the Democrat, was credited with winning 17 states having a total of 184 electoral votes, while the Republican, Rutherford B. Hayes, had won 17 states with a total of 163 electoral votes. One hundred and eighty-five electoral votes were needed to became president. The votes of fours states, Florida, Louisiana, South Carolina, and Oregon were in dispute, each party claiming to have won. The resolution of the national crisis yielded by the disputed outcome came to center on the votes from the three Southern states. Hayes supporters claimed a margin of victory of less than 1 percent in Florida and South Carolina, and less then 2 percent in Louisiana.

In reality the crisis was probably yielded as much by the outcome in the ex-Confederate states Hayes had lost by a wide margin as the outcome in the three states where he claimed narrow victories. The difference between the 1872 and 1876 tallies in Mississippi, Alabama, and North Carolina speaks to the possible consequences of the antiblack terror attending the 1876 campaign. In 1872 Grant won Mississippi with more than 60 percent of the vote, but in 1876 30,000 fewer votes were counted for the Republican candidate, Tilden winning 70 percent of the total vote. Grant had taken Alabama with 53 percent of the vote, but four years later

22,000 fewer votes were cast for the Republican candidate as Tilden won 60 percent of the vote. In North Carolina 70,000 more votes were counted in 1876 than had been counted in 1872, three-quarters of the increase going to Tilden.

The deadlock yielded a crisis replete with threats of violence by partisans of each candidate. Tilden supporters assured him of their readiness to march on Washington, while Ben Butler and a few like-minded colleagues called for installing Hayes by force if necessary. Congress met in early December to devise a way out of the impasse as an assortment of schemers and main-chance artists intrigued behind the scenes to effect an outcome serving private and special interests. In early January a proposal was put before the Republican-controlled Senate and the Democratic-controlled House for the creation of a fifteen-member "electoral commission" to study the returns from the disputed states and make a decision as to the victor. The commission was made up of five senators, five congressmen, and four designated members of the Supreme Court. Stephan Field and Nathan Clifford were known to be Democrats while William Strong and Samuel Miller were Republicans. Initially David Davis was to be the fifth justice, but he resigned from the Court in order to take a seat as the new senator from Illinois. The remaining four justices, after what was later described as "a long struggle," chose the fifth justice, Joseph Bradley. Professor Fairman, in his extraordinary account of the commission remarked that "Although every member of the Commission took the oath 'impartially (to) examine and consider . . . and a true judgment give . . .' it was assumed from the outset that this imposed a unique duty upon the fifth justice, Bradley."[54]

Tilden partisans were wary of the commission in that eight of its members were Republican while only seven were Democrats. They drew hope however from the selection of Bradley as the fifth justice. As Fairman recounts, the Nashville *Daily American* lauded him as a judicial statesman whose *Cruikshank* opinion saved "innocents almost the victims of a foul judicial and political conspiracy . . . from punishment." Earlier the *Cincinnati Commercial* claimed Republican apprehension that Bradley was not a good party man and that he would "not hesitate to give the presidency to Tilden if the technical points should be in his favor."[55] Within days the perception of Tilden partisans would change and within weeks as rumor and innuendo spread there would be calls for an investigation and possible impeachment of the fifth justice.

On Monday and Tuesday, February 5 and 6, the Commission

considered the Florida case, a decision to be rendered on Wednesday February 7. The distinguished historian Alan Nevins recounted that, "All day Tuesday, while it deliberated in secret from ten in the morning until eight o'clock at night, the keenest anxiety prevailed among party leaders as to the stand it would take. Everyone believed that the fourteen members first named would align themselves seven to seven, and the decision would rest with Judge Bradley."[56] And as the members of the commission dispersed into the February night, no one knew what the fifth justice intended.

Accounts as to what transpired later differ markedly. Professor Nevins repeated and credited the account given by Abram Hewitt, chairman of the Democratic National Committee at the time. According to Hewitt he was visited late Tuesday night by John Stevens, a Bradley friend, who indicated in his presence and that of two other men that the justice intended to support Tilden's claim to the Florida votes and that indeed he, Stevens, had read Bradley's statement. "We parted therefore, with assurance that all further doubt as to the Presidency was at rest." The Nevins-Hewitt account claimed that Bradley was visited some time between midnight and dawn however by his life-long friend and fellow member of the Commission, New Jersey Senator Frelinghuysen and by cabinet Secretary Robeson who, joined by Mrs. Bradley, implored him to change his position.[57]

On Wednesday, February 7, Bradley spoke next to last. At that point the commission was divided seven for Hayes and six for Tilden. Nathan Clifford was to speak last and was known to support Tilden's claim. Thus, Bradley's position would decided the matter. A little after three o'clock the doors of the meeting room were thrown open and a waiting throng learned that the commission had voted eight to seven to let Florida stay in the Republican column. The outcome of the remaining disputed contests was no longer in doubt nor was the identity of the next president.

Amid demands that the Democrats in Congress repudiate the legitimacy of the commission and rumors of efforts to force a new election, negotiations were undertaken between Hayes representatives and key leaders among the Southern Democrats. The South would be content with "home rule." They would not stall the process or further battle Hayes's ascension if states could assume near total control of their own affairs in something like the old understanding of federalism. Hayes's people secured a promise from the Southerners that they would not abuse their blacks but agreed to remove the few remaining mechanisms for insuring that the promise was kept. The spirit of the emerging consensus was summoned up by the chairman of the Kansas Republican state committee: "I think the policy of the new administration will be to conciliate the white men of the south. Carpetbaggers to the rear, and niggers take care of yourself."[58]

In concrete terms appointments of people sympathetic to the Southern point of view were to be made by the new administration and federal troops in South Carolina and Louisiana were to return to their barracks. In his inaugural address President Hayes acknowledged the new order. "The evils which afflict the Southern States can only be removed or remedied by the united and harmonious efforts of both races. I am sincerely anxious to use every legitimate influence in favor of honest and efficient local self-government as the true resource of the States for the promotion of the contentment and prosperity of their citizens."[59]

Bradley denied any wrong doing and in the wake of a settlement satisfactory to both sides the denunciations waned. The Republicans gained the White House and the Southerners saw the last remnants of Reconstruction removed. The effect of the Court's decisions in *Reese* and *Cruikshank* had been to disarm effective law enforcement relative to antiblack terror in any event. To all intents and purposes Reconstruction was already dead. The compromise of 1877, made necessary by an electoral stalemate due, it can be argued, to the consequences of the Court's decisions relative to suppression of the black vote, ended the last vestiges of a policy already rendered incapable of securing safety in general for blacks or access to the ballot in particular.

Court's holdings in the key cases of first impression coming before it dealing with race and rights were not inevitable nor were they dictated by the canons of legal analysis. A complex of factors related to the underlying views of key members of the Court on matters of race and the dynamics of Court interaction yielded holdings which largely nullified the potential of the Fourteenth and Fifteenth Amendments and crippled efforts at enforcement. For the foreseeable future there would be no new legislative initiatives to establish black rights, leading *The Nation* to observe in the year after the election and after the major civil rights cases: "The negro will disappear from the field of national politics. Henceforth, the nation, as nation, will have nothing more to do with him."[60]

Chapter 4

From *Pace* to *Plessy*:
If Not Slavery—What?

I t may be useful to review the ground traversed up to this point. The role of the Court in resolving the post–Civil War issue of black status and the meaning of freedom has to be understood against the background of the shifting political dynamic in the country in the fifteen years following Lee's surrender at Appomattox Court House. The political elements that assumed control of government in the states of the defeated Confederacy in the aftermath of the war proceeded rapidly to pass laws intended to restore blacks to a type of bondage. The Northern reaction to these efforts yielded the Civil Rights Act of 1866, the Thirteenth, Fourteenth, and Fifteenth Amendments, and the Reconstruction Act of 1867, which mandated a federal military presence in the South to sustain black rights, particularly access to the polling booth.

The effort to bring blacks into the political arena had major consequences. Their votes helped ensure Grant's victory in the 1868 presidential election and also brought Republican governments into office in the Southern states, some of these governments having progressive agendas going to such matters as founding and funding public school systems. In addition, a number of black office holders were elected at the local, state, and federal levels.

The effort to affect social and political changes in the South and to define the meaning of freedom in expansive terms spawned a counterrevolution. The Ku Klux Klan and other night rider orga-

nizations undertook a sustained campaign of murder and intimidation aimed at driving blacks from the political arena and driving
their white supporters from the South. The attempted counterrevolution in turn yielded the Enforcement Acts of 1870 and 1871
intended to facilitate the apprehension and conviction of terrorist
elements by empowering United States attorneys to bring charges
in federal court under federal law given that local law enforcement
could not be relied upon to maintain order or pursue felons.

   In the volatile political arena of the postwar decade the decisions of the Supreme Court contributed significantly to shifting the
delicate and unstable balance of power toward forces hostile to
black interests. The *Slaughterhouse, Reese,* and *Cruikshank* decisions narrowed the reach of the Civil War amendments by positing
that they empowered Congress only to protect blacks against state
encroachment on a few vaguely defined rights of "national citizenship." Otherwise, the states retained jurisdiction with regard to
most of the criminal abuses to which blacks were subjected. These
decisions gave a kind of moral as well as legal affirmation to a conception of federalism which subordinated black safety and civil status to state autonomy.

   The decisions in *Cruikshank* and *Reese* promoted the removal
of black concerns from the national political arena. The status of
blacks and the meaning of freedom had informed presidential politics and fueled the struggle between the Democrats and the Republicans from the end of the war through the tortured and disputed
1876 presidential election. Black access to the polls had been crucial to Republican success in the presidential elections of 1868 and
1872 and had accounted for winning the governor's mansion in a
number of Southern states. The party, therefore, had a pragmatic as
well as a practical interest in protecting the black voter.

   The practical political effect of the Supreme Court's approach
to the issue of intimidation of black voters, signaled early in
Bradley's circuit court holding in *Cruikshank,* was to undermine
the Republican party in the South by crippling the effort to prosecute the elements responsible for driving Republican voters away
from the polls via the use of force and violence. Denied the possibility of enough of a black vote as otherwise might have been available to them, the party moved to sustain its position at the national
level by reaching an accommodation with elements in the South.
Elements of the old Southern elite, restored to grace, would be
appointed to high office. Southerners in Congress would be consulted on judicial appointments. And white Southerners would be

left alone to formulate their relations with blacks in their own terms.

The *Nation* magazine had been correct in predicting that "the negro will disappear from the field of national politics." The actions and passions of the decade of the 1880s at the level of national politics came to revolve around other issues, currency reform, tariffs, the regulation of corporations and the railroads. The fate of the parties at the national level was determined by the vagaries of the economy and their stance on these issues.

Hence, as the 1880s began, the crucial issues to come before the Court regarding race and rights related to the constitutionality of state legislature aimed at defining the meaning of black freedom—specifically, the issues related to the use by the states of their police powers to regulate social interaction in terms of racial categories. To what extent could state law, consistent with the language of the Thirteenth and Fourteenth Amendments, regulate the circumstances of black-white interaction? To what extent, if at all, did the Thirteenth and Fourteenth Amendments allow racial distinctions to be made in law?

These questions were yielded largely by the limited meaning the Court's holdings had given the Civil War amendments. If the civil status of blacks was largely a matter of state determination, what were the limits in terms of how the state might define that status? As they moved to answer this question in a new set of cases the Court was not constrained by elite or public opinion. There was no uniform elite or public opinion as the decade of the 1880s dawned.

A strong strain of paternalism colored the thinking of elements of the Southern aristocracy. Poor whites were criticized for their crude and gratuitous abuse of blacks, lament being offered for the indignities to which the "better class of colored people" were subjected. Reform elements survived among the Northern elders of the Republican Party and yielded a renewed effort at the end of the 1880's to enact new legislation to protect black voting rights. Railroads were either a party to or supported some of the cases to come before the Court challenging the constitutionality of state-mandated segregation in public carriers, driven by economic rather than humanitarian concerns, not wanting to provide two first-class cars where one might do.

There were different visions of America and different dreams as to what the nation might be. The role of the Court, apart from any technical mandate of the Constitution, is to affirm one of those visions. And in doing so, it shifts the balance of power sufficiently to allow one dream or another to become reality. In the decade of the 1880s the Court began to answer the question posed by its own emasculation of the post-Civil War laws: If not slavery, what? If blacks were not to be slaves, what were they to be? Federalists did not necessarily yield to the states' unlimited power to define the meaning of freedom. The Fourteenth Amendment prohibited states from denying to their citizens "the equal protection of the laws." The legislative history of the amendment supported an argument that racial distinctions in law were inherently violative of black rights. Yet on the other hand the language of the amendment did not explicitly prohibit the states from making racial distinctions.

As with the initial cases testing the meaning of the Civil War amendments, the answers to this second set of questions were to a significant extent shaped by the composition of Court. And to a significant extent the composition changed as the new decade dawned.

A New Court and New Issues

On Sunday, January 5, 1879, Justice Bradley noted in his diary that associate justice Ward Hunt, had been "struck speechless with paralysis." The next day Hunt's opinion was read by Chief Justice Morrison Waite. Later Bradley indicated that there was little hope of Hunt's recovering his speech or returning to the bench. Hunt's incapacitating illness initiated a two-year period of turmoil on the Court which eventually saw four new justices appointed. John Marshall Harlan had been appointed in 1877 following the departure of David Davis to take a seat in the Senate, Hence, between 1877 and 1881 more than half the justices were replaced. The political intrigues and personal calculations yielding the resignations and new appointments had significant consequence with regard to the Court's ongoing formulation of a definition of freedom.

Political and personal calculations deterred Hunt from resigning even though gravely incapacitated. At the political level he was pressured by friends to stay on the bench in order to deny the Republican president Rutherford B. Hayes the chance of making an appointment. His comrades anticipated Hayes being replaced in 1880 with a Republican more likely to choose a nominee to their liking. At the personal level Hunt was worried about not qualifying for a pension. Federal law at the time offered salary for life to any federal judge who had served ten years or who had reached the age of seventy. Ward was sixty-eight and had sat as a Supreme Court justice only six years. Hence, even though unable to sit, Hunt refused to leave.

On October 8, 1880, associate justice Nathan Clifford returned to Washington for the start of the Court's new term. Justice Samuel Miller later recounted the circumstances in a letter: "Judge Clifford reached Washington . . . a babbling idiot. I saw him within three hours of his arrival, and he did not know me or any thing, and although his tongue framed words there was no sense in them."[1] Nearing eighty, Clifford had been appointed to the bench in 1857 by James Buchanan, the last Democrat to serve as president. He had been sympathetic to the Southern cause and was deeply hostile to black rights. He had vowed to stay on the bench until another Democrat was elected and could appoint his successor. However grave his mental impairment he was aware that a Republican was in the White House and, hence, refused to resign his seat.

As the fall 1880 term began, the Court found its effective number reduced to seven, two impaired justices refusing to resign in hopes of favorable outcomes in the presidential election, although they had conflicting notions about what would constitute a favorable outcome. In addition, Hunt was worried about not qualifying for a pension.

As fall turned to winter, intrigue and sweaty calculation overtook the process. Extreme pressure was brought on the aging Noah Swayne to resign in order to allow Hayes, while still in office, to nominate his personal and political friend Stanley Matthews. Hayes and his advisors calculated however that in order to secure Senate confirmation of Matthews it would be necessary to also nominate someone pleasing to the Senate's Southern members. In pursuit of this grand design William Strong's resignation was accepted, Strong having evinced a desire to leave the bench and return to private life.

Two names went before the Senate. the President's friend Stanley Matthews and William B. Wood, protégé of Joseph Bradley, and recipient a few years earlier of Bradley's letter airing his views on race and the Civil Rights Act of 1875. As fate and the machinations attending political betrayal would have it, Wood, thrown in as a sop to placate the South, was confirmed while Matthews, for whom the scheme had been devised, was not. A year later, having been renominated by the incoming president, James Garfield, Matthews finally received Senate confirmation by one vote.

Nathan Clifford, unable to cling to life until another Democrat reached the White House, died on July 25, 1881, and was replaced later that year by Horace Gray, chief justice of the Massachusetts Supreme Judicial Court. And in January of 1882 a bill was introduced in the Senate to allow Ward Hunt to receive his salary for life provided he resign within thirty days. Hunt resigned and was replaced by Circuit Court Judge Samuel Blatchford.

The new members of the Court represented a generation for whom the war had been the defining event of the national experience as it had for the sitting members. To a significant extent their generation defined itself morally and politically by the issues attending the war and its aftermath. Inevitably those issues involved the meaning of freedom for blacks. In effect, the prior Court had said that the new postwar amendments did not expand federal rights, they merely restricted certain kinds of state action relative to blacks. But what could the states do and what was forbidden to them under the Constitution in terms of dealing with their black citizens?

None of the new members of the panel had been involved in the antislavery movement. William Wood had opposed the war, but later served in the Union army, before settling in the South and becoming a planter and later a judge. He had been disposed early on to take the view that the Enforcement Act provided federal jurisdiction for the prosecution of cases of antiblack terror. Over the years he had also sought Bradley's advice and counsel on matters of statutory interpretation and seems to have regarded Bradley as something of an intellectual mentor. It was not to be expected that on the bench he would stray from whatever path Bradley set in matters of race, rights and federalism.

Although professing personal opposition to slavery Stanley Matthews had enforced the Fugitive Slave Act by prosecuting a reporter who had helped two slaves escape. Horace Gray and Samuel Blatchford were the scion of prominent, business-oriented, monied eastern families. Their mental landscape does not appear to have embraced territory beyond the commonplace pieties and conventional wisdom of their class.

The fifth new member of the 1880s Court had been appointed in 1877. John Marshall Harlan's background was in many ways significantly different from that of his colleagues. As regards race he had been much more directly involved in the actions and passions of his time. Given his background, a simple-minded determinism would have suggested that he would have been an obdurate racist, bending the law to strained and implausible justifications of palpable day-to-day outrages. He was instead a counterweight to Bradley, offering readings of the law that honored the federalist ideal while exposing its use as a cover for state-sponsored racial abuse and state connivance in private abuse.

From the perspective of blacks of that time, Harlan's elevation to the Court must have seemed to offer little that was promising and much that was ominous. He had been born into a wealthy, slave-holding Kentucky family. There was little in his life prior to joining the Court to suggest dissent from the views or interests of his class. In 1860 he had supported the Constitutional Union Party, which called for a negotiated settlement between North and South. When the war came he remained loyal to the Union as did most Kentuckians and even served briefly in the Union army. He had voted for "peace" Democrat George McClellan in the 1864 election. His antipathy to Lincoln sprung from his opposition to the Emancipation Proclamation, which he viewed as "a direct interference, by a portion of the States with the local concerns of other States." He also opposed the Thirteenth Amendment abolishing slavery because of "the dangerous character of the principle embodied in it," meaning, presumably, the divestment of "property" without compensation.

A deeply religious person, his epiphany as regards slavery appears to have come when his church divided on the matter and he opted for the antislavery congregation. Following the war he became active in Republican affairs, culminating in swinging Kentucky's vote to Rutherford Hayes at a crucial moment in the 1876 Republican convention, setting in motion the tide that resulted in Hayes getting the nomination on the seventh ballot. In office, Hayes nominated him to succeed David Davis, and in September of 1877 he was confirmed by the Senate.[2]

Bradley and Harlan brought different modes of analysis to the issues posed by cases involving race and rights. Bradley's approach was formalist. It involved reading statutory language in a narrow manner. A word carried no meaning beyond its most restricted definition. A statute carried no meaning or purpose beyond those yielded by the most restrictive readings of the language. The meaning of a word in one clause was not to be inferred from a modifying adjective in front of that word in a related clause.

The Civil War Amendments expanded the powers of Congress and the executive branch of the federal government under the Constitution to pursue racial justice. Insofar as the republic had moved into new political territory the meaning of the language yielding expanded authority was subject to clarification. Bradley led the Court in clarifying in such a way as to limit the meaning of the language and thereby the authority granted the federal government. This approach ignored the substantive conditions of abuse that yielded the amendments and their attendant laws in favor of a reading of language that reduced the laws to formal declarations with little meliorative effect.

Harlan seemed to appreciate the fact that the laws had something to do with a set of ongoing violent abuses and ritualized indignities. The laws were about "something" and if properly interpreted had been and could be instruments for racial reform without doing violence to principles of federalism or the individual rights of private, white citizens.

Their clashing views were joined in the last major case to come before the Court involving the reach and meaning of the post–Civil War amendments, the *Civil Rights Cases of 1883*. These cases dealt with the daily, ritual degradation of blacks rather than intentional racial violence directed at keeping blacks away from the ballot box. They spoke to the meaning of freedom in the new United States in a more profound manner than had *Cruikshank* and *Reese*. In terms of judicial doctrine they closed out one era and began another.

Civil Rights Cases of 1883:
The Symbolic Meaning of Caste

"It was a great case," according to Charles Fairman in his monumental work on the Supreme Court, ". . . great beyond the awareness of the participants." (3) In historical retrospect *Plessy* looms larger, but at the time The *Civil Rights Cases* drew much more attention. The press reaction to each suggests that the *Civil Rights Cases* defined a turning point for people at the time in a way in which *Plessy* did not. The cases were matters of intense public debate, to the extent that Benjamin Harrison, then a leading member of the Senate, five years later president of the United States, made it a point to be in the courtroom the day the decision was read.[4]

The cluster of suits that became the *Civil Rights Cases* illuminated the meaning of racial caste distinctions in the everyday lives of blacks and whites. Whereas many whites might have viewed a case like *Cruikshank* as dealing with bloody events in a faraway place, the *Civil Rights Cases* spoke to how they would relate to the blacks in their city, town, or village in the everyday transactions that comprise social life.

It was a case which also went to the feeling and tone of everyday life for blacks. Racial violence had ebbed with the restoration of the redemption governments in the South, while, outside the South, sustained, organized antiblack terror had never been part of the political scene. In the years following the *Reese* decision the Court had heard cases involving the exclusion of blacks from grand juries. In the nature of things, however, few blacks were involved with grand juries, thus the subtleties and implications of *Rives* and *Strauder*[5] had little to do with the facts of day-to-day black existence. On the other hand, any black traveler, tired at the end of a long day's journey into night, might wish to rest at the nearest wayside inn; any black laborer, spent at the end of the days work, might wish to drop into the nearest tavern; any black family might wish to take the children to the local theater or circus.

The *Civil Rights Cases* spoke to the issue of caste and an evolving etiquette of status degradation. They raised and partially answered the question of whether caste subordination could be reconciled to the egalitarian language of the new amendments added to the Constitution. And they continued the Supreme Court's formulation of the meaning of freedom in post–Civil War America. The decision was handed down on October 15, 1883, Bradley writing for the majority. There were five cases, each involving allegations of antiblack discrimination in access to public accommodations in violation of Sections One and Two of the Civil Rights Act of 1875. There was a New York case, a case from California, and cases from points in between.

The facts of the New York case mirrored the circumstances which brought the issue of the constitutionality of Sections One and Two before the Court. Did Congress have the power, under the Constitution, to prohibit racial discrimination in access to public accommodations such as inns and theaters, upon pain of civil and criminal penalties? The events yielding the case began on Saturday morning November 22, 1879. William R. Davis, a twenty-six-year-old black man living on West 27th Street in Manhattan was joined by a friend, a young woman of African American heritage, but sufficiently light skinned to pass for white. Earlier that day, at his request, Davis's friend had bought two tickets for the matinee performance at the Grand Opera House in mid-Manhattan. When

Davis and his companion arrived at the theater they were told by the ticket taker that their tickets were no good but that they might get their money back at the box office.

Davis returned the tickets to the box office but suspecting racial discrimination refused to take his money back. Outside the theater he hailed a small boy, had the lad go to the box office and buy two tickets for him, giving him some change for his trouble. Davis and his companion returned to the theater, where, according to the *New York Times* account of the incident: "The lady was admitted, or was not prevented from passing, perhaps because her fair complexion deceived the door-keeper, but when Davis, two or three feet behind her, offered the tickets, the door-keeper informed him that these tickets, also, were not good. Davis said they had been bought only a few minutes before at the box office . . . at the same time attempting to press his way through the gate. The gate-keeper took hold of him and forced him out and called a policeman to remove him. When Davis protested the policeman told him that the managers did not admit colored people to their theater. Davis again protested, and said that perhaps the managers did not admit colored people . . . but the laws of the land did . . . and he would try to have them enforced."[6]

On Monday morning, November 24, Davis consulted the United States attorney, Mr. Fiero, and initiated a suit against Poole and Donnelly, the managers of the Grand Opera House, under provisions of the Civil Rights Act of 1875, which guaranteed equal access to places of public accommodations, including inns, hotels, and theaters.

The accounts of the incident suggest that Davis knew that the Grand Opera House barred blacks from entry and that had he presented himself at the box office he would not have been sold tickets, hence the need to have them bought by an African American who could pass for white or by any white person, even a small boy. Educated and a business agent for the *Progressive American*, a weekly newspaper devoted to the interests and advancement of blacks, Davis was active in the struggle for equal rights.

Insofar as he knew that the theater would exclude him for reasons of race, Davis was initiating a test case. The Civil Rights Act of 1875 guaranteed access free of racial bias and the only way to bring about equal access was to initiate a suit which would bring the weight of sanctions to bear against offenders.

Taking Davis at his word, he believed he had the law on his side, as had William Garner six years earlier in Louisville when he initiated a test case knowing that Hiram Reese would refuse for reasons of race to receive his ballot, and as would Homer Plessy thirteen years later when he initiated a test case by refusing to move to a segregated car knowing that Judge John Ferguson would surely find against him.

In each instance the blacks initiating the test case also knew that the ultimate arbiter of the meaning of the amendments and statutes that appeared to convey rights to blacks and provide for their protection would be the United States Supreme Court. Ironically, their actions and the cases they initiated reflected a deep belief in the integrity of the system, a belief that the law meant what it said, and that an affirmation of equal rights for blacks could be derived from the Constitution as interpreted by the Supreme Court.

Filed on March 10, 1880, the Davis case joined other cases posing claims based on the public accommodations provisions of the Civil Rights Act of 1875 guaranteeing "That all persons within the jurisdiction of the United States shall be entitled to the full and equal enjoyment of the accommodations . . . of inns, public conveyances . . . theaters, and other places of public amusement."

U.S. v. Michael Ryan had come up to the Court from San Francisco on an appeal by the government from the decision of the California Circuit Court, which had dismissed charges against Michael Ryan for forcibly preventing George Taylor, a black man, from taking a seat at Maguire's Theater for which he had purchased a ticket.

In Kansas, Bird Gee, a black man, had been turned away from the dining room of an inn. Next door in Missouri, Samuel Nichols, owner of Nichols House, had denied lodging for the night to W. H. R. Agee, a black traveler. In *Robinson v. Memphis and Charleston RR*, Sallie Robinson, a black woman traveling from Grand Junction, Tennessee, to Lynchburg, Virginia, had been denied admission to the ladies car by a train conductor and had sued for civil damages.[7]

The cases had as their common denominator challenges to the constitutionality of Sections One and Two of the Civil Rights Act of 1875 prohibiting racial discrimination in public accommodations. Solicitor General, Samuel Field Phillips, as the government's chief lawyer carried the argument in defense of the statute. A Southerner by birth Phillips had opposed secession and had, after the war, become active in Republican affairs. Seven years earlier he had stood before the Court arguing that William Cruikshank and his accomplices had been properly convicted for their part in the Colfax massacre. A Court different in composition and an issue not implicating federalism perhaps promised a more successful outcome. He advanced two major arguments.

The Fourteenth Amendment prohibited the states from denying to their citizens the equal protection of the laws. Although privately owned and operated, most public accommodations required state licensing or otherwise were constrained to adhere to state rules, regulations, statutes, and inspection. State oversight of privately owned businesses serving the public derived from the fact that the operation of such businesses involved significant state interests such as the maintenance of public health, the promotion of commerce, and the facilitation of travel. Hence, in turning away the black man W. H. R. Agee, Samuel Nichols was not acting in a wholly private capacity, "but in one devoted to a public use and so affected with a public., i.e., state interest." Similarly, the theater owner, the hotelier, and the railroad conductor's racially discriminatory actions had consequences with regard to those state interests which yielded the rational for state regulation or licensing of their activities. State acquiescence in racial discrimination in businesses otherwise subject to state oversight constituted the kind of denial of equal protection of the law to which Congress could properly speak by a statute creating civil and criminal penalties.

Phillips second argument derived from the Thirteenth Amendment and was more subtle. Whereas the Fourteenth Amendment placed limits on state governments, the Thirteenth was intended to place limits on the actions of private individuals. Widespread antiblack feeling translated into near universal patterns of private discrimination denying blacks access to public accommodations, thereby, in effect, imposing upon blacks the kind of badge of servitude the Thirteenth Amendment was meant to prohibit.

The Court met in conference on consecutive Saturdays in late September and early October and on October 10, 1883, announced its holding. By a vote of 8 to 1 Sections One and Two of the Civil Rights Act were held to be unconstitutional. Justice Bradley's opinion is at first dispassionate and focused, but at the end becomes a reflection of the sentiments set forth in his 1876 memo. He developed the majority's position as follows.

The Fourteenth Amendment's implied prohibition on racial discrimination went mainly to the matter of preventing the states from making invidious racial distinctions in law: "The prohibitions of the Amendment are against state laws and acts done under state authority." The alleged offending parties in the cases before the Court were not acting under state law nor were they acting pursuant to any express authority invested in them by the state. On that ground alone Congress lacked the authority to prevent private entrepreneurs from acting on the decision that they did not wish to serve a black clientele.

Further, while the language of the Fourteenth Amendment invested Congress with the power to prohibit racial discrimination by the state or its agents, it did not give Congress the power to therefore mandate integration. In effect, the Fourteenth's ban on state-sponsored segregation created the conditions under which integration might occur. Congress had no authority to affirmatively mandate integration. It did not follow that "because the denial by the State to any persons of the equal protection of the laws is prohibited by the Amendment (that) Congress therefore may establish laws for their equal protection."[8]

The government's Thirteenth Amendment argument presented a different kind of hurdle for Bradley and the majority. While the Fourteenth Amendment spoke to the actions of state governments and their agents the Thirteenth could be construed as placing limits on the actions of individuals acting in a private capacity insofar as their action imposed involuntary servitude upon blacks or conditions which constituted a badge of servitude.

Bradley dealt with the matter by stating that while being turned away from a theater or an inn or put out of a railroad car might be unpleasant, "Many wrongs may be obnoxious . . . which are not, in any sense, incidents or elements of slavery." The Fourteenth had spoken to the positive rights that the freed slaves had acquired—the privileges and immunities of citizenship—and none of those rights necessarily entailed access to theaters, inns, or other places of public accommodation on the same terms as whites.

And at the end, Bradley's deeper views found expression: "It would be running the slavery argument into the ground to make it apply to every act of discrimination which a person may see fit to make as to the guests he will entertain, or as to the people he will take into his coach or cab or car, or admit to his concert or theater, or deal with in other matters of intercourse or business."[9] Mere discrimination on account of race was not and had never been regarded as a badge of servitude, he opined, and hence the Thirteenth Amendment did not provide Congress with the authority to prohibit it.

He evinced a certain impatience with the continued black

quest in the Courts for an expanded definition of freedom. "When a man has emerged from slavery, and by the aid of beneficent legislation has shaken off the inseparable concomitants of that state, there must some stage in the progress of his elevation when he takes the rank of a mere citizen, and ceases to be the special favorite of the laws." In other words, Anthony Davis's suit was not merely wrong on the law, it was impertinent. John Marshall Harlan was the lone dissenter, undertaking what would be one of a number of dissents in race cases as the years unfolded.

Harlan opened his dissent by going to the real heart of the matter: "It is not the words of the law but the internal sense of it that makes the law: the letter of the law is the body; the sense and reason of the law is the soul." The case was about caste. At its heart that is what it was really about, and the majority had found language and a mode of reasoning allowing for the reality of caste to be reconciled to the egalitarian objectives of the Thirteenth and Fourteenth Amendments.

They had accomplished this feat by engaging in a kind of formalist analysis: "I cannot resist the conclusion that the substance and spirit of the recent amendments of the Constitution have been sacrificed by a subtle and ingenious verbal criticism . . . the court has departed from the familiar rule requiring, in the interpretation of constitutional provisions, that full effect be given to the intent with which they were adopted."[10]

Harlan then proceeded to address the issue of whether Congress had exceeded its power in prohibiting discrimination in public accommodations. The Thirteenth Amendment "did something more than to prohibit slavery as an institution. . . . it decreed universal civil freedom throughout the United States." It would be foolish, he argued, to hold that the amendment merely forbade one person from owning another, but otherwise tolerated the recreation of practices very much like slavery in all save formal ownership. The amendment must, of necessity, have been directed at forms of black servitude beyond literal human bondage.

Congress therefore under its power to enforce the terms of the amendment could "enact laws to protect people . . . against deprivation *because of their race*, of any civil rights granted to other freemen in the same state." And such laws could operate directly upon the states and upon private parties exercising public functions, such as inn keepers, theater managers, and the proprietors of railroads.

An extensive body of case law established beyond cavil, Harlan argued, that inns, theaters, and the like had been viewed by the Supreme Court itself as quasi-public in character in previous holdings dealing with nonracial matters: "The authority to establish and maintain them comes from the public. The colored race is a part of that public. The local government granting the license represents them as well as all other races within its jurisdiction. A license from the public to establish a place of public amusement, imports, in law, equality of right, at such places, among all members of the public." Hence, under either the Thirteenth or the Fourteenth Amendments the complained-of forms of discrimination could be reached by Congress and prohibited.

And at the end Harlan addressed Bradley's comment regarding blacks being "the special favorites of the law," indicating that were it not for deep resistance to allowing blacks to assume the rank of "mere citizens" the laws would not be necessarily, but in the face of that resistance the legislative struggle became a necessity. "The underlying purpose of congressional legislation has been to enable the black race to take the rank of mere citizens. The difficulty has been to compel a recognition of the legal right of the black race to take the rank of citizens."[11]

Although from the standpoint of legal doctrine *Plessy* was to prove more important than The *Civil Rights Cases,* the *Civil Rights Cases* were perceived by people at the time as having much more to do with how they conducted their everyday affairs than was to be true at the time regarding *Plessy*. The black reaction to the decision reflected pain and deep despair. On October 22, 1883, a week after the decision, more than two thousand people, black and white, met at Washington Hall in the capital to voice protest. Hundreds more were turned away for lack of space. A number of speakers, including Frederick Douglass voiced passionate denunciation. The psychic havoc wrought by the outcome of the cases was reflected in Douglass's words. "The temptation at this time . . . is to speak more from feeling than reason, more from impulse than reflection. We have been, as a race, grievously wounded, wounded in the house of our friends, and this wound is too deep and too painful for ordinary and measured speech." But Douglass then proceeded to dissect the holding and the impulse driving it: "When a colored man is in the same room or carriage with white people, as a servant, there is no thought of social equality, but if he is there as a man and a gentleman, he is an offense."[12]

Away from Washington, out in the states and local communities, dismay and despair also vied with one another. The *North Car-*

olina Republican quoted Bishop Henry Turner's reaction to the case: "Nothing has hurt us so much since the day we were emancipated as the decision of the Supreme Court. Since that cruel decision I have heard nearly every colored man I meet traveling, abusing the Supreme Court justices. I have never heard so many . . . prayers offered to heaven against any body of men."[13]

Whereas the *Plessy* holding drew little press attention in the days following its announcement there was extensive press reaction to the *Civil Rights Cases* holding, most editorials in white newspapers expressing approval. According to the *Wilmington Gazette* the now unconstitutional statute had placed power "in the hands of malicious negroes to make trouble for white business men." The *New York Times* opined that it very existence had "kept alive a prejudice against the negroes and against the Republican Party in the South." Reflecting a perspective articulated almost twenty years earlier by Andrew Johnson, the *Virginia Free Press* viewed efforts to secure rights for blacks as giving them "privileges far-reaching and beyond anything to which the white people were entitled." The *Sentinel* newspaper quoted future president Benjamin Harrison's speech before a mixed audience in an Indiana Baptist Church seeking to calm black alarm, urging compliance with the law, and holding out the hope that state legislatures would undue the damage by passing local public accommodations laws. But the *State* published out of Richmond, Virginia, provided the definitive comment: "The amendments did much, but they did not make the Ethiopians skin white."[14]

Although only dimly perceived at the time, the *Civil Rights Cases* marked the end of a chapter in the struggle for equal rights. The Court had delimited and constricted the meaning of the post–Civil War amendments in terms of black rights. According to the Court, patterned, institutionalized discrimination, as long as private in emanation rather than state sponsored, was beyond the reach of Congress and the Constitution.

More significantly, the formal equality obtained only with regard to certain vaguely defined rights of "national citizenship." The states were constrained from denying their citizens enjoyment of these rights of national citizenship and from making explicit, invidious racial distinctions in law. In other words, they were prohibited from reenacting the black codes. It was not clear otherwise whether the states were prohibited from making any racial distinctions in law at all. *Slaughterhouse, Cruikshank*, and *Reese* had consigned to the states the major responsibility for overseeing black rights. Within the wide margins yielded by this federalist approach, what were the state's powers regarding race? Specifically, to what extent could the state regulate social life and civil rights based on explicit racial distinctions in law?

The Coming of Jim Crow

Redemptionist governments were by no means settled on answers posed by the situation confronting them with regard to race and rights. The tentative move of Tennessee toward embodying racial distinctions in law reflected the absence of a clear conception of the power of the state in regulating on the basis of race. In 1881 a law took effect which did not mandate separation of the races on railroads and public carriers but merely called on the railroads to provide first-class facilities for blacks. Although regarded by historians as an early Jim Crow law it differed in tone and mandate from the laws that were to follow toward the end of the decade after the Supreme Court had spoken further on the matter.

In practice a majority of the trains in the state continued to admit "well dressed and behaved colored" to ladies cars, according to John MacGowan, the editor of the Nashville *American*. But at the same time there were too many unfortunate instances of "the shoving of colored people who pay full fare into cars hardly fit for hogs and cattle."[15]

Other redemptionist figures such as David Key of Tennessee, a Democrat who had served in President Hayes's cabinet, also viewed race through the prism of social class. In an 1885 speech before the Tennessee Bar Association, Key ridiculed public accommodations laws that would condemn all blacks to inferior facilities, indicating that he "should prefer to sit by a genteel well bred Negro than by a dirty, filthy, disgusting white man."[16]

Key and MacGowan represented an elite Southern view which looked down upon and abhorred poor whites and which traced some of the racial tensions of the region to that class. Key stated that his observations had led him to conclude "that those who are most horrified by the presence of the Negro and find so much that is offensive in him have very often the least to boast of in the way of birth, renown, or achievement." But he also cautioned that if the views of the rabid black-haters were to be embodied in law, if the law were to make distinctions based on a race it could neither mandate nor tolerate substantively different conditions or outcomes for blacks and whites. In other words, if there was to be legally man-dated separation, the accommodation afforded blacks had to be equal.

Paternalists such as Key were moved to this view by consid-erations of fairness rather than calculations as to the calibrations allowed under the Fourteenth Amendment. But it was not clear at the time that the Fourteenth Amendment would tolerate racial dis-tinctions. Indeed, the contemporaneous holding of the Supreme Court itself in the *Strauder* case suggested that explicit racial dis-tinctions in law might be problematic.

Taylor Strauder, a black West Virginian, had murdered his wife. A West Virginia statute of March 12, 1873, limited jury selec-tion to "white male persons who are twenty one years of age and who are citizens of this State." Strauder moved pretrial for removal to federal court pursuant to 641 of the Revised Statutes on the grounds that he was to be tried under a jury selection law which violated the "equal protection" clause of the Fourteenth Amend-ment. The motion was denied. Strauder went to trial, was con-victed, and appealed to the United States Supreme Court, contend-ing that the denial of the removal petition forced him to be tried under explicitly discriminatory state law, thereby violating his right to the equal protection of the laws.

Justice William Strong delivered the opinion of the Court, indicating that the denial of Taylor Strauder's petition to move his case to federal court fatally prejudiced his case insofar as the West Virginia law explicitly barring blacks from jury service violated his right under the Fourteenth Amendment to the equal protection of the law.[17]

The Court had refrained from an expansive reading of the Civil War amendments and laws over the decade in which cases had come before them, but they were not yet ready to affirm exclu-sion based on race. But even though the states could not exclude on the basis of race, could they make any racial distinctions in law? In addressing the matter as a legal question, the Supreme Court was also writing a political agenda for the South. It either would or would not affirm the legality of making racial distinctions in law and in doing so it either would or would not provide political impe-tus to the proponents of a race-based political agenda.

The issue was joined early in 1883. Alabama, like many states, criminalized adultery and fornication, fixing the penalty for a first offense at a small fine and a term of six months in the county jail. The criminal code also contained a provision under which adultery, fornication, or intermarriage between "any white person and any negro, or the descendant of any negro to the third generation" carried a mandatory minimum two-year sentence.

In November, 1881, Tony Pace, a black man, and Mary J. Cox, a white woman, were convicted under the statute and sentenced to two years each in the state penitentiary. An unsuccessful appeal to the Alabama Supreme Court brought the case to the United States Supreme Court where John Tompkins, representing Pace, argued that any law that based the severity of the punishment on the race of the offender manifestly violated the Fourteenth Amendment's Equal Protection clause.

The Supreme Court disagreed. Justice Stephen Field for the majority indicated that the Alabama law was entirely consistent with the Fourteenth Amendment. If a black couple committed adultery they received the same six months each as a white couple would receive, and if the adulterous couple was interracial each party received two years, hence, there was no equal protection issue, a black receiving the same punishment for the same offense as a white.

Implicitly, the Court granted the legitimacy of a state's use of its criminal code to shape and delimit patterns of black/white social interaction, opening up the question of the scope of state powers relative to defining the "place" of blacks in the social system. The Court did not address the issue of why the racial distinction existed in law in the first place. Nor did it address the issue of whether the distinction implied a badge of servitude in violation of the Thirteenth Amendment, but the Court had nevertheless for the first time crossed an important threshold by endorsing the argument that there was a legitimate state interest in discouraging race contact. *Pace* involved an indirect disincentive in the form of differential punishment depending on the racial composition of the offending parties. The logic of the holding also suggested that a state might claim a legitimate interest in mandating racial separation without offending the Constitution.

It was not to be until the end of the decade six years after The *Civil Rights Cases* and *Pace* that the Court was to address that issue. Also it was to be a Court somewhat changed in composition, three new members being appointed within a two-year period, the appointments being driven by political calculations unpromising to black interests.

The death of William Wood gave Grover Cleveland, elected in 1884 as the first Democrat to occupy the White House since before the Civil War, the opportunity to make an appointment. Rutherford B. Hayes and James Garfield, the Republicans preceding Cleveland, had nominated John Marshall Harlan and William Wood to the bench in failing efforts to curry favor with Southern voters and win the support of Southerners in Congress. Cleveland as a Democrat move to fill Wood's seat with a Southerner whose background was more representative of the region whose votes had put him in the White House.

Georgia-born nominee Lucius Quintus Cincinnatus Lamar had been a state's rights extremist before the war. He had drafted Mississippi's secession ordinance in 1861 and later served as a colonel in the Eighteenth Mississippi regiment and as an aide in Robert E. Lee's Army of Northern Virginia. A lawyer by training, he had slowly rebuilt his career after the war and by the mid-1870s had positioned himself as the "great pacificator," an advocate of reconciliation between North and South. By the mid-1880s he had come to symbolize a "new South" deemed capable of working out its race problems on its own, free from Northern interference.

More fateful was Cleveland's nomination of Chicago corporate lawyer Melville Weston Fuller as chief justice to replace Morrison Waite who had died. Fuller was the kind of Northern commercial figure happy to turn over affairs of race to Southern elites such as Lamar. He had no commitment to any particular notion of racial equity. His record is bare of involvement in the kinds of racial uplift programs in which Waite was immersed. The former chief justice had subscribed strongly to the notion that education was key to black progress.

As a young man Fuller had managed Stephen Douglas's campaign against Abraham Lincoln in 1858. Unlike Douglas he regarded slavery as morally wrong but attacked opponents of the peculiar institution as "abolition madmen." While serving in the Illinois legislature he proposed a constitutional amendment barring federal interference with slavery and he had attacked the Emancipation Proclamation for many alleged defects including depriving "loyal men of their property." The ambiguity of his wartime views led critics of his nomination to accuse him of having been anti-Union. That he had never held a judicial post was offset by being an elite member of the Northern business community with a record of sustained loyalty to the Democratic Party and friends in high places. On April 12, 1888, fellow Chicago attorney Daniel Goodwin had written to him to inquire as to whether his friends were pressing for his nomination as chief justice, offering to lend his own weight to the effort, based on having kinship ties to two of the men who would pass on the nomination.[18]

But Fuller's prospective colleagues were less forgiving. Late in April Bradley sent a letter to Stanley Field consoling him for being passed over and belittling Fuller: "I have no doubt that he is an estimable man, and a successful practitioner at the local bar. But this hardly fills the public expectations for the position of Chief Justice of the United States." Nevertheless Fuller was confirmed and Bradley would later offer him intellectual guidance.

The death of Stanley Matthews and Cleveland's defeat in the 1888 election at the hands of Benjamin Harrison gave the Republicans a chance to fill a seat on the Court. While personally liberal on race issues by the standards of the time, Harrison was also committed to the interests of business. Hence, he nominated David J. Brewer, a Kansas judge, impeccable in his views on the sanctity of property and an implacable foe of state efforts to curb corporate power via legislating an eight-hour work day or regulating railroad rates. A committed social Darwinist, he was hostile toward working-class and poor people and abhorred the instruments and tactics they employed to better their lot. The impact of these views on his jurisprudence led him to find that the Constitution also abhorred unions, strikes, and state efforts to meliorate the condition of the working class.

His views on race were complicated but, essentially, regressive. While sitting as a Kansas judge he was the lone dissenter in a case challenging racial segregation in an Ottawa, Kansas, school, contending that the Fourteenth Amendment did not prohibit racial segregation. But, on the other hand, he had been instrumental in opening the first school for black children in Leavanworth, Kansas, shortly after the war. Later in life he drafted remarks for a speech which probably summed up his life-long views on race: "We are told that the colored people are of an inferior race . . . why waste time and money in attempting to prepare them for anything . . . a short but sufficient answer is: conceding their inferiority . . . yet the Master said, 'unto one of the least of these, my brethren, unto me.'" But, in any event, he speculated, apparent black inferiority might be the result of a harsh environment: "How much essentially inferior are these people? Who can tell? . . . Let history answer." Great strides had been made since the end of the war as evidenced by the success of Hampton Institute. It was the duty of whites, he offered, to support such institutions, recognizing that nature might have limited the black potential, but it was God's work and good for the society to help these deprived creatures.[19]

There was a kind of cruel paternalism in his views. Blacks were degraded creatures, but not all bad: "Sometimes I fancy that their warm-hearted, affectionate disposition—and the devotion and loyalty which spring from them—may bring a special blessing to the nation." Along with Fuller, Brewer would hear Homer Plessy's challenge to Louisiana's Jim Crow law.

Fuller, Lamar, and Brewer joined a Court which had not heard a case on black rights and state prerogatives since *Pace* in 1883. The right of states to make racial distinctions in law had been affirmed, but the implications of that holding had not yet unfolded before the Court. As the legal contours of segregation were being formed the Supreme Court did not reflect elite opinion, it fueled the momentum toward legal case restrictions even against an important sector of elite opinion. While *Pace* had said that a state could make race distinctions in law without offending the Fourteenth Amendment, it did not address circumstances where the substantive consequence of the distinction imposed a cost on white businesses. And indeed Mississippi, in moving to regulate race contacts by law, appeared to have done precisely that. In effect, the Mississippi law inadvertently gave a sector of the white business community an incentive to resist a segregationist mandate apart from any consideration of racial equity.

Louisville and Railway Co. v. Mississippi was a precursor to *Plessy* but is also important in terms of facilitating a greater understanding of the role of the Supreme Court in driving the society toward segregation. The ultimate plaintiff in the case was a railroad company resisting the expense of adhering to a Mississippi law passed on March 2, 1888, requiring the presence of a separate but equal car for blacks on routes within Mississippi: "all railroads carrying passengers in this State . . . shall provide equal, but separate, accommodation for the white and colored races, by providing two or more passenger cars for each passenger train, or by dividing the passenger cars by a partition, so as to secure separate accommodations." Failure to adhere to the terms of the statute subjected the offending carrier to a fine for each offense.[20]

The Louisville, New Orleans, and Texas Railroad Company owned and operated a continuous line running from Memphis, Tennessee, through Mississippi, to New Orleans, Louisiana. Upon its failure to either attach a segregated car to its train or partition an exiting car, the railroad was indicted for violating the statute and convicted. The conviction was upheld by the Mississippi courts, whereupon the railroad sought relief from the United States Supreme Court.

Economic rather than humanitarian concerns motivated the railroad as it challenged the constitutionality of the segregationist law on the grounds that it violated the commerce clause of the Constitution under which Congress has the sole authority to regulate the conditions of commerce among the states. The railroad argued, in essence, that Mississippi usurped that authority insofar as it was unrealistic to assume that each train would stop at the Mississippi border and attach another car. Compliance with the law would, of necessity, impact significantly on the way in which the railroad operated lines in other states feeding into Mississippi.

The issue had been building throughout the decade. In 1881 the Louisville, Kentucky, *Bulletin: Devoted to the Interest of the Colored People* had carried a story blasting "the assault upon Mrs. Ed Smoot, by a conductor of the Kentucky Central Railroad, the other day (as) an infamous outrage." Mrs. Smoot had a ticket for a first-class car, but had been ordered into a smoking car. Support was urged for the coming court fight.[21]

Three years later the *North Carolina Republican* carried a story recounting numerous incidents of black travelers being forced into segregated and inferior cars despite possessing first-class tickets. The editor of the paper had himself had a confrontation with a conductor over his refusal to take his sick wife into a second-class car, He had indicated that were the conductor to attempt to use force there would be a funeral the next day at one household or the other.[22]

Bigotry codified in statute commanded that the railroads provide specifically segregated cars. Deterred by considerations of cost as against volume of use. Louisville railroad sought relief in court. The opinion of the majority can only be regarded as "result driven." In other words, there was an inclination apart from any judicial concern to accommodate racial segregation. The justices were not stupid or unsophisticated men and thus must have grasped the nature of their own evasion. The basic problem confronting the majority can be summed up as follows: The Supreme Court in 1878 in *Hall v. DeCuir* had held a Louisiana law prohibiting racial discrimination in public carriers unconstitutional on the grounds that it usurped the authority of Congress to regulate interstate commerce. How could it now do other than find the Mississippi law requiring segregation unconstitutional on the same grounds?

In effect, the Court reconciled *Louisville* with *Hall* and upheld the constitutionality of the Mississippi law by passing the judicial buck. Prior to *Hall* coming to the United States Supreme Court, the highest court in the state of Louisiana had held that the integrationist law "applied to interstate carriers, and required them, when they came within the limits of the State, to receive colored passengers into the cabin set apart for white persons. This court, accepting that construction as conclusive, held that the act was a regulation of interstate commerce, and therefore beyond the power of the State."[23]

Twelve years later, in the proceedings leading up to *Louisville* being argued before the United States Supreme Court, the highest court in the state of Mississippi had held that the segregationist law "applied solely to commerce within the State" and hence did not implicate or violate the commerce clause. And, according to David Brewer in his first holding as a member of the Court, "that construction being the construction of the statute of the State by its highest court, must be accepted as conclusive here." Brewer then stated the pleasant conclusion to be drawn from this construction: "If it be a matter respecting wholly commerce within a State, then, obviously, there is no violation of the commerce clause of the Federal constitution."[24]

In his dissent Harlan indicated that this strategy led the Court to affirm substantively contradictory state court opinions, it not being immediately clear to the simple mind as to why a state law forbidding segregation in public carriers within a state constituted regulation of interstate commerce while a state law mandating segregation within a state did not.

Only four members of the *Hall* Court remained on the bench for *Louisville*, Harlan, Bradley, Samuel Miller, and Stephen Field, and for these four the cases must have presented peculiar issues in terms of intellectual rigor and consistency. Precedent is important in that it lends stability to the law and to the social system. Similar facts should yield similar legal outcomes. Whereas the newer members of the Court were attempting to reconcile a present inclination with a prior decision by their predecessors which, if followed, would thwart that inclination, Bradley, Miller, and Field were confronted with the necessity of personally affirming flatly contradictory positions, of looking at similar facts and reaching different legal conclusions. Only Field and Miller could do it. Whatever his personal inclination, Bradley joined Harlan in dissent, allowing his old antagonist to add his name to the observation that "It is difficult to understand how a state enactment, requiring the separation of the white and black races on interstate carriers . . . is (not) a regulation of commerce among the States," while an enactment forbidding racial separation is such a violation.

The line from *Louisville* to *Plessy* is direct. The *Louisville* decision was handed down on March 3, 1890. Two months later a bill was introduced in the Louisiana state legislature mandating separate but equal accommodations in public transportation in the state and in July 1890 the legislation was approved. Six years later the challenge to the law would wind up in the Supreme Court and would yield the decision which finally determined the meaning of freedom for blacks for half a century.

Plessy v. Ferguson

Race is a construct, a creation of the human imagination. It is an idea rather than a genetic or biological reality. Societies that attempt to categorize "races" on the basis of skin color face an intractable problem. People distribute themselves along the color spectrum in a continuum, whereas the concept "race" suggests discrete, discontinuous categories. Where "race" is a legal category lawmakers have to make decisions about how to divide the color spectrum. This becomes particularly important where different racial categories enjoy different rights, benefits, and privileges. South Africa's apartheid regime recognized several different "races" for legal purposes. By contrast the United States has always favored a system of racial classification which is both dichotomous and relatively exclusive with regard to the preferred category. One is either "white" or "black." And for purposes of categorization, limited and generationally remote "black" ancestry has been legally sufficient for designation as "black."

Systems of racial classification are related to the dynamics of protest against race-based oppression. South Africa's multifaceted system of legal racial classification tended to split off more favored nonwhites from less favored nonwhites in terms of degree of resistance to the old regime. The United States' system of dichotomous classification has generated black organizations cutting across all hues of the color spectrum, dedicated to resistance. Hence, the immediate circumstances in which *Plessy* developed involved organized resistance by the Creole population of New Orleans to the state's move to segregate nonwhites in public carriers. The challenged statute called for conductors to make a judgment as to the race of passengers for purposes of racial assignment. Many Creoles were light, shading into white; hence, as they formulated strategy the arbitrary character of the legal classification became itself a possible issue to press in resistance to the law. In addition, it became clear to the putative plaintiffs that they would not be able to go forward without the assistance and tacit support of the public carrier responsible for implementing the law. In other words, the railroad also saw itself as having an interest in overturning the separate car law.

Plessy's historical significance was not immediately grasped. As late as the 1940s *Plessy* was not included in anthologies of the most important Supreme Court cases. In contrast to the *Civil Rights Cases of 1883* it received relatively little attention in the newspapers at the time, the *New York Times* alluding to the holding in passing days after it was handed down. Nor was it perceived at the time that a formula had finally been adduced for reconciling the egalitarian language of the Civil War amendments to the reality of an evolving caste system.

The bill introduced in the Louisiana House mandated separate but equal accommodations for black and white passengers on all public railways in the state except street cars and imposed penalties upon railroad personnel refusing to enforce the law and upon passengers who refused to be assigned. The Creoles had been a privileged population, favored socially somewhat by skin color. But the dynamics of racial classification, embodied in increasingly restrictive laws, placed them on the wrong side of the color line. Some were light enough to blend into the white majority, others were not. Nevertheless, broad-based opposition to the new law developed among them.

The Creole-based American Citizens Equal Rights Association denounced the law within days of its introduction, and in the months following its approval a "Citizens Committee to Test the Constitutionality of the Separate Car Law" was formed. Albion Tourgee, lead attorney in the fight against the new law later spoke of "an association of about 10,000 colored men of Louisiana who raised the money to prosecute these and other cases." The objectives in the fall of 1890 were to raise the money for a challenge to go all the way to the Supreme Court, to find constitutional grounds for making that challenge, and to find attorneys capable of making the most effective representation possible in a hostile judicial climate.[25]

A successful test case required a plaintiff whose grievance derived solely from the operation of the law. Thus, Louis Martinet, Rodolphe Dusdenes, and others planning strategy contemplated the possibility that one of their number, refusing racial assignment, might simply be ejected from a carrier by angry passengers or put off the train by the conductor. These circumstances would create a grievance relative to the ruffianly behavior of particular people rather than the operation of the law. Eventually the Louisville and Nashville Railroad itself agreed to cooperate in the staging of an incident yielding a test of the law.

On February 24, 1892, Daniel Desdunes, the twenty-one-year-old son of one of the organizers of the court challenge was arrested for taking a seat in a white car on a Louisville and Nashville train, having bought a first-class ticket for the trip from New Orleans to Mobile, Alabama. Arraigned on March 18, Desdunes pleaded not guilty, fully expecting to be convicted in later proceedings, setting the stage for an appeal to the Supreme Court.

With the basic facts necessary to challenging the law in place, Louis Martinet, who was both a physician and an attorney, and other members of the protest group had to contemplate the legal basis for arguing that those facts demonstrated the unconstitutional character of the law. The ground was shifting under their feet. Early on in the fight Martinet had observed that "people of tolerably fair complexion, even if unmistakably colored, enjoy here a large degree of immunity from the accursed prejudice." The new law swept all who were not white into a separate place and must have seemed a harbinger of worst to come. In extreme circumstances the threatened may find hope in unlikely places. Thus, Martinet and his Citizens' Committee saw in *Louisville* reason to believe that the Supreme Court had left an opening for an argument against the Louisiana law.

Desdunes attorneys intended to argue that the Mississippi law at stake in *Louisville* merely required the railroad to add a car, an added expense perhaps, but not one which would put the line out of business thereby impacting on interstate commerce. Nor did the mere fact of adding a car necessarily have any other consequence with regard to interstate travel. By contrast, the Louisiana law clearly impinged on interstate commerce in a factual sense in that the defendant, bound for an out-of-state destination, had been arrested in Louisiana for refusal to comply with its racial assignment law. In the nature of things, the implementation of the law relative to any interstate passenger whose journey started in Louisiana had to impinge on interstate commerce.

This argument and the first test case collapsed however with the ruling of the Louisiana Supreme Court in the *Abbott* case. In

Abbott a conductor on the Texas and Pacific Railway had violated the new law by admitting a black passenger to a white car. On appeal from a conviction the conductor's attorneys contended that insofar as the black passenger had a ticket for a destination in Texas the new law did not apply to him, or if it did it violated the Interstate Commerce Clause. The Louisiana Supreme Court agreed and the conviction was reversed.[26]

Insofar as Daniel Desdunes had bought a ticket for an out-of-state destination his case would have been decided under the precedent of *Abbott* by any Louisiana court. Hence, the committee was constrained to devise a new scenario for a challenge to the law. Within two weeks of the *Abbott* decision the Citizens' Committee set machinery in motion for Homer Plessy's encounter with John Ferguson.

On June 7, 1892, Homer A. Plessy purchased a ticket for a trip from New Orleans to Covington, Louisiana, on the East Louisiana Railroad. Upon refusing racial assignment Plessy was arrested and eventually arraigned before Judge John H. Ferguson in the Criminal District Court for Orleans Parish. A complex legal dual ensued at the state level. Eventually the Supreme Court of Louisiana upheld the constitutionality of the law setting the stage in 1893 for Plessy to seek review by the United States Supreme Court.

Martinet and the Citizens' Committee had recruited local counsel, but the struggle was to be carried at the national level by sixty-year-old Albion Tourgee, Union army veteran and former judge in Reconstruction North Carolina who had continued the struggle for racial justice in a series of best selling books after the collapse of Reconstruction. *A Fool's Errand* lamented the meager harvest of racial justice yielded by reconstruction, while *Bricks Without Straw*, was an attack on prejudice. Tourgee understood the stakes in the case, reflecting that "it was of utmost consequence that we should not have a decision against us." He foresaw a negative decision as freezing in place the legitimacy of invidious race distinctions in law into the distant future: "it is a matter of boast with the Court that it has never reversed itself on a constitutional issue."[27]

Although docketed in the spring of 1893, the Court's crowded calendar made it possible that the case would not be scheduled for oral argument until the fall term 1895. Even though the Judiciary Act of 1891 had expanded the federal circuit court of appeals system, the backlog at the Supreme Court level was still extremely heavy. It was possible however to advance a case on the Court's calendar by petition from the contending parties for good cause shown. Given the day-to-day humiliation of his clients as a consequence of a law of questionable constitutionality, Tourgee contemplated seeking to have the case advanced, but held back given a reading of the composition of the Court. He counted one justice as favorable to Plessy and four against, leaving victory to hinge on winning over all four of the remaining justices. In the year or more before the case came to be heard by the Court, perhaps one or more of the more hostile justices would leave the bench and be replaced by someone more likely to be sympathetic to Plessy's cause.

Henry Billings Brown who had replaced Samuel Miller in 1890 was among the justices who had not yet been called upon to speak to the issue of race and rights and whom Tourgee perhaps counted among those who might be brought to Plessy's side. Wealthy and nearing sixty he had been nominated by Benjamin Harrison, a president relatively sympathetic to the black struggle for rights. He had avoided service during the Civil War by hiring a substitute in order to pursue his career in the law. He had made his reputation in admiralty law and had considerable tenure as a federal judge in the eastern district of Michigan but had no visible record regarding black affairs. On the Court his was to be a key voice on matters pertaining to race and rights.

The major change as regards race however had occurred with the death in 1892 of Joseph Bradley. As the dominant intellectual figure on the Court over a period of two decades Bradley had articulated and legitimated a conception of federalism that allowed states to retain near total jurisdiction over blacks despite the language of the post–Civil War amendments. If he did not invent formalism he had certainly perfected a type of judicial analysis which brought to bear on black issues. In interpreting the protective reach of the post–Civil War amendments and laws he employed a reading of a statutory language which ignored the substantive abuses that language was intended to address in favor of a narrow, pseudo-precise, literalism which divorced language from the inevitable ambiguities and imprecisions of day-to-day life. Almost, inevitably he found substantive abuses to be beyond the jurisdiction of the reformist language and intentions of the post–Civil War laws.

Bradley was replaced by George Shiras, a wealthy corporate lawyer, with little in his public record to speak to his views on race and rights but who could not have been seen as holding out less hope than the departed Bradley.

And so the decision was made not to try to advance the case

on the Court's calendar, but to await whatever fate would yield as regards the Court's composition when the case was called and whatever public climate would attend the appearance before the Court of the contending sides. Additionally, Tourgee believed that public opinion might swing to his side. "The Court has always been a foe of liberty until forced to move by public opinion," he observed, noting that it had affirmed the regulation of railroad rates and state authority to prohibit liquor only "because the general sentiment of the country was so unmistakably expressed as to have an enlightening effect." He saw similar hopeful prospects in the context of race, his optimism being nourished by signs interpreted as hopeful. The election of the Republican Benjamin Harrison in 1888 after four years of Grover Cleveland's retrograde administration was greeted with high hopes and great expectations by blacks and their friends. Harrison's views on matters of race seemed to have been deeply affected by having witnessed the heroism and sacrifices of black troops during the war. He had long evinced an interest in racial reform. Upon his election to the presidency he was strongly urged by Albion Tourgee, among others, to renew the struggle for civil rights. A series of new bills were introduced in Congress, backed by the president and intended to strengthen federal protection for black voters in federal elections. The Enforcement Act of 1890 passed the house by a margin of 155 to 149 but failed in the Senate.[28] Despite the outcome Tourgee, apparently, did not view the public as uniformly in support of every segregationist mandate.

On Friday, April 10, 1896, Tourgee boarded the train in Mayville, New York, headed for Washington, D.C., *Plessy* being on the Court calendar for oral argument on Monday morning, April 13. Louisiana was represented by Alexander Porter Morse, a transplanted native of that state with a practice in Washington, while Tourgee carried the burden for Plessy and the Citizens Association. Tourgee's argument drew on the Thirteenth and Fourteenth Amendments, the major points being as follows:

1. The Fourteenth Amendment was intended to end the exclusive control by states over citizens within their borders by identifying certain actions states could not pursue, among these the classification of citizens by race for purposes of distributing rights and opportunities. The Supreme Court itself in *Strauder* had stated that the Fourteenth Amendment "prohibited legislation prejudicial to any class of citizenship whether colored or not."

2. Insofar as the Louisiana statute made race per se the essence of a crime under circumstances which connoted the stigmatizing of the black population, it violated both the Fourteenth and Thirteenth Amendments, the latter because the stigma inherent in enforced segregation both symbolized and partially recreated the former condition of servitude.

3. The law could not be seen as a legitimate exercise of the state's police powers relative to the promotion of the health, safety, and welfare of the general population insofar as it was not obvious why interracial contact on railroads should be more contaminating or dangerous than interracial contact on the street or in the work place. And indeed if enforced racial separation represented a legitimate use of state police powers in terms of the maintenance of health and safety, then, "Why not require all colored citizens to walk on one side of the street and whites on the other? Why may it not require every white man's house to be painted white and every colored man's black?" That there would be "equality" of treatment would not vitiate the absurdity of the contention that legitimate police powers were being exercised.

4. The ultimate purpose of the Louisiana law was to degrade and stigmatize blacks. Hence it violated the Thirteenth Amendment. The purpose of that amendment "was not merely to destroy chattelism and involuntary servitude but the estate and condition of subjection and inferiority of personal right and privilege, which was the result and essential concomitant of slavery."

There were also a host of more technical arguments going to the issue of due process as raised by a train conductor's power under the law to make racial classifications which resulted in the loss of property (a right to a seat in the car for which one had purchased a ticket) and exposure to criminal liability for immediately contesting the accuracy of the classification.

Louisiana's argument as it emerged before the Court and in their briefs advanced three major points:

1. Relying on Bradley's holding in the *Civil Rights Cases of 1883* Milton Cunningham and Alexander Porter Morse argued the absence that the separate car statute did not violate the Thirteenth Amendment in that racial distinctions having consequence with regard to public conduct did not impose a badge of servitude on blacks.

2. With regard to the contention that the law violated the Fourteenth Amendment prohibition against denial of the equal protection of the laws, they drew on *Pace* and other cases to establish that the Supreme Court itself had averred that racial distinctions in law did not per se pose an equal protection problem. Such distinctions were valid provided they were made in pursuit of a legitimate state objective.

3. A considerable body of case law established that the Supreme Court had explicitly or implicitly recognized state authority to promote racial separation in the interest of the maintenance of peace and harmony. Indeed, in finding that Mississippi's separate car law did not violate the Interstate Commerce Clause in *Louisville*, the Court implicitly affirmed the racial purposes for which the law had mandated separate cars even though that issue was not directly being debated, while in *Hall v. DeCuir* the Court had allowed that "to some extent at least and under some circumstances, such (racial) separation is allowable."

The decision was handed down on May 18, 1896. By a vote of eight to one the Louisiana statute was found not to violate Homer Plessy's rights under either the Thirteenth or the Fourteenth Amendments. Henry Billings Brown delivered the opinion for the majority. John Marshall Harlan was the only dissenter.

It is not clear whether the majority merely concurred in the outcome or shared in Brown's assumptions. Brown was a man of many parts. He had been active in the American Social Science Association and, by all accounts, took a keen interest in the major intellectual trends of the day. He was familiar, therefore, with the thinking of Yale professor William Graham Sumner, regarded as one of the fathers of American sociology. The language setting forth his basic assumptions constitute a virtual restatement of Sumner's basic proposition. In Brown's words: " Legislation is powerless to eradicate racial instincts or to abolish distinctions based upon physical differences, and the attempt to do so can only result in accentuating the difficulties of the present situation. . . . If one race be inferior to the other socially, the Constitution of the United States cannot put them upon the same plane."[29]

Or in the language of Sumner, "Law-ways cannot change Folkways." If enough people fervently hold to a particular belief, law can do nothing to curb the behavior which flows from that belief. The Brown position followed from this basic premise. If law-ways could not alter folkways the Fourteenth Amendment could not be sensibly construed as if it were meant to do so. A number of cases from state and lower-level federal courts were cited in support of the proposition that racial distinctions in law and segregation of the races had not been found to offend statutes otherwise mandating equality before the law: "The object of the Amendment was . . . to enforce the absolute equality of the races before the law, but in the nature of things it could not have been intended to abolish distinctions based on color, or to enforce social, as distinguished from political equality, or a commingling of the two races upon terms unsatisfactory to either."[30]

In other words, the state retained, or had never lost, the power to make racial distinctions in law for the public good. His assumption with regard to racial instincts yielded the view that the Louisiana law was reasonable. It promoted peace by keeping the races apart: "So far, then, as a conflict with the 14th Amendment is concerned, the case reduces itself to the question of whether the statute . . . is a reasonable regulation, and with respect to this there must necessarily be a large discretion on the part of the legislature. In determining the question . . . it is at liberty to act with reference to the established usages, customs, and traditions of people and with a view to the promotion of their comfort and the preservation of public peace. . . . Gauged by this standard, we cannot say that a law which . . . requires separation of the races . . . is unreasonable or . . . obnoxious to the 14th Amendment."[31]

But might not a separate car law, however reflective of racial instincts, violate the Thirteenth Amendment by imposing a badge of servitude on black citizens? Brown found an easy answer to this question: "That it does not conflict with the Thirteenth Amendment . . . is to clear for argument." He interpreted the Thirteenth Amendment literally and averred that the Louisiana law did not impose involuntary servitude, it merely restricted choice with regard to where one sat on a public carrier. He then moved on to an unfortunate and notorious assertion. Drawing on Bradley's argument in The *Civil Rights Cases of 1883* he repudiated the notion that a racial distinction in law necessarily impinges on the equality of the minority race. "We consider the underlying fallacy of the plaintiff's argument to consist in the assumption that the enforced separation of the races stamps the colored race with a badge of inferiority. If this be so, it is not by reason of anything found in the act, but solely because the colored race chooses to put that construction on it."

Harlan provided the lone dissent. He advanced a number of arguments. The Court was inclined to give deference to state legislatures even where the statutes in question might be foolish or ill-conceived: "If the power exists to enact a statute, that ends the matter so far as the courts are concerned." However, where the law bears no relationship to any legitimate state objective, the courts may find the law invalid. In those terms, the Louisiana law could not be deemed a rational means for realizing a legitimate state objective. No state interest was promoted by mandating separate cars: "What can be more certain to arouse race hatred . . . than state enactments which . . . proceed on the ground that colored citizens are so inferior and degraded that they cannot be allowed to sit in public coaches occupied by white citizens?"[31]

Additionally, the law clearly violated the Thirteenth Amendment. "The arbitrary separation of citizens on the basis of race, while they are on a public highway, is a badge of servitude wholly inconsistent with the civil freedom and the equality before the law established by the Constitution." And also the Fourteenth Amendment. The right to travel on publicly licensed carriers was a civil right according to Harlan. Hence, "In respect of civil rights . . . the Constitution of the United States does not . . . permit any authority to know the race of those entitled to be protected in the enjoyment of such rights." But in the end, he acknowledged that he had lost: "It is . . . to be regretted that this high tribunal, the final expositor of the fundamental law of the land, has reached the conclusion that it is competent for a state to regulate the enjoyment by citizens of their civil rights solely upon the basis of race."

Six years before Justice Brown expressed being astonished that blacks should feel stigma at being singled out for segregation by law, the black newspaper the *Richmond Planet* had spoken to the matter. Early in the 1890s, about the time that Louisiana was passing its law, whites in Richmond called for a separate car law, arguing that blacks should not feel humiliated by a law excluding them from places where they were not wanted. The *Planet* offered the black perspective on the matter: "Pass a law debarring a certain class of white men from entering Pullman Parlor cars . . . because they cannot trace their white lineage to the revolutionary fathers and this class of white men would feel humiliated."[32] But the Brown perspective, gratuitously offered, reflected the limits of majority views on the matter.

Albion Tourgee died in 1905 in Bordeaux, France, where he had lived for eight years. He had foreseen *Plessy's* dark consequence, but far from domestic shores was perhaps only dimly aware of the sad accuracy of his forecast. Homer Plessy died in 1920 and thus was more directly witness and victim of the full meaning of his case as the Court spelled it out three years after affirming the legitimacy of state-mandated segregation as long as the facilities and services offered were equal.

And So It Ends: *Cumming v. Board*

"The mere statement of the case, in view of what this court has already decided, condemns such conduct," or so thought George Edmund as he implored the Supreme Court to find on behalf of a group of black parents and against the Richmond, Georgia, school board.

The conduct of which Edmund was complaining had occurred in July and August of 1897 and seemed clearly unconstitutional in the light of the Court's holding in *Plessy* a year earlier. And so Edmunds stood before the Court on October 3, 1899, urging the case of his clients, contending that *Plessy* "is entirely consistent with and supports our contention." And it would appear to have been so. *Plessy* stood for the proposition that government could mandate racial separation provided the facilities and services available to each of the races were substantially equal. The events that had transpired in Richmond County, Georgia, seemed clearly to have contravened this principle. The decision of the Court would speak to the meaning of the term *equal* in the equation *separate, but equal.*

The events setting *Cummings v. Board* in motion had a stark simplicity. In June of 1897 a subcommittee of the Richmond County school board had recommended the closing of the public high school for black students. At the time sixty black students were attending the black high school. The full board accepted the subcommittee's recommendation. Financial exigency was stated as the reason for the closing, the board not wanting to raise taxes in order to continue to support the black high school.

On July 10, 1897, the board levied a tax of two and two-tenths mills on every one hundred dollars of taxable property in the county, this levy falling on black property owners and white alike. The tax was to be used for the support of the public school system in the county, including two high schools solely for white students, one of which enrolled only girls and was free, the other of which enrolled boys and which charged a small tuition.

In August of 1897 a number of black parents went before the

board pleading that the decision to abolish the black high school be rescinded. After a two-hour meeting the board voted to affirm their earlier decision, contending that space would be allocated for a larger number of black children to receive an elementary school education and that, in any event, there were three black public high schools in Augusta to which local black students might repair. The board later acknowledged that the Augusta schools were private, church-related, tuition-charging entities.

In September, 1897, the black parents sought out legal help. Affidavits were drawn up by local attorneys indicating that J. W. Cumming, James Harper, and John Ladeveze were taxpayers, that they had, in fact, been taxed for the support of the local school system, that they had children in the black high school, that high school was now to be closed while their tax money was to be used to be used to keep two white high schools open.

They sought an injunction or court order barring Charles Bohler, the county tax collector from collecting taxes, and barring the school board from spending any of the revenues collected until the matter was resolved. They based their claim for relief on the contention that the actions of the school board violated the mandate of the Fourteenth Amendment that "no State shall deny any person within its jurisdiction the equal protection of the laws."

The superior court of Richmond County agreed with the black parents, ordering the board to "provide or establish equal facilities in high school education as are now maintained by them for white children for such colored children of high school grade . . . as may desire a high school education." The argument of the black parents and the holding of the superior court were both offered within the framework of the *Plessy* holding. The constitutionality of separate facilities was not challenged. An arm of the state was being asked to honor the mandate of "equal" facilities. In the light of the facts the validity of the complaint would have appeared to have been self-evident. However the Supreme Court had not yet ruminated on what it meant by "equal."

The board appealed to the Supreme Court of the state of Georgia, which reversed the decision of the superior court whereupon, the plaintiff moved to seek relief from the United States Supreme Court, thus bringing George Edmunds before the bench on a fall day, early in Court's term. He came back time and time again to the same basic facts, "the parents of . . . colored children (are) being taxed and their money expended to maintain . . . higher grade white school." And, "the board of education has undertaken to discriminate . . . between the two races, and to impose upon one burdens of taxation from which they and their children receive no benefit, for the purpose of giving educational benefits . . . to the white children alone."[33]

He seemed to believe that the language of the Fourteenth Amendment and the Court's own holdings, including *Plessy*, spoke to the matter in a manner which could yield only one outcome.

The holding read on December 18, 1899, proved Edmunds wrong. Resting in part on federalist principles and in part on alleged defects in the plaintiffs' pleadings the holding of a unanimous Court did not find anything in the Richmond school board's transactions offensive to the Constitution. Technically, what was at issue was the legitimacy of the Georgia Supreme Court holding reversing the decision of the local superior court. About half of the Supreme Court holding is given over to lengthy quotation from the Georgia court holding. The attorney for the plaintiffs had complained of a violation of the Fourteenth Amendment but had not made it clear whether the equal protection clause or the due process clause was violated. The alleged substantive abuse with regard to the distribution of tax money for purposes of education went to matters traditionally left to the discretion of local authorities, the courts not deeming to tell people at the local level how much money to raise or how to spend it.

The Supreme Court holding built on the Georgia court repudiation of the plaintiffs' complaints. There was no Fourteenth Amendment equal protection issue because "the education of the people in the schools maintained by state taxation is a matter belonging to the respective States, and any interference on the part of Federal authority with the management of such schools cannot be justified except in the case of a clear and unmistakable disregard of rights secured by the Supreme law of the land."[34] And given that there was no constitutional right to be the equal beneficiary of tax funds on racial or other grounds nor a right to a publicly funded high school education, the school board could not be said to have done violence to the plaintiffs under the law.

The Court holding was written by Harlan, the lone dissented in *Plessy*. Many decades later Benno Schmidt offered a plausible explanation for Harlan's frame of mind in writing the decision. The equal protection clause of the Fourteenth Amendment was violated where a state statute seemed to have the racial degradation of blacks as its major objective, but mere racial classification itself unaccompanied by hostile, denigrating action did not pose an issue.

The decision of the school board to convert the high school serving sixty black children into an elementary school serving more than two hundred black children was interpreted as reasonable and free of base motives despite the fact that white girls had a residual tax-derived benefit at the high school level not available to black girls.

Schmidt also acknowledged that it was the perceived meaning of *Cumming* which lent it consequence with regard to what followed, rather than its factual nuances. Whatever Harlan intended, cruel perception on the part of elements hostile to black interests led to the holding being seen "as upholding . . . blatant inequality."[35] In other words, the separate aspect of the separate-but-equal equation survived, while the equal dimension seemed to merit little more than a nod and a wink.

Cumming came on the eve of a new century. In just over twenty years, beginning with *Cruikshank*, the Supreme Court had restricted and delimited the reach of the post–Civil War laws in matters of race, invoking federalist principles in support of this endeavor. Irrespective of the language and intent of the reforms the states retained jurisdiction over their black populations in virtually all matters civil and criminal. National citizenship, subject to federal protection, was a vague and limited entity.

The Court did not ride a wave of public sentiment in doing its work. Elite views on matters of race and rights was divided. A few Northerners such as Albion Tourgee kept the old abolitionist dream of a color-blind society alive. Southern paternalists such as David Key decried segregation as an abuse of "the better element" among blacks but offered no alternative, coherent, or defined vision of a "just" yet race-conscious society. Railroad interests in two states involved themselves directly or indirectly in contesting separate car laws for reasons of money and ease of operation rather than a commitment to egalitarian principles. As late as 1890 an impulse to humanitarian reform led to the introduction in Congress of new measures to protect black rights, supported by Republican President Benjamin Harrison.

The weight of the Supreme Court's decisions on the political fulcrum helped tip the balance of power and influence to the most repressive and virulent antiblack elements in the political arena. The language of constitutional federalism was used to repudiate racial equality and legitimate the institutionalization of caste subordination.

The Court's holdings shaped and formed a definition of freedom for blacks in the post–Civil War era. They facilitated the development of a new and unique status in American society. Blacks were not chattel lacking the status of citizen as was the case before the war. They were citizens of the nation and of the state, but the states were free to mold the contours of citizenship in racial terms. The assumptions of some the justices with regard to racial instincts and black inferiority yielded the judicial conclusion that mandated racial separation of the races was within the police powers of the state given a state obligation to maintain peace and harmony.

The Court had not been hesitant, however, to find that the due process clause of the Fourteenth Amendment and various provisions of the Constitution placed limits on state power with regard to such matters as regulating the length of the work day or regulating railroad rates in the interests of farmers. Just as assumptions about race had consequence with regard to judicial reasoning on matters of race and states rights, so also did assumptions about the sanctity of property have consequence with regard to the Court's view that state attempts to curb corporate power constituted a deprivation of property without due process of law. That their application of federalist principles in the area of race was inconsistent with the application of those principles to matters of the state and private industry does not seem to have entered the consciousness of the justices.

A week after the decision in *Cumming* came down, George Edmunds provided the coda: "I was grieved to see in the newspapers that the Supreme Court had defeated my poor colored clients . . . in their aspirations and efforts for equal rights in public education."[36]

Chapter 5

American Apartheid

On September 25, 1913, a new law went into effect in the city of Baltimore intended to "prevent conflict and ill-feeling between the white and colored races . . . (and) . . . preserve the public peace and promote the general welfare by making reasonable provisions requiring the use of separate blocks for residences by white and colored people respectively."[1]

Baltimore had taken the lead in passing laws creating black zones and white zones, having passed its first ordinance three years earlier. Richmond, Ashland, Roanoke, and Portsmouth, Virginia; Winston-Salem, North Carolina; Greenville, South Carolina; Atlanta, Georgia; Birmingham, Alabama; and St. Louis, Missouri, had also moved to pass such laws as had a number of other cities, principally in the Southern and border states, although movement had begun to spread north by 1915.

The impetus for these new laws was the shift of an increasing percentage of the black population from rural areas to the cities of the South and the urban centers of the Midwest and North. Census data on the black population was not entirely reliable. The five decades following the end of the Civil War showed "figures as whimsical as if produced by the sport of the gods."[2] The black population was alleged to have increased by only 400,000 between 1860 and 1870, but by 1,700,000 between 1870 and 1880. It then allegedly increased by only 900,000 between 1880 and 1890, only to grow by 1,300,000 between 1890 and 1900. But between 1900 and

1910 growth was supposed to have fallen back to 990,000.[3] These seesaw figures belied the notion that anyone had any idea of what the size of the black population was. But the everyday experience of people in the cities of the South, Midwest, and East Coast suggested that the number of blacks living in urban centers was increasing markedly.

The movement of more prosperous blacks beyond the informal boundaries of the "colored section" of town was the immediate impetus for Baltimore's racial zoning law. The first issue of *Crisis*, the magazine of the National Association for the Advancement of Colored People, published in November, 1910, outlined the events leading to the proposal of the statute: "An inevitable step in anti-Negro prejudice is being taken in Baltimore. . . . The colored folk of that city long ago became dissatisfied with a particularly bad system of alley homes. They saved their money and purchased nearly the whole length of Druid Avenue. . . . They began to expand into parallel streets, one of which was McCullah. . . . The white people of McCulloh street rose in indignation and are importuning the City council to pass an ordinance prohibiting colored people from "invading" white residential districts."[4]

The purchase of a home on McCulloh Street in a hitherto all-white neighborhood by a black doctor and his school teacher wife prompted street protests and harassment of the newcomers and also inspired George W. West, a member of the city council, and Milton Dashiell, an attorney, to call for a law whereby the city would designate black zones and white zones and prohibit anyone to live outside their racial zone.[5]

The Baltimore struggle yielded similar efforts in other parts of the country, the movement to zone by race beginning in the South then spreading North and West. These were quite simply, apartheid laws intended to restrict blacks *by law* to given areas of residence. Indeed, some of the advocates of the new movement had been influenced by South African white supremacists. After meeting with Maurice Evans, a South African advocate of racial separation, Clarence Poe, a North Carolinian and editor of the *Progressive Farmer*, called for development of a domestic plan limiting ownership of most farm land in the Southern states to whites, blacks becoming, in effect, tenants confined to domestic Bantustans. At its 1914 convention the North Carolina Farmers' Union endorsed this proposal.[6]

In 1916, St. Louis put the matter to a test of the popular will. Two ordinances appeared on the ballot proposing that blacks be barred from moving into neighborhoods in which 75 percent or more of the occupants were white. The *Literary Digest* reported that for several days before the election "negro girls and women handed out circulars on the streets bearing a cartoon depicting a white man driving a negro before him and lashing his bare back, with the inscription 'Back to Slavery.'"[7] But if this was an appeal to conscience it was to no avail. The segregation measure carried by a margin of three to one.

These laws reflected the fact that there was no necessary or logical terminus to the degree, extent, and kind of racial separation that could be mandated in law once the basic premise of segregation as a legitimate expression of state police power was accepted. Already law and custom throughout the South dictated a separate and subordinate existence for blacks. In many public and private buildings blacks and whites could not use the same entrances, stairs, or exits. Schools were segregated as were hospitals and penal institutions. Blacks were either barred altogether from public parks and places of amusement or were admitted only on a segregated and restricted basis. Often the institutions and facilities available to blacks were grossly inferior to those afforded whites or were absent altogether.

Laws mandating black zones and white zones were a logical extrapolation of the premise of *Plessy* and were upheld as such in some of the initial court challenges to their constitutionality, the Virginia Court of Appeals finding that the premise of *Plessy* established the constitutionality of Richmond's apartheid law.[8] The laws also reflected the continued twenty-year drive by the successor governments to the old reconstruction regimes to define freedom for blacks in ever more restrictive terms.

The absence of an inherent terminus to the logic of segregation yielded enormous importance to the racial zoning cases as they made their way to the Supreme Court. If racial peace was promoted by creating white zones and black zones, would it not also be promoted by requiring blacks to be within their zone by a certain hour? If blacks had to be within their zones by a certain hour, would the peace and tranquility of the races not be promoted to an even greater extent by requiring passes of those who had need for reasons of employment to be outside their zone at forbidden times?

The logic of the Supreme Court position relative to state power and racial classification in law yielded a political dynamic moving inevitably toward an apartheid system. Social attitudes and taken-for-granted beliefs accommodated a move toward ever greater racial subordination and exclusion. There was movement toward the crystallization of a status for blacks equivalent to that of India's caste untouchables, an increasingly abhorred and degraded population, restricted by law and custom to the margins of the economy and the fringes of civil society, their interaction with members of higher castes mediated by an elaborate set of rituals of deference and by terror.

The abolitionist generation had largely passed from the scene. There were few in the new, postwar generation of whites willing to speak for equal rights with the fervor of a Charles Sumner, Ben Butler, or Albion Tourgee. The world view of this new generation had been shaped, in part, by an increasingly popular reinterpretation of the Reconstruction era and the prewar slave South. Revisionist works of scholarship and the diversions of popular culture promoted a view of race relations in the antebellum South as idyllic, populated by childlike, happy darkies, toiling willingly for kindhearted masters.

At the level of professional scholarship the work of the Southern-born, Columbia University historian Ulrich Phillips disseminated the same view of the Reconstruction era as did the novelist Thomas Dixon in his rabidly antiblack bestseller *The Klansman*.[9] The white South had been subjected to the misrule of venal black dolts, cheated by nature of the wit, judgment, and maturity to play a responsible role in a modern society.

In the first decade of the twentieth century the racial world the Supreme Court helped create was convulsed by violence as antiblack pogroms broke out. More than fifty blacks were killed and hundreds injured or made homeless in Atlanta in 1906. And in 1908 Springfield, Illinois, saw a raging antiblack pogrom, three days of violence resulting in dozens being killed and many put to flight. Pogroms are cathartic for their perpetrators and convey a message to victims. Violence is communication as is all forms of human behavior. Atlanta and Springfield spoke to blacks with regard to their subordination and helplessness. They survived by sufferance of the majority. Neither the law nor God would shield them from righteous wrath were they to transgress their caste boundaries or fail to honor the rituals and symbols of their subordinate status.

A letter addressed to President William Howard Taft by a coalition of 150 black ministers following a pogrom in Anderson County, Texas, in the summer of 1910 voiced desperation and sought intervention.

In the past we have put confidence in Statecraft to save us from exploitation at the behest of the strong, but the best we have ever received from it is not enough to deliver us from the troubles of which we now complain. we sought strength thru edution, but the more we advanced along this line, the greater the discrimination. We have bought land, built homes and established churches, but those states as desire to do so go on disenfranchising us, lynching our men on frivolous charges and unproved allegations, and widening the chasm which race differentiation has already made broad enough. When progress does not promise to save a people, that people is near desperation. But let us appeal to the best instincts of men as long as reason has a chance or argument a hearing.[10]

President Taft did not respond to the letter but had expressed himself elsewhere on the matter of race. He had doubted the wisdom of the Republican Party's lingering association with black aspirations and ruminated on the virtues of a lily-white Republicanism.[11]

Neither popular sentiment nor the language of the Constitution as interpreted by the Supreme Court impeded the momentum of segregation as the first decade of the new century ended. Indeed, the premise of the Court's major holdings on state power and racial organization yielded the legal rational for ever more extensive racial exclusion. The Court's premise yielded no inherent end-point and as the second decade of the century began the impulse and will to segregate seemed inexhaustible.

Between 1910 and 1920 the Court was presented with a series of cases which, while not as well known as *Plessy* and The *Civil Rights Cases of 1883*, were to prove equally decisive. Precise legal issues were contested in each of the cases but the common underlying issue was whether the logic of *Plessy* would play itself out.

As Long As Reason Has a Chance: A Pivotal Decade

At crucial times and on crucial issues the Supreme Court has made the United States. It has not made the country alone, but its holdings have been decisive with regard to the direction the nation took. Perhaps there would have been a Civil War without the *Dred Scott* holding, but *Dred Scott* made war inevitable. Perhaps the national momentum toward apartheid of the South African charac-

ter or a dual caste system with blacks occupying a status compara-
ble to that of India's untouchables would have abated. This can
never be known. But what is known is that in the second decade of
the new century the Court's approach to matters of race and rights
began to change. As legal historian Benno Schmidt indicated, "it is
surely not reading to much into the decade" to state that "under
the leadership of a Chief Justice from the deep South (the Court)
began a halting recognition of the promises of justice for black people contained in the Thirteenth, Fourteenth, and Fifteenth amendments."[12] The Court's tentative effort to redeem a vision of racial
reform during that decade is all the more remarkable because it was
achieved against the opposition of the most celebrated jurist to
wear the robes of an associate justice of the United States Supreme
court—Oliver Wendall Holmes.

Edward Douglass White had been on the Court sixteen years
at the time President William Howard Taft nominated him to be
chief justice. There was little in his background to hold out hope to
the ministers who had petitioned Taft for justice or for others sympathetic to the cause of racial justice. A native of Louisiana, White
had been studying at Georgetown in Washington, D.C., when Fort
Sumpter was fired upon in April of 1861. He had left school,
returned to the South, and enlisted in the Confederate army. On
July 8, 1863, he was one of more than 7,000 rebel soldiers captured
with the fall of Port Hudson, the last Confederate stronghold on the
Mississippi River.

Peacetime brought him a checkered but generally successful
career in law and politics culminating in his elevation to the Senate in 1888. Six years later he was President Grover Cleveland's
third choice for a seat on the bench after a feud between New York's
two senators prevented Cleveland from making an appointment
from the empire state to what was then regarded as the "New
York" seat.[13] In his sixteen years on the Court preceding his selection as Chief Justice, White had voted consistently against a generous interpretation of the Constitution relative to black rights.

The Court over which White was to preside had changed in a
matter of months. Four new justices were sworn in 1909 and 1910
transforming the "Fuller Court" into the "White Court." There
was little reason for contemporary observers to believe that the
White Court, even with three new members, would bring a generous view to matters of race and rights. Perhaps no one so reflected
the Court's impulse to reject pleas for racial equity as White's fellow Civil War veteran, Oliver Wendall Holmes.

Holmes is universally regarded as the greatest jurist ever to sit on the Supreme Court. Formerly a Harvard law professor and chief justice of the Massachusetts Supreme Court, a collection of his lectures published as *The Common Law* had brought him acclaim before he was forty. He had grown up on Boston's Beacon Hill, the son of a distinguished father, an heir to privilege.

The Civil War had broken out the year he graduated from Harvard. He had joined the 20th volunteers, the Harvard regiment, and had seen action in some of the war's fiercest battles. In the fall of 1862 Robert E. Lee and the Army of Northern Virginia launched the first Confederate invasion of the North, crossing into Maryland, hoping to collapse civilian morale in the loyal states and perhaps even seize Washington. The decisive battle took place at Antietam during three bloody days in September. Holmes's regiment entered the fight early on after a long forced march. As the convulsive struggle approached its apogee he was shot in the neck. It was a very close call. A fraction of an inch and he would have joined the swollen ranks of those killed in the single bloodiest day of combat in American military history.[14]

The future Supreme Court justice survived the wound only to be hit later by Confederate shrapnel at Fredericksburg. Wounded three times he was mustered out in 1864 and returned to Harvard to get his degree in law and embark upon the career which would later bring him national homage.

Holmes also reflected the deeply paradoxical nature of the progressive movement of the first two decades of the twentieth century. As a Massachusetts appellate court judge he had written opinions which were, by the standards of the time, regarded as favorable to labor rather to corporate and railroad interests. These holdings brought him to the attention of President Theodore Roosevelt, ardently seeking to invoke law and the power of the national government to protect working people against the depredations and exploitation of big business. The Supreme Court had been a foe of progressive change, tending to see efforts to limit corporate power or regulate their activities as contrary to the Constitution.[15] The Court entertained the fiction that the individual worker and the corporate employer bargained as equal entities on the terms of employment. It tended, therefore, to hold that state laws limiting the length of the work day or otherwise touching on the conditions of employment violated the constitutionally guaranteed right to contract.[16] Holmes, comparatively liberal views were welcomed by Roosevelt and facilitated his nomination to the Court in 1902.

Holmes was without question the best mind to ascend to the Court since the passing of Joseph Bradley, but like Bradley he was not committed to a vision of society entailing equal rights for blacks and whites. While reflecting the progressive vision on matters of social policy regarding corporate power and the public interest, he also reflected its dark side in matters of race. From his earliest days on the bench he brought his formidable intellect to bear against the claims of black plaintiffs.

One of Holmes early holdings as a member of the Court spoke to his view of blacks seeking redress under the Constitution. Like all of the states of the old Confederacy, Alabama had moved to exclude blacks from voting. Uncommon candor in the legislative debates given over to considering various schemes revealed a motive to come up with seemingly race-neutral procedures which would exclude most blacks while allowing most whites to slip through the net. A law which combined elements of the later challenged "grandfather statutes" combined with a grant of authority to local officials to weed out intelligent, civic-minded citizens from the illiterate and corruptible promised to meet these objectives.

The descendants of persons who had served in the military in various national conflicts, including service in the Confederate army during the war, were deemed eligible to vote. Otherwise local registrars were given the authority to determine whether potential voters were of sufficient character and competence as to be able to exercise the franchise in a responsible manner. Anyone who qualified under either test was on the rolls for life. In addition, after January 1, 1903, a set of very stiff property requirements was to come into effect.

No blacks qualified as descendants of Confederate veterans and, not unexpectedly, in the eyes of local registrars, few were deemed to be of sufficiently sturdy character as to merit the right to exercise the franchise. Among the blacks deemed unfit to exercise democracy's proudest function was Nathan Giles, turned away by the registrar of voters in Montgomery County in March of 1902. Suit was brought in the Federal Circuit Court by Giles on behalf of himself and five thousand other blacks denied access to the ballot, seeking equitable relief. The petitioners asked the Court to order that they be put on the rolls. They could not be made whole by monitary damages nor would punishment of the registrar have constituted adequate relief. They wanted to vote and hence they asked the Court to override the state's scheme and place them on the voter rolls. The circuit court demurred on the grounds that it lacked the power to grant the kind of relief the petitioners sought and, in the course of time, the case came before the United States Supreme Court on appeal from the decision of the circuit court.

In April, 1903, Justice Holmes offered the opinion of the majority. Neither case law nor statute supported the contention that the circuit court had the power to grant equitable relief in response to alleged political wrongs, he opined. And had it been left at that it would have been a succinct although questionable holding. But Holmes went on to gratuitously ridicule the plaintiffs and their claims. They had claimed that the Alabama law constituted a scheme to provide the franchise to whites while denying blacks the opportunity to vote, yet they were asking the Court to put their names on the rolls created by this fraudulent scheme. If the law was a fraud how could they ask to be its beneficiary, but if it were not a fraud, as implied by a demand to be put on the rolls it created, why would they complain about being excluded by its operation. And, if "the conspiracy and the intent exist" to unjustly exclude blacks, the plaintiffs would have to look for relief from the white citizens of the state and state government, or from the federal government.[17] The suggestion that Alabama blacks seek redress from their fellow white Alabamians was either facetious or was disdainful of the claims of the petitioners, given that there is no evidence that Holmes was so obtuse as to not grasp the nature of the political and social systems in that state.

It is one of the deep ironies of Supreme Court history that a son of abolitionist Massachusetts, regarded with awe and reverence by wise and accomplished persons since his death in 1932, should have been a constant foe of black claims on a Court presided over by a son of the South inclined, finally, to take a more sympathetic view of those claims.

Thirty years earlier Joseph Bradley had come to dominate Chief Justice Morrison Waite intellectually. While Waite had shown a personal interest in the expansion of opportunities for blacks, his behavior on the Court never took him beyond the reach of Bradley's shadow. Holmes brought to the Court the same potential for intellectual domination of the genial but modestly gifted White when the ex-Confederate became chief justice in 1910.

In the seven years preceding White's elevation, the racial conservative Melville Fuller had been chief justice. Holmes might have anticipated the same relationship with White as he had enjoyed with the midwesterner. Holmes biographer G. Edward White indicated that "It was as if Holmes enjoyed playing Sherlock to Fuller's

Dr. Watson: the one brilliant, eccentric, whimsical, detached; the other solid, conventional, prosaic, warm-hearted."[18]

Upon White's ascension Holmes moved to establish a harmonious relationship with him. While not the greatest of jurists White was a good administrator and strove to move the Court's work ahead expeditiously. Holmes's style lent itself to this effort. He was a fast writer and managed to draft and deliver his opinions to his colleagues very rapidly. He believed that this facility was greatly appreciated by the efficiency-minded chief justice. While not given to forming warm relations with his colleagues and somewhat guarded in his comments about them, Holmes spoke of the vastly different White as a good friend. There was both irony and calculation in this in that Holmes, according to biographer G. Edward White, thought of himself as "one who dwelt in the realm of high intellect and was disinclined to devote his energies to extended companionship with lesser minds."[19] Edward Douglass White was not the sort of man Holmes would ordinarily have cultivated. It was also the greatest of ironies that the gifted union veteran was reflexively more hostile to black rights than the modestly talented veteran of the Confederate army.

The dynamics of the Court on matters of race were significantly impacted in 1910 however by the addition of a second major intellect, committed to a vision of racial reform and capable in that small group of men of providing conceptual ballast to Holmes's tilt. Twenty years younger than Holmes, Charles Evans Hughes was a member of the postwar generation. He had shown great intellectual gifts very early on. He found school boring and was taken out after three weeks, completing the balance of his education at home until he entered college at fourteen. He graduated from Brown University as the youngest member of his class and later graduated from Columbia Law School. Within a few years he became a partner in the prestigious law firm of Chamberlain, Carter, and Hornblower, along the way marrying the daughter of one of the partners. He was a young man with immense talent moving ahead in a hurry in a world of power and privilege.

At twenty-nine he seems to have undergone something of an epiphany. He left the world of corporate practice and took a post teaching law. He returned to the legal wars after a few years but devoted a good deal of his time to what would later be termed "public interest" law. As counsel to committees investigating the insurance industry and the setting of gas and electric rates he was instrumental in exposing the shameless bilking of an unprotected public by powerful private interests. Good works brought him to the attention of political king makers and in 1906 he defeated newspaper magnate William Randolph Hearst in the race for governor of New York. He was reelected in 1908 and in 1910 was nominated to a seat on the Supreme Court.[20]

As had been the case with Holmes, an early opinion written by Hughes dealt with race. The holding portended a new approach to issues of race and rights and also brought him into conflict with Holmes who dissented strongly, acknowledging that the seemingly neutral law in question was applied only to blacks, but that it was the law nevertheless.

Bailey v. Alabama began the day after Christmas in 1907 when Alonzo Bailey, a black man, signed a contract as a laborer with the Riverside Corporation, receiving $15 at the signing and committing himself to work for a year on their plantation at Scotts Bend Place in Montgomery County for $12 a month from which a portion was to be deducted each month by the employer, presumably for services provided.

Early in February Bailey left the plantation and was promptly arrested and prosecuted under an Alabama law which created a presumption of an intent to defraud where an employee left the service of his employer before the contractual duration of his obligation had run. Given that an Alabama rule of evidence entertained in such cases denied the accused an opportunity to testify as to his "uncommunicated motives, purpose, or intention" at the time of contract signing, to be charged was to be found guilty.[21]

Bailey was found guilty and sentenced to a term of imprisonment at hard labor. The Alabama Supreme Court sustained the constitutionality of the statute against claims that it violated the due process and equal protection clauses of the Fourteenth Amendment, and that it imposed involuntary servitude in violation of the Thirteenth Amendment. The case then came before the United States Supreme Court.

Hughes made short work of the matter. He approached the issue in terms of the Thirteenth Amendment: "The State may impose involuntary servitude as a punishment for a crime, but it may not compel one man to labor for another in payment of a debt, by punishing him as a criminal if he does not perform the service or pay the debt."[22] And "What the State may not do directly it may not do indirectly. If it cannot punish the servant as a criminal for the mere failure or refusal to serve without paying his debt, it is not permitted to accomplish the same result by creating a statutory presumption which upon proof of no other fact exposes him to conviction and punishment."[23] And the underlying reality did matter: "Without imputing any actual motive to oppress, we must consider the natural operation of the statute . . . and it is apparent that it furnishes a convenient instrument for coercion which the Constitution and . . . Congress forbid."[24]

Holmes did not agree. His dissent was all elegant formalism with blithe disregard for the brutal factual realities attending the disputed issue. The crux of his dissent lay in professing to see little difference between civil and criminal penalties for breach of contract. The state had an interest in encouraging private parties to honor contractual obligations and hence made the courts available to plaintiffs seeking monitary damages. The addition of criminal penalties simply furthered that worthy end: "I do not blink (at) the fact that . . . liability to imprisonment may work as a motive when a fine without it would not, and that it may induce the laborer to keep on when he would like to leave. But it does not strike me as an objection to a law that it is effective."[25]

Whatever progressive views Holmes might have had, race was different. He virtually acknowledged the reality of caste abuse but dismissed the possibility of legal redress in terms that bordered on amused contempt for black plaintiffs. It is not possible to know what direction the White Court would have taken on racial matters had Holmes assumed the same degree of influence over the chief justice that Bradley assumed over Morrison Waite.

It can be surmised however that the addition of Hughes, Holmes's intellectual equal and a man of greater national stature who would go on to become a presidential candidate, changed the dynamic of the small group of men meeting weekly to decide what the nation stood for. Hughes brought to the table a mind which would begin to formulate a new jurisprudence of race and rights. The first faint hint, the first inkling of the judicial reasoning that would lead eventually *Brown v. Board of Education*, was advanced by Hughes in November, 1914, in response to Oklahoma's efforts as a state only recently admitted to the union, to erect a solid legal wall of racial segregation.

McCabe: A Modest Beginning: A Long Journey

It was an unlikely victory—a case that should have been lost. It was also the case which, in the words of legal scholar Benno

Schmidt, made "a breech in the aura of permanency that surrounded the regime of Jim Crow in the second decade of the twentieth century."[26] In a specific sense the case dealt with the constitutionality of an Oklahoma law. In a more fundamental sense it went to the question of the ultimate viability of *Plessy.*

In *Plessy* the Supreme Court had stated that state laws mandating segregation of blacks from whites were reasonable means for pursuing such legitimate state objectives as the maintenance of racial peace and that such laws did not offend the equal protection clause of the Fourteenth Amendment provided the separate facilities afforded black were equal to those afforded whites. The Court did not indicate its posture where practical circumstances or economic considerations made it difficult or impossible to provide equal facilities. Would the Equal Protection clause dictate equal access, or would the meaning of the clause be further eroded by finding only a limited state obligation to provide equal access? Hughes sought to answer this question in *McCabe.* The answer had limited immediate consequences, but it advanced a doctrine powerfully called upon by Hughes twenty-four years later in the *Gaines* case, which made the first serious crack in the legal foundation of segregation and which set the Court on the road that led to *Brown.*

McCabe began in 1907 with an awkwardly worded Oklahoma law that sought to reconcile Jim Crow sentiment and economic realities. Railroads operating within the state were constrained to provide separate but equal coach accommodations for black and white passengers. Noncoach accommodations—sleeping, dining, and parlor cars—were to be used exclusively by either whites or blacks and could not be partitioned, but the law did not require separate sleeping, dining, and parlor cars for each race.[27]

The strained language attempted to reconcile Jim Crow legislative intent to certain economic facts—there simply was not a large black demand for noncoach accommodations, hence, to require the provision of separate luxury and dining facilities for a minimal black clientele would have been to impose an economic burden on the railroads.

Shortly before the new law was to take effect, five black plaintiffs went to court seeking to enjoin its implementation. They challenged the entire statute on the grounds that it constituted state action denying citizens the equal protection of the laws for racial reasons, in violation of the Fourteenth Amendment. They also challenged the luxury car clause of the statute, arguing that the "equal provision" elements of the *Plessy* formula be honored were the courts to sustain the state's right to make racial distinctions in law. Objections were also raised under the Commerce Clause, relative to one state controlling the conditions of commerce in another state.[28]

The Federal District Court denied the injunction as did the Circuit Court of Appeals, both citing *Plessy* for the proposition that racially separate facilities did not violate constitutional rights, and holding that minimal black demand was a sufficient reason for not providing equal facilities for those blacks who might wish to use luxury facilities. And indeed, the legal precedents as the case moved to the Supreme Court were not at all promising.

In 1909, the Interstate Commerce Commission in *Cozart* and *Airline Railroad* had found the denial of equal accommodations due to small black demand not to constitute "undue prejudice."[29] While not bound by the holdings of either the Interstate Commerce Commission or the Federal Courts the Supreme Court itself had only recently reaffirmed the validity of the Jim Crow principle as regards travel.

On the last day of the 1909 Supreme Court term, the final day of Melville Fuller's tenure as chief justice, the Court had handed down the *Chiles v. Chesapeak and Ohio Railway* J. Alexander Chiles, a black graduate of the University of Michigan Law School who had bought a first-class ticket for a trip from Washington D.C. to Lexington, Kentucky. Upon taking his seat in the first-class car he was directed to a separate black car, a smoke-filled and noisome place, and moved under protest only when the police were called. In the subsequent suit the Supreme Court upheld the Kentucky court's decision absolving the railroad of any liability. Rather than relying on the state's Jim Crow law the railroad had argued that Chiles was moved pursuant to its own regulations regarding the safety and comfort of its passengers. The Supreme Court affirmed the reasonableness of race as a factor in the assignment of passengers, citing *Plessy* for the proposition that racial differences were real and could reasonably be reflected in law, policy, and regulation.[30]

Only months before *McCabe* was argued, the Court had addressed the issue of separate but unequal facilities in transportation in *Butts v. Merchant and Miners Transportation Company* and had no trouble in not finding a constitutional violation. In *Butts* a black woman, Mary F. Butts, had boarded a boat plying the seas between Boston and Norfork, Virginia. Despite her first-class ticket she was put below decks with the second-class passengers and constrained to dine after the first-class passengers, using the soiled table linen left by them.

Her subsequent suit derived from the Civil Rights Act of 1875, the argument being that Congress had the power to forbid acts of discrimination in areas directly under its jurisdiction such as Territories, the District of Columbia, and United States waters. In effect, she was arguing that the act should be viewed as something akin to a state civil rights law. In the context of the legal framework of the time it was equivalent to arguing that although Congress might not have power under the Constitution to forbid a merchant in New York from engaging in racial discrimination, the New York State legislature could prohibit invidious racial distinctions in access to public accommodations within the state. By analogy Congress could prohibit racial discrimination in the domains under its jurisdiction—Territories, the District of Columbia, and United States waters.

The Supreme Court disagreed. Writing for a unanimous Court, Justice Van Devanter held that while Congress did indeed have the power to prohibit discrimination in public accommodations in the areas under its jurisdiction, Joseph Bradley's majority holding in the *Civil Rights Cases of 1883* striking down of the public accommodations provisions of the 1875 law constituted a total judicial repudiation of the statute. Nothing in the language of the statute had suggested that it was separable into clauses applying to the states and clauses applying to areas under Congressional jurisdiction. The law was dead. It was not a vehicle through which Butts could pursue her claim.[31]

Given the recent judicial past there was reason for the railroad to be hopeful as *McCabe* approached the Court. Both the railroad and the state argued that racial segregation was essential to the interests of whites and blacks, that it promoted racial harmony and grounded the social order in the immutable differences of race which all sensible people recognized to exist. They argued further that it was unreasonable to expect luxury provisions to be provided for black passengers given comparatively light demand. They were particularly incensed by the lone dissenter at the appeals court level who had argued under the language of *Plessy* that the railroad should not provide luxury cars for whites if was not prepared to provide them for blacks.

In his majority holding Hughes went directly to the central issue—could the "equal" provision of the *Plessy* formulation be foregone on grounds of thin black demand for the service in question? Apparently there had been disagreement on the answer as Hughes in a letter to Holmes had stated the plain meaning of the state's argument: "All agree . . . that a black man must sit up all night just because he is black, unless there are enough blacks to make a 'black sleeping car' pay."[32] Hughes majority holding found reason to deny constitutional affirmation of that reality.

The state's argument failed in that it would make the availability of a constitutional right a function of the number of people seeking to enjoy that right. In reality, the majority held, constitutional rights are personal. "It is the individual who is entitled to equal protection of the law."[33] It followed, therefore, that it made no difference that the black demand for luxury accommodations was meager—the individual black seeking such accommodations still had a right under the constitution to a car at least as well appointed as that enjoyed by the white holder of a first-class ticket.

McCabe did not end discrimination in transportation. Pressure, intimidation, and local defiance still consigned black travelers to inferior accommodations. The importance of it at the time it was decided lay in the fact that it refused to affirm state legislation that would have eroded even the *Plessy* standard. It rejected the proposition that not only could a state make racial distinctions in law, it could also, within the framework of the Fourteenth Amendment and the Equal Protection clause, refuse to make service or accommodations available at all.

Not evident at the time was the fact that it articulated a doctrine to which Hughes was to return more than twenty years later after a run for the presidency, a return to private practice, and a reappointment to the Court as chief justice. In 1938 the Court took up the case of Lloyd Gaines, denied admittance to the all-white University of Missouri and unable otherwise to attend law school within the state because none existed for black students. The state argued that thin demand made creation of a black law school unfeasible. In finding for Gaines Hughes, speaking for the majority, cited *McCabe* and used the language he had used a quarter of a century earlier. Constitutional rights are personal. They do not wax or wane by the number of persons who might benefit from their exercise. The individual is entitled to the equal protection of the law and the state's obligation does not vanish because few persons might seek equal treatment along a particular dimension.[34]

The harshest challenges to black status were yet to come however. There had always been a schizoid quality element to the mode in which the nation sought to reconcile racial reality to the values and purposes that defined the country. On the one hand, blacks were outside the affective bonds of the national family, despised members of a semipariah caste. On the other hand, the nation defined itself as unique among the community of nations in that it defined all its members as equal before the law. By stating as a matter of constitutional doctrine that legal distinctions might be made on the basis of race without doing violence to the Constitution provided the races were treated equally, *Plessy* constituted an exercise in national self-deception.

At one level the laws at stakes in the next set of cases to come before the Court constituted efforts on the part of the most dedicated among the legions of segregationists to end the deception, to make it as clear in law as it was in fact that blacks were a pariah caste. Hence, *Guinn*, and particularly *Buchanan*, were regarded as pivotal at the time they were argued and decided. The participants and the national community broadly understood that the Court's holdings spoke to whether the exclusion could be formalized in law without any reference to "equal"; whether as a matter of law blacks could be excluded from the political arena and restricted by law to all-black communities.

The Grandfather Clause Cases

In the fall of 1910 an article appeared in the *Harvard Law Review* entitled "The Latest Phase of Negro Disfranchisement." Its author, Julien C. Monnet, of the University of Oklahoma, was moved to ask whether the country was approaching the last phase of black disfranchisement by virtue of the statute only recently passed in his state which promised to effect complete black exclusion from electoral politics. A clear set of historical events had brought Oklahoma to its pivotal place in the surge toward constitutionally sanctioned racial exclusion, leading Monnet to the sad speculation that Professor Arthur Machen might have been correct when he asserted in an earlier *Harvard Law Review* article that the Fifteenth Amendment is dead.[35]

The Radical Republicans of the 1860s had regarded access to the ballot as one of the keys to black liberation. Armed with the vote blacks could protect and advance their own interests. Despite the redemptionist countertide of the early 1870s the Fifteenth, implemented via the civil rights act of 1870 and other legislation, and by a federal presence in the states of the old Confederacy, had discernable consequences. In the presidential election of 1880 a majority of black males in the South voted. By the end of the 1880s however a sustained assault on the black franchise, made possible in part by Supreme Court decisions, had reduced black participation significantly. In *Reese* and *Cruickshank* the Supreme Court had limited the reach of federal law-enforcement efforts, fixing responsibility for dealing with local terror aimed at driving blacks away from the polls on local officials, persons who might themselves be involved in the violence.

Additionally, the detente between North and South and the reading of blacks out of the political community was promoted by successful redemptionist efforts to define the activities of the reconstructionist governments as corrupt and foolish, manifestation of black incompetence and proof of the wisdom of excluding them from the deliberations of thoughtful and serious men, able to behave responsibly in the political arena. In this spirit, Congress in 1878 prohibited the use of the army to oversee elections, and ten years later defeated new proposals for federal supervision of elections.

Terror and the manipulation of criteria such as literacy and payment of poll taxes had the consequence of driving black electoral participation downward significantly by the turn of the century. An inherent problem with such restrictive devices however was that they also put a substantial number of whites at risk. As the legal historian Benno Schmidt observed, "Property, literacy . . . ,or good character tests could normally or by administrative manipulation exclude virtually all black voters, but poor, unschooled whites also had good reason to fear these disenfranchising mechanisms."[36]

The "Grandfather Clause" was born in the twists and turns of Southern states to find a constitutionally valid way of disfranchising black voters without also excluding white voters. Mississippi pioneered in the effort to purge blacks from the rolls, its 1890 constitutional convention calling for the right to vote to be conditioned on the payment of a poll tax months in advance, production of the receipt for payment at the time of voting, and one-year residence in the election district, in addition to two years residence in the state. In addition, would-be voters were required to be able to read, write, and interpret any section of the state constitution to the satisfaction of the registrar. South Carolina adopted the Mississippi plan in 1895 and introduced further restrictions.

Concern about the potential of literacy tests and poll taxes by white elites to disfranchise poor whites generated enormous controversy at the Louisiana convention called to consider the Mississippi plan, leading the state to become the first to enact a grandfather clause as a temporary measure to get whites on the rolls. North Carolina followed in 1900, Alabama in 1901, and Virginia in 1902.

There was little effort to disguise the intention of the new laws, the *New Orleans Times Democrat* stating that the objective was to place "every white voter on the poll list and keep out nearly every negro, without violating the federal constitution." According to the Birmingham *Age-Herald* state officials were looking for a scheme "which will let every white man vote and prevent any negro from voting."[37] The before and after differences in black political participation were dramatic. More than 130,000 blacks voted in Louisiana in 1896, two years before the new law. In 1900, two years after the law, 5,320 blacks voted. A similar impact was had in Alabama.

Oklahoma came late to the process, adding a grandfather clause to the state constitution in 1910 as a permanent element of the election law, in effect creating a circumstance in which a white would be able to secure a place on the rolls no matter what, while blacks faced permanent exclusion. An unusual set of circumstances brought the law before the Supreme Court, the Court being called upon to decide whether black disenfranchisement would be written into law with something approaching a literal declaration of intent.

The Oklahoma Cases

Even by the standards of those sympathetic to the move to disenfranchise black voters, the Oklahoma law was extraordinary. According to Professor Monnet of the University of Oklahoma, writing as the events unfolded, "A comparison of this clause with its predecessors shows the Oklahoma amendment to be the most sweeping attempt yet made constitutionally to include all whites and exclude all blacks from the privilege of voting."[38]

Drawn up by the legislature in January of 1910 and put to the voters in August of that year, it declared, in part, that no one would be allowed to register to vote unless he was able to read and write any section of the Oklahoma constitution. On the other hand, no person who had been eligible to vote on January 1, 1866, or who at that time resided in a foreign country, nor the descendants of such persons would be denied the right to vote because they could not read or write any section of the Oklahoma constitution. In other words, a black graduate of Harvard Law School could be found ineligible to vote while an illiterate, white immigrant faced no barrier at all. But despite its extraordinary character the prospects of the new law being declared unconstitutional were not promising.

The initial struggle revolved around getting the matter into federal court at all. Blacks made up less than 9 percent of the population of the state, most black voters being Republican. State Republican officials, although not problack, understood that the black vote could make a difference in close elections and thus became alarmed at the implications of near total black disenfranchisement.

Efforts on the part of state Republican officials to get the Taft administration to challenge the law in court prior to the 1910 state elections failed, President Taft pursuing an early version of the "Southern strategy," hoping to rebuild Republican strength in the Southern and border states by being accommodating on racial matters. As the 1912 presidential election approached, an ominous situation loomed before Taft. His mentor, former president Theodore Roosevelt, accused him of betraying the principles of progressivism, the use of government on behalf of consumers and ordinary people to counterbalance the awesome power and influence of big business. The fiery ex-president was threatening to challenge Taft for the Republican nomination or mount a third party movement and was attracting widespread support for a run against his former protege. Faced with the prospect of losing support in traditional Republican strongholds, Taft turned a covetous eye to the South. If he showed himself sympathetic to white interests, perhaps he would be remembered on election day.

In the Oklahoma state elections of the fall of 1910, conducted under the terms of the clause, the black vote was virtually eliminated from local politics to the detriment of Republican candidates, spurring new demands by state officials that the national administration take action. Again, the administration hesitated, Taft fearing that an aggressive stance would jeopardize whatever chance he had of persuading the white South that he was indeed a friend.

Despite the warning of Taft's Justice Department with regard to the possible negative political consequences at the national level of an aggressive administration stance, local United States attorneys John Embree and William Gregg, under pressure from local Republicans concerned about their own political fate, moved to initiate a case. Two local election officials Frank Guinn and J. J. Beal were indicted, charged with conspiring to deny blacks their right to vote. Seeking solace in the belief that no local jury would convict, the administration acquiesced in letting the case go forward. On September 29, 1911, to the great surprise of Washington, Guinn and Beal were convicted in the Federal District Court for the Western District of Oklahoma of violating Section 19 of the Federal Criminal Code punishing conspiracies to prevent any citizen from enjoying constitutional conferred rights. The conviction set the case on the road to the Supreme Court.[39]

Unable to articulate a clear rationale for his candidacy in the bitterly contested 1912 presidential campaign, Taft was routed, finishing third in the election as the Republican candidate behind Theodore Roosevelt and his Bull Moose Party and the winner, Democrat Woodrow Wilson. Taft had proved an unconvincing Southerner and had been unable in the months before the election to reposition himself as a champion of the common man after all. The old Confederacy had opted for a genuine Southerner in Wilson, a son of old Virginia, albeit transplanted to New Jersey. But with Wilson's victory the *Guinn* case passed into the hands of a new justice department and a new administration having neither a moral nor a political commitment to black interests.

Wilson had been elected with the votes of states which had pioneered in devising legal mechanisms for disfranchising blacks. It had neither a stake nor an interest in challenging Oklahoma's device for accomplishing a racial purging of the rolls. Its chief legal officers were both committed sons of the Confederacy. Attorney General James Clark McReynolds would later be appointed to the Supreme Court and would over the span of his two decades on the bench reveal himself to be a rigid white supremacist. Solicitor General John W. Davis, the son of proslavery parents, would become a presidential candidate a decade later on the Democratic ticket, losing to Calvin Coolidge, but would also be remembered for arguing the South's case for segregation before the Supreme Court in *Brown v. Board of Education* some four decades after coming to Washington to serve Wilson.

Concerned that the incoming administration would not push the case, Oklahoma Republicans had pressed the outgoing Taft administration to request its advance on the Supreme Court's calendar. The Court refused to move it forward for argument before the new administration took office and thus the matter passed into the hands of Davis and McReynolds.

It is not clear what Davis's state of mind was as he approached the case as solicitor general. On the one hand, he believed blacks to be unfit for the responsibilities of citizenship, but on the other, according to some historians, he did not want to make his debut before the court as solicitor general with an obviously lame performance. Argument was heard before the Court in October, 1913, in a cultural climate not hospitable to black concerns. Elite and educated opinion had reached a consensus on black inferiority and the necessity therefore of racial segregation. The Wilson administration itself had moved to eliminate the last vestiges of racial inclusion in Washington by mandating the segregation of federal employees.

Among the populace at large the diversions of popular culture reflected the contours of popular thinking about matters of race. As the parties gathered in Washington in October, 1913, to argue the merits of a bar to black voting, the pioneer director David Wark Griffith was completing filming of *Birth of a Nation*, a paean to the Ku Klux Klan as rescuer of the white South from the ruin visited upon it by primitive blacks and venal carpetbaggers. It would feature many scenes of corrupt and ignorant black politicians, no more fit for office than orangutans, bringing a nightmare of misrule upon a suffering but courageous white population inspired finally to fight back by the heroism of the Klan. The film would also become the first feature-length mega-hit in American screen history.

In defense of Oklahoma Joseph W. Bailey argued that the Grandfather Clause did no violence to the Fifteenth Amendment because it did not restrict anyone's right to vote on racial grounds. Oklahoma's accompanying literacy test restricted access to the ballot, but the Supreme Court itself twenty years earlier in *Williams v. Mississippi* had found that state literacy test requirements did not offend the Constitution despite the fact that they seemed to snare blacks almost exclusively. The Grandfather Clause merely opened up another avenue to political participation. That it might benefit whites disproportionately did not deprive blacks of the right to vote in that they might qualify by other means.[40]

In the months between oral argument and the handing down of the decision, national attention came to focus again on the search for a "Great White Hope" to beat the black heavyweight champion Jack Johnson, the fervor brought to the task reflecting majority sensibilities on matters of race as the Court moved to resolution in deciding on the fate of Frank Guinn and J. J. Beal. Indeed the enormous wave of passion generated by the quest had drawn the Court itself into its wake.

Few single events in the nation's history up to that point had generated as much anticipation nor so focused national attention as the July 4th championship fight between Johnson and Jim Jeffries in Reno, three years earlier. Former white heavyweight champion Jim Jeffries had come out of retirement to fight Jack Johnson, in order to restore the crown to the white race and put aside any suspicion that the black race might not be inferior after all. The fight generated an enormous live gate and took place before a huge, unruly crowd, almost entirely white, hot with anticipation of racial triumph. It was also one of the first media events in American history, crowds gathering around telegraph offices throughout the country to follow the fight blow-by-blow via wireless.

But in the fifteenth round Jeffries lost, knocked out by the younger, stronger, faster Johnson and antiblack riots followed. The *New York Herald* headline indicated "Africans dragged from New York Street Cars and Attacked in Streets in Fury of Whites Over Jeffries' Defeat . . . Negroes Also Attacked and Lynchings Threatened in Philadelphia, Washington, Pittsburgh, Chattanooga, Atlanta, St. Louis and Many Other Points."[41]

The fight had been filmed, one of the first major sporting events to be recorded by the crude new medium, motion pictures. And Jeffries and Johnson were among the first, or were perhaps the first athletes to sell the film rights to their contest. But just as the outcome of the fight itself had led to riots and mayhem so also did the exhibition of the film spark racial violence. A number of states, including Ohio, passed legislation requiring the licensing of films to be exhibited commercially in-state. Licenses were denied films deemed immoral or improper on sexual grounds and for exhibit of the Johnson-Jeffries fight. An Illinois-based film distributor, Mutual Corporation, challenged Ohio's licensing law, and by implication those of other states, on the First Amendment grounds and on a claim of improper state interference with commerce.

In *Mutual v. Ohio*, decided in 1915, the Court held that filmmaking was a business rather than an artistic enterprise and that the states could regulate the conditions of their operation as they regulated the conditions of operation of other businesses.[42] And as the decision was being handed down in the long months between the oral argument in *Guinn* and the final holding, the passions that animated the quest for a redeemer of the white race were rising again. It appeared Johnson would soon fight another White Hope. The Chief Justice and his colleagues deliberated in a cultural environment animated again by dreams of triumph in racial combat as a confirmation of racial superiority.

A trio of "grandfather clause" cases were before the Court as the racial temper of the nation rose. In addition to *Guinn* the Court had before it *Myers*, a case coming out of Maryland addressing the possible liability of election officials should the clause fail the constitutional test, and *Mosley*, also out of Oklahoma, dealing with whether an old anti-Klan Act could be applied to the derelictions of election officers.[43]

More than a year elapsed between oral argument and the handing down of a decision as a behind the scenes struggle developed. Chief Justice White sought unanimity. Associate justice Horace Lurton, ailing but still combative, refused to join the majority. White urged him to resign but he refused to do so. White held back on the decision, not wanting to go before the country with a Court divided on the issue. And then Lurton died.

On June 21, 1915, Chief Justice White delivered the opinion of the Court. The terms in which Oklahoma had defended the law in its briefs and oral argument and by which the Court addressed the issue foreshadowed the terms of debate decades later relative to "disparate treatment" as against "disparate impact" discrimination. Even if disparate treatment in the sense of overt and intentional racial discrimination is made anathema to the law, it does not necessarily follow that racially different outcomes yielded by neutral procedures or processes are matters for legal redress.

In a brief thick with citations Oklahoma argued that the Fifteenth Amendment had not deprived states of their right to set voter qualifications, it merely constrained them from making race a qualifying or disqualifying factor. The grandfather clause applied "without distinction of race, color, or previous condition of servitude" and although whites might be its primary beneficiary it was neutral in character and therefore passed constitutional muster.

In effect, Oklahoma was arguing that while there might be disparate outcomes in the sense that a much larger percentage of blacks than whites were ineligible to vote under the new law, the courts were not looking at disparate treatment—and hence a violation of the Fifteenth Amendment—because the law was facially neutral. In principle, a black could meet its terms and vote just as those whites who voted had met its requirements. Neither did it matter that whites could qualify under this objective test while blacks were left to the mercy of a more subjective test resting on the judgment of registrars. If that were a problem it was a problem, in its own terms—it did not undermine the constitutionality of a race-neutral grandfather clause.

In addressing the Oklahoma argument White spoke for a Court finally unanimous. While the state's argument had a surface plausibility, White indicated, it was necessary to look beyond the mere words of the Oklahoma law and go to the purpose of the state legislature in adopting it in the first place. If the law's purpose had not been to nullify the effect of the Fifteenth Amendment, what reason had there been for fixing the date for ancestral qualification at January 1, 1866—a date preceding the adoption of the Fifteenth Amendment?

The language used by the Court was unusually strong and without precedent in an opinion upholding black rights: "How can there be any room for any serious dispute concerning the repugnancy of the standard based on January 1, 1866?" And further on, "We have difficulty in finding words to more clearly demonstrate the conviction we entertain" that the state standard was intended to evade the intent of the Fifteenth Amendment, "we seek in vain for any ground which would sustain any other interpretation."[44] In companion holdings, *Myers* and *Mosley*, the civil liability of the Maryland election officials and the exposure of the Oklahoma officials under the anticonspiracy Klan Act were affirmed.

Contemporary observers understood the decision to be of vast importance, but disagreed as to why. The New York *Evening Post* hailed the decision, declaring it to "mean as much forward as the Dred Scott case did backward."[45] Others pointed out that it did not confer the vote on one black who did not already have it. Perhaps its greatest import was psychological. It slowed the momentum of segregation, the sense that it was an unfolding and inevitably triumphant system, not yet complete in its molding of the place of blacks in the society.

But segregation continued to be a dynamic, resilient system. As *Guinn* was being handed down events were unfolding in Louisville, Kentucky, which were to bring to the Court a case understood at the time and viewed by every contemporary observer as pivotal in the resolving the meaning of freedom for the nation's black population. Events were also unfolding on the Court, bringing a significant change in its composition.

Prior to Charles Evans Hughes's tenure, John Marshall Harlan, had been the only justice to consistently articulate an interpretation of the Constitution which limited state power and spoke in sympathetic terms to black rights. Hughes joined a Court having a constellation which allowed him to marshal majority support in *McCabe* and *Bailey*. William Day, appointed to the Court a few years earlier than Hughes, brought a perspective to issues of race that allowed him to see beyond the formalist sophistries reconciling caste subordination to the egalitarian language of the Constitution. And most unexpectedly, Edward Douglass White, the ex-Confederate trooper, a faithful soldier in the army of orthodoxy throughout his career in Congress and on the bench, lent himself to the effort to hew out a new path on matters of race, against the opposition of stubborn colleagues.

But shortly after *Guinn* the delicate balance was altered. In 1916 Hughes resigned from the Court to run for president on the Republican ticket against Woodrow Wilson. While the resignation posed Wilson with a challenge from a popular opponent it also gave him the chance to make his second appointment. In filling the seat Wilson selected James Clark McReynolds, his attorney general, a man referred to by an astute scholar as an "obdurate racist."[46]

While not hopeful in terms of black interests it was not clear what the McReynolds appointment did to the overall cast of the Court and its delicate balance on matters of race given that Wilson's first appointment a year earlier to replace the deceased Horace Lurton had been Louis Dembitz Brandeis, a nomination reflecting the deep contradictions of progressivism. Brandeis had made his reputation as an articulate, forceful, and effective champion of the public interest against corporate privilege. He had written a book called *Other Peoples' Money—And How the Banks Use It* and a number of popular and scholarly articles exposing the arrogance and abuses of banks and the lords of industry. Their venom toward him was a function of the fact that he was effective. Hence a vicious campaign had been mounted to block his nomination.

The rage of former President William Howard Taft, who had himself nurtured hopes of being appointed to the bench, reflected the stinging hostility of many Republicans. Upon hearing of the nomination he denounced Brandeis to a friend as "a socialist . . . a hypocrite . . . a man of infinite cunning . . . a dishonest trickster." Even Brandeis's Jewish identity was seen as a sham, only recently assumed for whatever political advantage it might bring. "The intelligent Jews of this country are as much opposed to the Brandeis nomination as I am. . . . There is a great feeling of antagonism toward Brandeis among the leading Jews, because his present superlative and extreme Judaism is a plant of very late growth." And given that the friend to whom he was denouncing Brandeis was Jewish, he resorted to Yiddish in raging against the situation. "When you consider Brandeis's appointment, and think that men were pressing me for the place, *es zum lachen.*" To his brother he indicated being deeply concerned "to have such an insidious devil in the Court."[47]

Four years later, with a Republican restored to the White House, Taft was to be appointed to the Court and become Brandeis's colleague. But the sentiment which animated Taft's rage was widespread among Senate Republicans, representatives of business and commercial interests, making the Brandeis confirmation a near thing, the move to turn him back at the level of the Judiciary Committee failing by only one vote.

Wilson had been drawn to Brandeis because of his progressive views and because Brandeis had been an advisor in the 1912 campaign. But as a Jew Brandeis brought a very different historical lineage to the issue of caste abuse than did Wilson. The Georgia lynching of the young Jewish businessman Leo Frank in 1910 had shaken Jewish communities nationwide. Although not known to be deeply observant, Brandeis did move in a circle that included some of the major Jewish intellectuals of the day and thus, without doubt, pondered the genteel and sometimes not so genteel anti-Semitism found in the academy and in the commercial and social worlds.

There was also reason to believe that he would not indulge the evasions of formalism where the interests of the weak were at issue. In 1910 he had been approached by his sister-in-law Florence Goldmark, an activist in progressive organizations, to look into the case of a poor, Portland, Oregon, working mother, Mrs. Elmer Gotcher. Oregon had only recently passed a law limiting the number of hours women could work per day in factories or laundries to ten, but Mrs. Gother's employer, Curt Muller, owner of the Grand Laundry, had forced her to work longer hours in defiance of the law. Upon being fined, Muller indicated his intention of seeking the overturn of the statute, going up to the Supreme Court if necessary to free himself and other employers of the shackles of state legislation limiting the number of hours in a day they could work an employee.

The Supreme Court had shown itself sympathetic to employer arguments relative to state infringement on their right to form contracts with their employees and their rights under the Fourteenth Amendment, having recently declared a New York State law limiting the work day for men to ten hours to be unconstitutional. Thus, Muller had every expectation of winning and of overturning Oregon's law and the laws of nineteen other states seeking to create more humane working conditions for women and children.

Brandeis had not been the first attorney approached about helping Oregon defend the law. Joseph Choate, a distinguished attorney and former ambassador, had indicated when asked to enter in defense of the state that he could not understand why a big, strong Irishwoman could not work more than ten hours a day if her employer wanted her to.[48] Brandeis brought a different perspective to the matter. He read the Court's prior holdings as admitting of state regulation if it could be established that regulation was reasonable and represented a limited and rational means of realizing a legitimate state objective.

To establish the reasonableness of the Oregon statute Brandeis turned to the research literature of the social and biological sciences rather than to prior legal pronouncements about women, the state, and the law. The brief submitted to the Supreme Court contained a few pages of legal argument and over one hundred pages of citations to research literature bearing on the deleterious effects of excessive female labor in the workplace on the stability of the family, on a woman's children, and on her health. Drawn by the brief and by oral argument to look at the issue in terms of the realities concerning the workplace, employer demands and their social consequences, and state efforts to regulate in reasonable terms, the Court held that the Oregon law was not in violation of the Constitution.

On matters of race and rights Brandeis's realist judicial approach and broader, reformist social philosophy offered at least the possibility of balancing off James Clark McReynolds's known hostility to black interests. Thus, as the Court moved toward its encounter with the growing move to write black zones and white zones into law, its composition had changed in ways that made it unclear as to where it might stand on this or other segregationist measures to achieve the caste society implicit in the logic of *Plessy*.

American Apartheid

In 1909 a group of black intellectuals, activists, and reformers met at Niagara Falls, New York, on the Canadian border, to discuss a new organization and a new political agenda. Random terror had given away to the pogrom. In Atlanta the black quarter had been burned and blacks driven from the city. In Springfield, Illinois, eighty-five blacks had been killed and masses of blacks driven out into the countryside. Calhoun County, Georgia, moved to make itself racially pure by driving away all blacks.

In an atmosphere of racial terror, a shriveling of the opportunity for political participation, and shrinking legal rights, a mix of white philanthropists and reformers, and black intellectuals and activists held a series of meetings to chart a course designed to sustain what remained of black rights and, if possible, breath new life into the post–Civil War amendments. The move to create an American-style apartheid provided the circumstance for the new organization—the National Association for the Advancement of Colored People—to take hold in black communities.

The Association's legal defense work was initiated in the summer of 1910 with the Pink Franklin case out of South Carolina. Franklin, a plantation field hand had violated a peonage-like "agricultural contract" and had shot the sheriff sent to enforce it. An NAACP petition before Governor Martin Ansel had resulted in commutation of the death sentence to life in prison. A year later the organization secured life in prison for two blacks condemned to death in Delaware, and in 1914 lobbied successfully for the defeat of bills before Congress which would have excluded blacks from military service. But the decade-long struggle against the attempt to create legally designated black zones contributed to the long-term survival of the association.

The first chapter of the NAACP was organized in Baltimore in 1910 to fight that city's residential segregation law. Other chapters came into existence in cities adopting laws creating black zones and white zones. The Louisville, Kentucky, chapter, under the leadership of William Warley, dedicated itself to challenging that city's ordinance in court.

The Louisville law was plainly worded. No black could move into and occupy a house in any block in which a majority of the occupants were white and no white could move into a residence in a block in which the majority residence was black. As with other such laws the purpose, presumably, was to promote racial peace and harmony and protect the value of property. Additionally, the ordinance held out the prospect of a legally mandated black shanty town crystallizing as a satellite of the white metropolis.[49]

In the years following the passage of the Baltimore statute national attention came to focus on Louisville and the fate of its ordinance in court. A number of communities in the South had followed Baltimore's lead, but the test of the issue in the Supreme

Court was developing in Louisville. Baltimore's city attorney wrote to James Maher, the clerk of the Supreme Court in March of 1916 indicating that "many cities throughout this country have similar (segregation) ordinances now in force and the cities of Baltimore and Richmond are vitally interested in the outcome of this litigation."[50]

The struggle in Louisville had begun in mid-November, 1913, with the appearance before the weekly luncheon of the Louisville Real Estate Club of W. D. Binford, a white employed by the local papers. Binford raised the specter of blacks moving into white neighborhoods and wreaking havoc with property values, causing whites to lose the fruits of their lives' work as their homes plummeted in worth. He called for racial zoning as the solution. Although the Real Estate Board remained noncommittal, white support began to grow for Binford's proposal and the struggle moved to the political arena as the city council took up the matter of an ordinance to create black zones and white zones.

After a series of open meetings heavily attended by blacks as members of the new National Association for the Advancement of Colored People, and by whites expressing fears regarding property values, the city council by a vote of 21–0 approved an ordinance creating a process that would yield legally mandated black zones and white zones. On May 11, 1914, the measure was signed into law by the mayor.

Sectors of the black community and the NAACP mobilized to fight the new law in what was to become one of the first cases bringing the new organization before the Supreme Court. August 9th was designated "segregation Sunday," black ministers in Louisville being asked to preach on the subject. At the same time plans were made to challenge the ordinance in both civil and criminal court via test cases. Two weeks after "segregation Sunday" Arthur Harris, a black, moved into 630 Nineteenth Street, a house in a white zone. He was arrested, found guilty, and fined, thereby providing the NAACP with one of its cases.[51]

The events yielding the civil case, *Buchanan v. Warley*, had also been set in motion. On October 31, 1914, William Warley, president of the newly formed chapter of the National Association for the Advancement of Colored People, entered into a contract with Charles Buchanan, a white realtor, to buy a lot in a block in which there were eight white families and two black. Part payment was to be made upon the delivery of the deed with the balance being paid off over a two-year period. While the block was majority white the lot in question was adjacent to the two lots occupied by blacks. The offer in writing to purchase the property contained words to the effect that Warley would not be required to accept a deed unless he had the right under the laws of the State of Kentucky and of Louisville "to occupy said property as a residence."

On November 2, 1914, Buchanan excepted Warley's offer and on November 10 tendered a deed and sought the initial payment. Citing the new ordinance which declared it to be "unlawful for any colored person to move into and occupy as a residence any house upon any block in the city of Louisville upon which a greater number of houses are occupied as residences by white people than are occupied as residences by colored people," Warley refused payment. Whereupon Buchanan promptly sued him in the Jefferson County Circuit Court for "specific performance," a court order that Warley honor the terms of the agreement. Buchanan argued that the ordinance was in conflict with the Fourteenth Amendment to the United States Constitution and therefore was no defense to the action for specific performance.

The circuit court disagreed with Buchanan as did the Kentucky Court of Appeals. In a unanimous opinion handed down on June 18, 1915, Judge J. B. Hannah stated Kentucky's position. The new law was held to be consistent with the language of the Fourteenth Amendment as interpreted by the Supreme Court in the numerous cases which had upheld the constitutionality of laws mandating racial segregation. It bore equally on both races, it had a rational basis related to the maintenance of racial peace, and it entailed the exercise of zoning powers which, undeniably, the state had. The law could also be affirmed on the basis of the Berea College case, decided only a dozen years earlier, in which the United States Supreme Court had held that the Fourteenth Amendment is not offended where "the State is fully committed to the principle of the separation of the races whenever and wherever practicable and expedient for the public welfare."[52]

The losses at the state level set the stage for the battle to move to the Supreme Court. Ironically, given the posture of the parties in the Kentucky court battles, Warley, the black man, was raising the Louisville ordinance as defense to Buchanan's breach-of-contract claim, while the white realtor was challenging the constitutionality of the law, arguing that invalid laws cannot be a defense to failure to honor the terms of a contract. Warley found himself, on paper, allied with the Louisville City Counsel attorneys defending the law. Whatever the psychological or strategic impact of the strategy, the opponents of this profoundly antiblack law had structured the challenge to it in such a way that its constitutionality was contested by a respected white man.

The case was understood at the time to be pivotal. In March, 1916, Pendleton Beckley, city attorney for Louisville sent a letter to James Maher, chief clerk of the Supreme Court, regarding other cities wishing to file briefs in support of the ordinance: " Although this is the first case involving the segregation of the races under city ordinance to reach the Supreme Court, many cities throughout this country have similar ordinances. . . . Naturally, on account of the importance of the question involved we feel that these cities will wish some form of representation at the hearing of this case. If the legal representatives of these cities request it, will the Supreme Court likely grant them an opportunity to be heard? To be perfectly candid we would be glad to have the cooperation and help of other municipalities which have for some years past been working out the segregation problem along lines similar to that adopted by the City of Louisville."[53]

And indeed a number of supporting briefs were filed. Baltimore, perhaps the pioneer city in racial zoning, argued strenuously in its brief, offering both legal and practical arguments.

Using the reasoning employed by the Supreme Court thirty-five years earlier in *Pace v. Alabama*, Baltimore's brief contended that there was "no such discrimination as is prohibited by the Constitution or statutes securing civil rights" to be found in racial zoning ordinances. What was denied one race was denied the other. What was allowed one race was allowed the other. Blacks could not buy or live in white zones, but then, whites could not buy or live in black zones. Hence, both races were being treated equally. In addition, the statutes met a reasonableness test in that they promoted racial peace.

But it was, perhaps, the practical arguments offered by Baltimore that supporters of racial zoning looked to have an impact on the Court. The Louisville ordinance had only recently been implemented, but Baltimore was able to assert that "For nearly four years these ordinances have been in force in Baltimore City, and have been almost universally obeyed, only one case having reached the Courts of any person violating the provision of the ordinance." And, the city argued, that one case had been the work of an outside agitator from the North who had come to Baltimore and stirred up local blacks.

In defense of Louisville, City Attorney Pendleton Beckley

went to the heart of the legal issue. The Supreme Court itself had affirmed the constitutionality of laws making distinctions based on race. Laws requiring separate railroad accommodations, separate schools, and forbidding interracial marriage been held to be valid exercises of police power. If the language of segregation laws treated the races alike and if those laws had a reasonable purpose they passed constitutional muster. It followed, he argued, that what was true of other Jim Crow laws was also true of the Louisville ordinance. On its face it treated the races alike and it had a legitimate objective well within the police powers of the state, the maintenance of racial peace.

Finally, Beckley contended, zoning laws always compromise property rights. In the nature of things zoning laws tell people what they can and cannot do with their property. Even though Jones may devoutly wish to open up a store in his spare room, if the neighborhood is zoned "residential" he cannot legally do that. Buchanan therefore was not being subjected to a disability greater than that placed on any owner of property.[54]

Clayton Blakey, Moorfield Storey, and Harold Davis, speaking for Buchanan, made three main points. After asserting that Buchanan was indeed being deprived of a property right they moved to a dissection of the racial realities underlying the passage of the statute: "The general assumption is that a law is enacted in good faith for the purposes declared, but where, as in this case, it is obvious that the real purpose was very different, the courts will determine the purpose from the natural and legal effect of the language employed when put into operation."

The natural and legal effect of the language when put into operation was to deprive Buchanan of the opportunity to sell his property. Given that the lot in question was adjacent to two lots occupied by blacks even though the block was majority white, "If he cannot sell to a colored person, he cannot sell at all, for the lot is so situated with reference to other colored men's residences that no white man would buy it."

At the same time the law forbade "under penalty of criminal proceedings, an owner of land in many parts of the city to live thereon if he happens to be a negro, although he would be free to do so if he were white. . . . A plainer case of racial discrimination cannot be well imagined." Hence, even if Warley were to honor the terms of the contact the ordinance forbade him from moving onto the lot or renting it to another black despite the fact that he would not be able to find either a white buyer or renter.

The plaintiffs then moved to counter the argument that the law represented merely the logical extension of the principles of racial separation affirmed by the Supreme Court in numerous prior cases. The school segregation cases were inapposite, they argued, because the state was not obliged to provide schools for anyone: "Statutes regulating attendance at schools do not cut down rights previously recognized, but grant privileges which would not otherwise exist." Cases banning interracial marriage were also irrelevant, they argued, "since marriage is a matter of status in which the interests of the State are vitally concerned."[55]

As the case went to the Court for its deliberations it was not clear that the plaintiffs had made a case demonstrably superior to that of Louisville. Surely the existence and constitutionality of zoning ordinances indicated that the state was vitally concerned with the uses to which land was put. Surely the underlying logic of the Louisville statute was similar to that of the Alabama antimiscegenation statute which had passed constitutional muster in *Pace*. If, by law, whites could only marry whites and blacks could only marry blacks, did it not follow that there was no constitutional problem with a scheme asserting that only whites could live in white zones while only blacks could live in black zones?

Due in part to the absence of Associate Justice William Day the case was reargued, final argument being heard on April 27, 1917, a year after the initial argument. Four months later Day delivered the Court's holding. The initial issue addressed by the Court was Charles Buchanan's standing to raise the challenge at all. Louisville had consistently argued as the case moved up to the Supreme Court that Buchanan lacked standing—that he was pressing a grievance on behalf of another party in defiance of a basic proposition in American law—that one must be an injured party in order to sue in an American court. Buchanan's real argument, the Louisville attorneys contended, was that the law violated the rights of blacks to the equal protection of the law under the Fourteenth Amendment. He was therefore asserting a violation of the rights of other parties rather than himself and therefore lacked standing to contest the constitutionality of the statute.

Had the Court chosen to exercise the option, the standing issue provided it with a way of avoiding addressing the constitutionality of the Louisville ordinance. It could have held that Buchanan as a white man pressing claims on behalf of blacks lacked standing and that his suit, therefore, had been improperly brought. And indeed one member of the Court had proposed that the Court take that route. Oliver Wendall Holmes drafted a dissent in which he argued that even though he had been injured by the law, the purpose of Buchanan's argument and the thrust of his claim was to redeem black rights. Less than two weeks before the decision was handed down Holmes contacted Day indicating that he was still debating whether to go on record with his dissent. In the end he did not, for reasons about which historians are uncertain.[56]

The consequence of Holmes's approach, had he been able to bring a majority along with him, would have been to leave the Louisville ordinance in effect, its constitutionality undetermined, pending the bringing of a case by a black plaintiff. The popular perception probably would have been that the ordinance had survived constitutional challenge and that it was proper therefore for other communities to proceed with racial zoning.

The handling of the standing issue signaled that the Court intended to address the racial realities attending the Louisville law. Without question, but for the ordinance, Buchanan would have been able to secure an order for specific performance from the court below. The courts below denied this relief only because the other party to the contract was black, Warley plainly had breached the contract.

If the ordinance was unconstitutional the harm it generated devolved not only upon blacks but also upon Buchanan in that he was now left with a piece of property which he could sell neither to a black nor, in all likelihood, to a white. In that sense he, and other similarly situated owners of property, were potentially aggrieved parties under the Fourteenth Amendment. The law potentially abridged Buchanan's right under the Constitution to acquire and enjoy property.

Having disposed of the standing issue Day moved to the merits of the case. He conceded that local authorities have vast powers to regulate their own affairs provided only that the means adopted are reasonably related to legitimate and lawful state objectives. On the other hand, the protections afforded to citizens by the Constitution place limits on government with regard to both means and ends.

Louisville had argued that the ordinance represented a reasonable mechanism for realizing legitimate objectives. The law was intended to maintain racial peace, promote racial purity, and maintain the value of property owned by whites, decline being sure to follow upon the influx of blacks into a neighborhood. The law represented merely an exercise of the accepted power of government to regulate the uses to which property can be put relative to notions of the public interest.

Conceding the authority of government to place restrictions on property owners with regard to the purposes for which they might use or dispose of their property, the issue posed by the Louisville ordinance, Day indicated, was whether the occupancy of property could be lawfully inhibited "solely because of the color of the proposed occupant of the premises."

Day then proceeded to review a variety of cases from *Slaughterhouse* through *Ex Parte Virginia*, establishing that the protective language of the Fourteenth Amendment applied to both blacks and whites and that the right to contract without inhibitions imposed by race was constitutionally protected. Case law and an analysis of legislative intent strongly suggested that statutes limiting contractual access to and occupancy of property breached the language of the Constitution.

Day then sought to distinguish *Plessy*, *Berea*, and the other Jim Crow cases upon which Louisville had relied. These cases did not revolve around the right to use, control, or dispose of property. In other words, they did not implicate rights explicitly recognized in the Constitution, the right to contract and property rights. Hence, the issue of the limits of state power relative to the Louisville ordinance had to be viewed somewhat more restrictively. In addition, the Jim Crow cases imposed an obligation on the state to provide equal, albeit separate, services for blacks and whites. In the nature of things, this principle could not apply where a law generated circumstances in which an owner could not dispose of his property at all because of the race of the buyer in relation to the racial composition of the proposed area of sale.

Granting the importance of the objective of maintaining racial peace the Court concluded nevertheless: "We think this attempt to prevent the alienation of the property in question to a person of color was not a legitimate exercise of the police power of the State, and is in direct violation of the fundamental law enacted in the Fourteenth amendment . . . preventing state interference with property rights except by due process of law."[57]

The overwhelming importance of the case was well understood at the time. Said the Baltimore *Afro-American* on November 10, 1917, "The joy in (mudville) when home run Casey came to bat in the final inning of a famous game with the bases loaded is nothing compared with the rejoicing in Baltimore, Richmond, St. Louis and other Southern towns over the outcome of the Louisville segregation decision." On the same day the Richmond *Planet*, a black paper, opined "God bless the Supreme Court of the United States. . . . We have always believed that God in his own time would make the crooked ways straight and have meted to Etheopia that justice for which she has so many years prayed." The *New York Age*, also a black paper, declared that the decision proved that the Constitution had "not yet become a scrap of paper but can still exert a vital, living influence for the maintenance of right and the annulment of wrong."[58]

It was also understood by the white commentators to be a case of enormous significance, the most important Supreme Court decision on race since *Dred Scott* said some. It was understood consciously or implicitly that the creation by law of black zones and white zones, while yielded as a goal by the underlying assumptions and legal rationale for segregation, represented the crossing of a line into new and unknown racial territory. In historical retrospect the rush of laws from Baltimore in 1910 through Richmond can be seen as a formal step toward a system of apartheid later constructed in South Africa.

Later commentators, far removed from the passions of the time, tended to view *Buchanan* as a case having to do with the right to contract rather than with racial issues. The case was not viewed in that manner at the time, although the later observation is probably correct in one limited respect. James Clark McReynolds would not have knowingly struck a blow for racial justice. Undoubtably, MacReynolds had to resolve the matter in his own mind in a manner which removed any glow of racial uplift. Perhaps he saw it as a matter of contract.

Although the enormous importance of *Buchanan v. Warley* was grasped at the time in terms of the immediate harm it prevented, a fuller grasp of its impact required the passage of time. Although the decision turned back the immediate wave of ordinances intended to create black zones and white zones, the impulse to legal apartheid did not die. In 1922 New Orleans passed a racial zoning law and was followed a few years later by Dallas, Texas, and Norfolk, Virginia. In 1927 the Indianapolis City Council also passed an ordinance intended to create black zones and white zones, and in 1940 Winston-Salem, North Carolina, sought to link race and residence by law. *Buchanan v. Warley* as precedent binding on lower-level courts defeated all of these efforts. None made headway in the judicial system as the ordinances were struck down on constitutional grounds under the holding of *Buchanan*.[59]

Also unknown at the time was that *Buchanan* represented the beginning of a turning point for the Supreme Court in matters of race and rights. The Supreme Court had rarely ruled in favor of black plaintiffs over almost four decades. Having restricted the reach and meaning of the Civil War amendments in the fifteen years following the war, the Court had proceeded to affirm an interpretation of the Constitution which accommodated state-mandated organization of society based on race. The racial zoning ordinances, based on constitutional principles which the Waite and Fuller Courts had affirmed, simply represented the extension of state-mandated racial organization to ever greater areas of social life. Given the underlying logic of segregation there was no inherent limit to the racial structuring of social life. The legal premises justifying segregation yielded arguments for the total racial structuring of society.

Only the Supreme Court could indicate the limits of its own constitutional premise. In *Buchanan v. Warley* it began that process. After *Buchanan* it began to find limits to segregation in other areas. The decision did not undermine, criticize, or reverse the underlying premise of *Plessy* and Jim Crow but found limits in the real world in terms of the areas of life and social organization to which the premise could be extended. Indeed, that the decision did not go to the legitimacy of the *Plessy* premise might have been a condition of Day and White being able to secure a majority. McReynolds was an inflexible segregationist, a fervent believer in white supremacy. An argument in terms of the "rights of property" could sway McReynolds's, whereas an argument in terms of the rights of blacks would not. Whatever McReynolds's motives for joining the majority, the practical effect was to lend weight to a decision crucial to limiting further the interpretation of the Constitution relative to the rights of blacks.

Finally, the decision proved crucial in terms of the fortunes of the National Association for the Advancement of Colored People, the organization later to bring before the Court the major civil rights cases of the twentieth century. The black struggle from the end of the Civil War onward had been hard and painful and had been mainly a history of defeat in the halls of the Supreme Court.

Organizations had come and gone in the face of the discouraging struggle. The National Association for the Advancement of Colored People, only recently formed when the *Buchanan* struggle was joined, was only the latest to take up the struggle for racial justice. Its initial approach was not markedly different from that of earlier organizations which had struggled and been broken against the wall of racial hostility, ever more fully supported by law. It had brought a test case, knowing that loss at the local level was certain, and hoping for the vindication in the Supreme Court.

The outcome before the Court had been different and, perhaps, the fate of the NAACP as compared to earlier organizations which had taken up the struggle. In the months following the widely publicized victory, membership rose and new chapters came into existence. By the end of the first decade of its existence the organization was poised to become a major player before the court in the ongoing struggle over race and rights.

Conclusion

At crucial times and in crucial ways the Supreme Court has made the United States. The second decade of the twentieth century was a crucial time. Neither law, logic, nor the national impulse set a limit on the reach of segregation. The ever more encompassing laws as they came on the books represented logical extrapolations from the basic premise of *Plessy* and from the evasions of subsequent cases with regard to whether the "equal" aspect of the "separate but equal" equation was to be honored.

The Fuller Court had comfortably read a state obligation to maintain equality out of the law. The Court's leading intellect, Oliver Wendall Holmes, seemed dismissive of black claims, amused contempt for the plaintiffs and their arguments sometimes creeping into his holdings. As the new century entered its second decade there was no brake on the engine of history.

The holdings of the White Court did not put a single new black voter on the rolls. They did not open up opportunity for a single black homeowner to escape the limits of choice imposed by customary segregation. But they did slow the engine. The created the sense on the part of blacks and their few white allies that a strategy might be found to redeem the promise of the past.

Wilson's term ended in 1920. The Republicans regained the White House, Warren Gamiel Harding beating William Cox and his vice-presidential running mate, former Secretary of the Navy, Franklin Delano Roosevelt. Several months after the inauguration Edward Douglass White died. And thus as the new decade began both the Court and the country faced a new era on race and rights.

Chapter 6

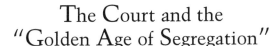

The Court and the
"Golden Age of Segregation"

By 1918 and the end of World War I the redemptionist impulse had begun to wane. The urge to enact ever more laws restricting and denigrating black rights was in decline. The Civil War had ended a half century earlier. The generation which had fought the war and which had come of age in its turbulent aftermath was passing from the political stage. In February of 1917 Samuel Ferguson, one of the last surviving Confederate generals died. A distant relative of Robert E. Lee, he had been among the firebrands who instigated the war by firing on Fort Sumpter, and four years later as a member of the legion guarding Jefferson Davis's flight from Richmond had seen the Confederate dream die. His death symbolized the passing of the confederate era.

By 1920 and the end of Woodrow Wilson's second term as president the demands of caste had come to inform virtually every facet and nuance of black life. Where one was born, grew up, and lived, where one went to school, assuming a school for blacks existed, where one worked, how one addressed whites, adults as well as children, where one was buried at the end of one's mortal journey, were all shaped by the demands of segregation and caste.

The 1920s ushered in what might be termed "the golden age of segregation." By that time the system had come to enjoy a degree of national acceptance which had always eluded slavery. From the earliest days of the republic the dispute over slavery had threatened to tear the nation apart By contrast, in the decades following the

Civil War, something close to a national consensus evolved regarding the legitimacy of segregation. It was deemed morally correct, socially desirable, and legally consistent with the language and intentions of the Constitution. In the half century from the end of the Civil War to the end of World War I the Supreme Court had played no small part in bringing about this state of affairs. It holdings provided both a legal foundation for segregation and moral affirmation of its behavioral imperatives.

In 1919 and 1920 a series of race riots having more the character of antiblack pogroms broke out in a number of big cities including Chicago, Cincinnati, Washington D.C., and Tulsa, and eventually came to engulf small towns and rural hamlets. The riots came in the context of two events which inspired the white majority to a sense of the need to reinforce the rules of caste subordination. The ten years period between 1910 and 1920 had seen a massive migration of blacks out of the South into the cites of the North and Midwest. Informal rules of interaction had enforced the rules of caste subordination outside the South, but as tens of thousands of blacks poured into the cities the old rules were no longer widely understood nor scrupulously adhered to. A report out of Michigan commented upon in the *New York Times* reflected the official view of the situation: "Young negroes are flocking to Michigan industrial centers by the hundreds, according to a report made to the State Administrative Board. The report . . . blames unrest prevalent among young negroes since the war, and conditions in the South for the influx."[1]

In the South decades of terror defined the limits of black liberty and the terms of black-white interaction. Outside the South, the antiblack pogrom served to reinforce the boundaries of caste. Tulsa, Oklahoma, witnessed a riot in May, 1921, leading to the burning of the city's Greenwood district, dubbed at the time "the black Wall Street" because of the number of successful black businesses serving a growing black population.[2] Coming late in the cycle of postwar antiblack pogroms, the Tulsa riot was similar to outbreaks that had occurred in a dozen other cities.

The war itself was the second factor yielding the wave of terror that ushered in the 1920s. Thousands of black troops served in Europe. Whatever the racial climate in France, they had at least not been exposed to the straightjacket of Southern-style caste segregation. Fears were openly expressed in the South that black men returning from overseas would prove to be troublemakers, unwilling to adjust to the strictures of caste subordination, and given to poisoning the minds of other blacks with thoughts of social equality. Indeed, the *New York Times* of February 11, 1921, carried a story regarding mass letter-writing campaigns directed at members of Congress by Americans of German descent calling on the American government to pressure France to remove black troops from its African colonies from the French force occupying the Rhineland. These "uncivilized or semi-civilized" blacks were alleged to be attacking white women and children. The view was widespread in the United States that French laxity in matters of racial separation had corrupted black American troops. There was a heightened sense of the need to enforce and reinforce the rules of the caste game and to react swiftly to signs of black insubordination.

A manuscript by the celebrated black writer Zora Neal Hurston, rediscovered years after her death, described the riot at Ocoee, Florida, typical in its unfolding of the pattern of racial violence attending the years immediately after the war.

"This happened on election day, November 2, 1920," Hurston began. Despite threats, a black farmer named Mose Norman came into town determined to cast his vote in the Harding-Cox presidential race. Attacked and driven away, Norman later returned and was again set upon, but managed to flee. Then, according to Hurston, "the white mobs began to parade up and down the streets and grew more disorderly and unmanageable." Fearing what was to come, blacks in the area began to flee into the woods. Toward evening the mob decided that Norman must be made to pay for his effrontery and upon learning that he had taken refuge with a black farmer and contractor named Jules Perry they headed for Perry's residence. By the time they reached Perry's home, Norman had joined other blacks seeking safety in the swamps and woods. As the assault on Perry's farmhouse ensued the black quarter was put to the torch, blacks unlucky enough to have hidden in barns or under porches being shot as they fled the flames. A wounded Perry was seized following a sustained assault and taken to the jail in Orlando. Just after sun-up a mob stormed the jail, dragged him out, killed him, and left his body hanging from a telephone pole. "That," according to Hurston, "was the end of what happened in Ocoee on election day, 1920."[3]

But the tide of antiblack violence involving the burning of blacks' communities, the flight of blacks from mob violence, and in some cases the expulsion of blacks from communities, was waning. As the new decade unfolded, a kind of racial peace settled on the land, punctuated only by the occasional lynching rather than by the organized pogrom. The violence of 1918 to 1921 reflected a spasm of anxiety directed in the South at reinforcing the rules of caste, and in the North at defining those rules more clearly. For example, in Tom's River, New Jersey, a swelling of the black school-age population led to the mid-year removal of black students from the existing public schools and a transfer to a new, all-black school. The protests of black parents were met with varying answers: "Local school authorities denied that the Ku Klux Klan was behind the forming of the negro school. They said that the negroes had been put in a school by themselves because most of the negro students were not as far advanced as the other students, having come from the south recently, and were thus hampering the progress of their white classmates."[4]

In numerous decisions the Supreme Court had legitimated segregation and had emasculated whatever impulse the federal government might have had toward intervention on behalf of black rights. In numerous holdings it had held laws intended to promote racial equality unconstitutional and affirmed the constitutionality of state statutes mandating racial separation. It had declared that states had a legitimate interest in keeping the races apart and that the law could not make equal those whom nature had made different and unequal.

By 1920 this was settled legal doctrine and had promoted the development of circumstances whereby blacks had disappeared from the political arena and had virtually disappeared from the courts as litigants for equal rights. The legitimacy accorded segregation is reflected in the fact that in the entire decade of the 1920s only a few cases involving issues of race and segregation came before the Supreme Court. An examination of the racial climate of that decade is essential to grasping the cultural and political context in which the Court began to gradually reexamine the realities of segregation in relation to the language of the Constitution and lay the foundation for a revolution in judicial doctrine relative to race and rights.

This chapter is organized in four sections. The first section focuses on the accepted, taken-for-granted social and sociological premises that underlay the legal doctrines of the twenties regarding race and rights. The second part of the chapter examines the justices sitting on the bench during the "golden age of segregation." Who were they? How did they interact? What views did they bring with them? How was the Court's later address to issues of race and rights impacted upon by these men and their approaches? Part three of the chapter reviews the comparatively small number of cases on race and rights coming before the Court during the twenties. The Court deal with refinements in the constitutional rules regarding race, including the question of whether the United States was as a matter of law a "white" country. The chapter closes with a discussion of where the Court, the law, and the country stood on matters of race and rights at the end of the decade, that summary giving an indication of the steepness of the mountain to be climbed in the subsequent challenges to the racial status quo.

Legal Doctrine and Social Myth

From the earliest days of the Republic there had been a reciprocal relationship between the legal status of blacks and the image of blacks in the public mind. In the public mind blacks were calibanlike figures lacking the intellect and the maturity necessary for responsible participation in civil society. The denial to them of the status and legal rights attached to citizenship after the Civil War was not deemed a betrayal of the national purpose, given the presumed marginal claim blacks were assumed to have on attributes of character and intellect necessary to the competent exercise of citizenship.

The minstrel show tradition, a vastly favored element in popular culture from the early nineteenth well into the twentieth century, is an apt exemplar of "race" as a set of cultural symbols. The minstrel show projected and elaborated upon various images of the black as simpleton and buffoon. Originally, the sole province of whites in black face, by the 1890s minstrel shows had become the only theatrical vehicle in which the white audience was willing to tolerate black performers. This audience was loath to expose itself to any image of blacks in popular entertainment that did not conform to its view of blacks as the fools, amusing in their absurd pretensions and ludicrous efforts to approximate civilized behavior.

To the extent that opportunities were controlled by whites, blacks were constrained to behave before whites in conformity with the white image of blacks as degraded specimens of human material. Indeed, attempts to break away from the stereotype were met with hostility, as occurred with the comments of the *Variety* critic Jack Lait, directed at the New York production of the all-black revue *Put and Take*, which sought to move away from the "coon show" formula. Lait was not pleased. The men in the show "hacked away in dress suits, when it would have been a success in plantation jumpers. The girl's wardrobe run to tawdry gowns and frocks, when they should have been fancifully dressed as picks, zulus, cannibals, and cotton pickers. There wasn't enough true colored stuff in the show—until the finale."[5]

The enforced selective view of the black persona reinforced the belief that the racial stratification system rested on innate differences, and for those who pondered such matters, probably strengthened the conviction that the Supreme Court's interpretation of the Constitution rested on a sober recognition of the reality of basic differences between the races which could not be willed away by the hopeful language of the Fourteenth Amendment.

And as the historian Nathan Huggins observed: "Many black performers were content to add only style to the caricature. Indeed, some seemed to have discovered that the formula for success was Negro depreciation, and they capitalized on it."[6] Taking advantage of the one narrow, shadowed passage to relative theatrical success open to the black performer, black minstrel Ernest Hogan wrote and performed "All Coons Look Like Me," which introduced the "coon song" as a style, ragtime songs having lyrics about black life. At about the same time Robert Cole's *A Trip to Coontown* achieved great popular success, while Bert Williams and George Walker, destined for stardom in the Ziegfeld follies, began their road to twentieth-century success by billing themselves as "two real coons," offering themselves to white audiences as the genuine article rather than mere whites in blackface.[7]

By the early 1920s the minstrel show was waning as an element of popular culture, and indeed the character elements inherent in various images of blacks had coalesced into a kind of theory subscribed to by white moderates and conservatives alike. Popular culture during the "roaring twenties" reflected the shared and taken-for-granted character of the racial views that yielded the golden age of segregation. They also provide a context for understanding the Court's deliberation on matters of race and rights during that era as well as a grasp of the starting point of the journey it was to make in the next decade.

The myth of black primitivism, widely subscribed to during the twenties, put a more complicated and sophisticated spin on the minstrel show image of the black as buffoon. This myth posited a dichotomy. On the one hand, there was industrial civilization with its stifling of the emotional and intuitive facets of the human personality and with its regimentation of people, the factory assembly line and the masses of desks in rows and columns in the business office being major symbols. This image of industrial life was projected in Fritz Lang's enormously popular and influential film of the period *Metropolis*. On the other hand, there was primitive man, not shackled by the constraints and pressures of industrial civilization, less inhibited, in greater touch with his emotional life, guided more by affect than intellect. At once more childlike than his civilized counterpart and less able to shoulder responsibility, but thereby also freer and perhaps happier.

In varying modes and with greater or lesser degrees of elaboration and pretension the view of the black as primitive came to characterize much of the white view of blacks during the golden age of segregation and provided the cultural context within which the Court did its work. In the hands of the writer Carl Van Vechten, author of *Nigger Heaven*, and other members of the white world of the arts, the assumed primitivism of blacks took on a romantic and vaguely tragic aura. The black by virtue of his greater emotionality was somehow more "authentic" than the white but was also, thereby, less able to fully shoulder responsibility as a member of modern society with its strong emphasis on impulse control and the deferral of gratification. Indeed, the black who lost his "primitive" birthright by acquiring the genteel manners of the white world was deemed to have surrendered ghetto passion for the pale and fake satisfactions of the drawing room.[8]

In the hands of the revisionist historian Ulrich Phillips, the assumed primitive characteristics romantisized by the liberal intelligentsia became elements that justified the legal and social subordination of blacks, shading over into images of the black as brute, kept in check by the law when possible, and by the lyncher's rope when necessary.

A series of hit Broadway shows reflected the popularity of the image of the black as romantic primitive. The all-black musical "Shuffle Along" opened in New York in the spring of 1921, playing at the 63rd Street Theater in Manhattan to audiences in which blacks were confined to the balcony. According to the *New York Times* critic, "Quite a bit of melody popularly supposed to be inherent in the negro . . . is to be found in the melodies of 'Shuffle Along.'"[9] "Shuffle Along" was followed a year later by the all-black productions "Strut Miss Suzie" and "Liza," and a few years later by "Blackbirds." That the black was the "other" was an assumption shared by the public and the artist alike. Thus, the title of Eugene O'Neill's hit play *The Emperor Jones* played on the irony of the notion that a black could be or aspire to be an emperor and, in the unfolding of its plot, chronicled the stripping away of the veneer of civilization from the black pullman porter Jones to reveal the primitive beneath.

In similar fashion legendary film director King Vidor's *Hallelujah*, an early sound extravaganza, conveyed a confirmation of the image of the black as primitive. *New York Times* film critic Mordaunt Hall reflected and conveyed the popular view: "Throughout this talking and spasmodically singing study one appreciates that Mr. Vidor knows his subject. . . . Perhaps a few of the passages are a trifle dull, but in portraying the peculiarly typical religious hysteria of the darkies and their gullibility, Mr. Vidor atones for any sloth in preceding scenes. . . . The audience was much amused by the scenes dealing with the baptism of the darkies, especially the first and second immersions."[10]

As persons participating in the actions and passions of their times the justices of the Supreme Court were exposed to and in varying degrees, seemed to have internalized, popular views of the black as "other." The underlying thrust of their decisions from *Cruickshank* onward had rested on the assumption that blacks were somehow not like other people and that this fact could be reflected in the actions of state legislatures and the actions of reasonable white citizens, without doing violence to the Constitution.

Against the tide, the White Court of the immediately preceding decade had applied judicial breaks to the movement toward apartheid dictated by the logic of the Court's own holdings in the cases that had undermined the racial protection afforded by the Fourteenth Amendment and by the Court's social theories regarding intrinsic, basic, and immutable differences between blacks and whites. But while vitally important to preventing the further deterioration of black status, the White court's holding in the Grandfather Clause cases and in *Buchanan v. Warley* had not spoken to the continuing validity of the assumption that state laws mandating segregation were consistent with the Equal Protection clause of the Fourteenth Amendment. Those decisions did however coincide with and probably contributed to the spending of the redemptionist passion.

The South had lost the war but won the battle. And so five and a half decades after the guns fell silent at Appomattox Court House peace had returned to the land. The Supreme Court had undermined measures intended to protect black rights. Their work facilitated the social isolation of blacks. That isolation had facilitated widespread internalization of already existing images of the black as "other." By the dawn of the 1920s and the golden age of segregation a near national consensus existed regarding the black as other, as Caliban, as part child, part brute. That consensus supported laws that kept the black in his place and sanctioned means and methods outside the law where necessary to hold "the beast" in check. Although not celebrated, lynching was accepted and in its frequent occurances was reported in the newspapers without national outcry or revulsion.

On May 9, 1920, the *Atlanta Constitution* newspaper reported the Florida lynching of black pullman porter Henry Scott. The *Brooklyn Times* of June 16, 1920, carried a story detailing the lynching of three black youths in Duluth, Minnesota. The lynching of Philip Gathers in Bulloch County, Georgia, was a featured story in the *Atlanta Journal* for June 21 of that year. Three weeks later the *New York Mail* carried a story regarding the Roxboro, North Carolina, lynching of Edward Roach, while the *Kansas City Times* reported the lynching in Paris, Texas, of Irving Arthur and Herman Arthur. The October 29 edition of the *New York Mail* reported the Tennessee lynching of Cooksey Dallas, while the *Atlanta Constitution* for November 24, 1920, carried a story regarding the Mississippi lynching of Harry Jacobs. The *New York Times* one day later reported the lynching in Dewitt, Georgia, of Curley McKelvey.[11]

Eighteen states experienced one or more lynchings that year but none of these incidents, nor the myriad other less lethal circumstances of caste subordination, gave rise either to popular condemnation or mass protest save among blacks. Shortly after the East St. Louis riot black leaders, including W. E. B. DuBois, organized a silent protest march down New York's Fifth Avenue, said to be the largest black protest in American history up to that time.[12] Ten thousand blacks took part, their passage marked by mournful drum beats. No reprisals occurred, but neither was the majority conscience stirred to action. An antilynching bill died in Congress for want of support.

It is not clear whether any of the justices ever passed Armstrong High School on their way to and from the Court nor is there any reason to believe that any of them read Marita Bonner's short piece "On Being Young—A Woman—And Colored," which appeared in the NAACP's magazine *Crisis* in December, 1925, a few weeks before they heard oral argument concerning John Buckley's grievance against Irene Corrigan. As the black woman seeking to buy

Corrigan's house it is more likely that Helen Curtis would have been familiar with *Crisis* and with the segregated high school, and possibly with Bonner.

Bonner's piece captured an inner world shaped by the realities of the system affirmed by the Court, the psychological reality behind minstrel show images of blacks to which most of the white world confined itself.

> You start out after you have gone from kindergarten to sheepskin covered with sundry phrases. At least you know what you want life to give you. A career as fixed and as calmly brilliant as the North Star. The one real thing that money buys. Time. Time to do things. A house that can be as delectably out of order and as easily put in order as the doll-house of "playhouse days." And of course, a husband you can look up to without looking down on yourself.

Bonner was a recent graduate of Radcliffe College and had taken a job teaching English in a Washington, D.C., high school after living for some years in Massachusetts.

> If you have never lived among your own, you feel prodigal. Some warm untouched current flows through them—through you—and drags you into the deep waters of a new sea of human foibles and mannerisms; of a peculiar psychology and prejudices. And one day you find yourself entangled—enmeshed—pinioned in the seaweed of a Black Ghetto. . . . Cut off, flung together, shoved aside in a bundle because of color and with no more in common.
> Unless color is, after all, the real bond.
> Milling around like live fish in a basket. Those at the bottom crushed into a sort of stupid apathy by the weight of those on top. Those on top leaping, leaping; leaping to scale the sides; to get out.
> There are two "colored" movies, innumerable parties—and cards. Cards played so intensely that it fascinates and repulses at once.

The essay had won first prize in a contest organized by W. E. B. DuBois, editor of the *Crisis.* It reflected a complex view, loyalty to the race yet a longing to be free of considerations of race, anger, and bitterness and a resistance to being engulfed by bitterness.

Why do they see a colored woman only as a gross collection of desires, all uncontrolled, reaching out for their Appollos and the Quasimodoes with avid indiscrimination.

Why unless you talk in staccato squawks . . . unless you "champ" gum—unless you cover two yards square when you laugh—unless your tastes run to violent colors—impossible perfumes and more impossible clothes—are you a feminine Caliban craving to pass for Ariel.

Every part of you becomes bitter. . . . But—in heaven's name do not grow bitter. Be bigger than they are—exhort white friends who have never had to draw a breath in a Jim Crow car. . . . You long to explode and hurt everything white; friendly and unfriendly. But you know you cannot live with a chip on your shoulder. . . . For chips make your body bend to balance them.

Be quiet . . . like Buddha—who brown like I am . . . sat entirely at ease, entirely sure of himself. . . . Perhaps Buddha is a woman. . . . And then you can, when Time is ripe, swoop to your feet—at you full height—at a single gesture.

Ready to go where?

Why. . . . Wherever God motions.[13]

But by the dawn of the 1920s a near national consensus had developed regarding the otherness of blacks and the soundness of constitutional doctrine that took that into account. Segregation entered its golden age.

After White: The Four Horsemen of the Apocalypse

The Court, which was to consider issues of race and rights during the "roaring twenties," changed radically within the space of a few years. History is chance and chance is indifferent to merit or morality. Thus, within a few years of his election in 1920 Warren Gamiel Harding, universally judged the worst president in the history of the Republic, was to have the opportunity to shape the Court by nominating four of its justices.

In 1921 Edward Douglass White died and was succeeded as chief justice by William Howard Taft, the expresident finally realizing his ambition to sit on the high Court. Five years earlier Taft expressed his disappointment at not being selected to the Court by privately abusing Louis Brandeis, the successful nominee, in anti-

Semitic terms. He now found himself a colleague on the same Court, but estranged ideologically from the progressive Brandeis. As fate would have it new appointments were to cede to Taft a working arch-conservative majority within a few years of his becoming chief justice.

The essence of Taft's conservatism lay in his hostility to the use of state power to meliorate the circumstances of working and poor people in a rapidly developing industrial economy. In 1894, while sitting as a federal judge he expressed his views on the great Pullman strike in a letter to his wife: "it will be necessary for the military to kill some of the mob. . . . They have only killed six . . . as yet. This is hardly enough to make an impression."[14] Early in his tenure as chief justice he had the opportunity to speak again to the interests of labor. He led a bear majority of the Court in striking down an Arizona statute that limited the use of injunctions as an instrument to break strikes. The activities of strikers constituted "moral coercion by illegal annoyance and obstruction" he proclaimed in *Truax v. Corrigan*.[15] A short time later in *Bailey v. Drexel* he declared a federal statute seeking to curb the use of child labor via the imposition of a tax on the income of persons who benefited from such labor to be unconstitutional on the grounds that the Framers intended the federal government to have only very limited powers in the area of taxation.[16]

Taft's views on race were of a part with his views on class. Class privilege was not problematic, neither was racial privilege. Both reflected the fact that God and nature made some people more intelligent and deserving than others. His judicial views on race and rights reflected his views on blacks. A year after becoming chief justice he gave a speech at the unveiling of a monument honoring post–Civil War Chief Justice Salmon Chase. He used the occasion to attack the postwar efforts to achieve racial reform. The congressional effort to protect black rights "was fanatical, a kind of frenzied religion." Congress "adopted reconstruction measures whose weakness time has proven and historians recognized."[17]

One year after Taft's ascension to the Court George Sutherland took a seat on the bench. Sutherland, who was to write the first major holding of that decade having to do with race and rights, was a person whose contradictions were mirrored in some respects six decades later by Clarence Thomas. Sutherland had grown up poor even by the meager standards of the nineteenth-century Pacific Northwest. Thomas grew up poor in rural post–World War II Georgia. Sutherland had been put out to fulltime employment before entering his teens, subject to merciless conditions and wages short of supporting subsistence. He was exposed to the ravages of class exploitation in frontier America as Thomas was later to be exposed to the brutalities of racial subordination in the segregated South. A combination of personal drive and the support of various benefactors and mentors allowed him to acquire a modest education and eventually enter the practice of law. Decades later a host of benefactors and various affirmative action efforts supported Thomas in his quest for educational attainment.

And as was true with Thomas half a century later, Sutherland's personal ascent coincided with the expression of views ever more hostile to organizations and groups purporting to advance the cause of the downtrodden class from which he had come. By the time he reached the Court Sutherland was committed to a mode of constitutional interpretation which held that state efforts to mandate better working conditions for employees was a violation of the constitutionally guaranteed right to contract, the implicit assumption being that the conditions under which laborers toiled were yielded by mutual agreement between boss and worker rather than by the bosses power and the workers weakness and desperation.[18]

In his first term on the Court Sutherland was asked to write the majority opinion in what was recognized at the time as one of the most important cases of the decade, *Adkins versus Children's Hospital.* At issue was a congressional law setting a minimum wage for women and children in the District of Columbia. That a higher wage might be desirable in terms of the "subsistency, health, and morals" of the workers was, according to Sutherland, an "extraneous circumstance." Presumably, any worker not satisfied with the terms of employment was free to quit, hence the "contract" with the employer had been freely entered into. Any state attempt to mandate wage levels infringed on the Constitution's guarantee of a right to freely contract.

The decision drew bitter denunciation from labor. American Federation of Labor leader Samuel Gompers excoriated Sutherland for comparing "the labor of a woman to the purchase of a shin bone over the counter to make soup." And there were calls for a constitutional amendment allowing Congress to override Supreme Court decisions.[19]

With *Adkins* Sutherland assumed intellectual leadership of the Court's conservative bloc. In addition, he was a pleasant individual and therefore was more effective in bargaining with other justices than his fellow arch-reactionaries James Clark McReynolds and Pierce Butler.

Butler, who joined the Court shortly after Sutherland, was a railroad lawyer whose nomination provoked widespread opposition from labor and progressive circles. In addition to having a history of single-minded devotion to the interests of the railroads with regard to rates and regulation he had given speeches denouncing liberal professors as a threat to the Republic. As a Regent of the University of Minnesota he been implicated in the firing of several professors whose views were regarded as "radical."[20]

Edward Terry Sanford, the last man appointed to the Court within the span of Harding's presidency, brought a different temperament and set of interests to the bench. He had served years on the federal bench rather than as the servant of corporate interests. His appointment was political but represented something other than obeisance to powerful business interests. Harding had gotten a good many votes from the South and his handlers believed it might be prudent to appoint a moderate Southerner to the bench.

Along with holdovers Willis Van Devanter and McReynolds, Sutherland, Butler, and Taft came to form a self-identified conservative majority. Late in the decade, as age and infirmity increasingly brought thoughts of retirement or death to Taft's mind he wrote to fellow conservative Pierce Butler regarding the survival of the bloc. He denounced President Herbert Hoover as a progressive who would put "extreme destroyers of the Constitution" on the Court. It was important therefore "that members of the prevailing bloc remain on the Court as long as possible," to beat back any effort Brandeis or other liberals might make to bring about "reversals of present positions."[21]

An essential element of the judicial conservatism brought to the Court by the new justices was hostility toward any effort at state intervention, either federal or local, to mitigate the harsher aspects of industrialism—low wages, dangerous working conditions, lack of job security, lack of benefits, and child labor. And hence, it follows that they would also be reluctant regarding the use of government as an instrument for reform regarding race, even had they conceived of the need for reform.

A grasp of the intellectual and judicial climate of the times and of the minds of the justices who were to address black-inspired issues of race and rights during the decade is facilitated by review of a series of cases coming before the Court posing the question, essentially, of whether the United States was, as a matter of law, a "white" country.

The Court and the "White America" Cases

From its earliest days the nation had conceived of itself as "white" and this conception was embodied in law. Until 1870, citizenship by naturalization was denied to any persons other than "free whites." The racial assumptions of the Court and the country were made explicit in a holding written by Sutherland in his early days on the Court.

In 1922 the Court heard Takao Ozawa's appeal from a district court decision in Hawaii affirming the denial of his application to become a naturalized citizen. Ozawa had resided in the United States for twenty years, had graduated from high school in Berkeley, California, and educated his children in American schools. Denial of his application rested on the United States Attorney's contention that under federal law naturalization was limited to white persons, the only exception being an 1870 amendment which included persons of African descent and nativity essentially as an accommodation to incorporating a particular segment of the newly freed black population. Acknowledging that there had been significant amendments to the Naturalization Act as late as 1906 and some broadening of eligibility for citizenship, the United States Attorney contended however that nothing in the language of the amended statute suggested that the bar on Asians had been lifted.

Writing for a unanimous Court, Justice Sutherland approached the issue as one of legislative intent. What did Congress mean when it passed the law? There was nothing in the record, Sutherland stated, which suggested that Congress intended to extend opportunities for nonwhite naturalization beyond what it had already done. Even though the amended statute did not use the term *free white person* it was reasonable, Sutherland observed, to assume that Congress intended to retain the racial preference in the absence of an express declaration to the contrary.[22]

Two years later, Pierce Butler followed Sutherland's lead in the matter of the racial identity of the nation. in *Toyota v. United States* the Court reaffirmed the exclusive racial nature of access to United States citizenship. Under a law passed in the spring of 1918, as American casualties mounted in the bloody struggle in Europe, aliens who served in the military were eligible to apply for citizenship. Hidemitsu Toyota had served in the United States Navy from 1913 through 1923, from before the date of United States entry into the war until well after the signing of the armistice.

In 1921 Toyota applied for and was granted citizenship, but

shortly thereafter a petition was filed by the United States to withdraw naturalization on the grounds that it had been illegally procured. The issue before the Court was whether Toyota could acquire citizenship under the law affording such an opportunity to aliens who served honorably in the military.

Writing for a Court majority Justice Butler indicated that there was nothing in the 1919 law that suggested that it did not incorporate the racially exclusive terms of previous naturalization statutes and that Toyota being Asian and not fitting into any other category of exemption was indeed not eligible for citizenship.[23]

In his decade as chief justice he spoke in a significant way only once to matters of race. At the level of legal doctrine his holding in *Gong Lum* reaffirmed the validity of *Plessy's* central premise regarding the absence of conflict between state-mandated racial separation and the meaning and purposes of the equal protection clause. At the level of social doctrine it reinforced the premise that the United States was meant to be a "white" nation.

In the fall of 1924 Martha Lum, born in the United States of Chinese parents, presented herself for enrollment at the Rosedale Consolidated School in Bolivar County, Mississippi, her father being a merchant in that community. Jeannie Rhee's penetrating article "In Black and White: Chinese in the Mississippi Delta" in *Journal of Supreme Court History* deals with this case. The Chinese escaped the caste abuse visited upon blacks and in some cases regarded themselves and came to be seen as "honorary whites." Hence the Lum parents thought that their daughters could attend the white school.

Not all whites agreed that honorary extended that far. At the noon recess Martha Lum and her sister were notified they would have to leave the school because they was not members of the white race and hence was not eligible under Mississippi law to attend school with white children. They were directed instead to a segregated black school.

Martha Lum's father filed a petition for Mandamus in the state circuit court seeking a court order to allow Martha to be enrolled at Rosedale, arguing that as a taxpayer he helped support the school, that the right to attend it was a valuable right, and that Martha in being turned away was being denied equal protection of the law in contravention of the Fourteenth Amendment. Taft did not regard the issue as a difficult one to resolve. "The question here is whether a Chinese citizen of the United States is denied equal protection of the law when . . . classed among the colored races," he wrote on behalf of a unanimous Court. It was a settled matter, he observed, that it was within the discretion of the states to regulate their schools and that classification and assignment by race did not conflict with the Fourteenth Amendment. It is not clear that Gong Lum ever argued that the available black school was objectively inferior to the white school, hence Taft explicitly asserted that the only issue was assignment by race and that Martha Lum not being white could not reasonably be expected to have access to the facilities afforded whites.[24]

Race and rights were not central to the Court's agenda during the golden age of segregation. All the questions seemed to have been answered. The great flurry of cases enshrining racial distinctions in law had occurred a generation earlier. The White Court had resisted the redemptionist thrust toward ever greater legal confinement of blacks. But by the time Taft took his seat redemptionist fervor was waning. The racial war had been won. During the decade the Court was presented with two major challenges to the racial order. Both holdings had long-range and important consequences for blacks. One holding looked back to the emasculating doctrines of the past, the other began to lay the foundation for an eventual change in judicial approaches to issues of race and rights.

Buckley v. Corrigan:
The Birth of the Restrictive Covenant

In 1904 the Supreme Court in *Berea v. Kentucky* had denied a private institution the prerogative of operating on a nonracial basis if state law mandated racial separation. Thirteen years later in *Buchanan v. Warley* the Court under Chief Justice White had turned back the creation of a formal system of apartheid by declaring racial zoning to be unconstitutional. Seven years later the Court in *Buckley v. Corrigan* moved to extend the underlying principle of *Berea* to housing, holding that private agreements not to sell across racial lines could be enforced in the courts even if a particular white owner wished to sell to a nonwhite.

While the White court had prohibited the law from mandating black zones and white zones it had not, in words spoken in an earlier era, "made the ethiop white." And hence private guile sought to achieve what the law was forbidden to do. In the wake of the *Buchanan v. Warley* decision declaring racial zoning laws to be a violation of the constitutionally guaranteed right to contract, a movement toward the formulation of private agreements not to sell across racial lines developed, agreements being called "restrictive covenants." It is an elementary principle of law that a contract to do an illegal act is not enforceable, hence it was inevitable that the constitutionality of restrictive covenants would be challenged.

In 1921, three years after *Buchanan*, a group of white home-owners in Washington, D.C., entered into agreement regarding the disposition of their property. Thirty in number and residing on S Street between 18th and New Hampshire Avenues, they drew up a document in which they mutually agreed that none of them would sell, lease, or rent their home to "any person of the negro race or blood." This covenant, duly recorded, was to be binding on their heirs and assigns for twenty-one years from the date of its being signed. Among the signataries were Irene Corrigan and John Buckley.

In 1922 Irene Corrigan signed a contract in which she agreed to sell her house to Helen Curtis, knowing that Curtis was a person "of the negro race." And at the time of signing Curtis knew that the restrictive covenant, entered into by Corrigan's neighbors, forbade sale to her of Corrigan's house. Protests ensued as knowledge of the impending sale spread, but both seller and buyer held fast to their intentions.

Acting on his own behalf and that of the homeowners John Buckley sought relief in the District of Columbia court, asking that Corrigan be enjoined by court order from breaching the agreement by selling her home to Curtis. In other words, Buckley sought equitable relief. There was no law prohibiting Corrigan from selling her home to Curtis, residential restriction by statute had failed in *Buchanan*. But breach of the covenant via sale of her home to a black would cause irreparable harm to the other parties to the agreement, Buckley argued, and hence the court should, in the interest of fairness, hold Corrigan to the pact by enjoining her from going through with the sale.

In effect, what was at stake in *Buckley* was the power of the community to enforce the constraints of segregation even upon those whites who might wish to breach its limits. Given the realities of income differentials and job discrimination there were not large numbers of blacks likely to seek residence in white neighborhoods, but the move toward restrictive covenants reflected an impulse toward an absolute in terms of exclusion, even the occasional black who might be able to buy and the maverick white who would be willing to sell were to be denied the opportunity to contract to meet their mutual objectives.

As in *Buchanan* eight years earlier there was also an issue related to the relationship between race and property values. Buchanan had argued that were he to be denied the right to sell his property to a black he would not be able to sell it at all given the probable refusal of whites in the market to buy on a block in which there were already black homeowners. The issue was never stated directly in *Buckley*, yet an implicit reason for the covenant on the part of the white homeowners was to prevent the occurance of a circumstance they believed would lower values. Whatever the validity or lack of validity of this concern it did not yield a grievance of constitutional dimensions, hence the thrust of Buckley's argument in court went to the matter of the enforceability of the private agreement rather than the reasons for its racially exclusive particulars.

On other hand, Irene Corrigan and Helen Curtis directly confronted the racial nature and objectives of the agreement in their argument against its enforceability. The agreement in its nature imposed upon Curtis "a badge of servitude" in violation of the language of the Thirteenth Amendment, it was argued, and also violated certain constitutionally derived statutes conferring upon blacks the same right to form contracts as enjoyed by whites. If Corrigan could have freely contracted with a white for the purchase of her property there was, she argued, a constitutional issue relative to a bar on her being able to contract just as freely with a black.

The District of Columbia court agreed with Buckley and enjoined the sale, and the decision was affirmed on appeal by the Court of Appeal of the District, which acknowledged however that its "attention (had) not been called to any decision of the Supreme Court of the United States involving the exact question before" posed by the case. And indeed the United States Supreme Court had not spoken, although in the wake of *Buchanan*, cases spurred by private agreements to exclude the transfer of property to blacks had come before the courts of Michigan, California, Louisiana, and Missouri. It was inevitable that the matter would have to be settled at the highest judicial level.

Oral argument in the case of *Corrigan v. Buckley* was heard on January 8, 1926, with Moorfield Strorey and Louis Marshall, supported by the NAACP, appearing for Corrigan and Curtis. The outcome, according to the *New York Times*, represented a test of the constitutionality of restrictive covenants in ten other cities. The volatile nature of residential segregation was reflected in the other major housing case occupying the attention of the NAACP. Five days before Storey and Marshall stood to offer argument before William Howard Taft and the assembled justices a rally was held at the Mt. Olive Baptist Church at 120th Street and Lenox Avenue in Manhattan in support of Ossian Sweet, his wife, and nine other blacks. Sweet, a doctor living in Detroit, had bought a home in a white neighborhood. Other blacks guilty of the same offense had been driven from their homes by mobs, but when the mobs came for Sweet he, his wife, and his supporters stood their ground in his barricaded home. In the ensuing melee a member of the mob was killed. Sweet, his wife, and nine other blacks were tried in a trial that ended with a hung jury. On January 3, Sweet and his wife appeared at the Harlem rally.[25] Five days later the Supreme Court heard oral argument regarding a different strategy for keeping blacks out of the neighborhood.

Louis Marshall contended that if such agreements were affirmed regarding blacks they could be extended to other groups and that the Court itself in *Buchanan* had held municipal ordinances mandating residential segregation to be invalid and had "provided that no instrumentality of the state could be so used." Under questioning he conceded that owners of property might bar use as a slaughterhouse or store, but contended that "no agreement should be allowed to exclude a certain race, nationality, religion, or political faith."[26]

Five months after oral argument Justice Sanford handed down the decision of the majority, addressing mainly the constitutional claims raised by Helen Curtis. In effect, Sanford held that two of the provisions of the Constitution Curtis had cited as affording her the right not to be barred from buying Corrigan's home by virtue of race—the Fifth Amendment's prohibition on the deprivation of liberty or property without due process of law and the Fourteenth Amendment's guarantee of the equal protection of the law—spoke only to state action, not to the actions of private citizens, however much those actions might limit the options of blacks solely for reasons of race. The *Civil Rights Cases*, decided four decades earlier, were cited as authority for this proposition: "It is State action of a particular character that is prohibited. Individual invasion of individual rights is not the subject of the Amendment."

Curtis's reliance on the Thirteenth Amendment was misplaced, Sanford held, because that amendment was intended to bar "a condition of enforced compulsory service of one to another" but did not, in other respects, confer any positive rights upon blacks. Whatever harm might have been done to Curtis, Sanford concluded, it was not of such a nature as to allow for redress under any provision of the United States Constitution. Indeed, there may have been an understandable racial grievance but the Constitution did not afford a remedy, and hence redress, if any, was outside the jurisdiction of the Supreme Court.[27]

Within a week of the decision a telegram arrived at the Supreme Court: "We the Progressive Federation of Improvement Associations of California, representing over five million dollars of residential property owned by colored citizens of Los Angeles . . . do most earnestly protest against the decision of the United States Supreme Court in the Curtis case denying fundamental Constitutional relief against race segregation by block agreement. We urge . . . a final appeal of this modern Dred Scott decision to the Christian conscience of the American people, the court of last resort for the amicable adjustment of all violations of fundamental human rights."[28]

But there was nothing to suggest that John Buckley and the other parties to the agreement lacked a Christian conscience. The decision reflected the popular will. The restrictive covenant provided a formal mechanism for sustaining racial boundaries in residential dwellings. Insofar as the covenants were legally enforceable against signatories who sought to violate their racially exclusive terms, the courts as agents of enforcement and as agents of the state became the instrument for sustaining apartheid for the next two decades.

The Nixon Case and the Waning Redemptionist Impulse

About two months after the *Buckley* holding came down, events began to unfold that reflected the evolution of one of the Court's most influential members. Oliver Wendall Holmes had not been an ally in the black struggle to resist caste imprisonment. His evolution suggested a slow, barely discernable beginning of a new jurisprudence of race.

On July 26, 1926, L. A. Nixon, a black doctor residing in El Paso, eligible in every particular to participate in the Democratic Party primary save that he was black, presented himself at the polling place in Precinct 9 to vote in the election to select nominees for Congress, the Senate and various state offices. As with William Garner in Louisville half a century earlier in the *Reese* case, Nixon was under no illusion that he would actually be allowed to cast his ballot. The anticipated denial was to indeed to provide the basis for a challenge to the new Texas law having to do with race and voting.

In the years following the end of the Civil War the Democratic Party became the dominant political force in all of the states of the old Confederacy, the Republicans being associated with the defeat of the South and with Reconstruction. One-party politics came to predominate in most of the Southern states, victory in the Democratic primary being tantamount to victory in the subsequent election. In the *Grandfather Clause* cases the White Court had turned back an effort to write black political exclusion into law, but economic intimidation, manipulation of voter qualifications, and terror still kept black political participation at a minimal level. Hence, from a white supremacist point of view there was no need for Texas statute 3093a. Nevertheless in May, 1923, the Texas legislature passed a law declaring that "in no event shall a negro be eligible to participate in a Democratic party primary election held in the State of Texas." The effect would not go so much to the matter of reducing black political participation as it did to formalizing that exclusion in law, making it a matter of statutory mandate rather than dubious practice. And of course, if let stand, it would have provided a precedent for other states to write black political exclusion into law.

As the drama unfolded C. C.Herndon and Charles Porras came to play the role that Hiram Reese had played in the earlier case. Acting pursuant to instructions from E. M. Whitaker, chairman of the Executive Committee of the Democratic Party in El Paso County, they turned Nixon away, thereby becoming the named parties in the suit Nixon brought to have the law barring blacks from voting overturned. Five days after having been denied access to the polling place Nixon filed in the United States District Court seeking $5,000 in damages from Herndon and Porras. He alleged injury under the United States Constitution, arguing that Texas Statute 3093a violated the Fifteenth Amendment prohibition against state interference with voting rights and the Fourteenth Amendment guarantee of the equal protection of the laws. Texas raised a number of objections in response, claiming that the District Court had no jurisdiction to hear the case, but that if it did, Nixon had not stated a claim for which relief could be granted in that a primary election was not an aspect of the political process that the post–Civil War amendments were meant to encumber. The District Court agreed with Texas and dismissed the suit, whereupon appeal was taken by Nixon directly to the United States Supreme Court.

Before the High Court, Texas repeated and elaborated upon its previous argument: "A nominating primary of the Demoractic Party in Texas is not a public election under the Constitution of that State . . . nominating primaries were unknown at the time of the adoption of the Constitution of the United States and the Constitution of Texas . . . the nominating primary, like the nominating convention . . . is not the 'election.' Nomination is distinct from election and has been so differentiated from the beginning of our government." It followed therefore that "The refusal of local officers of a political party to permit a negro to participate in the nominating primary of that party . . . does not abridge the right to vote under the Fifteenth Amendment, nor does it deny the equal protection of the law guaranteed by the Fourteenth Amendment to the United States Constitution."

Oliver Wendall Holmes delivered the opinion of the Court making short work of the Texas argument, indicating that it was "hard to imagine a more direct and obvious infringement of the Fourteenth." The blunt, straightforward declaration was notable. Holmes was in his third decade on the Court. He had been a celebrated, respected figure at the time he assumed his seat at the turn of the century. Although he had called on judges to appreciate the social realities reflected in the cases coming before them, throughout his first two decades on the Court he had avoided facing those realities in cases dealing with race and rights. In his first years on the bench he had avoided facing up to the fact of black peonage by resort to the fiction that the black laborer and his white master bargained as equal partners in terms of labor agreements, and he had evaded the reality of racial exclusion from the political process solely for reasons of race by pretending that the neutral language of voter requirement laws could be taken at face value. In his second decade on the Court he had threatened to become the lone dissenter in *Buchanan v. Warley* as the Court rejected municipal efforts to create black zones and white zones, by law. But in his third decade on the bench he began to show a willingness to take the lead in arguing for holdings that reflected an honest acknowledgment of some of the grim realities and open atrocities attending the day-to-day enforcement of a racial caste system.

Dempsey v. Moore came before the Court during the 1922 term as the conservative bloc was forming. The case had grown out of a notorious occurance in Elaine, Arkansas, three years earlier when a group of rural blacks meeting in a church to discuss organizing to seek better terms from landowners were set upon by a white mob. In the ensuing melee a number of blacks and some whites were killed. Forty-nine blacks had been brought up on murder charges and all convicted, twelve of them receiving death sentences. The ensuing appeals had brought *Dempsey* before the United States Supreme Court in challenge to death sentences of five of the defendants. Their trial had lasted forty-five minutes during which their court-appointed attorney neither consulted with his clients nor called any witnesses, perhaps intimidated by the raging mob outside threatening mayhem and a mass lynching unless the accused were convicted. The record as it came before the Court contained copies of a letter to the governor of Arkansas from the American Legion Post in Helena, three hundred members strong, protesting a delay in the executions, "solemn promise was given by the leading citizens of the community that if the guilty parties were not lynched, and . . . the law take its course . . . justice would be done." The Helena Rotary Club and the Lions Club of Helena had sent letters to the governor in support of the American Legion Post.

Holmes majority decision set aside the verdict, McReynolds and Sutherland dissenting, arguing that there was little to suggest that accused had not been dealt with fairly. The state had failed to establish that the hasty trial and quick verdict were not the result of mob pressure: "it does not seem to us sufficient to allow a judge of the United States to escape the duty of examining the facts for himself, when, if true, as alleged, they make the trial absolutely void." The case was remanded for further proceedings. An NAACP memo written shortly thereafter summarized the events in the aftermath of the reversal: "Of the sixty-seven men sentenced to prison terms 59 have been freed." With regard to the entire group, "Of the seventy nine . . . sixty three are free today."[29]

The hallmark of formalism as a mode of analysis in cases involving race and rights, from Joseph Bradley onward, involves a refusal to look to the motives behind statutory language and therefore the realities attending the implementation of that language as it involves blacks. Analysis stops at the level of language and if the language appears not to be inconsistent with constitutional imperatives, the realities behind it are either ignored or explained away. Holmes had shown a predisposition to engage in this form of analysis in his first decades on the Court, as had Joseph Bradley before him, and as would William Rehnquist after him. As he approached the end of his third decade on the bench the willingness revealed in *Moore v. Dempsey* to look at the horific realities behind the statutory facade carried through to events attending L. A. Nixon's effort to vote.

Unlike his prior judgments in matters of race, Holmes's *Nixon* holding departed from a purely formal analysis abstracted from the underlying reality of racial oppression. In defending its statute Texas Attorney General Claude Pollard invited the Court to ignore reality by contending that, "A nominating primary of the Democratic Party in Texas is not a public election under the Constitution of that State." Nixon was free, presumably, to vote in the general election and, hence could claim no injury under the Fourteenth or Fifteenth Amendments to the United States Constitution.

Holmes clearly recognized that the vote in the Democratic primary determined the outcome of the final election, hence exclusion from that forum constituted exclusion from the political arena. The statute constituted state action denying the equal protection of the law. "States may do a good deal of classifying that it is difficult to believe rational," he observed, "but there are limits, and it is too clear for extended argument that color cannot be the basis for a statutory classification affecting the right set up in this case."[30]

Texas lost. But the meaning of that loss in terms of the ongoing struggle over race and rights and the role of the Supreme Court has to be placed in context. Holmes's majority holding did not place a single additional black voter on the rolls in Texas. It did not increase the sum of black political power in that state or anywhere else one iota. Nevertheless, in the ongoing struggle for justice it was a significant victory. The Court's two housing decisions in the preceding decade, *Buchanan* and *Buckley*, had dealt with a situation that was fluid. Blacks were moving into cities in increasing numbers. There was increasing residential overlap. The two housing cases dealt with black efforts to reduce the fluidity via measures intended to enforce residential segregation. By contrast, the political situation in Texas, and in the other states of the old Confederacy, was not fluid. Blacks played no role in the political process. In that sense, the Texas law was gratuitous. It was not needed relative to excluding blacks from the political process. It represented an effort to codify the exclusion, to write the terms of exclusion into law.

Viewed in context, the Holmes majority decision did not represent an advance in terms of black interests, it prevented further decline. To the extent that the decision denied the state the opportunity to make black exclusion from the political process an explicit matter of law, it was an important decision. And viewed in historical context, it came in the twilight of the golden age of segregation. Important changes were soon to occur in the composition of the Court. The terms of the struggle before the Court relative to race and rights were soon to change.

The Death of Taft: An End and a Beginning

On Monday, February 3, 1930, late in the afternoon, William Howard Taft, accompanied by family and doctors, boarded a train in Asheville, North Carolina, for Washington, D.C. Earlier that day his letter of resignation from the Supreme Court had been handed to President Herbert Hoover, his rapidly failing health being cited as the key factor in reaching the decision to step down. He had come to Asheville three weeks earlier hoping that rest and a milder climate would restore his vigor, but after a brief period of improvement had taken a sharp turn for the worse. As word of his resignation and his imminent departure spread, newsmen gathered at the Asheville train station hoping for a statment. They were told that his physical condition prevented him from talking to anyone and that he was able to make known only his simplest needs.

The sky was overcast as the train carrying Taft approached the capital Tuesday morning and by the time it arrived the weather had worsened. Taft was carried from his railroad car to a waiting automobile "to drive through fog and a steady rain to his home on Wyoming Avenue." Few doubted that the end was near for a man who had loomed large on the national stage for two generations. The perorations began immediately and came from all quarters. He was praised for his ideas, for his judicial acuman, for his administrative innovations as chief justice, for his nobility of character and "wonderful ability." But no reference was made to a Taft decision, idea, or holding regarding race. In the public mind and in Taft's the race issue was settled. Legal segregation was consistent with the language and intent of the post–Civil War constitutional amendments and reflected the immutable fact of black incapacity to meet the demands of civilized society. In legal terms, segregationist laws had a rational basis insofar as they derived from and reflected certain inevitable social and biological realities.

Taft's underlying social philosophy reflected elements of the social Darwinist ideology widely subscribed to in many quarters in his formative and mature years. At the level of social analysis this translated into the view that the distribution of power, privilege, and wealth pretty much reflected and derived from differences between people and classes in terms of traits of character, drive, and intellect. The social order had a moral dimension insofar as privilege was yielded by and reflected the possession of preferred habits and attributes. At the level of judicial philosophy this outlook yielded a reluctance to affirm state efforts to intervene on behalf of the less privileged via the passage of progressive legislation. Taft consistently found such legislation to be unconstitutional. At the same time neither Taft nor his fellow conservatives on the Court nor the legal community at large found any inconsistency in affirming state power regarding the mandated separation of the races given assumptions with regard to blacks being fundamentally "the other." Hence, as the testimonials accumulated in the grey days following Taft's return to the capital his views on race as reflected in his jurisprudence were passed over as matters of no consequence.

Given the irrelevance of race in the weighing of public men it was not perceived that the passing of Taft also presaged the opening of a long and bitter struggle to reshape the judicial framework within which matters of race and rights were considered. The immediate and key instrument of that struggle was Herbert Hoover's choice to replace Taft. Charles Evans Hughes's career had been as extraordinary as Taft's. He had served on the Court from 1910 to 1916 having been appointed by then President William Howard Taft. He had resigned on June 10, 1916, to run for president on the Republican ticket against the Democratic incumbent Woodrow Wilson and had lost by a scant twenty-three electoral votes. With the election of a Republican president in 1920 he had returned to public life, serving with distinction as Secretary of State in the Harding and Coolidge administrations and had beeen elected a member of the World Court in 1929.

Within hours of Taft's resignation Hoover nominated Hughes to succeed him and from his office at 100 Broadway in Manhattan Hughes accepted. Two weeks later he was sworn as the new chief justice before five hundred well wishers. He moved immediately to assume a role as a Court leader. "Twenty eight decisions were handed down by the court and as the new Chief Justice read the orders of the day, his voice rang out with the vigor of old."

Taft had not been willing to think about race and rights in a new way. Hughes had. Sixteen years earlier as a member of the Court presided over by Edward Douglass White, Hughes had provided the intellectual leadership in terms of moving away from a formalist analysis of discrimination cases to inquire into the fundamental realities yielded by segregation. In legal terms, he had asked whether "separate" was or could be "equal." In the new decade this question was to be posed again and was to provide the initial wedge in the long struggle to topple legal segregation.

Chapter 7

⊂∞◇∞⊃

From *Scottsboro* to *Gaines*

The freight train had left Chattanooga almost a half hour behind schedule. More than forty cars long and slow moving, its route was to take it down to Memphis and from there southward into Alabama through the Tennessee Valley. Winter had been mild and on this March day the green buds were beginning to sprout on the hickory and poplar trees that carpeted the valley.

Train conductor Robert Turner ignored the score or more of hoboes who scrambled on board the train at Chattanooga. It was 1931 and the depression was deep into its second year. Tens of thousands of young men, homeless and destitute, road the rails looking for work, a drama captured by Hollywood in *Wildboys of the Road*. And there were also wild girls of the road. Somewhere along the line after the train left Chattanooga but before its rendezvous with history at Scottsboro in Alabama, two young women dressed in mens overalls also scrambled on board the freight.

Shortly after the train left Stevenson, Alabama, a startled station master was approached by a group of white hoboes claiming that there had been a fight onboard the train with some blacks and that they wanted to press charges. A call to the next town down the line, Scottsboro, revealed that the train had passed through minutes earlier on its way to Paint Rock. By the time the train reached Paint Rock Deputy Sheriff Charlie Latham had deputized every available white man with a gun. As the lead cars pulled to a stop adjacent the water tower the deputies swarmed aboard. In short order nine young blacks, ranging in age from thirteen to twenty were pulled off the train and lined up under guard. And to the surprise of the posse two young white women were also found.

As the story would later be told in parlors and poolrooms across the South, about twenty minutes after being removed from the train one of the young women, identifying herself as Ruby Bates from Huntsville, Alabama, asked to see deputy Latham. She and her companion, Victoria Price, had been raped by the black youths, overpowered, held down, and brutally assaulted. Latham and his deputies immediately placed the nine young men under arrest and rushed them to the Scottsboro jail. Word of the atrocity spread rapidly and as evening approached an angry mob began to assemble in front of the lockup. A mass lynching seemed imminent as the mob grew in number and anger turned to fury.

As evening turned to night Sheriff M. L. Wann barricaded the rickety jail and placed a call to Governor Ben Miller urging mobilization of the nearest national guard units. As the night deepened and apocalypse loomed, support arrived in the form of the national guard. The added guns turned the mob away from thoughts of violence as did assurances from public officials that the law would take its course, the nine blacks would surely not escape justice. They would be punished for their outrage. justice would be done. In the morning the mob began to drift away, confident that the courts, although slower, would write the same end to the story that would have been written had the guardsmen never arrived on the scene.[1]

It was late March 1931. The *Scottsboro Boys Case* would grip the national attention for a decade. It would make repeated trips to the United States Supreme Court, and would not finally come to an end until 1950 with the release of the last of the accused from prison. It would spark the first multiracial mass protests against racial injustice since the days of abolition. It would become the focus of international protest as rallies in support of the Scottsboro boys were held across Europe and would presage the cold war in making America's racial practices matters of national embarrassment.

The courts of Alabama spoke for Southern justice. It fell to the United States Supreme Court to contemplate the articulation of an alternative national ethic. In late March, 1931, it could not be said whether the Supreme Court would affirm Southern justice as it had on so many prior occasions or provide moral weight and legal force to the black struggle for change.

Alabama in 1931 mirrored the South. Race relations were governed by an elaborate code of white-black interaction which exacted from blacks the sustained performance of deferential behavior. Blacks addressed whites, even children, as "Mr" or "Miss," but were addressed themselves by their first name, language being an instrument symbolizing and reinforcing caste subordination. White customers were served in stores before blacks. Blacks could not try on clothing, but had to buy in the hope of a proper fit. Restaurants and diners did not admit blacks, some allowing them to purchase food only to take out. Customarily two to five times as much was allocated to schools for the education of white children as compared to black children, blacks attending separate and unequal institutions.

Neither were there green pastures in the north. The struggle over the fate of the Scottsboro boys developed in a context in which the Southern way of life only reflected in sharper relief patterns found elsewhere. Black New York's major newspaper *The Amsterdam News* recounted the refusal of a Horn and Hardart's restaurant at 125th street and 5th Avenue to serve the prominent black, Dr. Channing Tobias.[2] In Chicago, Jack Blackburn, trainer for the promising new heavyweight Joe Louis, filed suit against a restaurant with a policy of "no service to colored people." In Jamaica, Queens, the local NAACP spear-headed protest against the firing of three black elevator operators and a black woman restroom matron by the Montgomery Ward department store. Ward's, like other department stores, did not hire blacks as sales clerks. There was also protest against Columbia University's Teachers College for denying Ruth Simon, a black applicant, the opportunity to participate in a five-week overseas program.[3]

Popular culture reflected and reinforced the view of blacks as fools and children. Under the stage name "Stepin Fetchit" the black actor Lincoln Perry brought the minstrel show coon to the silver screen. He shuffled and mumbled through a series of films in a slow-witted daze. The poorest white sharecropper, bereft of education or property, wit or good looks, could feel superior to him. The American mind could neither grasp nor accept the more heroic persona of Stepin Fetchit's contemporary, Paul Robeson. Hence, Robeson pursued his career in film as a leading man largely overseas.

There was little national dissent from the Southern system. Blacks were viewed as a degraded breed, a childlike race, deficient in intellect and with the child's incapacity to harness impulse in the service of responsibility. Although there were to be mass

protests in support of the Scottsboro boys there was much sentiment in the North sympathetic to the Southern point of view. The
Supreme Court, again, was not a mere reflection of the public ethos
but was to play a major role in reshaping that ethos.

The events that began in the late afternoon on March 31,
1931, were to create a fissure in the national consensus regarding
race and rights and the Supreme Court was to play a role in creating that fissure. As the Scottsboro boys case evolved, the grim realities it reflected posed a counterpoint to the myth of the romantic
South propagated in the major pop culture work of the decade,
Gone with the Wind. Those grim realities had always been an
aspect of the Southern way of life, but the Court's formalist analysis of issues of race and rights, the fiction of separate but equal, had
allowed the South and the nation to avoid reconciling those realities to the language and purported meaning of the Constitution.

The role of the Supreme Court in the Scottsboro struggle as it
unfolded was both symbolic and substantive. In the symbolic
sense, the Court gave moral affirmation to the view that an injustice of monstrous dimensions was being perpetrated in a small
town in Alabama. That injustice was not peculiar to that town but
was endemic in the system. In substantive terms the Court began
to question the legitimacy of a judicial process which had ceased to
heed any stricture of the Bill of Rights regarding respect for the
rights of the accused.

Although passions ran high through the spring, the temptation to resort to mob justice via a mass lynching was stilled by the
assurance from local authorities that the judicial system would do
its job and spare the state and the town the opprobrium that might
attend the seizure and hanging of the nine boys without a trial. The
local paper reported that"The general temper of the public seems to
be that the negroes will be given a fair and lawful trial in the courts
and that the ends of justice can be met best in this manner,
although the case charged against the negroes appears to be the
most revolting in the criminal records of our state, an certainly of
our country."

Within days of the arrest Judge Alfred E. Hawkins took over
the case. The law called for the grand jury to be convened to hear
the evidence against the accused and return an indictment if the
evidence so warranted. Sensing that the case would draw an intense
spotlight Hawkins vowed that the proceedings would not dishonor
Southern justice. Anticipating an indictment and a trial in which
the boys would face the death penalty Hawkins viewed the first

order of business as the securing of defense counsel. As the date for the grand jury to be reconvened approached, however, it was proving difficult to find a local attorney willing to defend the boys. They were penniless and the community wanted to see them die. The *Daily Times* in nearby Huntsville referred to them as "beasts unfit to be called human." An attorney taking their case would work for little or nothing and face the wrath of the community.[4]

In the absence of an apparent alternative Hawkins appointed all seven Scottsboro attorneys to represent the boys only to see them one by one invoke reasons for withdrawal, some for good cause others without. It was alleged later that John Snodgrass, numbering the Alabama Power Company among his clients, sought withdrawal because he stood to gain were the boys to be electrocuted.[5]

In the end only Milo Moody remained. Nearing seventy and near the end of a career which even by the undemanding standards of the small-town South had been undistinguished, he was also regarded as in decline mentally. He had a reputation for sometimes championing unpopular causes but it was also suspected that straightened circumstances might have made the state's small fee attractive. Whatever the reasons for his stepping forward, as the day of the grand jury proceedings approached Milo Moody was all that stood between the Scottsboro boys and eternity.

Barely a week and a half passed between the arrests and the convening of the grand jury on Monday, March 30. As a restless crowd milled outside the courthouse while the panel prepared to hear from Victoria Price, a new attorney Stephan Roddy appeared to represent the boys. Roddy had driven down from Chattanooga, having vowed he would not let the boys be victims of a legal lynching. At least two of the Scottsboro boys were from Chattanooga and as word of the mass arrest and impending mass trial and execution spread in the Chattanooga black community, an alliance of black ministers organized an effort to raise a defense fund.

Stephan A Roddy was one of the few white attorneys who took "colored cases" and perhaps the only one willing to work for the $120 fee the depression-stricken, impoverished community struggled to raise. He had never handled a serious felony case and he had a serious drinking problem. Less than a year earlier he had been jailed on a charge of public drunkenness and seemed unable, despite periodic hospitalization, to maintain sobriety.[6]

And so he appeared on Monday, March 30, as the grand jury convened.. The outcome was a foregone conclusion. The boys would be indicted and the State would seek the death penalty. The trial date was set for a week later, Monday, April 6. Roddy returned to Chattanooga without having participated in the proceedings.

Between five and ten thousand people gathered outside the courthouse in Scottsboro on the day the trial was to begin. National guardsmen were on patrol and machine guns protected the doors to the building. Whatever resolve Roddy brought to his job was severely tested under the barrage of verbal abuse directed at him by the mob upon his arrival and had, perhaps, evaporated entirely by the time Judge Hawkins began the day's proceedings by asking counsel for both sides to step forward. Roddy did not move, and under Hawkins questioning equivocated as to whether he was or was not there to represent the boys. He claimed lack of knowledge of Alabama law and suggested that it might be better for the boys if he stepped "entirely out of the case." Matters were at an impasse until Milo Moody stepped forward to assist Roddy. Satisfied that the boys had representation Hawkins commenced the proceedings. The nine boys conferred with their attorneys for a few minutes then the trials began.

They were tried in batches over a four-day period. Victoria Price and Ruby Bates repeated their stories before sets of juries, peripheral details being corroborated by other witnesses. There had been a fight between black and white hoboes. The whites had been ejected from or had fled the train. A mass rape had occurred. As one jury left the courtroom to begin deliberation another was being selected. As one jury returned to the courtroom to deliver its verdict it would pass another on the way to deliberate. The last to be tried was Roy Wright, the thirteen year old. Roddy had refused the state's offer to allow Wright to plead guilty in return for a life sentence realizing that Wright would thereby have waived a right to appeal. In summation Edward Knight, representing the People, asked for a life sentence in any event in view of Wright's youth. With eight guilty verdicts returned save for that of Wright, Judge Hawkins had the Wright jury returned to the courtroom around noon on Thursday, April 9, the fourth day of the trials. Despite the state's willingness to take less, seven of the jurors were still holding out for the death penalty for the thirteen year old. Their hopeless deadlock led Hawkins to declare a mistrial.

Roddy and Moody had tried as best they could to mount a defense. Roddy had asked for a change of venue but in the tinderbox atmosphere of the trial's first day had not pursued the matter under the state's challenge. He had called some of the boys to the stand to testify on their own behalf but had obviously not had time to go over their testimony with them or prepare them for withering cross examination. Neither he nor Moody had the time or the resources to seek out witnesses who might have undermined the girl's claims.

In the late afternoon of April 9, four days after the opening gavel, eight of the nine Scottsboro boys were brought before a distressed Judge Hawkins, apparently overwhelmed by the implications of his judicial duty. Eight death sentences were pronounced.[7]

Hawkins's sense of the case had been correct. Its meaning would come to transcend and dwarf any of the immediate participants. Even as news of the case spread, Alabama governor Ben Miller began to receive letters of protest. Some were from private citizens, others from organizations, often with a disclaimer as to harboring radical sentiments, but all with a plea to Miller to avert a legal lynching. Aroused sentiment did not automatically translate into an effective, organized effort. The struggle for leadership in the fight to save the boys following the convictions set in motion a bitter struggle between moderate and radical elements in the civil rights movement which was to have consequence with regard to the long-term struggle of blacks before the Supreme Court.

The train that brought the boys to their appointment with history had commenced its journey in Chattanooga and as circumstances would have it, the struggle for control for their legal fate also commenced in Chattanooga. Two days before the trial had started P. A. Stephens, the black doctor who had mobilized the Ministers Alliance in support of the boys and sought out Roddy as one of the few attorneys immediately available to represent them, sought help from the national office of the NAACP in New York City. Barely twenty years old, the organization was gaining in influence and effectiveness as a champion of black rights. In 1930 it had spearheaded the successful drive to block the appointment of John J. Parker to the Supreme Court, the North Carolinian being accused of favoring grandfather clauses and of having made antiblack statements over the years."[8] It was not now anxious to be seen as a champion of black rapists if the boys were in fact guilty. Walter White, executive secretary of the organization asked Stephens to secure more information before the NAACP decided whether to commit itself to the struggle.[9]

James Alen and Helen Marcy were also in Chattanooga during that winter of 1931 working as organizers for the Communist Party. They had heard about the arrests on the radio a few hours after they had occurred. The next day as rumor of mob action and a mass lynching hung in the air they wired the International Labor Defense committee in New York, ostensibly noncommunist, but actually controlled by the party. One week later Lowell Wakefield and Douglas MaKenzie, Southern representatives of the ILD, departed for Scottsboro to witness the trials. On Friday, April 10, the day after eight death sentences had been handed down, the ILD voted to offer its services to the Scottsboro boys for the difficult appeals process to follow.[10]

Appalled by the swift trial, the mob atmosphere, and the uncertain nature of the state's case, the NAACP also moved to become involved, setting in motion a complicated struggle as three sets of attorneys vied to represent the boys. The growing notoriety of the case with its attendant national exposure and, perhaps, the possibility of vindicating himself, drove Roddy to insist on continuing to speak for the boys. The NAACP was merely pursuing its mandate to vindicate black rights in the face of grievous assault. Opponents charged that the ILD brought mixed motives to their quest to champion the condemned boys. If the appeals succeeded, the Communist Party would be able to present itself as an effective champion of the masses in the struggle against capitalist oppression. On the other hand, were the appeals to fail and the boys be executed, the ensuing mass anger, particularly in the black community, would provide very fertile ground for the party to recruit and mobilize.

In part, because their representatives were able to get to the boys and their parents first the ILD eventually won out in the struggle to assume their cause as the case moved forward through a hearing on motions for new trials and the filing of briefs before the Alabama Supreme Court when the motions were denied. Thus, as the Alabama Supreme Court convened in January, 1932, Joseph Brodsky, a skilled New York criminal lawyer, and Gerald Chamlee, a Southerner, sensitive to the nuances of Southern sensibilities, but a sometime maverick and spokesperson for unpopular causes, rose to argue for the condemned boys. Alabama attorney general Thomas G. Knight, represented not only the state but a social system whose morality was in doubt and legitimacy in question.[11]

Nothing so articulated the larger issues of justice and the legitimacy of the Southern way of life than the deluge of letters and telegrams that had flooded the offices of the seven justices of the Alabama court. But that deluge also made an unsympathetic court even more hostile and defensive. On the first day of the court's new session, January 21, 1932, Chief Justice John C. Anderson denounced what he deemed were efforts to "bulldoze" the court by flooding it with "highly improper, inflammatory and revolutionary" missives.[12]

Brodsky and Chamlee divided oral argument before the court and concentrated on three points. Blacks had been excluded from both the grand jury and the petit jury in violation of their rights under the Fourteenth Amendment to the United States Constitution. The trial had been conducted in an atmosphere of incipient mob violence, making it impossible for any jury to deliberate impartially for fear of being the target of mob wrath were anything other than a verdict of "guilty" returned. And given the confused and hasty manner in which Roddy and Moody had assumed responsibility at the trial and the inadequate nature of their preparation the boys had been denied effective assistance of counsel in violation of their rights under the Sixth Amendment of the United States Constitution. The state's reply the next day denied the validity of each contention.

On March 24, 1932, almost a year to the day after the arrests at Paint Rock, the Alabama court handed down its ruling. Eugene Williams was granted a new trial on the grounds that he was a juvenile, but otherwise the death penalties stood. The absence of blacks from the jury merely reflected the fact that none were qualified to serve. The speed of the trials spoke to a commendable desire to see justice done swiftly. The presence of the national guard merely ensured that the proceedings would take place in an atmosphere unaffected by the heat of public passions. Only the chief justice, John Anderson, dissented. The case was on its way to the United States Supreme Court.

Monday, October 10, 1932, was an overcast day in Washington, D.C. The United States Supreme Court still met in the old Senate chambers, dark, cramped quarters which led the justices to do much of their work at home. The seven months that had passed since the Alabama Supreme Court had affirmed the convictions and death penalties of seven of the eight boys had seen the continuation of the intense international campaign on their behalf. Albert Einstein, Thomas Mann, Theodore Dreiser, and other prominent members of the intelligentsia had weighed in on their behalf. Leave for further appeal had been granted and hence on the second Monday in October the court convened to hear oral argument in the case of *Powell v. Alabama*. Walter Pollak, highly skilled in the art of advocacy and George Chamlee, stood for the Scottsboro boys. Alabama attorney general Thomas Knight carried the burden for the state. Outside the cloistered chambers the presidential campaign was in full swing as Democratic nominee Franklin Delano Roosevelt opened a fourteen-state final drive for votes, while incumbent Herbert Hoover, the target of abuse at campaign stops, sought to sustain hopes being dragged down by an ever worsening depression.

Pollak repeated and elaborated on the arguments advanced earlier with regard to the violation of the constitutional rights of the accused: the trial process had been tainted by mob intimidation, there had been no opportunity to consult with counsel nor had there been opportunity for counsel to prepare, and qualified members of the petitioners race had been excluded from jury participation.

Knight argued essentially within a federalist and formalist framework. Although the Fourteenth Amendment placed some limits on state authority, nevertheless states retained a great deal of autonomy. Indeed, there was neither language nor case law in support of the proposition that the provisions of the Bill of Rights, meant in their inception to protect citizens from congressional abuse, extended automatically or in their entirety to states and the actions of state government. Hence, the only real question was whether the accused had received due process under state law.

Knight then proceeded to a formalist argument. The trials had been conducted "in accordance with the constitution and statutes of Alabama, the provisions of which are in no way attacked as being unconstitutional." Under Alabama law an indigent accused had a right to appointed counsel in a capital case and counsel had been appointed. Indeed, one of their attorneys had "enjoyed a long and successful practice before the courts of Jackson County." And as for effectiveness of representation, "Counsel, by their own statements, showed that they not only had time for preparation of their case, but they knew and proceeded along proper lines for a week prior to the trial."[13]

On Monday, November 7, shortly before noon a crowd carrying banners and placards in support of the boys began to gather in the plaza adjacent to the east entrance to the Capital building. Word had spread that the Supreme Court was about to hand down its decision in the Scottsboro case. The police came and, using tear gas and clubs, disbursed the crowd, making fourteen arrests. An hour later in hushed Supreme Court chambers Edward Sutherland, long a conservative stalwart, read the decision. In the words of the *New York Times*, "Not a whisper disturbed the solemnity. Present were many sympathizers with Scottsboro defendants."[14]

Sutherland began with a long recitation of the facts, The arrests, the indictment, the circumstances surrounding the imprisonment and trial of the accused. He then moved closer to the issue as the Court had seen it. 'The sole inquiry we are permitted to make is whether the federal constitution was contravened." And as to that charge they had confined themselves to a single issue among the three raised by the boys: were "the defendants . . . in substance denied the right to counsel, and if so, (did) such denial infring(es) the due process clause of the Fourteenth Amendment?"

Sutherland then proceeded to a detailed reading of the record recounting the circumstances attending the issue of counsel. There had been confusion and delay. In the absence of counsel being present to represent the boys Hawkins had initially appointed all of the attorneys in Scottsboro which was, according to Sutherland, to fix responsibility on no one. On the day the trial commenced Roddy had equivocated as to whether he did or did not represent the accused.

MR. RODDY: Your Honor has appointed counsel, is that correct?
THE COURT: I appointed all the members of the bar for the purpose of arraigning the defendants and then of course I anticipated them to continue to help if no counsel appears.
MR. RODDY: Then I don't want to appear then as counsel but I do want to stay in and not be ruled out in this case.

Sutherland continued to read the increasingly opaque exchange between the bench and the assembled lawyers in the courtroom the first day of the trial as the nine defendants sat huddled awaiting their fate while a restless mob patrolled the streets, their numbers spilling over into the courtroom. At one point Roddy declared: "I have not prepared this case for trial . . . they have not given me an opportunity to prepare the case. . . . If there is anything I can do to be of help to them, I will be glad to do it; I am interested to that extent." In the course of the same response to Roddy's equivocations Hawkins had seemed at first willing to grant him a limited role then in the next sentence to reverse himself: "how can I make a qualified appointment or a limited appointment." At that point aging Milo Moody had expressed a willingness to help Roddy, satisfying Hawkins that the boys at last had adequate representation. Neither Roddy nor Moody had done any investigation nor had they had time to counsel and prepare the accused for cross examination.

There still remained the issue however of whether these facts translated into a violation of any rights the boys might have under the United States Constitution. Indeed, the Supreme Court's *Hurtado* decision of several decades earlier, cited as precedent by Knight, seemed to say that federalist principles denied the proposition that the due process clause of the Fifth Amendment was binding on the states. Whatever the term *due process* meant in the Fourteenth Amendment it did not necessarily mean the specific rights enumerated in the first eight amendments of the Bill of Rights.

Speaking for the majority Sutherland indicated that while this might be true there were, nevertheless, certain rights which were of such a character that they could not be denied "without violating those 'fundamental principles of liberty and justice which lie at the base of all our civil and political institutions.'" A considerable review of case law suggested that the right to representation in the face of a major accusation might be one of those rights. It was not a matter, Sutherland observed, of extending to the states the obligations placed on Congress and the federal government by the due process clause of the Fifth Amendment but of construing the meaning of the term in the Fourteenth Amendment. Historical and case review established that at a minimum it meant representation by counsel when on trial for one's life.

The analysis yielded the holding, "we are of the opinion that under the circumstances . . . the necessity of counsel was so vital . . . that the failure of the trial court to make an effective appointment . . . was . . . a denial of due process within the meaning of the Fourteenth Amendment." The court was not prepared to articulate a general right to counsel in serious felony cases. "All that it is necessary now to decide . . . is that in a capital case, where the defendant is unable to employ counsel, and is incapable of making his own defense because of ignorance, feeble mindedness, illiteracy, or the like, it is the duty of the court . . . to assign counsel for him as a necessary requisite of due process of law; and that duty is not discharged by an assignment at such time or under such circumstances as to preclude the giving of effective aid in the preparation and trial of the case."[15] The Scottsboro case was headed for a second trial.

A number of publications including the *New York Times* hailed the decision as a landmark. Alabama greeted it with anger. In Birmingham handbills were rained down upon blacks gathered in the streets as word of the decision spread. They read in part,

"Negroes of Birmingham, the Ku Klux Klan is watching you."

Conservatives Pierce Butler and James Clark McReynolds had dissented, while fellow conservative Edward Sutherland had delivered the opinion for the majority. Understanding that the decision broke new ground constitutionally and created a new right, Chief Justice Charles Evans Hughes had sought to give it added weight by having it delivered by a conservative like Sutherland rather than by one of the court's liberals. It was the first major decision on race and rights of the new Hughes Court and marked the beginning of a judicial approach that was to take the Court through a second Scottsboro decision three years later as it moved along a road of constitutional interpretation, charted by Hughes, which would culminate three decades later in *Brown v. Board*.

The Hughes Court

Charles Evans Hughes had returned to a Court and a country much changed from what they had been at the time he resigned in 1916 to run for the presidency on the Republican ticket. The race had been close but in the end Woodrow Wilson had won reelection. With the restoration of Republicans to the White House during the 1920s he had, been summoned again to public service, filling the Secretary of State post under Calvin Coolidge and acting as Herbert Hoover's representative to the Hague Conference. Hoover had nominated him to replace William Howard Taft as chief justice upon Taft's death in 1930.[16]

In the fourteen years between leaving the Court and returning, the enormous influx of immigrants into the country from southern and eastern Europe had slowed to a trickle as a result of restrictive immigration laws passed in 1921 and 1924. Americans of older lineage had expressed fear of national collapse were the country to continue to receive waves of migrants from that part of the Old World. They were backward people from countries enured to centuries of authoritarian rule and were, it was argued, incapable of assuming the responsibilities of citizenship in a democracy. And besides, newly designed paper and pencil tests designed to measure intelligence established that they were innately inferior mentally.

But while those immigrants who had made it into the country before the legal gangplank was pulled up were absorbed into civil society, blacks continued to be the special objects of social contempt and legal exclusion. In his first term on the Court Hughes had played a key role in blunting a dynamic leading to ever greater legal crystallization of a pariah, apartheidlike status for blacks—physical residence in the country, but stripped of all legal claims to any of the privileges or protections of citizenship.

The collapse of Reconstruction had seen ever greater efforts to exclude blacks, by law, from civil society. *Plessy v. Ferguson* with its fiction of "separate but equal" had been merely a way station on a legal track leading inevitably toward something equivalent to an American version of the apartheid system developed later in South Africa. In his six-year stint on the Court from 1910 to 1916, Hughes had played a major role in putting a break on the legal momentum speeding inevitably toward legal apartheid and social caste. Purported to be the finest mind on the Court, Oliver Wendall Holmes had seen nothing wrong with the failure of railroads to even make a pretense of honoring the separate but equal doctrine while Hughes had persuaded a majority to hold to at least a formal affirmation of the doctrine rather than affirm further circumstances in which it might be legally abandoned all together. He had persuaded a majority to avoid a de-facto repeal of the Thirteenth Amendment by rejecting the constitutionality of grandfather clauses aimed at legally barring blacks from the polling place.

Underlying Hughes jurisprudence relative to race and rights was a rejection of formalism. Justice Holmes's comments in the peonage cases thirty years earlier had been an exemplar of the formalist approach. Holmes's observations rested on the assumption that agreements between black labor and white mill and plantation owners in the segregated South represented contracts freely entered into between equals. Hughes seemed always to look to the underlying realities in matters of race rather than formalist fiction. This approach had provided the few Supreme Court vindications of black rights during the progressive era, and upon his return to the Court laid the foundation for a new jurisprudence which was to culminate with the toppling of legal segregation.

In a formal sense the Scottsboro boys had counsel. Two attorneys stood for them, made motions, cross examined witnesses, argued their innocence. In reality, the circumstances in which this occurred denied them the assistance of counsel save in the most formal sense. James Clark McReynolds and Pierce Butler reflected the approach of the Court throughout the decades following the passage of the post–Civil War amendments. In some sense, the formal amenities had been observed.

Hughes had brought the majority of his colleagues, including the conservative Edward Sutherland, to look at the underlying realities and to begin to derive a jurisprudence of race and rights from those realities. He had succeeded in *Powell* and in the course of doing so had promoted the articulation of a new right. But the matter of the fate of the Scottsboro boys was soon to be engaged again.

The Deepening Tragedy

The second trial opened on March 27, 1933, in a different venue and before a new judge, James Edwin Horton, scion of an old Alabama family. Samuel Liebowitz, an experienced and noted trial lawyer, regarded by some as a successor to Clarence Darrow, represented the accused. International protest and the swelling tide of national indignation among moderates and progressives had generated momentum for the provision of a more adequate defense. Despite their bitter differences over overall strategy the Communist Party and the National Association for Advancement of Colored People had cobbled together an arrangement under which Leibowitz agreed to defend.[17]

On Monday, March 27, 1933, just over two years after the arrests at Paint Rock, proceedings began anew. The state had decided to retry Heywood Patterson first. Liebowitz made a motion to quash the original 1931 indictment on the grounds that blacks had been excluded from sitting on the Jackson County grand jury that issued it in violation of the "due process" clause of the Fourteenth Amendment. Jackson County had 7,800 males qualified by age to serve, of whom over 600 were black, but no black was on the jury roll. In support of his motion he called a reluctant witness to the stand, James Benson, editor of the Scottsboro *Progressive Age.* Under gentle but persistent questioning Benson grudgingly acknowledged that blacks were kept off the rolls because they were black, no thought being given to character or intellect. He displayed the bewilderment of a man who viewed the virtue of excluding blacks from civic life for reasons of race alone as self-evident, but who now had to pretend that considerations of character or honesty or intellect were what really accounted for black exclusion.[18]

Leibowitz next called two members of the jury commission who had neither a grasp of the legal requirements for jury service nor any clear reason other than race as to why no blacks appeared on the rolls. He then followed with the testimony over two days of nine blacks from Jackson County who appeared to be men of good character and sound judgment. Although Thomas Knight, representing the state, was able to show gaps in their knowledge of civic affairs, it was clear that they were no less qualified than the run of white men who were on the rolls. On Tuesday, March 28, Horton cut short the proceedings and denied the Leibowitz motion.

With the denial of both motions, the trial began anew with the testimony of star witness and putative rape victim Victoria Price. It was clear immediately that the defendants had counsel in a substantive rather than a merely formal sense. Under sharp questioning Price's story began to crumble. Other prosecution witnesses proved equally unreliable. But despite Liebowitz's vigorous defense the outcome of the case was determined in the end by events which transpired outside the hearing of the jury.

The prosecution was prepared to call two doctors who had examined the girls proximate to the time of the charged rapes. The testimony of the first doctor, corroborating the occurrence of rape, was offered late in the afternoon of the first day of trial and completed in the morning of the second day. Rather than call the second physician, Dr. Marvin Lynch, the prosecutor asked for a conference. Meeting privately with the judge, other attorneys, and Lynch, the prosecution indicated that Lynch's testimony would merely duplicate the first physician's and expressed the intention of excusing him from taking the stand. Horton saw no problem with this.

As the parties were returning to the courtroom Lynch asked judge Horton if he might speak with him privately. In a small room, away from the others, an agitated Lynch bared his anguish. He did not believe that a rape had occurred. He had examined the girls within an hour of the alleged attacks and there had been no physical evidence to corroborate their story. He had confronted the girls with this fact and they had laughed at him. A shaken judge Horton asked Lynch to testify, but he refused. He could not. He lived in the community. Were his testimony to free the boys he would be a pariah.[19]

The trial proceeded another two weeks, the defense did an excellent job of undermining the state's case. After bitter closing arguments, tinged with antisemitic attacks upon Leibowitz by the prosecution, the case went to the jury on Saturday afternoon, April 8.The following morning the jury indicated that it had reached a verdict. Shortly after 11:00 A.M. the verdict was read. "We find the defendant guilty as charged and fix the punishment at death in the electric chair."

At the beginning of the trial judge Horton had believed the boys guilty. The first day's testimony and cross examination raised doubts in his mind. The Lynch admission established their innocence, but he had let the trial proceed, hoping against the odds that the jury would find Patterson not guilty. The verdict and sentence narrowed the options available to him. The Alabama Supreme Court might reverse or the United States Supreme Court might. Or they might not. In the end the only just and certain outcome was up to him. The defense made a motion to set aside the verdict as against the weight of the evidence and on June 22, 1933, after a long and detailed recitation in open court of the inconsistencies and improbabilities in the state's case, he granted it.

The decision effectively ended his career. Shortly thereafter he was voted out of office and returned to private life. Interviewed many years later he expressed no regret over setting aside the verdict rather than hoping that a higher-level court would grant relief. He also indicated that he thought his action would end the state's efforts to convict the boys. And in that he proved wrong.[20]

In November, 1933, the third set of Scottsboro boy trials began, Heywood Patterson and Clarence Norris in the dock, the other boys to be tried later, Judge William Washington Callahan presiding. Once again Leibowitz made a motion to set aside the original indictment on the grounds that blacks had been excluded from the grand jury from which it issued. He also made a motion to quash the Morgan County venire because of the exclusion of blacks from jury service. Callahan denied the second motion but agreed to review the records relative to the Jackson County grand jury. Over the next few days the names on the Jackson County rolls were reviewed in open Court by the head of the Jackson County jury commission and the clerk of the county court, the names of several blacks eventually being found. There was also strong evidence however that the rolls had been doctored, the names of potential black jurors being added at some point in time after that of the whites and after the date on which the original Scottsboro case grand jury had met. After reviewing the evidence, including the testimony of a handwriting expert called by Leibowitz to affirm that the black names had been fraudulently added to the list, Callahan denied the motion.[21]

Patterson was tried first and then Norris. On December 1, 1933, the jury came back with a verdict of guilty and recommendation of the electric chair for Patterson, and a few days later a second jury came back with the same verdict and recommendation for

Norris. Again, appeals were undertaken on behalf of the condemned boys. Hence, the convictions of Patterson and Norris proceeded to the Alabama Supreme Court for review. The boys had been convicted in successive trials on the same evidence. Norris's conviction and death sentence were affirmed on the basis of a review of the record. The court refused to review Patterson's appeal, however, on the grounds that it had been filed after the statutory deadline. Their refusal let the conviction and death sentence stand.

Alabama law required that a "bill of exceptions" be filed within ninety days of the day from which judgment was entered. The jury had returned its verdict on December 1,1933, and sentence had been imposed on December 6. If December 6 was taken as the day on which judgment had been entered, the appeal had been filed on time. On the other hand, if December 1 was taken as that date it had not. The Alabama Supreme Court took the position that December 1 was the day on which judgment had been entered and that Patterson had therefore waived his right to appeal.

Late in the year the United States Supreme Court granted certiorari in *Norris v. Alabama* and *Patterson v. Alabama*. On February 15, 1935, oral argument was heard anew on behalf of and against the Scottsboro boys. On April 1, 1935, Chief Justice Charles Evans Hughes read the separate majority holdings for each appeal.

He began with *Norris* in a masterpiece of exposition: "There is no controversy as to the constitutional principle involved." Where the state excludes "all persons of the African race" from participation on either grand or petit juries, "the equal protection of the law is denied to him, contrary to the Fourteenth Amendment to the Constitution of the United States." Thus, there was the factual question as to whether such exclusion had occurred in this case. And although the Court's mandate was to examine questions of law, "That the question is one of fact does not relieve us of the duty to determine whether in truth a federal right has been denied." And in that inquiry the Court was constrained to go beyond the ritualism of formalist analysis, "it is our province to inquire not merely whether it was denied in express terms but also whether it was denied in substance and effect."[22]

He then moved to an analysis of the facts. Testimony offered on Leibowitz's motion to quash prior to the second trial and stipulated as part of the record of the third trial had established that no blacks had ever served on a Jackson County grand jury and that there were a number qualified to do so. Evidence offered prior to the third trial spoke to a fraudulent effort to make it appear that the names of blacks had been on the rolls.

The Alabama Supreme Court had disposed of these matters in short order. The responsible officials had testified that they never discussed racial exclusion and, indeed, there were many white men similar situated with regard to qualifications who were not on the roll and hence it could not be assumed or inferred that black absence was yielded by racial decision making.

Speaking for the majority, Hughes disposed of these arguments in equally short order. The testimony as to not discussing race seemed to reflect the taken-for-granted nature of racial exclusion. There was no need to discuss matters that were not at issue. If there was never any thought given to placing blacks on the rolls there was no need to discuss excluding them. Nor did it seem plausible that factors unrelated to race would yield the total exclusion over generations of blacks who seemed otherwise to be qualified for service. The motion to quash the indictment was granted.

Similar facts and the same reasoning yielded a similar conclusion with regard to the motion to quash the Morgan County roll from which the trial jury had been selected. Clarence Norris's conviction was set aside and remanded back to Alabama for further proceedings in accord with the Supreme Court holding.

Hughes then followed with the majority decision as to Heywood Patterson. Although the facts of *Norris* and *Patterson* were identical, the second case was in a peculiar posture. Alabama contested Supreme Court jurisdiction, pointing to the rule that a convicted party must exhaust his state remedies before seeking relief from the U.S. Supreme Court and that Patterson in failing to appeal in a timely manner at the state level had failed to exhaust his state remedies and was now barred from going into the federal system. To have acceded to this argument would have been to let stand Patterson's death sentence despite the fact that an appeal based on an identical record established that the conviction had been obtained in violation of his rights under the United States Constitution. Without question, this outcome could not be allowed.

Hughes disposed of the matter in a straightforward manner. The Supreme Court ultimately has an "interest of justice" jurisdiction, he asserted. "We have frequently held that in the exercise of our appellate jurisdiction we have power not only to correct error in the judgment under review but to make such disposition of the case as justice requires." Where a subsequent change in law impacts on the meaning or consequences of a prior state court action, the state court might wish to reconsider. Given that the Supreme Court had now held that the process yielding the panels from which the indictment and the trial decision had issued had violated the equal protection clause of the Fourteenth Amendment, did the Alabama Supreme Court wish to remain in the posture of affirming the actions of these improperly constituted panels?

The judgment below was vacated and the case remanded to the state court for further proceedings.

In the Wake of Scottsboro

And then it was over. *Scottsboro* continued to be a rallying cry on the left, allowing the Communist Party to both attack the capitalist exploitation said to be the root cause of the phony case and to point to the survival of the boys as evidence of the power of an aroused proletariat inspired by the party's leadership. Only a few scenes remained in the drama. The state of Alabama gave up the struggle to execute the boys but sought to vindicate itself by exacting further jail time from them. The last of the boys was not released until 1950, nineteen years after the train had been stopped at Paint Rock on a Monday afternoon in March.

The Supreme Court also lived with the consequences of its twin holdings. The Court had articulated a rule with regard to the composition of grand juries and petit juries. The exclusion of blacks solely on grounds of race violated the due process clause of the Fourteenth Amendment to the United States Constitution. In principle, those jurisdictions not in compliance with the rule should have sought to reconstitute their panels. In reality, given the fanatic commitment to white supremacy, the holding was ignored. Hence, the Court was constrained to bring recalcitrant jurisdictions to heel on a case-by-case basis.

Undeterred by *Norris*, McCracken County, Kentucky, prosecutors successfully sought the indictment of a young black man from a grand jury that had not had a black member within anyone's memory despite the presence in the population of many blacks statutorily qualified to serve. The Supreme Court set aside the subsequent conviction.[23] Two years after *Norris* a St. John's Parish, Louisiana, grand jury on which no black had sat for the preceding forty years indicted a black male. Again, the Supreme Court vacated the conviction.[24] A few years later a racially exclusive Harris County, Texas, jury convicted a young black man of murder. And once again the Supreme Court reversed.[25]

The Court's *Scottsboro* holdings promoted delegitimization of the South's system of institutionalized racism. Prior to *Scottsboro* there had been no widespread white involvement in antiracist protest since the days of abolitionism eighty years earlier. In the wake of the redemptionist triumph following the war, history had been reinterpreted in such a way as to romanticize the Old South and discredit Reconstruction's brief experiment with multiracial government. *Powell* and *Norris* acknowledged an ugly and unacceptable reality the North had hitherto evaded and the South had rationalized.

Scottsboro also represented the last major holding on race and rights by a Court about to undergo major change. From his earliest days on the Court Charles Evans Hughes had articulated a jurisprudence of racial reform. Circumstances had never yielded a combination of justices sufficient to yield a majority consistently in support of Hughes approach to issues of race and rights. As *Scottsboro* was unfolding, events were also transpiring which were, unexpectedly, to begin to put that majority in place.

The Court-Packing Scheme

Presidential nominations to the Court made in pursuit of one set of objectives may have enormous consequences for a different area of the law. In the years between 1935 and 1937 a series of events took place which were to lay the foundation for a Supreme Court majority hospitable to the jurisprudence which eventually yielded the holding of *Brown v. Board of Education*. The events were precipitated in large part by the Courts response to the Roosevelt administration's efforts to respond to the crisis presented by the depression. The Court!s composition had remained fixed for an unusually long period of time. An old and tired bloc on the Court seemed unable to grasp the need for new policy and new ideas to cope with the unfolding collapse of the social system.

Upon Oliver Wendall Holmes's retirement from the Court in 1932 at the age of ninety-two, Herbert Hoover had nominated the distinguished New York jurist Benjamin Cardozo to replace him and the Senate had confirmed. From that period onward into Franklin Roosevelt's first term there had been not been a change in the composition of the Court, nor did any appear imminent.

Roosevelt had taken office in the midst of the worst national crisis since the Civil War. Millions of the unemployed roamed the highways. Farmers faced foreclosure and expulsion from the land. The banking system had collapsed. The cries of demagogues and charlatans were heard in the land offering wild nostrums and dangerous remedies to a frightened and desperate population. Herbert Hoover had been in the grip of ideas that limited his capacity to understand the crisis or conceptualize an effective response. He counseled inaction. Surely the crisis would soon end. Good times were just around the corner. And he had been decisively defeated. The people wanted leadership and they wanted action.

In his first months in office Roosevelt took a series of steps intended to deal with the crisis. The blizzard of new legislation, agencies, and policies derived from the premise that the federal government was the only institution capable of organizing and implementing an effective national response to a crippling national crisis. Structurally, the new policies and programs expanded the role of the federal government in the management of the economy and redefined federalism in such a way as to reduce the autonomy of states and the private sector.

After a brief hopeful response by the Supreme Court to challenges to the legitimacy of the new powers assumed by the federal government the situation deteriorated. A Court majority set its face against change. Drawing on decades of jurisprudence rationalizing corporate interests, the Court in a series of swift moves, systematically invalidated New Deal efforts to invoke the power of the federal government on behalf of the weak, the dispossessed, and ordinary workers.

In March, 1935, attorneys for the railroads appeared in Court to argue against the Railroad Retirement Act of 1934, under which Congress, using its power to regulate interstate commerce, had mandated a pension system for railroad workers. Resolution of the issue had implication for a new system called "social security" which had not yet been enacted into law. In May, 1935, a five-to-four majority held for the railroads.[26] In the exercise of its power to regulate interstate commerce Congress had to respect the Fifth Amendment due-process rights of those regulated. For various reasons the majority found mandated employer contributions to a retirement fund to be a taking of property without due process of law. The establishment of eligibility for a period of years prior to the passage of the law constituted additional forced payment to workers who had already been fully compensated. The establishment of a government-administered fund into which all railroads paid placed the successful companies in the position of compensating the employees of failed companies, this also constituting the taking of property without due process of law.

A series of decisions followed on the heels of *Railroad Board* putting in further jeopardy federal efforts to address the crisis. The thrust of Roosevelt's policies to cope with the crisis entailed enlarging the federal role in the dynamics of the economy, the introduction of a set of regulations intended to provide more security and greater bargaining power for labor, and economic support for particularly vulnerable players such as farmers. The policies were embodied in a series of new laws including the National Industrial Recovery Act, addressing the problems of industry and the Agricultural Adjustment Act, creating farm subsidies. By the end of Roosevelt's first term a Court majority had invalidated much of this legislation, arguing a theory of federalism stretching back to Melville Fuller, which limited Congressional and Executive Branch involvement in the management of the economy by giving the Commerce Clause a very narrow reading, thereby limiting the range of economic activity Congress could address under its Constitutional power to regulate the conditions of commerce.[27]

National dismay at the Court's wrecking of the New Deal is reflected in one of the letters received by Chief Justice Hughes. George Mott spoke to the meaning of the Courts actions for workers: "By the decision of yourself and your colleagues on the N.R.A. you have stretched my hours of labor from 46 to 54 hours a week at the same wage, although the firm was willing to give us the shorter hours, with the cutthroat competition eliminated by the N.R.A. I am only one of millions of workers in this Country, that with eight other men you have had the power to put such a burden upon: if this is what the Constitution of my Country stands for wouldn't it be a blessing to scrap the same. I am writing you this letter hoping you will consider the unrighteousness of the Act."[28] And compounding the problem, state meliorative policies were also found to be unconstitutional. Almost exactly one year after the railroad cases the Court heard a case addressing New York State's effort to shore up its economy.

Joseph Tibaldi was in jail in Brooklyn awaiting trial. The state of New York had passed a law mandating a minimum wage for women and minors employed in any "Industry, trade or business or branch thereof" save for domestic service. Joseph Tibaldi as manager of a laundry had refused to pay the minimum wage and had been put in jail. A lower court had dismissed his writ seeking relief only to be reversed by the New York Court of Appeals on the grounds that the statute Tibaldi had violated was "repugnant to the due process clause of the state and federal constitution." The state appealed this decision to the United States Supreme Court. Hence, on April 25, 1936, attorneys for New York stood before the Court arguing the constitutionality of minimum wage laws in a case that had attracted enormous attention and a number of supporting briefs on each side.[29]

On June 1, 1936, Pierce Butler delivered the majority opinion for a sharply divided court. The statute had a number of defects, not the least of which was that it harmed women: "minimum wages for women alone would unreasonably restrain them in competition with men and tend to arbitrarily deprive them of employment and a fair chance to find work." In other words there was nothing in the law preventing an employer from paying men an even lower wage. Hence, in addition to injury to Tibaldi and his class the law also deprived women of the chance for a livelihood without due process of law in violation of the Fourteenth Amendment. Hughes spoke for the dissenters arguing that neither case law nor the Constitution denied states the power to protect women being exploited by unscrupulous employers.

Throughout the summer and fall of 1936 Roosevelt met with his advisors trying to formulate a strategy for confronting the Court. Although the Court was unpopular he refrained from making it an issue in the fall election in the absence of a clear plan as to what to do. After a resounding victory over Republican Alf Landon he felt emboldened. On February 5, 1937, he sent a special message to Congress calling for the composition of the Supreme Court to be altered. Using the lame and transparent rationale of an excessive workload Roosevelt argued the need for more federal judges. The president could nominate an additional judge where a federal judge reaching the age of seventy did not retire within a short period of time. The scheme would have allowed him to nominate up to six additional Supreme Court justices.[30]

In part a victim of circumstance, Roosevelt had been the first president within memory not to have had the opportunity to make an appointment within a full term. The axis of his dispute with the Court related to the meaning of federalism. A majority of the Court viewed the federal governments constitutional power to regulate industry and the activities of states as very limited. Successful pursuit of New Deal recovery programs required an expanded federal capacity to regulate the affairs of private firms, individuals, and the states. Although Roosevelt's concerns in his dispute with the Court were related entirely to economic issues and had nothing at all to do with civil rights, the premises of the mode of judicial philosophy he was seeking were necessary to any rethinking of the constitutional rights of blacks.

The Civil War amendments and the antiterror and civil rights laws of the decade following the Civil War presupposed an expanded federal role in the affairs of states, businesses, and private individuals. They posed a conception of federalism inconsistent with an expanded notion of state's rights and inhospitable to the notion that private decisions having major social consequences could not be made subject to a degree of oversight.

Although civil rights was not on his mind, Roosevelt had in mind a type of judicial philosophy whose premises would be necessary though not sufficient to yield a change in constitutional interpretation involving race and rights. But whatever hopes he had that his overwhelming electoral victory would translate into quick passage of his proposed court reorganization legislation quickly vanished as bitter, loud, and tenacious opposition developed.

In the end fortune turned Roosevelt's way. The struggle had been directed at Van Devanter, Sutherland, Pierce Butler, and James Clark McReynolds, and within a short period time all save McReynolds were gone. The scheme to change the Court died but in the end Roosevelt got the opportunity anyway to create a "Roosevelt Court," a Court having a judicial philosophy contemplating an expanded federal role in the pursuit of policies having progressive and reformist objectives. And although race was not on Roosevelt's mind, that mode of judicial philosophy was necessary to a reading of the Constitution consistent with racial reform.

Willis Van Devanter resigned from the Court in May, 1937, in the midst of the "court-packing" crisis, giving Roosevelt his first opportunity to name a justice. Ironically, his eventual choice—however promising in terms of the judicial fate of the new deal—appeared publicly at the time to be a disaster as regards race and rights.

A New Court Forms

Hugo Lafeytte Black appeared to embody the contradictions of the progressive impulse in the era between the end of the Civil War and the end of World War 11. Born into meager circumstances in rural Alabama, he had struggled mightily for the meager two years of formal education in the law that was to suffice through decades on the Supreme Court. In his early days as a lawyer he had championed the interests of poor whites and, as a consequence, had come to be viewed as a radical and a Communist by local elites born to privilege. But in the pursuit of political power and a career that would take him away from the dirt streets and tumbled-down shacks of Harlan, Alabama, he had also accommodated the white supremacist passions of the local electorate.

Voted into the United States Senate in 1926 and reelected in 1932, he had been a passionate champion of the New Deal, exceeding his colleagues in the pursuit of radical change. He had called on the floor of the Senate for a thirty-hour work week and pursued investigations into the power of business to influence and corrupt the political process. He subscribed to the view that the federal government had the power under the Constitution to regulate the economy and the affairs of business for the purpose of mitigating the harsher aspects of capitalism and to create a greater measure of security for working people. It was not apparent from anything he had ever said or done publically that his conception of social justice embraced blacks. There was no public hint of dissent from the religion of segregation.[31]

In the summer of 1937 Franklin Roosevelts main objective was the seating of a justice whose conception of an expanded role for the federal government in national affairs matched his own. Roosevelt was not hostile to minority interests. It was simply that he was unconcerned with any potential nominees' views on race, as Grant decades earlier had been unconcerned about the racial views of Bradley and Strong. Following the death of Joseph Robinson, to whom he had promised the first Court opening, Roosevelt nominated Black, and after a short but spirited debate the Senate in August, 1937 confirmed, whereupon Black and his wife departed for a vacation in Europe.

There had been hints and rumors, but no proof. Then matters began to come to a head. On September 11, 1937, a letter from Paris-based *New York Times* correspondent Lansing Warren was delivered to Black at the Hotel George the Fifth. Warren was anxious to be in touch with the new associate justice regarding a message he had received from the *Times* New York office. On Monday they were planning to run a story alleging that Black had been and still was a member of the Ku KLux Klan. A photostat of his membership card and other documentary evidence was alleged to be available. The *Times* wanted to secure Black's comments on these charges. To that end Warren indicated, "I shall telephone you again this afternoon and evening, and will be in my office between 5 and 7 and after ten p.m. tonight."[32]

The issue of his possible membership in the Ku Klux Klan had surfaced briefly in the confirmation debate but died quickly in the absence of anything definitive. Yet a joke went around Washington after the confirmation vote: "Hugo will not have to buy a robe, he can dye his white one black."

Four weeks later the story broke. In a series of stories developed by investigative reporter Ray Springle, for which he later received a Pulitzer Prize, the *Pittsburgh Gazette* laid out the details of Black's Klan membership. He had joined the Robert E. Lee klavern in Birmingham, Alabama, on September 11, 1923, pledging to advance the cause of white supremacy. He had resigned in 1925 but in 1926 had received a "Grand Passport," a special life membership and a signal honor within the invisible empire. There was no record or evidence that he had rejected or returned the Grand Passport and thus he was still, arguably, a member of the Ku Klux Klan.[33]

Within days criticism swelled to tidal-wave proportions. Reporters pursued Black to Europe amid cries for his resignation. Black returned to the United States on September 30, 1937, and on October 1 went on the radio to give his side of the story, polls showing that 59 percent of the public thought he should resign. He admitted former Klan membership but disclaimed present association. He proclaimed his commitment to fairness and disclaimed hostility to any racial or religious group. He had been on the radio before and was an effective speaker. Following his talk polls indicated that 56 percent of the public felt he should not resign. Three days later he took his seat as a member of the Supreme Court.[34]

Ultimately, the story with regard to Black and the issue of race was more complicated than it appeared to be publicly. Without question any ambitious white politician in the Alabama of the 1920s had to express public support for the pieties of white supremacy. There was a nonpublic side to the matter however, unknown to Black's white electorate and not made public at the time to limit the damage yielded by the revelation of Klan membership because it would have created a different kind of problem.

While in the Senate he had met and begun to develop a relationship with NAACP secretary Walter White. In June, 1936, White had written Black a letter commenting favorably on an earlier meeting in Philadelphia and commending the Senator for his apparent greater understanding of the NAACP's philosophy.[35] A year later as the Klan controversy was unfolding he cabled Black congratulations on his confirmation and expressed confidence that he would take "not only a liberal but the broadest interpretation of the due process and equal protection clauses of the Constitution," particularly regarding "the rights of the Negro and other minorities."[36]

Irrespective of White's private confidence the public test of Black's judicial philosophy as regards race and rights would be his stance on cases as they came before the Court. And indeed a test came very quickly but in a form that compromised the meaning of the outcome as regarded Black's ultimate notions of racial justice.

Throughout American history law had been an instrument placing workers at a disadvantage relative to owners. The 1807 effort of a group of Philadelphia workers to organize—perhaps the first in the country—resulted in prosecution for engaging in a conspiracy to raise wages.[37] On numerous occasions in the ensuing decades law and the courts defeated labors' efforts to organize against brutal conditions. A secure base in law for pursuing efforts to organize and bargain on an equal footing was not won by labor until the early 1930s as part of the political and social revolution spawned by the New Deal in its effort to cope with the collapse of the economy.

In 1937 Congress had passed the Norris-LaGuardia Act allowing for peaceful picketing in situations involving labor disputes. The act provided labor with leverage in contesting the terms and conditions of work by denying management the capacity to have peaceful labor protest defined as criminal activity. As a friend of labor Hugo Black had been a champion of legislation intended to arm labor with more weapons in its struggle against management.

Unions, by and large, like every other institution in the country were racially exclusive. The Marxist dream of working-class solidarity had foundered on a reality grounded in intense racial hostility toward blacks on the part of white labor. Blacks had been pushed to the margins of the economy. Unions made no effort to recruit black members and indeed had played a role, historically, in driving blacks from the few niches in the industrial economy where they had secured a place. To champion the cause of labor as Hugo Black had done in his days in Congress was not necessarily to champion the cause of black workers or black rights. Nor had Black and other champions of the new legislation contemplated being confronted with a situation in which the rights of blacks would be inextricably interwoven with the rights of labor, a circumstance in which support of the rights of labor necessarily also strengthened the black struggle against the kind of racial exclusion the unions represented.

In the fall of 1938 the *New Negro-Alliance* case came before the Court on appeal from the District of Columbia Court of Appeals. The New Negro Alliance had lost in the court of appeals as it had in district court and had sought relief now in the United States Supreme Court. The immediate circumstances yielding the conflict involved blacks. Their fate in the courts implicated labor.

The conflict had grown out of a common condition. The Sanitary Grocery store chain operated 255 retail outlets in the greater Washington, D.C., area. Sanitary did not hire black clerks for any of its stores, even those in black neighborhoods in the Capital. Sanitary's practices merely mirrored those of other retailers nationwide. Black clerks were not employed in any of New York City's downtown department stores, managers contending that their white clientele would object, nor were blacks hired in retail outlets in Harlem or other black communities. In the larger stores there might be a black presence as washroom attendants or running freight elevators, in smaller outlets there was likely to be no presence at all.

The New Negro Alliance had been formed with the objective of cracking the wall barring blacks from a place in the labor force, at least for employers doing business in black neighborhoods. The immediate precipitant of conflict with Sanitary involved the opening of a new store at 1936 Eleventh Street, N.W. in the District on April 3, 1936, in a black neighborhood but for which no black clerks were hired. William Hastie and Harry Honesty, the Alliance's principle officers, had sought to meet with and press upon the officers of Sanitary a request that at least some black clerks be hired for at least some of the outlets in black Washington, D.C., particularly the new store. Sanitary refused to acknowledge the request and on April 4, the day after the new store opened, a picket appeared carrying a large placard urging "Do Your Part! Buy Where You Can Work! No Negroes Employed Here!" Whereupon Sanitary successfully sought redress in district court in the form of an injunction or court order barring the New Negro Alliance from picketing. The refusal of the Court of Appeals to overturn the district court order brought the case before the Supreme Court.

In a technical sense the issue was related to whether the district court had jurisdiction in the first place to issue an injunction. Attorneys for the New Negro Alliance argued that the Norris-LaGuardia

Act barred federal courts from issuing injunctions curbing peaceful activities on behalf of workers in bonafide labor disputes. The injunction had been a favorite tool of business, employed historically to block all forms of peaceful labor protest, picketing, leafletting, boycotts, marches, rallies. Violation of an injunction provided grounds for more forceful types of repression. The purpose of section 13(A) of the 1932 act had been to stay the hand of the courts where workers sought peacefully to pursue their legitimate interests.

The district court, supported by the court of appeals, had denied that the conflict between the New Negro Alliance and Sanitary was a labor dispute. In their view it was simply a racial dispute, not involving terms and conditions of employment such as wages, hours, working conditions, or union status. From the perspective of the black seeking entry to the workplace the implications of these holdings were devastating. Blacks were barred from employment because of race, hence they could not be in a circumstance where they were disputing conditions of labor as regards wages, hours, and the like. If they were denied the use of the picket line or the boycott to protest their exclusion because their grievance was merely racial rather than reflective of a bonafide labor dispute, they were consigned to perpetual outsider status.

The task confronting the Supreme Court was one of statutory construction. What did it choose to infer as to the meaning intended by Congress relative to the language of the act where the issue before them had not been specifically addressed by that language? The Court engaged in this task had undergone an additional change in the year since Hugo Black had ascended to the Court. Shortly after Black had joined the Court, George Sutherland, another of the judicial foes of the New Deal retired. Fate having given him opportunities denied by the failure of the court-packing scheme, Roosevelt made another shrewd nomination to the Senate for confirmation.

Stanley Forman Reed was a Kentuckian by birth but had traveled broadly in the world. Educated at Yale, Columbia, and the Sorbonne, he had returned to Kentucky and a career in law and politics. By the standards of the time he was a progressive on certain economic and social issues, supporting legislation in the state legislature curbing child labor and providing workmens' compensation. He had been appointed to the Federal Farm Board by Hoover in 1929 and had remained in Washington after Roosevelt's ascent, first as head of the Reconstruction Finance Corporation and then as Solicitor General charged with defending the New Deal's policies against legal assault. As the government's chief lawyer he had championed the New Deal cause before the Supreme Court in the losing cases that led Roosevelt to advance the court-packing plan. Roosevelt seems not to have held the losses against him and to have viewed him as committed to the New Deal's vision of federalism. His views on race and rights were not seen as central to a consideration of his candidacy. He easily won nomination without there being any indication of the meaning of his ascension for issues of race and rights.[38]

The matter before the Court had not been addressed by the drafters of the Norris-LaGuardia Act. The Court could let the matter stand and affirm the decision of the court of appeals in not setting aside the district court injunction. On the other hand, it could infer an intent as to a matter not specifically addressed. They chose to do the latter even though had their reading of the underlying intent of Congress relative to race and jobs been put to a vote in Congress it would, undoubtably, have lost.

Justice Owen Roberts delivered the opinion of the majority.[39] They recognized implicitly that the district court and court of appeals interpretations of the law robbed blacks of legal means for openly protesting exclusion from the workplace given that any protest could be defined as a "racial" rather than a labor dispute and therefore not be protected under the act. Speaking for the majority, Roberts took a leap from the actual language of the statute. True, the act was intended to prevent employers from using the Courts as an instrument to bludgeon workers seeking to unionize or seeking better working conditions. In that sense, it was intended to get at and curb a certain type of bad motive that management might have. The implicit, antitrade union, bad motive sought to be curbed by the act did not exhaust the repertoire of bad motives management might bring to a dispute however. A wish to exclude because of race presented the same issue of fairness in terms of those adversely affected as a wish to exclude because of union activity. If the acts underlying intent of providing fair rules for dispute resolution applied relative to the trade unionist it followed that it also applied for the black contesting racial exclusion by an employer.

Roberts then went on to express a view surely not likely to have been supported on the floor of Congress, by the trade unions or by the white public: "Race discrimination by an employer may reasonably be deemed more unfair and less excusable than discrimination against workers on the ground of union affiliation." The statement was dicta and not law. It was a point of view, an expression of sentiment. The case itself had dealt with a matter of statutory interpretation having great pragmatic significance as regards black strategy in terms of employment discrimination—indeed whether there could be a legal strategy—but it did not go to the fundamental legal underpinnings of the separate but equal doctrine.

The practical significance of *New Negro Alliance* is not to be overlooked however. "Buy Black" campaigns became an aspect of protest against employment discrimination in the cities of the North over the next twenty years. Several years after the Supreme Court had lifted the injunction barring William Hastie and Harry Honesty from picketing Sanitary stores a similar campaign helped launch the political career of a young Harlem minister named Adam Clayton Powell.

As *New Negro-Alliance* was unfolding in the nation's capital, events were also transpiring half way across the continent that were to yield the beginning of broad Court acceptance of a jurisprudence of race and rights building on the principles Charles Evans Hughes had begun to apply twenty years earlier in holding that separate must in fact be equal and, where separate cannot be made equal, separate must give way.

The Gaines Case

On June 12, 1935, Lloyd Gaines, a twenty-five-year-old black man, wrote to the registrar of the University of Missouri at Columbia, S.W. Canada, asking for a law school catalog and on June 18 a catalog was forwarded to him. On August 19 Gaines wrote to the registrar requesting law school admissions application forms and indicated shortly thereafter that he was having his undergraduate transcript forwarded to the law school as part of the process.[40]

Gaines was an ambitious young man from an ambitious family. He had graduated from Lincoln University in June, 1935, a state-supported, all-black institution. His brother George, a pullman porter, had paid his expenses and he anticipated that George would continue to provide support were he admitted to the University of Missouri Law School and that he might also receive a scholarship allocated by the black fraternity Apha Phi Apha for students of high scholastic standing.

Inevitably the registrar learned that the new applicant was black. Irrespective of his good academic record and his degree from an accredited, state-supported institution he was barred under Missouri law from attending a white institution. On September 16, Canada sent Gaines a telegram suggesting that he take up the matter of studying law with President Florence of Lincoln University.

By its own light Missouri was progressive in matters of race and education. It supported its black institution, Lincoln University, more generously than other Southern or border states supported their segregated schools. It had empowered Lincoln University as early as 1921 to seek a charter for a law school were black demand sufficient to justify the expense of building a law school for blacks. It was one of only two Southern states providing out-of-state scholarships, West Virginia being the other—although it was understood that these applied only in adjacent states.

Gaines had straightforward and uncomplicated motives. He lived in Missouri. He wanted to make his career in Missouri. The best place to learn Missouri law was the University of Missouri Law School. In addition, going to school out of state imposed expenses on a modest budget that studying in state would not impose. Indeed, state support might itself prove illusory given that the legislature had only recently amended the law, obliging Missouri to pay only the differential between tuition out of state and tuition at the university for the same course of study. Thus, if Kansas, or Illinois, or other adjacent states were charging less for the same program the black student forced to go out of state would receive no financial help from Missouri.

He seems also to have initially believed that reasonable people would see the merits of his case. On September 24 he sat down at home and typed out a letter to the president of the University of Missouri pleading his case. But three days later he sent a letter to the national offices of the National Association for the Advancement of Colored People in New York.

Gaines query had come at a crucial time for the Association. Under the courtroom leadership of Charles Houston, Dean of the Howard University Law School, it had initiated a series of cases intended to strike at the heart of the separate-but-equal doctrine. *Plessy* had held that equal conditions were necessary to save state-sponsored racial separation from constitutional default. There was no question but that the Jim Crow states had failed in every respect to meet the "equal" dimension of the separate-but-equal equation. This failure had been only fitfully tested in the courts and only Charles Evans Hughes, in his first term on the Supreme Court two decades earlier, had spoken to the implications of that failure. That there might be small black demand for a service did not relieve the state provider of the obligation of providing it at the same level of quality as afforded whites, and if that could not be done for economic reasons then the racial bar to access must fall.

As a strategic matter Houston felt that the focus should be on the failure of Jim Crow at the level of graduate and professional studies, particularly with regard to the opportunity to study law. The legal implications of possible success were profound yet the arena of struggle would be remote from the view of the demagogues, klansmen, and mob orators likely to sweep angry crowds into the streets were the issue possible integration of elementary schools.

In 1935 as the education campaign began, no Southern state supported a graduate or professional school for blacks. All barred blacks from attending in-state graduate and professional schools and only Missouri and West Virginia provided out-of-state scholarships. In that year Oklahoma introduced an out-of-state scholarship program as did Maryland, but the Maryland state legislature voted no funds for its implementation. Kentucky also appeared to be moving in the direction of a program, but also seemed intent on deducting the funds from the support it provided for its black institution, Kentucky State College.[41]

Three months before Gaines sent his letter to the national office, the Association had won a victory in Maryland in a case embracing some of the same issues. Donald Murray had wanted to attend law school in Maryland but the University of Maryland Law School barred blacks and indeed had denied admission to nine in the two years preceding Murray's application. In a scenario somewhat similar to the one that unfolded in Missouri several months later, Murray had sought admission and had received a letter from the University of Maryland registrar closing off the process and advising him to contact the local black institution, Princess Anne Academy, which, as with Lincoln University in Missouri, did not have a law school. Murray had then written to the university's Board of Regents pressing his case only to receive a letter from the president referring him again to Princess Anne Academy, but also suggesting that he consider going to Howard.[42]

Supported by Belford Lawson, a Washington attorney and one of the organizers of the New Negro Alliance, as well as by Houston and Thurgood Marshall, Murray brought suit seeking entry and in June of 1935 the case was argued in Baltimore City Court. Houston called University of Maryland President Raymond Pearson to the stand and under fierce questioning wrung crucial admissions from him. Princess Anne Academy was not a sensible option given Murray's objective and, indeed, was not even in its own terms a quality institution. And while the state had voted to set up out-of-state scholarships they had provided no funds so that as they spoke, had Murray followed the suggestion to go to Howard University Law School he would have had to pay out of his own pocket. There was no factor other than Murrays race that had brought the assembled group together in contentious encounter on this day in early June.

Houston next had called to the stand Roger Howell, Dean of the University of Maryland Law School. The questioning made clear that a desire to practice law in Maryland was best served by the opportunity to study law at the University of Maryland. The dean objected to Murray however on the grounds that there was not sufficient demand to justify creating a separate black law school and that custom dictated excluding blacks from the existing law school. Without mentioning Hughes's holding of two decades earlier, Houston posed the question of whether lack of demand for a service by a plaintiffs group robbed the plaintiff of an individual, constitutional right to enjoy that service, to which Pearson did not have a satisfactory answer.

Judge Eugene O'Dunne had seemed not unsympathetic to Murray's claim. His periodic interjections suggested lack of the kind of hostility to black plaintiffs pressing civil rights claims that Houston and Marshall had previously encountered. And indeed, Maryland had failed to respond to the constitutional issue posed by the state's failure to balance "separate" with a credible "equal." On June 25, 1935, O'Dunne issued a writ ordering President Pearson to admit Donald Murray to the University of Maryland Law School. The state attorney general appealed and sought an expedited hearing before the Maryland Court of Appeals, but the state's highest court refused to advance the case on the calendar and hence Donald Murray registered for the fall term.[43]

Murray had been sitting in class a few weeks when Lloyd Gaines's letter arrived at the NAACP national office, Gaines was still barred at the schoolhouse door. And while the outcome of Maryland's appeal before the Court of Appeals was unknown, the struggle in Missouri promised to be more tenacious. Generals do not always have the luxury of choosing the field on which to fight. Houston, Hastie, and Thurgood Marshall were all on the East Coast. They knew each other and knew something of Donald Murray. Always working in straightened economic circumstances and always having need to seek funds from sympathetic organizations to press major cases up through the legal system, Murray's case by its very location held appeal, close to the home base of the attorney's, close to Washington and the Supreme Court should it go that far. It had the potential of offering a major challenge to Jim Crow constitutionalism under favorable logistical circumstances. But on the other hand, victory while always sweet is not always filling. Should Murray prevail at the Court of Appeals level the broader challenge to the assumptions of *Plessy* might never occur, save should the state choose to press onward to the Supreme Court.

Gaines's letter suggested a case that might be engaged for the long haul, but the initial question was, Who was Lloyd Gaines? The national office forwarded Gaines's letter to Charles Houston. Gaines had asked in his letter whether he had a right to go to the University of Missouri Law School. Houston wrote back to Gaines expressing sympathy and suggested that he meet with Sidney Redmond, a St. Louis attorney and NAACP activist. Gaines satisfied Redmond and his partner Henry Espy as to his seriousness of purpose and they agreed to pursue his case with the backing of the NAACP. Hence on January 24, 1936, Redmond and Espy filed suit in the circuit court of Boone County against S. Canada as registrar of the university, asking the court to order him to act on Gaines's application.

Without awaiting the outcome of the court proceedings, the university's board met on March 27 and voted rejection of Gaines's application. Two weeks later Redmond and Espy went back to the circuit court seeking a writ of mandamus compelling the board to admit Gaines to the law school. The matter was finally joined in the courtroom on July 10, Charles Houston joining Redmond and Espy in support of Gaines. The university's attorneys, shrewd and accomplished practitioners, argued that the state had met its obligation to Gaines insofar as Lincoln University had been charged under law since 1921 with the responsibility of developing a law school for black students were the need made manifest. Gaines had not applied to Lincoln for professional study in law and thus could not claim that the state had defaulted. In addition, his failure to apply for an out-of-state scholarship to a law school in an adjacent state negated his claim that the state had denied him the opportunity to study law while providing such an opportunity to white students. The courts had affirmed that "separate but equal" meant substantially similar rather than identical opportunities.[44]

Houston, Redmond, and Espy sought to establish that both Lincoln University and the out-of-state tuition options were illusory. No institution could create a law school overnight or for one or two students, nor did the terms of the out-of-state scholarship program serve either the financial or career interests of a student who wanted to practice law in Missouri. But as the proceedings progressed, Houton sensed that the court's ruling would be adverse and sought, primarily, to establish a record for the inevitable appeal.

Several months later the Missouri Court of Appeals affirmed the decision of the court below. The state could not, consistent with the Constitution, deny Lloyd Gaines a right it afforded white students and, indeed, it had not done so. The laws of Missouri mandated separation of the races in schools at all levels and hence the University of Missouri could not, consistent with state law, admit Gaines or any other black to any of its programs. The state had taken reasonable steps, however, to honor the constitutional right of Gaines and other blacks to an equal opportunity to pursue graduate study.

Missouri and Maryland had come out differently on the issue, but Missouri's stance represented that of the South. In 1935 Oklahoma had introduced a scholarship program and in 1936 Virginia and Kentucky followed suit, the state legislatures perhaps having a perception of the underlying issues and dangers of *Gaines* and similar challenges presented as they worked their way up through the courts. Implicit in *Gaines* were questions going to the constitutionality and viability of "separate but equal." The University of Missouri's lawyers had been correct in arguing before the state courts that the equal dimension of the separate-but-equal equation had always been construed by the courts to mean substantial equivalence rather than absolute identity. But the NAACP on behalf of black students was countering that even within that framework it was, in the words of an internal memo, "unconstitutional to exile them out of state while white students were being educated at home."[45]

Defenders of the status quo understood the practical implications were the courts to accept that NAACP formulation. The Southern states would be constrained to do what none of them had done, fund in-state graduate and professional schools for blacks that could plausibly be defended as substantially equal to those provided for whites. William Redmond, a young black student had a case pending against the University of Tennessee School of Pharmacy and the assistance of the Association had been sought by black students seeking entry to the University of Virginia Graduate School and the University of North Carolina Medical School. It was not expected that a single case would necessarily determine the constitutional fate of separate but equal at the level of graduate and professional training; but it was clear that the outcome of *Gaines*, should the United States Supreme Court agree to hear it, would speak powerfully to the latitude available to the states under the constitution to institutionalize racial subordination.

In the summer of 1938 it was not clear to Houston and the NAACP that the Supreme Court would necessarily grant certiorari. The fight had been carried forward at the state level with the financial support of the progressive American Fund for Public Service. But by June, 1938, with no indication as to whether the Supreme Court would entertain the appeal from Missouri's judgment, the money had run out. Houston was informed by Roger Baldwin, the fund's secretary, that a special appropriation of $700 would be made available "conditioned upon the Association raising the same amount and upon the statement from any reputable counsel that there is a fair chance of winning the case."[46]

An exchange of confidential letters between Houston and various prominent attorneys of a liberal bent followed in which Houston expressed his position as he sought to secure the kind of third-party legal assurance that Baldwin and the fund were requesting. Perhaps the fund's resources need not be called upon unless the Supreme Court granted certiorari. "I think the Fund should help us at this point, if and when we reach it." He was not certain however that they would get to that point: "The chances of the court granting the writ are not as bright as we might wish . . . the court may find the subject too hot to handle." And if the Fund did not contribute because the case did not go forward, "I trust it will hold the money and set it aside for Negro work: say to challenge the question of Negro exclusion from labor unions, or disenfranchisement, or an economic problem of first importance to workers' rights."[47]

On October 12, Walter White of the NAACP wrote to Roger Baldwin, "I am happy to inform you that the United States Supreme Court on October 10 granted our motion for a writ of certiorari in the case of Lloyd L. Gaines v. The University of Missouri. . . . We would be very grateful if a check could be sent to us at your earliest convenience in order that preparations for the argument in the supreme court, which will take place about November 7, may not be handicapped by lack of funds."[48]

The same day Wilkins mailed his letter to the fund he received a letter from E. Washington Rhodes, editor of the black *Philadelphia Tribune*, regarding the possibility of the Supreme

Court hearing the case and indicating not without apprehension, "It will be interesting to observe the position justice KKK Black takes."[49] The Court was changing but it was not clear yet what those changes meant to black interests.

The case argued on November 9 before a Court with two justices certain to reject Gaines's claims. McReynolds remained as fierce a foe of black rights in his dotage as he had been in his youth. Pierce Butler, lacked an empathetic grasp of the black predicament and hence was indisposed to read the possibility of reform into the language of the law.

Four weeks after oral argument Charles Evans Hughes delivered the holding for a six-to-two majority. The blow was delivered swiftly. Following a brief delineation of the facts, Hughes moved to the majority's decision. The state's policy of providing in-state legal education for whites while denying it to blacks was "discrimination repugnant to the Fourteenth Amendment." Neither the intent to support a law school at Lincoln University pending sufficient demand nor the offer of scholarships to study law in adjacent states cured or negated the discrimination. Indeed, "We think that these matters are beside the point. The basic consideration is not what sort of opportunities other States provide, or whether they are as good as those in Missouri, but as to what opportunities Missouri itself furnishes to white students and denies to negroes solely upon the grounds of color." There was no way of viewing the racial bar other than as a denial of a privilege established by the state, "and the provision of payment of tuition fees in another State does not remove the discrimination."[50]

Nor did the lack of demand justify state policy relative to not having established an in-state option for black students. Hughes harked back to his holding in *McCabe v. Atchison* twenty years earlier. The lack-of-demand argument had been found unsatisfactory insofar as it made enjoyment of a constitutional right a function of the number of people discriminated against, "whereas the essence of (a) constitutional right is that it is a personal one." Gaines's right was a personal one. "It was as an individual that he was entitled to the equal protection of the laws."[51]

Nor was the denial temporary insofar as there appeared to be no immediate prospect that a black law school would be established in Missouri or that it could be done so in a timely manner relative to Gaines's claim. Hughes and the majority construed the Missouri Supreme Court as having said that the state had met its obligation under the United States Constitution by affording an opportunity for out-of-state study. However, "We are of the opinion that the ruling was error, and that petitioner was entitled to be admitted to the law school of the State University in the absence of other and proper provision for his legal training within the State."[52]

Fierce outcries were heard from many quarters. Student voices at the Missouri law school vowed to leave the institution rather than attend with blacks. A bill was introduced in the legislature to expedite making Lincoln University the equivalent of the University of Missouri, but only $200,000 was appropriated to accomplish this task, while $3,000,000 was given to the white institution.[53] Lost amid the clamor and the din was the editorial in *The Missouri Student*, the University of Missouri's student paper, appearing on December 10, two days after the decision was handed down. The student editor understood the implications of *Gaines*. "A report from the state capitol indicates the legislature may provide a law school for Negroes at Lincoln university. But what about journalism? What about Engineering? . . . To what extent can it provide equal protection in any of the studies outside of those taught at Lincoln University? . . . Here then we meet the question: Can Missouri provide for the Negro a University of the completeness of the State University? It is apparent the state will employ every trick in its hand to maintain its traditional policy of separation of whites and Negroes in schools. At the same time it is fighting an uphill battle. . . . The hill is steep, and rugged, and the fight looms as a losing battle."[54]

The anonymous student grasped the meaning of the case and was prescient. Missouri and other states would employ every stratagem at their command and the fight would be long and costly. And embedded in *Gaines* was the seeds of a jurisprudence which, if developed by subsequent justices, could collapse separate but equal.

Unlike Donald Murray, Lloyd Gaines did not enroll following the court victory. On July 13, 1938, while word was still being awaited as to whether the Supreme Court would hear the case, Charles Houston received a letter from Sydney Redmond regarding their client. "Gaines' family has not heard from him in over a month. The brother was in my office a few days ago and seems to think he has been kidnapped. They are having an investigation made. If I get any more information on the subject I will advise."[55]

He had boarded a train for Chicago and was never seen again. The statistics on lynchings in 1938 do not include his name.

Chambers and the New Court

The case had begun in 1933. Perhaps because the Scottsboro boys were still in the shadow of the electric chair it did not draw a great deal of attention. Perhaps because there were only four men in jeopardy rather than eight. Perhaps because it involved murder rather than rape. When it ended seven year later the *New York Times* headlined the decision, and spoke to the reasons it drew national attention: "It was voiced eloquently by justice Black, who admitted after his nomination to the high bench, that he had once been a member of the Ku Klux KIan. . . . The drama of the occasion, due to the . . . background of the justice rendering it . . . was not lost upon the audience which crowded the great marble court chamber."[56] It helped define Black and the new Court in terms of matters of race.

The facts were stark and straightforward and by the standards of the old South not exceptional. Robert Darcy, an elderly white man and a resident of Pompano, Florida, a small community just north of Fort Lauderdale, had been robbed and killed some time around 9:00 P.M., Saturday, May 13. Almost immediately a mass round-up of black men began as cries for blood were heard in the white community. As the mob's passions swelled, one J. T. Williams, a prison guard, came to assume an ever larger role in the hunt for the killers.

As Sunday evening turned to night the round up and jailing of black suspects gave way to sustained and vigorous interrogation of the forty or fifty men being held. According to the record "the officers of Broward County were in the jail almost continuously during the whole week questioning these boys." The record also indicated that "the prisoners at no time during the week we:e permitted to see or confer with counsel or a single friend or relative."[57] Yet a week's grilling failed to yield any confessions.

At about 3:30 in the afternoon on Saturday, May 20, J. T. Williams and the other interrogators began what came to be referred to as "the all-night vigil." They focused on a smaller number of prisoners, bringing them in one after another throughout the afternoon, into the evening, through the night, past midnight, and into the next day. At about 2:30 in the morning Walter Woodard broke under Williams grilling. The state's attorney was awakened and summoned to the jail to take down Woodard's statement. He broke off however in short order dismissing the "confession" as worthless and stalked out indicating "When you get something worthwhile, call me." Williams and his companions went back to work.

Later that morning the state's attorney was called back to the jail. The renewed labor of the interrogators had yielded fruit. Walter Woodard, Isaiah Chambers, Jack Williamson, and Charlie Davis confessed to having killed Robert Darcy. They were later tried, their confessions being the only evidence against them, convicted, and sentenced to death in the electric chair.

On appeal the condemned men claimed a violation of their right to due process of law insofar as their convictions had been secured on the basis of coerced confessions. Failing in the Florida Supreme Court they petitioned as paupers to the United States Supreme Court. Again Hughes had provided a framework within which to assess the validity of the constitutional claim. In *Brown* Hughes had spoken for a majority willing to extend to the states the Fifth Amendment prohibition on deprivation of life without due process of law in response to the conviction of a black man based on a confession exacted under clear signs of physical torture. The facts appeared damning in *Chambers* but for Black's fellow Southerner, McReynolds, there appeared to be no set of circumstances so outrageous as to tempt him to see a possible deprivation of rights because of race. In *Chambers* Black set aside the public notion that he might be a member of McReynold's fraternity on matters of race and that he was the kind of progressive who could combine support for the rights of labor and working people with hostility to efforts to extend those rights to blacks.

He began with a recital of the facts then moved to the question of law.[58] True, the facts were outrageous, but were they outrageous in a way that implicated a constitutionally protected right? The answer to that question hinged on the intent or purposes behind the Fourteenth Amendment. The matter was clear, Black asserted. "In view of its historical setting and the wrongs which called it into being, the due process provision of the Fourteenth Amendment . . . has led few to doubt that it was intended to guarantee procedural standards."[59]

Applying the legal principle to the extant facts there could be no doubt that procedural integrity had been violated irrespective of the fact that the condemned men did not bear the marks of physical torture. The language of analysis then gave way to the language of passion. 'Tyrannical governments (have) memorially utilized dictatorial criminal procedure and punishment to make scapegoats of the weak or of helpless political, religious, or racial minorities and those who differed, who would not conform and who resisted tyranny."[60]

Hughes and the End of the Beginning

Hughes was concerned about staying on the bench past his time. He had asked close members of his family to confer among themselves should they sense he was slipping into senility and to convey their collective sentiment to him. As the 1938–1939 court term passed its midway point however he appeared to still be vigorous physically and mentally at age seventy-seven.

In February, 1939, he collapsed briefly in the Court's conference room, only the court clerk, whom he swore to silence being present. Two months later he was briefly incapacitated with a bleeding ulcer but after an apparent recovery was again stricken as the Court's term came to a close. Pierce Butler came to see him at his home just before going on vacation and came away shaken, opining that he would "never see the Chief again." And indeed the prediction turned out to be correct. Butler died later that year, allowing Roosevelt to achieve a Court majority with the nomination and ratification of Frank Murphy to the bench.

Hughes returned for the 1939–1940 Court term, apparently restored to something like his old vigor physically and mentally. And by the time the 1940–1941 term began, thoughts of retirement appear to have been set aside save for urgent and vigorous importuning by Herbert Hoover that he step down in protest against Franklin Roosevelt's unprecedented bid for a third term in the White House. The former president and other voices in the land cried out against what they viewed as an incipient dictatorship.

By the end of the term Hughes himself had concluded however that he was no longer up to the task of guiding the Court. On June 2, 1941, he sent a note to Roosevelt indicating his intention of resigning, effective July 1, 1941. Sentiment was widespread among those in the legal fraternity and in political life that Hughes had been one of the greatest jurists to sit on the bench, perhaps equal in rank to John Marshall, His colleagues on the bench expressed gratitude for his leadership and the major commentators of the day saluted his sustained effort to move the country forward to realizing its unique promise. Biographers later described his contributions. He had played a major role from the bench in establishing the "freedoms of the First Amendment as guarantees to the citizen against state action . . . in the field of civil liberties his record (was) more consistent than that of Holmes . . . instead of becoming another great dissenter for freedom (he) succeeded in making most of his opinions the law of the lang."[61]

And perhaps there were other voices, black and unreported, also offering a salute.

Chapter 8

The Road to *Brown*

Franklin Roosevelt was at his ancestral home in Hyde Park, New York, when he received word in early June of 1941 that Chief Justice Charles Evans Hughes intended to leave the Court at the end of that month. Only months away from having been sworn in as the first man ever to be elected president three times, Roosevelt now had the opportunity of putting his stamp on the Court for generations to come. In his first term he had been defied by a Court committed to a vision of the nation fundamentally at odds with that of the New Deal and its efforts to provide a safety net for citizens against the destructive caprice of the economy. In his second term he had been able to make four appointments and had thereby moved the Court closer to his side as an ally in the struggle to redefine the meaning of federalism. Hughes's retirement gave him the opportunity to become the first president since Abraham Lincoln to nominate a majority of the Court, and only the third to do so, George Washington having been the first.

His prior choices had reflected a search for justices willing to define federalism in terms of an expanded role for the federal government in regulating the economy and insulating citizens against the ravages of economic downturns. Considerations relative to their positions on race and rights had not been a factor. With the exception of Hugo Black, none of his nominees had significant involvement in associations that spoke to any kind of racial ideology, either progressive or hostile. Frank Murphy, Hugo Black, and

Stanley Reed had ascended to a Court for which Charles Evans Hughes provided the intellectual leadership on matters of race and rights.

In an ironic twist, the last case in which Hughes addressed race and rights a few months before sending his note to Roosevelt was strikingly similar to *McCabe*. The similarity reflected two central propositions regarding the Supreme Court, race, and rights. If bigoted practice was fervently supported or deeply entrenched, a progressive holding had little impact. Nevertheless such holdings were important insofar as they became part of the doctrinal basis for incremental progressive change.

Second, given the commitment segregationists brought to the struggle to preserve the system and the fact that cases tend to address specific kinds of factual situations, any factual circumstances differing even slightly from those addressed in a prior progressive holding were deemed untouched by that holding. Hence, proponents of progressive racial change had to fight substantially the same battles again and again. Both propositions obtained in the last race case taken up by Hughes.

The Mitchell Case: Caste and Commerce

Although blacks made up a quarter or more of the population of many Southern states and although there were vast stretches in the big cities of the North and Midwest entirely populated by blacks, there was only one black in Congress in 1937. Violence and gerrymandering had done their work. Arthur Mitchell, representing the south side of Chicago, sat as the only black member of the House of Representatives. As such he was a celebrity in the black community. His comings and goings were noted in the black press. His fate was important to the black community in terms of its collective sense of self in a hostile land.

On April 20, 1937, Mitchell boarded the 6:05 P.M. train out of Chicago carrying a ticket for first-class accommodations, bound for Hot Springs, Arkansas. Early the next morning as the train crossed the Arkansas border, Mitchell was approach by train conductor Albert W. Jones and informed that pursuant to Arkansas law he could not ride in a pullman car in that state not withstanding the fact that he had purchased first-class passage.

According to the record as developed subsequently by the United States District Court, "Following objection by plaintiff to the conductor, the plaintiff was ejected from the car and was forced to ride to Hot Springs in a second class car."[1] Later testimony also established that the railroad did not provide first-class accommodations for blacks, confining them without exception, to a noisome, unpleasant second-class car, said in Mitchell's complaint to be "without wash basins, soap, towel or running water" or a flush toilet in two of the three restrooms and without air conditioning.

Mitchell filed a complaint with the Interstate Commerce Commission, the regulatory agency having jurisdiction over interstate travel, asking for "a rule that the railroad be compelled to desist from its practice." A hearing and rehearing conducted over the next two years resulted in dismissal of the complaint by a divided body of commissioners. Under the Interstate Commerce Act not all discrimination was unlawful, only discrimination which was undue, unreasonable, and unjust. In the view of the Commission majority the burden that would have been placed on the railroad by requiring the provision of segregated first-class accommodations to the relatively small number of blacks seeking to travel first class would have been too great.

Mitchell then sought relief in district court and at the hearing before a three-judge panel enlarged on the rationale for the relief sought: "I wish the Court would remember that they (Arkansas) enforce rigidly that part of the law which provides that they (blacks) must travel separately. As a group who have suffered the inconveniences of such a law, we contend that if you are going to 'Jim Crow' us and put us off, then we are entitled to the benefits of the law that we at least ought to have equal accommodations."[2]

That the number of blacks seeking first-class accommodations was small was not sufficient justification for the railroad to deny such accommodations to all blacks, Mitchell contended. And in support of this proposition he quoted Hughes: "The Supreme Court of the United States has said on more than one occasion that the constitutional rights of individuals are individual and personal, and they are not to be considered in bulk. They said that in a decision in 1916 handed down . . . by our present Chief Justice Hughes, and as late as 1939 this rule was repeated in the case of Gaines . . . by the same Justice."[3]

The commission had not abused its discretion in finding that the railroad's policy was reasonable and hence, according the district court panel, its dismissal of Mitchell's complaint was not subject to judicial review. Mitchell then sought relief in the United States Supreme Court and the case was argued on March 13, 1941.

Six weeks later on April 28, Chief Justice Charles Evans Hughes handed down his last ruling on race and rights. Speaking for a Court majority he went immediately to the heart of the matter: "The denial to appellant of equality of accommodations because of his race (is) an invasion of a fundamental individual right which is guaranteed against state action by the Fourteenth Amendment."[4]

In other words, the issue was not the constitutionality of the Arkansas segregation law. Under the *Plessy* interpretation of the Fourteenth Amendment, Arkansas could mandate racial separation on public carriers within its borders. However *Plessy* also mandated equality of circumstance, albeit within a context of racial segregation. The railroad had argued and the Commission had agreed that economic considerations made it impossible to provide equal accommodations to blacks seeking to travel first class. There were not enough first-class black travelers to justify the expense of a separate first-class, black car. In effect, they were arguing that volume of traffic provided reasonable grounds for being exempt from the "equal" mandate of the separate-but-equal equation even though the "equal" dimension of the equation was, presumably, necessary to reconciling the fact of separation with the equal-protection language of the Fourteenth Amendment. In dismissing Mitchell's complaint the Commission had accepted this argument and, hence, the issue before the Supreme Court was whether the Commission had erred.

Hughes turned to the precedent established by his own holdings in deciding the issue. A quarter of a century earlier in *McCabe*, "We thought a similar argument with respect to volume of traffic to be untenable . . . it made the constitutional right depend upon the number of persons who may be discriminated against, whereas the essence of that right is that it is a personal one." Two years earlier the same point had been made in *Gaines*: "It is the individual . . . who is entitled to the equal protection of the laws—not merely a group of individuals, or a body of persons according to their numbers." The district court was directed to set aside the order of the commission "and to remand the case to the Commission for further proceedings in conformity with this opinion."[4]

Hughes left a legacy of enormous consequence with regard to race and rights. The redemptionist tide was at its crest in his first term on the Court. Having propounded the separate-but-equal doctrine the Court had proceeded to render the "equal" dimension of the equation meaningless. There was no walk of life in which there was a pretense of equality with regard to services and facilities operated under the aegis of government. The "separate" dimension of the equation was fervently honored but the "equal" dimension was not.

As Hughes took his seat in 1910 the Court was presented with the issue of formalizing the denial of equal facilities, of rewriting *Plessy* in such a way as to provide huge exemptions from a state obligation to provide equal facilities. In *McCabe* Hughes persuaded a majority to avoid finding such exemptions, his success had long-term consequences even though the immediate consequences of *McCabe* were not great. At a minimum the legal principle was preserved, the state was obliged to provide equal facilities and services where it otherwise mandated racial separation. That principle eventually had profound consequences with regard to the long-term struggle against state-mandated segregation. If the state, for whatever reason, was unable to provide equal facilities for blacks it had no choice, under the Constitution, but to allow black access to existing facilities. The implications of the *McCabe* doctrine were realized in *Gaines* and set the Court on the doctrinal road to *Brown*.

The encomiums showered on Hughes reflected the widespread view that a major figure was departing the stage. He had contributed enormously to the Republic in many ways, yet the true meaning of some of those contributions as regards race and rights was to await the unfolding of future events.

In June, 1941, Roosevelt nominated two new justices. James Clark McReynolds had retired in February of 1941, two days short of his seventy-ninth birthday. Never a popular or congenial figure, he had become increasingly isolated and bitter in his final years on the Court. The *New York Times* captured the tone of his final days: "In delivering minority opinions Justice McReynolds frequently departed from the written opinion to express his sentiments in virulent, sarcastic words. According to the custom of the court, no stenographic record was made of his remarks."[5] In subsequent years no member of the Court would so openly and unashamedly put his racial animus on display.

McReynolds was replaced by James Byrnes. A South Carolinian by birth, Byrnes had risen from humble circumstances. He had worked as a reporter and a court stenographer and had studied law on his own. Entering politics just before the start of World War I he had risen through Democratic Party ranks to the Senate and had been a staunch defender of the New Deal. Although there was little reason for black optimism with his nomination, it was not always possible to discern what a man might do once elevated to the Court and freed of the immediate pressure of political survival. Hugo Black had not turned out to be a McReynolds. Politics intervened rather quickly however.

In 1942 Roosevelt importuned Byrnes to resign and assume a key administrative post as the nation mobilized to fight the war. In his one year on the Court Byrnes did not have much occasion to speak to race and rights. In 1951 he was elected governor of South Carolina and a few years later assumed a leading role in the South's bitter and brutal struggle to avoid the *Brown* holding. Had he remained on the Court he almost certainly would have fought tenaciously against finding legal segregation unconstitutional.

Robert Jackson, a worldly, sophisticated man with a complicated mind, was nominated to replace Hughes. Jackson's tenure on the Court extended through *Brown*. He was stricken with a heart attack as *Brown* was being debated by his colleagues and that, along with Earl Warren's simple but masterful draft of a majority holding, perhaps, deterred him from writing a concurring opinion asserting that the Court had acted correctly, wisely, and justly in outlawing school segregation even though there was not a strong basis for doing so in terms of conventional legal analysis. Such a holding would have further complicated the enormously difficult issue of how to secure compliance with a decision outlawing school segregation.

Jackson had worked with Roosevelt when Roosevelt served as assistant secretary of the Navy during the Wilson administration, and had campaigned for him when he made his political comeback after having been stricken with polio, and later joined the administration when Roosevelt became president. His career had not involved him in issues bearing on race and rights, but at the time of his nomination he was serving as solicitor general and his office had filed a memorandum with the Supreme Court in support of Arthur Mitchell and against the judgment of the district court dismissing Mitchell's complaint. He seems also to have been a man with a strong and unbending ethical sense, this leading him to come into bitter, prolonged, and public conflict with Hugo Black over Black's alleged conflict of interest in a case which came before the Court.

It was, perhaps also, the sense of Jackson as a man of impeccable principle and moral stature which led to his being selected as the chief United States prosecutor of the major Nazi war criminals at the Nuremberg trials. The experience of those trials confronted

Jackson with the ultimate consequences of organizing society around the principle of racial superiority. It would be extraordinary had the experience played no role in his view of the cases challenging America's racial hierarchy he confronted upon his return to the Court.

In a move eventually having relevance for race and rights, Roosevelt nominated Harlan Fiske Stone to succeed Hughes as chief justice. A veteran of sixteen tumultuous years on the Court, Stone had seen it go through at least two major transformations. He had been nominated to the bench by Calvin Coolidge in January, 1925, following a distinguished career as Dean of Columbia Law School and head of Sullivan and Cromwell's litigation department. A year earlier Coolidge had asked him to assume the post of Attorney General and head the justice department in the wake of the Harding administration scandals.

Throughout his first ten years on the Court conservative justices dominated the discussion and prevailed in most of the cases. In the 1920s, during William Howard Taft's tenure as chief justice, the Court's hostility to efforts to use law as an instrument to meliorate the condition of workers and the poor had been in accord with the values and policies of the Coolidge and Hoover administrations and was consistent with a generally conservative national mood. The collapse of the economy in 1929, the onset of the depression, and the rising tide of unemployment, mortgage foreclosures, homelessness, bank failures, and business closings brought public support for massive intervention at the federal level to meliorate the condition of the dispossessed via new rules and regulations setting minimum wages, better working conditions, and enhancing the right to organize.

The Court's continuing hostility to the use of government as an instrument for social and economic reform threatened New Deal policy and brought on the court-packing crisis. Stone had remained something of a moderate throughout his first decade on the bench, bringing him increasingly into conflict with McReynolds, Pierce Butler, Sutherland, and Van Devanter as their opposition to New Deal legislation seemed to stifle development of a national response to an overwhelming national crisis.

With the retirement of conservatives from the bench and the waning of the constitutional crisis occasioned by the court-packing scheme, Stone emerged as one of Roosevelt's favorite Republicans. When Hughes stepped down he became only the second chief justice to be nominated by a president of the other party, Edward Douglass White having been the first. As had been the case with White, Stone also assumed office at a crucial time in terms of race and rights. The issues that had driven the Court's agenda for a decade seemed to have been resolved. Federalism had been redefined by the Court such as to allow for an enormously expanded federal role in both regulating the economy and setting a floor below which no citizen was to be allowed to fall. The country was on the verge of war and the war years were to generate a new set of issues related to civil liberties and civil rights.

The War Years

As Byrnes and Jackson took their seats on the high Court in the Fall of 1941 American involvement in the war was three months away. The docket was clear of cases dealing with race and rights, but the war itself was to confront the Court with the question of the meaning of race in a nation combating the racial barbarism of its enemies. Irrespective of the specific legal issues at stake, the war cases posed questions about the moral integrity of the nation in maintaining a legally sanctioned system of racial subordination.

Three factors formed a backdrop against which the Court wrestled with the race cases coming before it during the war. First, the war against the Third Reich posed a moral challenge to the nation's racial status quo as well as a threat to national survival. In stark terms, Nazism gave racism a bad name. On the one hand, national propaganda assailed the Nazi menace for the racial abuse and torment it visited on conquered peoples, but on the other hand, the United States fielded an army segregated along racial lines for reasons akin in spirit to Nazism's racial mania. The moral claims advanced for pressing the struggle against Hitler made it increasingly difficult to take for granted or avoid confronting the moral perversion present in the nation's own system of racial hierarchy.

In addition, considerations of race played a complicated role in the war in the Pacific. It was not lost on segments of the nation's black population that the Japanese were a nonwhite people making a claim to freeing other nonwhite Asians from colonialism's shackles as they drove the British, French, Dutch, and Americans out of long-held domains and moved to establish what they referred to as the Greater East-Asia Co-Prosperity Sphere. Nor was the nonwhite status of the Japanese lost on the nation's white population. Japanese residents in the United States were regarded as a menace more so than persons of German or Italian descent. That suspicion yielded internment, which eventually yielded the *Koramatsu* case, occasioning the Supreme Court's first articulation of a judicial suspicion of race-based laws.

The third factor forming a backdrop against which the Court addressed race cases was the war at home involving race. In the second year of United States involvement in the global struggle the stresses imposed by the contradiction between an egalitarian ethic and racist practice at home generated escalating social conflict. On June 1, 1943, a conference of Catholic priests serving black parishes passed a resolution calling on President Roosevelt to ensure equal treatment for black servicemen, citing the racial "prejudice so evident at Camp Stewart, Georgia and Drew Field, Florida."[6] On June 10, black soldiers at Camp Stewart rioted in protest of the conditions they faced.

On June 16, marshal law was declared in Beaumont, Texas, because of "violence between Negroes and whites which caused one fatality, injured at least eleven persons, disrupted numerous businesses and virtually shutdown a shipyard."[7] On the same day in Chester, Pennsylvania, "Five Negroe workmen were shot . . . in a clash with guards in Yard No. 4 of the Sun Shipbuilding and Dry Dock Company."[8] And on June 22, Roosevelt ordered federal troops to take control of Detroit in the wake of massive race rioting.[9]

The contradiction between national ethic and habitual practice, accentuated by the moral dimension of the war against Hitlerism, yielded a set of cases which began to undermine both the legal foundation of segregation and its moral legitimacy. By 1943 and 1944 cases that had begun in a more complacent time as regards racial subordination had begun to appear on the Court's docket.

Smith v. Allwright

Voting is about power. The South's struggle to deny blacks the power of the vote had been long and tenacious. By the 1920s violence had given way to custom. And when custom was challenged in court, legal maneuver became the preferred means for sustaining a racial monopoly on access to the ballot box.

The South advanced a single basic argument with multiple, infinite variations in defending the exclusion of blacks from the political process. The Democratic Party was a private organization and as such was not constrained by the language of the Fourteenth Amendment with regard to "equal protection." A private club could select its members on a racial basis without implicating the Constitution insofar as the Fourteenth Amendment spoke only to state action and not to the acts of private entities. If the Democratic Party chose to exclude blacks from its ranks no state action was involved and, hence, there was no constitutional issue.

After two defeats the South appeared finally to have persuaded a majority of the Court to accept its definition of the situation in *Grovey v. Townsend,* decided in 1935.[10] Thus, when Lonnie Smith was turned away from the Harris County polling place on July 27, 1940, as he sought to vote in the Texas Democratic Party primary his prospects for success in court were not bright. Both the district court and the circuit court of appeals denied his five-thousand-dollar claim for civil damages on the basis of *Grovey v. Townsend.* But by the time the case reached the Supreme Court the country was deep in the struggle against the Axis powers.

Stanley Reed of Kentucky read the majority holding. Clearly, the claim that the Democratic Party was a private entity was a fiction. It was true that prior Supreme Court holdings had brought Texas to this strained and implausible claim, but it was a fiction nevertheless. The holding briefly reviewed the tortured history of the issue. Twenty years earlier Texas had by law barred blacks from participating in Democratic primaries. When this was deemed state action in violation of the equal protection clause of the Fourteenth Amendment in *Nixon v. Herndon,* Texas delegated the authority to bar blacks to the party's state executive committee. This evasion fell in *Nixon v. Condon,* the executive committee being deemed merely an agent of the state; whereupon continued black exclusion was defended on the grounds of having been yielded by a resolution passed at the state party convention, a gathering of private individuals not acting on state authority. This claim had survived constitutional challenge in *Grovey v. Townsend.*

Reed turned to a holding that had followed *Grovey* in terms of precedent for overruling that case. A few terms earlier the Court had held that primaries involving federal offices are an integral part of the election process for purposes of upholding a claim that federal fraud statutes applied in terms of chicanery at that stage. *Classic v. United States* now served as a basis for overruling *Grovey.* Lonnie Smith had grounds for going forward with his civil suit.[11]

Under the holding of *Grovey,* exclusion from the political

process was a wrong experienced by blacks without the possibility of legal redress. The effect of the new holding was not necessarily to expand black political participation, rather it avoided giving legal sanction to the denial of black participation and provided grounds for seeking legal redress. And in the racially volatile context of the war it avoided the contradiction which would have been occasioned by exacting blood sacrifice from a population in the name of humanistic values while providing legal sanction for the exclusion of that population from the most of fundamental political rights.

The selection of justices to read an opinion was sometimes governed by political considerations. A Southern justice might read a holding uncongenial to Southern conservatives in the hope of lending it greater legitimacy. In those terms Stanley Reed represented both the vision and the limitations of the moderate South. He was not a hardened bigot in the James Clark McReynolds mold. He seems to have been of a class that abhorred violence and brutality directed at blacks or crude and abusive interpersonal treatment. On the other hand, he seems also to have had a visceral reaction against anything that spoke of close interpersonal interaction between black and white on equal terms. Ten years later his limitations would compromise and threaten the outcome of *Brown*.

In the first year after the war he would be joined on the Court by Fred Vinson, a fellow Southerner of similar instinct. Their vacillation, doubt, and seemingly visceral reaction against close black-white interaction, possibly on equal terms, posed the cases grouped under *Brown* with an uncertain fate.

In the war years, however, the primary issues confronting the Court continued to relate to efforts to give racial exclusion the imprimatur of legal sanction. Again context put the issues into sharp relief.

Race and the Railroad Unions

Railroads have always occupied a prominent place in the American imagination. The train whistle in the night has been a symbol of the urge to move on, to find a new life and shape a new self. Railroads have also been crucial in welding a new and disparate nation together, in giving it a sense of being one place, one country, a set of hopes, possibilities, and dreams. But railroads have also been part of a number of grim American realities. As the tracks were laid West in the last half of the nineteenth century, towns not on a railroad line faced the possibility of death. In response the railroad companies often auctioned off a spur to a town making the highest bid, the winner sometimes coming to the brink of bankruptcy and sometimes finding that a line had been lain through a rival town in any event. Company owners charged farmers, ranchers, and mine owners extortionate rates to take their products to market, and sold investors stock at inflated prices. As would be expected, they also exploited labor to the fullest extent allowed by the law and public sentiment.

The bitter history of conflict between labor and management over the first century of the development of the railroad industry in the United States was punctuated by periods of convulsive violence and sharp betrayal, none worse than the period ushered in in July, 1877. An effort by the Baltimore and Ohio Railroad and other companies to further reduce wages already barely at a subsistence level set off a nationwide wave of strikes, violence, and the wrecking of railroad property. President Hayes mobilized federal troops and deployed them to key locales. The class nature of the conflict was made stark in some places by the use of militias such as Pennsylvania's Easton Greys, a gentlemen's regiment made up of the sons of privileged families. The black poet Albery Whitman penned a piece calling upon the owning class to "heed poor honest labor's call."[12]

Yet if capital did not heed labor's call neither did white labor heed any interest it shared with black labor. The white workers' struggle with management and with law as an instrument wielded by the powerful, via statutes criminalizing strikes and efforts to organize, rarely translated into an effort to make common cause with black labor, ceding to management the tactical advantage thereby of being able, on occasion, to use black labor to break strikes by white workers.

The railroad unions were more hostile to black interests than most. To the extent that their history of strife with owners had translated into a class identity, that identity was limited by considerations of race. Blacks were not part of their community of interest as workers. Their hostility to blacks went beyond mere exclusion from union membership to efforts to drive black workers from those niches to which they had clung. These efforts became part of an unfolding and expanding Supreme Court docket addressing the implications of the new federalism and the expansion of federal authority for issues of race and rights.

In mid-November, 1944, shortly after Franklin Roosevelt had been reelected for a fourth term, the Court heard oral argument in two cases bearing on unions and black workers, *Steele v. Louisville & Nashville Railroad* and *Tunstall v. Brotherhood.* The Railway Labor Act had empowered particular unions to act as the exclusive bargaining agents of given classes of railway workers, with majority consent. One of the purposes of the act had been to prevent the railroads from establishing sham "company unions ." Management was constrained under penalty of law to negotiate with the entity chosen by the majority of workers as their representative. In other words, the act was intended to strengthen the hand of labor in dealing with management.

On March 28, 1940, officers of the Brotherhood of Locomotive Firemen and Engineers had notified management of the Louisville and Nashville railroad and twenty other lines, operating principally in the South, of their desire to amend the existing collective bargaining agreement in such a way as to eventually eliminate all black firemen. The scheme involved extending and writing into the contract existing exclusionary practices. By custom, engineer positions were limited to white men and the engineer position was achieved by promotion from the rank of firemen. In other words, there was a ceiling on blacks at the level of firemen. Under the scheme the railroads would have been constrained to employ only "promotable" men as firemen, or, in other words, only white men. Only promotable men would be assigned to new runs or hired to fill existing jobs as they became vacant. On February 18 and May 12, 1941, the Brotherhood initiated agreements further restricting the rights of black firemen, failing in all instances to give the black firemen notice or an opportunity to be heard.

Black workers did not become aware of the scheme until it was put into effect. In April, 1941, pursuant to rerouting and mileage reductions, the railroad reorganized its assignment of firemen and in accord with the new collective bargaining agreement filled new and reallocated openings with whites having less seniority than black workers, now bumped back to local and less remunerative jobs.

In January, 1942, the black workers sought redress in court, asking for an injunction against enforcement of the agreement and for damages. Failing at the state level, they entered the federal system and on November 14, 1944, argued before the Supreme Court as *Steele v. Railroad.*

The union and the railroads argued, in essence, that the Railroad Act neither prohibited the union from bargaining to restrict the rights of black workers nor imposed an affirmative duty that they negotiate the same terms for those workers as they had for white workers. Four weeks after oral argument Harlan Fiske Stone delivered the holding of the majority, going swiftly to the basic issues.

The unions' argument was constitutionally insupportable. The union enjoyed powers no greater than those conferred on it by Congress via the Railroad Act. Congress cannot confer powers that it does not have. Congress itself would have been sorely pressed by the language of the Fourteenth Amendment were it to seek to write a law stating that black workers could be downgraded or terminated so that white workers could be hired and promoted. Hence, it could confer no such power on the union.

The language closely tracked a 1944 hand-written memo in William O. Douglas's papers: "There are certainly no more invidious discriminations than those based on race. We cannot believe that Congress gave authority to a bargaining agent to do what Congress itself is forbidden by the Constitution to do."[13]

The Alabama court's approach failed in terms of any reasonable understanding of statutory construction. A court cannot reasonably conclude that what is not specifically prohibited is allowed, without reaching absurd conclusions. In the facts of the present case, the lower court's approach would leave black workers with no alternative but to strike or employ some other type of disruption of train service, whereas one of the purposes of the Act had been to deter the interruption of commerce by providing workers with institutional means for pursuing their interests. *Tunstall v. Brotherhood* presented similar facts and was decided in a similar fashion.[14]

In his concurrent opinion Frank Murphy used unusually strong language in condemning the union: "No statutory interpretation can erase this ugly example of economic cruelty against colored citizens of the United States. Nothing can destroy the fact that the accident of birth has been used as the basis to abuse individual rights by an organization purporting to act in conformity with its Congressional mandate."

In the language occasionally but not frequently used, there seemed to be a sense of the human dimension of the outrage masked by the measured language of legal argument.

Korematsu: Race Is Special

On the same day that *Tunstall* and *Steele* were handed down, the Court also handed down its holding in *Korematsu*, a challenge ultimately to Franklin Roosevelt's Executive Order 9066 authorizing the designation of military zones "from which any or all persons may be excluded," which had served as the legal basis for the removal of the Japanese from the West Coast.

The executive order had been translated into federal statute by Congress on March 21, 1942, and the Congressional Act had in turn yielded Exclusion Order 34, setting forth the specifics of removal, when and where. The only known instances of attempted sabotage in the continental United States during the war involved persons of European descent. Midway through the war a Nazi U Boat had landed a group of saboteurs off the coast of Long Island; made up of German nationals and Germans reared in the United States but recruited to the Nazi cause, they were quickly apprehended and executed.[15] After the war a naturalized American citizen of Dutch descent was tried for collaboration with Italian naval intelligence.[16]

Inevitably, removal brought Court challenges and eventually brought the Supreme Court face to face with another race-based action done under cover of law. Despite its outcome the Court began to carve out race as a special area of concern, Murphy's passion in his concurrent opinion in *Steele* translating in more muted tones into judicial language.

Fred Korematsu was, at best, a reluctant hero. As implemented, the evacuation order pertained only to persons of Japanese descent, there being no opportunity for the effected parties to demonstrate loyalty or refute any suspicion of disloyalty. To be Japanese was to be suspect, and to refuse removal was to violate the law. Inevitably, the law was challenged as a matter of principle by some of the parties subject to its harsh terms. Minoru Yasui and Gordon Hirabiyashi, acting independent of each other, subjected themselves to arrest for purposes of challenging the constitutional particulars of the law.

By contrast, initially Korematsu had not been a prisoner of conscience. Unlike Yasui and Hirabiyashi, he was neither educated nor a professional and had not been raised in an environment stressing commitment to matters of principle. He was a high school graduate and a welder who by coincidence, a few weeks before the evacuation order had gone to a quack doctor seeking plastic surgery to make himself look less oriental. Seeking to persuade a young woman of Italian-American descent to elope with him to the Midwest, he had not turned himself in, trusting that the crude surgery on his nose and eyelids would save him from apprehension.

On May 16, 1942, he was stopped on the street in San Leandro, California, and was soon in jail facing a charge of having violated the order pertaining to him as a person of Japanese descent to turn himself in. Other Japanese apprehended under the law had been approached with an offer of help by the American Civil Liberties Union, but had refused to press a case.[17]

Korematsu seemed to be an unlikely prospect. His motive for violating the law had been personal; he was hoping to run away with his girlfriend. He had no history of commitment to political struggle. And, in any event, there was little enthusiasm in the camps for legal challenge, many feeling that it was best to refrain from appearing to be hostile to the government. Nevertheless, when approached Korematsu expressed interest in fighting his case. He was a law-abiding citizen. he knew no other country. He felt the law was unfair. His conviction in federal district court set the case on the road to the United States Supreme Court.

Argued in October, 1944, the case caused bitter dissension within the Court. Black and a tenuous majority favored resolving *Korematsu* as they had *Hirabiyashi* earlier. Having deliberately violated the curfew order, which preceded more sweeping evacuation orders, Hirabiyahsi had argued that the president and Congress had exceeded their authority under the Constitution in limiting the liberty of citizens without just cause. The government had argued that its actions were consistent with its obligation to protect the nation in times of peril and that the only question was whether the acts taken toward that end were reasonable. The Court had accepted the government's basic argument, indicating reluctance to substitute its judgment for that of General DeWitt and other military authorities on the scene charged with implementing an order intended to promote national security.[18]

Basically the same defense had been offered to Fred Korematsu's challenge to detention and removal, but to a more skeptical audience. Frank Murphy, Owen Roberts, and Robert Jackson would have none of it. A wavering chief justice assigned the opinion to Black, and Black sought as he circulated his various drafts to sustain an unenthusiastic majority in support of the government in the face of three problems. *Korematsu* challenged removal from one's home under the exclusion aspects of the order; whereas, *Hirabayashi*, having gone to court earlier, had challenged the preliminary and less onerous curfew law. Second, even granting expanded governmental authority in times of crisis, the argument that mass removal met a test of reasonableness under the circumstances as they existed seemed very strained. And third, there was no escaping the racial targeting attending implementation of the law. In the end Black and the majority fell back on a the need for judicial deference in the face of decisions of the military, which might have seemed reasonable at the time they were taken.[19]

The dissenters balked given that General Dewitt's *Final Report* on the actions taken in 1942 seemed to say that the Japanese were targeted because they were an "alien race" given to foreign and mysterious practices. The racial targeting drew bitter comments from Owen Roberts. Korematsu was convicted ". . . solely because of his ancestry, without evidence of inquiry concerning his loyalty and good disposition." Frank Murphy argued that the assumption of "racial guilt" belied any argument that the exclusion and removal met a test of reasonableness. And Jackson contended that the government's policy was contrary to the fundamental American assumption that guilt was personal and nor heritable.[20]

Attempting to address the concerns of the dissenters and of some of the majority, Black confronted the racial issue in his final draft: "It should be noted, to begin with, that all legal restrictions which curtail the civil rights of a single racial group are immediately suspect."[21] Whatever this language might have meant to lay persons, it carried great import in terms of legal argument and burden of persuasion. If adhered to by the Court, racial laws were to be subjected to strict scrutiny. The burden would be on the state to prove that such laws served a compelling state interest.

The majority had not itself held to this test in upholding the government's acts relative to Korematsu but they had articulated a standard by which the defense of race-based laws might be made more difficult. Race was special. It could not be presumed that racial distinctions in law were benign.

The Postwar Years

Harlan Fiske Stone died in the spring of 1946. His tenure as chief justice during the war years had seen the Court articulate an important doctrine, but the key challenges to segregation as legal principle lay ahead. Under Stone the Court had articulated a doctrine placing limits on the discriminatory practices of entities deriving their power or authority from either the executive or legislative branches of the federal government. Railroad unions could not connive against the interest of black workers without violating the Railway Act. Railroad companies could not deprive black passengers of equal accommodations on grounds of low demand without violating their federal charter. National emergency might justify policies otherwise violative of citizen rights but, in principle, where the policy or any law singled out a particular race the government bore a heavy burden of persuasion.

The fundamental legal doctrines supporting segregation retained their validity however. Hughes had pressed the Court over the years to take seriously the "equal" dimension of the separate-but-equal doctrine, but the implicit question in the Hughes formulation had not yet been posed—might it be that "separate" was inherently unequal where mandated on racial grounds, thereby negating the validity of the doctrine? Neither had the Court addressed a rather limited conception of "government" in terms of the Fourteenth Amendment's mandate that states not deny their citizens the equal protection of the law. To what extent was government an accomplice in private acts of racial discrimination occurring in settings or processes subject to government oversight, licensing, or approval?

With the death of Stone the composition of the Court again became an issue. The selection of Stone's successor was made difficult for Truman by feuding on the Court. A bitter public dispute had developed between Robert Jackson and Hugo Black over Jackson's belief that Black ought to have recused himself in a case where Jackson believed he had a conflict of interest. Word reached the president that there would be one and possibly two resignations were Jackson named chief justice.

Forced to look outside the Court, Truman settled on Frederick Moore Vinson, an unknown quantity in terms of race and rights. He had come from modest circumstances, his father having been a small-town jailer in Kentucky. He was a bright fellow, had done very well in the small college he attended, and had later obtained a law degree. As a member of Congress during the worst days of the depression he had stood solidly behind Franklin Roosevelt and the New Deal and had been rewarded with a seat on the District of Columbia Court of Appeals, often regarded as a stepping stone to the Supreme Court. The war years saw him diverted to important administrative posts and then to a position in Truman's cabinet as Secretary of the Treasury. He seemed to be a choice acceptable to the various factions on the Court and was eventually sworn in on the eve of what was to be the most important period in the Court's history as regards race and rights since the Reconstruction era.

Portrayed at the time as a decisive figure, capable of "walking into the middle of a fight and forcing a settlement," Vinson was to prove increasingly indecisive as cases posing ever greater challenge to the fundamental premises of legal segregation came before the Court.[22] In the end, his incapacity to lead became a major obstacle to moving forward on *Brown* and its companion school segregation cases.

In the five years since Hughes had retired the Court had fractured. Ideological divisions and personal enmities had come to the fore and Stone had been too weak a leader to quell them or even sustain a facade of civility. Although race and rights were by no means at the center of the issues dividing the Court, the justices brought different sensibilities to the issue. Frank Murphy and Robert Jackson seemed to be made angry by the indignities and abuses attending institutionalized racial discrimination, whereas Felix Frankfurter, ever conscious of being a member of an exposed and vulnerable minority group, supported the NAACP and other progressive groups but did not want to be perceived publicly as a left-wing ideologue in a climate when Jews were seen by elements of the public as purveyors of dangerous and subversive doctrines.

In the years since his appointment Hugo Black had surprised his critics by taking a stand against the more egregious abuses of blacks done under cover of law. He had written the holding setting aside the conviction of four blacks put in the shadow of the electric chair by proceedings constituting a legal lynching and had joined Hughes in finding that separate must give way to access where the state fails to provide equal facilities for blacks. He had not been asked however to repudiate the very doctrine of separate but equal.

Given the challenges likely to be posed in the cases certain to come before the Court in the postwar years, the Court's composition became vitally important. A year earlier Truman had made his first appointment, Harold Burton. Under pressure from some quarters to appoint a Republican and unsure of himself as a president who had come to office by the accident of Roosevelt's death, Truman had nominated Harold Burton, a Republican Senator who as mayor of Cleveland had been a progressive on social welfare policy. His tenure was to extend through *Brown* but in his first years on the bench he presented a mixed picture as regards his judicial stance on matters of race and rights, but was later to become a key player.

Between the end of the war and the beginning of the slow judicial revolution leading to *Brown* the Court began to assume a stance toward race and the law which both suggested the limits to which it was willing to go and the thinking of the particular justices. In the course of doing so they began to reverse some of the holdings of Joseph Bradley and his brethren. The formalist rationalizations for the more egregious abuses to dignity were repudiated and the cases that articulated those rationalizations reversed.

In moving as it did, the Court was both in tune with popular thinking and yet not in tune. The ideological dimensions of World War II and the struggle against Nazism generated popular repudiation of racism at the abstract level, yet there was no popular demand that any particular segregationist practice be abolished. The Court however was constrained to deal with the particular and in doing so began to push back the reach of segregation in the public arena. Certain public forms of racial status degradation peripheral to the everyday lives or needs of people were to be denied the sanction of law, while the institution of segregation itself was not undermined.

The four-year period between the end of the war and *Sweatt*, which set the Court directly on the road to *Brown*, was also the finest hour of the moderate Southerner as Supreme Court justice. Fred Vinson and Stanley Reed seemed able to repudiate the more gratuitous forms of racial stratification in the public sector, but later pulled back as the school cases challenged the more fundamental assumptions of segregation.

The cases between the end of the war and *Sweatt* reveal a Court whose holdings began in a slow and cumulative sense to weaken the legal foundations of segregation at the margins and to erode the consensus in support of it in terms of particulars. Three cases marked that passage and defined the stance of the justices.

In early June, 1946, as the session was coming to an end, the Court handed down its decision in *Morgan v. Virginia*. Irene Morgan had boarded a bus in Glouster County, Virginia, headed for Baltimore via Washington, D.C., but never reached her destination. Pursuant to Virginia law the bus driver had asked her to give up her seat as the bus filled and move to a seat further back. When she refused she was arrested, taken off the bus, and eventually fined ten dollars.[23]

Stanley Reed authored the Court's decision. As the decision was interpreted at the time, the Court was not speaking to the matter of racial equality but, rather, whether the Virginia law infringed on the authority of Congress to regulate interstate commerce. The law in operation did or could have bizarre consequences, according to Reed. A black passenger riding in Virginia might have to change seats several times as the racial composition of the passengers changed, but upon arrival in Washington, D.C., could occupy any vacant seat. Virginia's contention that mandated racial separation promoted racial peace, had to give way to the argument that pursuit of such an objective entailed enforcement of a law tending to pose a burden on interstate commerce. Insofar as the law in question did, it and similar statutes, were invalid.

Harold Burton dissented. There was no factual evidence supporting the contention that the law burdened interstate commerce in any degree and hence no real counter to Virginia's rationale for the statute related to the prevention of racial friction. The justice was willing to accommodate the South's *Plessy*-based rationale for legal segregation.[24] Eight years later he would be asked to consider the same argument in *Brown*. But the holding reflected the inclination of a majority of the Court to strip away peripheral affronts to racial dignity.

Within months, in a recapitulation of the scenario whereby the Bradley Court eighty years earlier had lent the Court's imprimatur to the impulse to exclude on racial grounds, they were asked to again consider the commerce clause argument in a racial context. If state laws mandating segregation on public carriers going beyond state borders violated the commerce clause did it not follow that laws prohibiting such segregation also violated the commerce clause?

Bob-Lo and a Day in the Country

It is an elementary principle of American federalism that a state may provide more rights to its citizens than is required by the Constitution as interpreted by the Supreme Court but it cannot provide fewer rights. Consistent with this principle, following the Court's decision in the *Civil Rights Cases of 1883* stating that Congress had no authority under the Constitution to limit the decisions of business people with regard to whom they would serve and who they would not serve insofar as their actions were not those of the state, a number of states in the North and Midwest moved to pass public accommodation laws. Honored more in the breach than in the observance in many places, they nevertheless remained on the books and provided the legal basis at the state and local level for challenges to the denial of services or access on racial grounds. A series of events began to unfold in Michigan in 1945 leading the

Supreme Court two years later to determine the constitutionality of one such law, the outcome having implication for similar laws in other states.

Sarah Elizabeth Ray worked for the Detroit Ordinance Department and also took a class offered under the auspices of the Department at Commerce High School. In the spring of 1945 the city was still in the process of trying to recover from a bloody race riot spawned in part by the migration to the city of large numbers of Southern whites, drawn by the prospect of work in the automobile and defense industries. At the same time the CIO, emerging from years of bitter and often violent conflict with management in the automobile industry, had staked out a progressive position on matters of race, in contrast to the older AF of L. By and large it fought for the interests of workers black and white, avoiding the efforts of other unions to either exclude blacks from membership or drive them from the workforce in favor of whites. The city and the state presented a complicated profile as regards race and rights.There were elements and practices which mirrored the rigid segregation of the deep South, but there were also organizations, workforce policies, and major political players who were very progressive by the standards of the time. Not the least among the elements in the complicated picture presented by the state and the city was the existence on the books of a statute dating from 1885 but amended as recently as 1937 prohibiting racial discrimination in the operation of public accommodations.

In June, 1945, as the school year ended, Sarah Ray's class planned a day trip, an excursion from Detroit to Bois Blanc Island, an amusement park fifteen miles upriver from the city, geographically part of the Province of Ontario, Canada. Two steamships owned by the Bob-Lo Excursion Company ferried passengers round trip between Detroit and the island, the first boat departing early in the morning. And hence, on the morning of June 21, students from the Commerce High class congregated on the dock in anticipation of a day at the fair. Collecting the eighty-five-cent fare from each girl, the teacher bought tickets, distributed them, and accompanied the group aboard the boat. Shortly after the young women had checked their coats and gone to the upper deck to relax, two men appeared.

Sarah Ray would not be allowed to accompany the group. Company policy barred people who were boisterous, rough, or rowdy and "colored people." Bob-Lo was a private concern and it did not have to serve coloreds if it did not want to. Ray would have to leave the boat. The young woman protested and at first refused to leave, but when it appeared that she would be forcibly ejected she went ashore. An offer to refund her money was refused and a promise to seek redress tendered to the two men.

Redress came in the form of criminal prosecution in Detroit's Recorder's Court under Michigan Statutes 146 and 147. The first statute provided a right of "full and equal accommodations" relative to inns, hotels, restaurants, public conveyances, and other public accommodations subject only to those conditions and limitations "applicable alike, to all citizens." The second made violation 147 a misdemeanor and also created a civil cause of action.

There had been no question of Sarah Ray being boisterous, rowdy, or disorderly and hence there was no question but that Bob-Lo was liable. The company waived a jury trial and was convicted at a bench trial and ordered to pay a fine of twenty-five dollars. Their appeal to the Michigan Supreme Court was motivated by the issue of racial exclusion rather than the small financial liability incurred by having thrown Sarah Ray off their boat on a fine June morning.

But the Michigan Supreme Court affirmed the lower court's judgment, leading Bob-Lo to then seek relief from the United State's Supreme Court, contending that the Michigan statute constituted a usurpation by the state of power reserved to Congress by the Constitution to regulate the conditions of foreign and interstate commerce. Indeed, Bob-Lo sought to persuade the Court that two cases widely separated in time, intent, and consequence ought to control its decision. In *Hall v. De Cuir* six decades earlier, the Supreme Court had held that a Louisiana statute prohibiting segration on steamboats moving between states was unconstitutional. A few years earlier in *Morgan v. Virginia* it had struck down a Virginia statute mandating racial segregation on interstate motor buses. Whatever the intent, state law could not command relative to race and travel, Bob-Lo contended, without intruding on an area left to Congress.

Vaguely softening racial sentiment but hardened racial practice characterized the world within which the Court addressed the new race cases. In Washington, D.C., black ticket holders were refused admission to George Washington University's Lisner Hall during Ingrid Bergman's two week run in Maxwell Anderson's "Joan of Lorraine." Following picketing, the school's board of trustees voted to lift racial restriction where the hall was rented for public functions. Given that the new policy limited future rentals to functions of a "general educational nature" the capital was still left with a situation in which there was no commercial theater that would admit blacks.[25]

Wiley Routledge delivered the holding in *Bob-Lo*. The cases Bob-Lo relied upon were distinguished on their facts. Neither involved the complete exclusion of blacks from the opportunity to travel but rather their isolation once on a carrier. And both involved interstate commerce in some more meaningful sense of the term rather than an essentially local business which happened to have one terminus in Canada. And at the end of the holding there was a restatement of the Michigan Supreme Court's rejection of the formalist element in the Bob-Lo argument. The practical consequence of upholding the constitutionality of the Michigan statute would be that Bob-Lo would have to carry black passengers and it was impossible to discern how that fact alone would impose an undue burden on foreign commerce.[26]

Morgan and *Bob-Lo* involved undoing or redefining the work of previous courts touching on the public sector. A third holding seemed to strike more at the sentiment undergirding racial exclusion and offered more promise in terms of Chief Justice Fred Vinson than events were to establish he was inclined or able to fulfill.

Shelley v. Kraemer began in September, 1945, barely a month after the end of the war, when a black family, Ethel and J. D. Shelley and their children, moved into a new home on Labadie Avenue in St. Louis, Missouri. Within days they received a summons to appear in court. A white couple living nearby, Fern and Louis Kraemer, were seeking to evict them. A restrictive covenant going back to 1911 covered the property. Fern Kraemer's parents and a number of other white homeowners had signed an agreement barring ownership or occupancy of homes in the neighborhood by persons of the "Negro or Mongolian Race."[27]

Twenty years earlier, William Howard Taft's Supreme Court had affirmed the legitimacy of such agreements by holding in *Buckley v. Corrigan* that they were enforceable in court. They involved private parties rather than the state, and private parties were perfectly able to express racial preferences in their business dealings without implicating the Constitution. Hence, Ethel and J. D. Shelley were hauled before the bar of justice in 1945 to answer as to why they should not be put out of their newly acquired home.

The initial proceedings in Circuit Court were favorable to the Shelley's as Judge William Koerner held that the initial agreement had not been signed by all of the homeowners of the area and, hence, was not valid. In December, 1946, the Missouri Supreme Court reversed Koerner, holding that the agreement was valid relative to the property of those who had signed it and that under *Corrigan* it was legally enforceable in court.

Relying on briefs which stressed the destructive consequences for blacks of residential segregation, as well as more conventional legal arguments, the NAACP pressed the matter before the Supreme Court in January, 1948. Oral argument was offered before six justices, surmise being that the remaining three excused themselves as signatories to deeds or leases having restrictive covenants.

Five months after oral argument the unanimous holding came down, authored by Chief Justice Fred Vinson. There was nothing in the Constitution that prevented private citizens from entering into racially exclusive agreements. Indeed, that was the holding of *Corrigan*. This case presented a different question however. Does court enforcement of a racially exclusive agreement constitute state action? The answer, according to Vinson and his colleagues, was yes. Court enforcement of restrictive racial covenants constituted state action in violation of the Equal Protection clause of the Fourteenth Amendment and those terms of the Civil Rights Act of 1866 guaranteeing blacks the same right to contract as white citizens. Hence, the agreement that would have barred the Shelleys from purchasing their home was not illegal or unconstitutional, but the Kraemers could not use the courts as an instrument to try to enforce its terms.[28]

The holding was widely hailed in progressive and civil rights circles. In the summer of 1948 both the Court and Chief Justice Vinson seemed to offer great promise in the struggle to come. The postwar Court, building on the progressive record of the war Court, had avoided formalist rationalization for egregious racial abuse. It had also redefined the relationship between the public and the private such as to diminish the role of the lower courts as instruments for enforcing caste degradation.

They had not yet addressed the question of the constitutionality of legal segregation itself however. They were approaching the Rubicon and would soon be asked to cross it. It was essential to success that the Rubicon be crossed by them as a unit if it was to be crossed at all. But a complex of cross pressures and personal doubts about the wisdom or desirability of crossing the river was to make the journey extremely difficult, and at points unlikely.

Sweatt: The Slow Revolution

As a legal doctrine "separate but equal" rested on two premises. *Plessy* and its progeny had asserted that the maintenance of peace between the races was a legitimate state objective and that laws mandating racial separation were valid instruments for realizing that objective. In other words, segregation as policy had a rational foundation. The states were constrained, however, to afford blacks services and facilities equal in quality to those afforded whites in conformity with the mandate of the Fourteenth Amendment that no state might deny its citizens the equal protection of the laws.

Within months of *Plessy* the states began to fall short with regard to the equal dimension of the *Plessy* equation. *Cummings,* handed down three years after *Plessy,* seemed to narrow the scope of the state's obligation, placing the Supreme Court's imprimatur on state reluctance to adhere to the holding's plain meaning. Over the decades, from *McCabe* just before World War I to *Mitchell* just before World War II, the thrust of the black struggle in the courts had gone to challenging state failure to provide equal facilities for blacks.

In his two terms on the Supreme Court, Charles Evans Hughes had been receptive to this argument and had articulated a legal doctrine that was progressive in the context of the times. States and state-regulated enterprises were mandated by the language of the Fourteenth Amendment to afford blacks equality, and that mandate held even in the context of legal segregation irrespective of the fact that a state or state-regulated enterprise might find it economically burdensome to do so. In the face of the reluctance of some of his colleagues to accept the notion that the law meant what it said, it would have been idle for Hughes to have argued a more progressive line directly and openly challenging the *Plessy* formulation.

Inherent in the Hughes doctrine however was a question which would go ultimately to the viability of legal segregation as constitutionally acceptable doctrine. Were there circumstances under which separate facilities were irretrievably inferior, circumstances under which they could not be made "equal" by any conceivable means? By buying more books for black schools, or by providing more science labs or more teachers or providing nicer buildings? The answer to these questions rested finally with the Supreme Court as it confronted a series of cases growing out of the issues posed by the *Gaines* holding.

The ultimate objective of the NAACP was to end legal segregation. The chosen instrument was the court challenge. The specific issues confronted the Court with the prospect of promoting a slow revolution in American society. In the years after the Civil War it had played a decisive role in eroding the protections the law had afforded blacks and in creating a new system called "segregation." In the years after World War II it was confronted with cases challenging the premises on which that system rested. A number of cases had built toward *Sweatt* and the pivotal issues it posed relative to the constitutional validity of segregation.

As a gesture toward meeting its obligation under the law to provide blacks the equal benefits and protections of the law, Texas offered financial assistance to blacks seeking graduate or professional training outside the state in fields where no in-state program for blacks existed. The Committee on Scholarship Aid for Negro Residents of Texas Attending Graduate and Professional Schools Outside the State employed a formula by which the student was paid the "increased cost of tuition and travel necessary to secure graduate or professional instruction, not provided by a publicly supported institution for Negroes in Texas, in an out-of-State school."[29] Even this effort fell short however. Approximately $25,000 was appropriated for the 1945–1946 academic year, about $7,000 below what should have been appropriated to meet the projected need. But even an adequate appropriation might not have saved the state in the coming challenge.[30]

On February 26, 1946, Hemon Marion Sweatt, a young black man, applied to the University of Texas Law School, the only law school in the state. He met the residential and scholastic requirements but was rejected on the basis of state policy with regard to racial separation. As Lloyd Gaines had done a decade earlier, Sweatt turned to the law, asking a local court to issue a writ of *mandamus*, an order directing officers of the University of Texas to perform their public duty and admit him to the law school. In June the court found that Texas had failed in its duty to provide blacks with the opportunity to study law in the state at a public school, but stayed a final order for six months pending any effort Texas might make to meet it responsibilities.[31]

Guided by the holding in *Gaines* the court understood that the provision of an opportunity to study in another state did not meet the requirement of the Constitution as interpreted by the Supreme Court. Gaines had wanted to practice law in Missouri and the Supreme Court had said that the best place to prepare for such practice was the University of Missouri Law School rather than a law school in another state. Sweatt had indicated that he wished to pursue a career in law in Texas and hence it could be expected that were the matter to reach the Supreme Court and were the Court to follow its own recent precedent, it would hold that the best place to prepare was at a law school in Texas.

The Texas State legislature knew that Missouri had enacted legislation to establish a black law school at Lincoln University in that state at some unspecified time in the future, but had not demonstrated seriousness of purpose. Purportedly, the law school had not been established because there was not sufficient demand. But it was unlikely, of course, that there would be sufficient demand until there was a law school. In any event no money had been appropriated.

Seeking to learn from Missouri's missteps, the Texas legislature moved with dispatch in the six-month grace period granted by the court. On March 3, 1947, it passed a bill creating the State University of Texas for Negroes, which was to consist of a law school located in Austin and a graduate school at Prairie View. Appreciative of the legal risks posed by a transparently insincere effort to meet the requirement that separate be equal, more than $100,000 was appropriated for the creation of the new law school and an effort was made to establish that it would be indistinguishable from the University of Texas Law School in resources and facilities. More than 10,000 books were purchased in order to meet the standards of the American Bar Association and the American Association of Law Schools. In addition, students were to have access to the library of the Supreme Court of Texas: "Courses of Instruction were set up identical with those offered in the University of Texas School of Law, and the identical professors of the University of Texas were assigned to instruct said courses."[32]

In December the parties returned to Court for a hearing, Thurgood Marshall representing Sweatt, Attorney General Price Daniel speaking for Texas. Testimony was taken from more than twenty persons as Marshall argued, over Daniel's objection, that the issue was not whether Texas had made an effort to create a law school for blacks but whether there was any rational foundation for having separate schools in the first place.

The Court declined to engage the larger question in favor of focusing on the state's effort to create an equal school within a separate context. In the end they agreed with Texas that, "the School of Law of Texas State University for Negroes offers education in law equal to that offered by the University of Texas" and denied Sweatt's request for *mandamus*.[33]

Sweatt had been notified by letter of the establishment of Texas State University Law School for Negroes shortly after the action of the state legislature six months earlier, but had declined the offer of admission to what was then an institution that existed only on paper. By December, 1947, there was a building, a faculty, a library, and other blacks who had been admitted as the first class to this new law school. In declining admission Sweatt was now prepared to pose a more fundamental kind of challenge to the *Plessy* doctrine. Without question, the Texas Law School for Negroes was not the University of Texas Law School but it seemed to represent an effort to provide competent, professional legal education for blacks. But if it could never *be* the University of Texas Law School could it ever be equal? Sweatt's appeal went to the Texas Court of Appeals, which affirmed the decision of the trial court denying the writ of *mandamus*, whereupon Sweatt sought review by the United States Supreme Court.

In the months between the grant of certiorari and oral argument before the Court the implications of the case became increasingly clear to ever-widening constituencies on both sides of the issue. A hostile and defensive air came to characterize Price Daniel's approach to groups and people on the other side. In December, 1949, four months before scheduled oral argument he chastised the Federation Council of the Churches of Christ In America for seeking to file a Friend of the Court brief on behalf of Sweatt, indicating he would consent only if they acknowledged that many of the member denominations of the federation practiced racial segregation.[34] Three months later his aid Joe Greenhill declined a request by Arthur Goldberg, General Counsel of the CIO and future Supreme Court justice, to file an additional Friend of the Court Brief on behalf of Sweatt.[35] At the same time the attorneys general of eleven Southern states filed briefs in support of Texas.

The case was argued in early April, 1950, and a decision handed down in early June. Chief Justice Fred Vinson spoke for a unanimous Court and began by comparing the University of Texas Law School and the Texas Law School for Negroes. There were certainly differences.

The University of Texas Law School had 16 full-time faculty members, 850 students, and library of 65,000 volumes, while Texas State had 5 full-time teachers, 23 students, and a library with 16,500 volumes. The new school was not without strengths however. It had a practice court, a legal aid society, and one alumnus who had been admitted to the Texas bar. It was "apparently on the road to full accreditation." On balance, however, Texas State could not be said to be equal to the University of Texas in objective terms.

Had the Court stopped at that point there would have been at least the theoretical possibility that Texas, or states facing a similar challenge, could bridge the gap in quality with a greater infusion of money and personnel. There would have been some possibility of making things "right" in equal protection terms. The Court did not stop at that point however. In its next words it took a step that collapsed even the theoretical possibility that separate could be made equal in the circumstances being addressed and, by extension, many other circumstances.

Bricks, mortar, books, and number of faculty were important, but "What is more important, the University of Texas Law School possesses to a far greater degree those qualities which are incapable of objective measurement but which make for greatness in a law school." Among these intangibles were the "position and influence of the alumni, standing in the community, tradition and prestige." Or, in other words, Texas State Law School for Negroes was deficient in ways that could never be bridged. In the nature of things, the state of Texas could not, beginning in 1947, create a law school for blacks which would be equal to the law school it reserved for whites.

The Court then moved on to articulate a further reason why it was inherently impossible to create a separate black law school equal to the University of Texas Law School. Blacks comprised only 15 percent of the state's population. Again, in the nature of things, the overwhelming number of lawyers, judges, and other officials with whom the black attorney would interact would be white, most of them graduates of the University of Texas Law school. "The law school, the proving ground for legal learning and practice, cannot be effective in isolation from the individuals and institutions with which the law interacts."[36] The black law student denied the opportunity to study with and come to know and understand the majority of his fellow practitioners could not be said to have been afforded equality under the law.

In practical terms Texas could not set it right. The Court had defined equality in a way that precluded the possibility of its being realized in a separate setting. By implication, other states, similarly situated, could not set it right by spending money and building new schools. Separate was inherently unequal.

Vinson then paid homage to Hughes. Citing *Gaines* he affirmed that Sweatt's rights under the Fourteenth Amendment were personal and could not be abridged because he was a member of a particular racial group. And in accordance with *Gaines* and the present holding, Sweatt could claim his right to attend the University of Texas Law School.

But at the same time Vinson and the majority backed away from the more profound implication of their own reasoning. They did not agree with Texas that *Plessy* compelled a finding in favor of the state. But, on the other hand, "Nor need we reach petitioner's contention that *Plessy v. Ferguson* should be reexamined in the light of contemporary knowledge respecting the purposes of the Fourteenth Amendment and the effects of racial segregation."[37]

But within months, circumstances would force that reexamination.

Constitutional Doctrine and the Road to Brown

In the fall of 1947 all of the states of the old Confederacy and some states outside the South had some form of legal segregation in education. South Carolina was typical of the old South in separating black and white children from the first grade onward and in funding black schools at a fraction of the level set for white schools. In Kansas, a border state, Topeka separated children by race only through elementary school. Segregation was also a legal mandate in terms of other public services and facilities. Hospitals, public parks, publicly supported swimming pools, libraries, and other public amenities either limited or barred black access.

The *Plessy* Court's interpretation of the equal protection language of the Fourteenth Amendment provided constitutional sanction for state-mandated racial separation, provided blacks were afforded equal services and facilities. In practice, of course, the states had not honored the equal aspect of the equation, but save for *Gaines* had not been brought to answer for the failure. On the eve of the new Court term in the fifth year after the war, *Plessy* was still Constitutional doctrine. No direct challenge had been made to the doctrine itself, rather the attack had centered on the failure of the states to provide equality.

Constitutional doctrine as regards race also accommodated a limited conception of national citizenship and therefore limited the claims to segregation and racial bias blacks could make. Seven decades earlier the *Slaughterhouse* Court had held that the Fourteenth Amendment constrained the states from abusing blacks in terms of the rights they enjoyed as citizens of the United States, and those rights were limited in number. The *Slaughterhouse* Court specifically rejected the idea that the amendment denied states their traditional authority to set their own rules and write their own laws with regard to most of the matters affecting the lives of their citizens.

As a consequence, the states felt free to adopt such measures as laws barring interracial marriage insofar as those laws were deemed to address concerns traditionally within the purview of the states. Under federalist principles, leaving a good deal of the handling of race and rights to the states, a few states moved to provide, at least on paper, more rights to blacks than required by the Constitution. A number of states in the North and upper Midwest had laws on the books barring racial discrimination in public accommodations. A few had laws or commissions charged with curbing discrimination in employment. Most states outside the South had no laws speaking to race and rights, while the Southern states filled the wide margin left by the limited conception of the reach of post–Civil War amendments with laws of a racially restrictive character.

In the *Civil Rights Cases of 1883* the Court had held that the post–Civil War amendments had not conferred upon Congress the Constitutional authority to limit or shape the decisions of entrepreneurs with regard to whom they would serve and whom they would not serve. There was an enormous amount of racially discriminatory behavior deemed "private" in nature and therefore beyond the reach or concern of the Fourteenth Amendment. Much or most of this private discrimination involved the decision not to serve black patrons or hire black employees. And private agreements between whites to discriminate, entered into with the formalities attending the drawing up of contracts, were as enforceable in court.

As a matter of Constitutional doctrine in the fall of 1947 states could make explicit racial distinctions in law provided the facilities and services yielded by those distinctions were equal without violating the equal protection clause of the Fourteenth Amendment. Such distinctions were made in virtually every sphere of life in the Southern states. The discriminatory behavior of individuals in the operation of their businesses was deemed beyond the scope of the Constitution, although a few states in the North and

West had antidiscrimination laws of varying degrees of impact on actual behavior.

During the term two cases came before the Court having different implications in practical terms, but both going to the matter of whether the Court was willing to reexamine Constitutional doctrine as regards race and rights in a fundamental way.

Chapter 9

Brown v. Board of Education

The year has a distinctive cycle for the parents of young children, as steady and predictable as the change of seasons. Fall
brings a dip in the temperature and a touch of brown to the
tips of leaves and also brings the opening of school. And if the child
is starting at a new school the annual ritual extends beyond shop-
ping for new clothes to also embrace registration.

And so early in the morning on a September day in 1950,
Oliver Brown took his seven-year-old daughter Linda by the hand
to walk the six blocks to the Sumner Elementary School to register
for the third grade. Several weeks earlier notice of registration had
been left at all of the homes in the Sumner school district, including Oliver Brown's neatly kept, one-family home at 511 First Street.

Although the neighborhood was mostly white there were also
a few black families in the Sumner district, and although the notice
had been left at the Brown home it was not meant for them. Elementary schools in Kansas were segregated by law. Lucy Brown had
attended Monroe, the black elementary school, in the first and second grades. In order to reach school by nine each morning she had
to leave the home before seven to catch the school bus. Reaching
the bus stop meant walking several blocks along a section of First
Street having no sidewalks or taking a route through the Rock
Island railroad switching yards. If the bus was late she had to wait
in the open in bad weather, if it was on time she arrived at school
early and had to wait half an hour for the doors to open.

Sumner was her neighborhood school. It was closer and appeared from the outside to be a nicer building than Monroe. Knowing that the notice of registration was not meant for his family, Oliver Brown nevertheless took Lucy by the hand and walked the six blocks to Sumner on the first day of school. Upon arrival father and daughter were brought to the principal's office. The father entered while the daughter waited outside. In a few minutes the father reappeared. He was upset, Lucy recalled many years later, and he became increasingly upset as they headed home.[1]

At the same time in other quarters a constellation of forces were coming together which were to allow Oliver Brown to translate his anger into a case that would join *Dred Scott* and *Plessy* as pivotal in the long, tortured history of race in the United States.

For as long as anyone could remember, blacks in Topeka and in the state of Kansas as a whole had been objects of amused contempt, shadow beings confined to the margins of social life. Relations between the races were not marked by the lethal violence of the old Confederacy nor was segregation quite as pervasive, but blacks as a rule were barred from restaurants and hotels as patrons, and were confined to segregated sections of movie theaters. The job market was largely closed, save for domestic or laboring positions. In Topeka no black worked as a sales person in a white-owned store nor as a bank teller or secretary or clerk. There was a small cadre of black professionals sustained within the framework of segregation, black teachers in the black school and one black lawyer.[2]

In the fall of 1948, two years before Oliver and Lucy Brown had walked the six blocks to the Sumner School, McKinley Burnett, chairman of the local NAACP, had presented a petition to the school board on behalf of a black "citizens committee" calling for an end to school segregation. In addition, Isabel Lurie, also a member of the NAACP, had sought the counsel and advice of the national office with regard to the possibility of filing a lawsuit against the board.

The Topeka board's summary dismissal of the citizens committee petition led to a series of increasingly bitter confrontations, the board claiming that Kansas law tied its hands in the matter. It could not end segregation even if it wanted to. Burnett and his people should take their grievance to the halls of the Kansas state legislature.

In the fall of 1950, about the time that Oliver Brown was seeking to enroll Lucy at Sumner, the national office of the NAACP received two letters from the Topeka NAACP describing a situation beyond redress by means of civil discourse and calm negotiation. Lucinda Todd, the chapter secretary, renewed the earlier request for guidance with regard to a possible law suit, while McKinley Burnett indicated that "words will not express the humiliation and disrespect in this matter" experienced by representatives of the citizens committee when they sought redress from the legislature.[3]

In the two years that had elapsed between the first communication from Topeka involving a lawsuit and the second set of queries, the legal landscape had changed. *Sweatt* and *McLauren* had been decided. The essential logic of *Sweatt* suggested that there were circumstances in which "separate" could never be equal at the level of graduate and professional education. But a strategy was developing involving the use of the results of projective tests on black children to argue that legal segregation at the elementary and secondary levels was also inherently unequal insofar as it had destructive consequences with regard to ego and "sense of self." Two of the Legal Defense Fund's growing cadre of courtroom veterans in the fight against segregation, Robert Carter and Jack Greenberg, were put in contact with local black attorneys to set the wheels in motion for a challenge to the Kansas segregation law.[4]

Experience had driven home the lesson that it was better to have more than one plaintiff in a suit challenging segregation. A single plaintiff was more vulnerable to threat or intimidation or might, on one legal pretext or another, be found to be ineligible to sue. The initial challenge to the refusal of the Clarendon County, South Carolina, school board to provide even a modicum of the support for black schools that it provided for white schools foundered when the single black plaintiff was found to live just across the line from the district encompassed by the school district.

Hence, in Topeka, McKinley Burnett set about attempting to persuade as large a number of people as he could to join the suit. The NAACP drew its membership from the minority in the black community willing to be active, vocal, and visible on matters of race. Most members of the community were not politically engaged. Most went about their day-to-day lives impacted by race and Jim Crow in its legal and normative guises, but not involved in the struggle to eradicate it.

In those terms Oliver Brown was not atypical. He had not been involved in the affairs of the NAACP. A lifelong resident of Topeka, he had grown up with the system and had been educated in its schools. His only extended experience outside of Topeka had come during his years of service in the war. Initially he was apart from the struggle unfolding around him. No one regarded him as a militant. He had married the former Miss Black Topeka, had a steady job working for the railroad, a family, and a nice home. A father's concern rather than ideology had impelled him to seek enrollment of his daughter at the Sumner School. But the humiliation and anger attending the dismissal of that effort made him receptive to McKinley Burnett's talk of a possible suit.

Twenty people in all were identified as willing to join in the challenge to the Kansas law. Although the specifics of their experiences varied, the common denominator was the claim that the law denied them a constitutional right because of their race. All of the parties brought deeply felt grievances to the process but as Brown's name came first alphabetically among the plaintiffs the suit assumed his name.[5] On February 28, 1951, the Legal Defense Fund filed *Brown v. Topeka Board of Education* in federal court.

Briggs: The Struggle Engaged

Revolutions rarely begin with the demand that the world be turned upside down. More often the initial request, timid and hesitant from below and turned away with scorn and disdain from above, is for a shade less hardship—half a crust of bread rather than a quarter of a crust. And after the world has been turned upside down erstwhile masters look back with dismay at having lost so much when they might have survived by giving so little. And so *Briggs*, the case providing the battleground on which the struggle over segregation was actually waged, began with a humble request.

In the summer of 1947 the Reverend J. A. DeLaine and two other black men went to see L. B. McCord, the white superintendent of schools in Clarendon County, South Carolina, and also a Presbyterian minister. Black children and white children attended schools vastly different in quality. Many of the black schools were old, leaky, run-down affairs with faulty plumbing and broken heating systems. The county paid the salaries of black teachers but provided no other support. White teachers were paid two-thirds more than black teachers.[6]

But the immediate problem bringing Reverend DeLaine and his associates to see L. B. McCord was transportation. The county provided buses for white children but not for black children. Many children from the scattered black communities had to walk miles to get to school and during the rainy part of the year the backwoods roads and byways were muddy and nearly impossible to traverse on foot. The superintendent was not sympathetic to their plight. No further support was to be forthcoming.

In the face of the refusal the scattered black community pooled its resources and bought a bus, old and rickety, but transportation nevertheless for the children. Again, a request was made of the superintendent. Perhaps the county could help pay for the gas. But again, the County said no.

Clarendon had a history of defiance with regard to black interests. It had said no to the courts and thus did not hesitate to say no to the black supplicants seeking money for gas for the black school bus. In 1940 the Fourth Circuit Court of Appeals, sitting in Richmond, Virginia, had ruled that black teachers must be paid the same salaries as white teachers and the ruling had been upheld by the United States Supreme Court. South Carolina's response was summed up by a member of the state legislature, "We would like to see them make us give the Negroes more money." A series of cases in the mid-1940s had forced Charleston and Columbia to comply with the court's ruling but in the rural areas black teachers continued to be paid less than white teachers.[7]

In the face of the school district's refusal to make even a gesture toward support of the black parents in their struggle to ease the transportation problem, talk turned to the possibility of seeking relief in the courts. Although all of the local black parents shared in the grievance, most were also dependent on whites for their livelihood. To become a named party in a suit was to risk economic reprisal or worse. Eventually however Levi Pearson, a black farmer with two children in the black high school and a contributor toward purchase of the bus, agreed to assume the role of plaintiff for a lawsuit seeking only equal support for transportation. The outcome of the effort was to reinforce McCord and the school board's sense of racial superiority. Their victory might also have dulled them to the need for the kind of compromise which might have sustained their defense of the segregation in the battles yet to come.

Harold Boulware, an experienced black lawyer and perhaps the only black attorney in the state, filed on behalf of Levi Pearson in March, 1948, seeking an injunction barring the school board from denying black children the free transportation it provided white children. Almost immediately reprisals were visited upon Pearson. His credit was cut off by every white-owned establishment. His effort to raise cash by cutting down some of the trees on his property and selling it as timber were thwarted when the local mill refused to haul the logs away. And in the end it was all for naught.

The case was scheduled to be heard in federal district court on June 9, 1948, but was thrown out on June 7. The attorneys for the school board had checked tax records. Pearson's property was on the boundary between two school districts. He paid property tax to district 5 but his children attended school in district 26. He had no standing to bring the case. The local state representative was later heard to remark with amusement and disdain, "our niggers don't even know where they live."[8]

In the ensuing months silent terror spread through the black community. Loss of livelihood was held out as the prospect for any-one engaging in further protest. But the lesson learned from the Levi Pearson's ordeal for those blacks inclined to press on was that the risk should be spread among a number of plaintiffs. In March, 1949, DeLaine and other Clarendon blacks met with state and national leaders of the NAACP, including Thurgood Marshall. Nei-ther *Sweatt* nor *McLaurin* had yet been decided by the Supreme Court. There was not yet a holding in which the *Plessy* formulation had been found unconstitutional in the context of education. The discussion turned therefore on moving beyond seeking support for transportation to seeking full equalization of the black schools, pro-vided a number of parents could be found to take on the burden and risk of being named parties in a suit against the school board. Twenty would be a good number.

Eight months later the twenty names had been compiled. And just as the alphabet singled out Oliver Brown to be the named party in the suit so also it singled out Harry Briggs. Both men were ordi-nary in their circumstance. The circumstances by which each came to the courtroom door reflected the ordinary, take-for-granted, rou-tine nature of the different worlds of black education and white.

Briggs had lived his entire life in Clarendon County save for service in the military during the war. He worked in a gas station in Summerton doing a variety of jobs from pumping gas to minor auto repair. His wife worked as a chambermaid at the Summerton Motel. Quality rather than transportation was the issue for the Briggs family. They lived adjacent to the black school, an enterprise as badly underfunded as all of the black schools in the county. Years later Harry Briggs indicated his motivation: "We figured anything to better the children's condition was worthwhile."[9]

In the spring of 1951, three years after the Reverend DeLaine had gone to see Superintendent McCord to ask for a modest bit of relief for black parents and their children, the case moved into federal court, the fate of legal segregation in the schools perhaps being at stake in that the plaintiffs were seeking an injunction barring racial segregation in South Carolina's public schools. On May 28 the parties gathered for a hearing before a panel made up of three distinctly different federal judges.

John J. Parker had been nominated for a seat on the Supreme Court by Herbert Hoover twenty years earlier. A concerted effort by the NAACP alleging a history of racial provocation, and attacks on his record as regards labor had defeated his candidacy. In the following two decades he had gained a reputation as a moderate on racial matters to the extent that Thurgood Marshall had indicated that he might not oppose him were he to be renominated.[10]

J. Waties Waring was regarded as a judicial radical by the white South and as disreputable in his personal life. He had ruled for black teachers in the equal pay cases and had found the white primary to be unconstitutional. He had divorced his first wife and married a Northern woman who moved in circles viewed as ultraliberal. Unbeknownst to his critics he was also secretly advising Thurgood Marshall and the NAACP relative to the Clarendon County case. He had urged Marshall to meet the South Carolina statute head-on by directly challenging its constitutionality, to argue that the issue was not equalization but segregation itself.[11] The third judge, John Bell Timmerman, was an unreconstructed racist in the James Clark McReynolds mold. He could not be expected to be sympathetic to the plaintiffs' case.

The black population of the region understood that much was at stake. An enormous crowd gathered in the halls and corridors of the courthouse and spilled outside into the May morning. Those who squeezed into the courtroom heard the opening arguments in a bitter and portentous legal debate which was to go on for another three years.

South Carolina's strategy was simple and straightforward. Representing the Clarendon County School Board, Attorney Robert Figg conceded all. The black schools were physically inferior. They had been underfunded. No doubt about it. But under the leadership of governor and former Supreme Court justice, James Byrnes, the state was moving vigorously to correct the situation. Substantial monies were to be allocated for a crash program to upgrade black schools. Indeed, half a million dollars was to be spent on upgrading the schools in Clarendon County alone. True, the state had been derelict in the past, but it was now moving with dispatch to honor its obligation under *Plessy* to provide equal facilities. Laws mandating segregation were reasonable insofar as separation was in the interest of both races. Race mixing would not improve the quality of education for children of either race and might lead white parents to abandon the public school system altogether.[12]

Implicit in the testimony Figg solicited was a reaffirmation of the sociological premise of *Plessy*. The races were vastly different and it would be folly for the law to not take that fact into account. Insofar as they derived from genuine and immutable differences between blacks and whites, segregation laws had a rational basis. The only real issue was whether "equal" was supplied within the framework of "separate." The state had been derelict in the past with regard to the "equal" dimension of the equation but was now prepared to meet its responsibilities under the law.

The state's concession blunted the impact of the evidence presented by the plaintiffs with regard to physical differences between black and white schools. In reality, whatever was intended, the plaintiffs arguments came to constitute a challenge to the constitutionality of segregation itself. Kenneth Clark, a social psychologist, was called to the stand to testify as to results of a series of doll preference studies he and his wife, Mamie Clark, had done which seemed to suggest that segregation generated a negative self-image in black children. Other testimony in the same vein was offered by social scientists called to the stand.[13] The inevitable conclusion of such evidence was that legal segregation was inherently and irretrievably unequal.

The three-judge panel split two to one, John J. Parker writing the decision, John Bell Timmerman, concurring. Parker moved to overcome the implications of *Sweatt* and *McLauren*. The issues attending equal access to graduate and professional schools are different from those related to elementary and secondary education. A segregated education at the postgraduate level might limit professional contacts and subsequent professional opportunities. Such considerations were not relevant at the elementary and secondary levels, rather the issue was quality. Surely a quality education could be provided to black children at that level within the framework of segregation.

In addition, the United States Supreme Court had not reversed *Plessy* nor had it ever held that legal segregation is unconstitutional. If circumstances rendered segregation unwise as public policy the legislature could abolish it, but until that day the Court was not empowered to declare unconstitutional a policy which had withstood the test of time and challenge before the Supreme Court.[14] Choosing instead to frame the issue within the confines of *Plessy*, Parker and Timmerman gave South Carolina time to upgrade the quality of the black schools in Clarendon County. Periodic reports were to be made to the Court as to their progress in that endeavor. In his dissent Waties Waring argued that racial bias was the true motive for segregation and that a school system structured on the basis of abhorrence of blacks was inherently unequal.[15]

In July, 1951, the NAACP appealed the ruling to the United States Supreme Court. Not yet ready to confront the issue the Supreme Court referred the case back to the three-judge panel for further hearings. At a second hearing in March, 1952, the Court pronounced itself satisfied that South Carolina was making substantial progress in improving the physical quality of the black schools. Again the NAACP appealed to the United States Supreme Court which, finally, set October 13, 1952, as a date to hear argument.[16]

The Other Front

At approximately the same time on the other side of the nation *Brown* was also working its way up the judicial ladder. On June 25, 1951, represented by Jack Greenberg and Robert Carter of the NAACP and by two local attorneys, John and Charles Scott, a number of black parents came before a three-judge panel to recount the problems and inequities imposed on them by Topeka's segregated school policy. Their children passed new schools with excellent facilities on their way to old buildings, inferior in design and short of supplies.

The plaintiff's attorneys also solicited testimony from Louise Holt of the University of Kansas bearing on the issues addressed by Kenneth Clark and the social psychologists in the South Carolina case. Whatever gloss was put on legal segregation, ultimately it rested on the assumption of black inferiority and, at heart everyone knew that, including black children. There could be no reasonable conclusion other than that state-sponsored segregation was destructive of the black child's sense of self-worth.[17]

Nevertheless on August 3, 1951, the panel came back with a reluctant holding against the plaintiffs. They felt that they were bound by *Plessy*. *Sweatt* and *McLaurin* had undermined *Plessy* at the level of graduate and professional education, thereby making it difficulty to see why state-mandated segregation would not also be a violation of the Equal Protection clause at the elementary and secondary levels. Nevertheless, the Supreme Court had not overruled *Plessy* and hence, they were bound.

Writing for the Court, Judge Walter Huxman, made it clear that even were the black schools to be deemed substantially equal to the white schools in physical terms, nevertheless legal segregation itself inflicted harm on the black child. In his memoirs, Jack Greenberg indicated that this pointed observation was not happenstance. Interviewed years later, Huxman stated that he was pushing the Supreme Court to face the issue of segregation directly, indicating in Greenberg's recounting of his remarks to NAACP expert Hugh Speer, "I tried to wrap it up in such a way that they could not duck it. They had whittled away at it long enough."[18] The NAACP appealed the panel's holding directly to the Supreme Court.

The case which came to be known as *Brown* was actually five cases, each presenting the issue of segregation in a different guise. The Topeka case and the *Belton* case out of Delaware challenged border state segregation. This involved racial subordination as a matter of custom but without the hard-edged hatred that attended segregation in the states of the old Confederacy. In Kansas racial segregation in the schools was permitted but not required for cities over 15,000. *Bolling v. Sharpe* challenged school segregation in Washington, D.C., and presented its own unique issues, but was closer in circumstance and mind-set to the border states than to the deep South. School segregation was neither prohibited nor required, it was simply custom.

The real battle involved two states emblematic of the "lost cause," South Carolina and Virginia. South Carolina had started the Civil War by firing on Forth Sumpter. Much of the war had been fought on Virginia's soil and the South's most enduring hero, Robert E. Lee, had been a son of Virginia. Along with South Carolina, Virginia would carry the standard for the South in the coming struggles. The issues attending separate but equal in Virginia's schools had been engaged at approximately the same time as it was crystallizing in the other jurisdictions.

In late February, 1952, argument was heard on both sides of the question in *Davis v. Prince Edward County School Board*. Substantial testimony was offered as to the inferiority of black schools. Social scientists who had testified in the South Carolina case were called to testify again as to the harmful psychological effects of segregation. Virginia was cruder than South Carolina in its defense of the old system, but also more sophisticated. On the one hand, the state's attorney openly attacked the plaintiffs' social science experts in antisemitic and racial terms, but, on the other hand, they called their own social scientists to the stand to testify that legal segregation had a rational basis and harmed no one.[19]

In March, 1952, the court found the black schools to indeed be inferior and ordered the state to undertake steps to achieve physical equality. On the other hand, legal segregation was held to be inoffensive to the Constitution and its possible elimination harmful to both races. *Davis* was on its way to the Supreme Court.[20]

The five cases had begun at different times and in different places, but like streams flowing down a mountainside they came together to form a single mighty river washing up against the bulwark of segregation.

The Cases Come to the Court: Days of Judgment

The issue would finally be settled by the United State Supreme Court. Thurgood Marshall, South Carolina Governor James Byrnes, Robert Figg, all of the parties understood that, as did the nine justices on the Court. The only questions were when and how. What question would be presented? How would the issue be phrased? How broad or narrow a ruling would the Court be asked to make?

As the final engagements loomed, the South believed that it had a winning three-part strategy. The first facet of the strategy lay in admitting past dereliction.

In 1950 former Supreme Court justice James Byrnes had been elected governor of South Carolina. Wily and shrewd, he understood the implication of *McLauren* and *Sweatt*. The South found it increasingly difficult to deny the bald reality of failure to honor the "equal" dimension of the *Plessy* doctrine and increasingly risky to hope that the courts would look the other way. Under a strategy blessed by Byrnes and pursued by Robert Figg, South Carolina admitted its past sins and asked only for the chance to make amends by appropriating large amounts of money for the building of up-to-date and well-equipped black schools.

The second and third parts of the strategy were to be carried forward before the Supreme Court by John W. Davis, former presidential candidate on the Democratic Party ticket, senior figure in a powerful and prestigious New York law firm, and respected advocate before the Court on behalf of the eminent and the influential.

Accepted canons of constitutional analysis commended the

court to reject the proposition that legal segregation in and of itself violated the Equal Protection clause of the Fourteenth Amendment. The Court was bound to give statutes the meaning their framers intended. There was nothing in the record of the debates attending the drafting and passage of the Fourteenth Amendment which suggested that its framers meant its language to apply to public schools. Neither had the Supreme Court itself ever held that the language of the Equal Protection clause prohibited the states from making racial distinctions with regard to the allocation of children in school systems, provided they were afforded substantially equal facilities. Thus, neither original intent analysis nor precedent supported the challenge to the constitutionality of legal segregation in elementary and secondary schools.

In addition, circumstances had not changed such as to now give the Supreme Court a basis for expanding the meaning accorded the Equal Protection clause. The social science evidence relied upon by the plaintiffs for support of the proposition that legal segregation was inherently destructive of the psyche of the black child was weak stuff indeed, contradicted by the work and testimony of other eminent social scientists. Hence, there were no grounds for finding that segregation did not continue to have a rational basis.

All of the parties understood that they were approaching a watershed, that a decisive battle was about to be fought, and that the world would be different in its aftermath no matter which side won.

Oral argument in the much delayed case was finally engaged in December, 1952. Over a three-day period the contending sides vied before the Court and underwent intense questioning, not reflective of the direction the justices might take. And at 3:50 on Thursday, December 11, 1952, it was over. The matter was now in the hands of nine men. John Davis was heard to remark on his way out of the Court that the South had won. It would be a split decision, but a win nevertheless.[21] Reverend DeLaine was also in the courtroom. Years earlier he had sought only a little more support from Clarendon County officials and now the system of school segregation itself was at stake. He remarked later that as he left the Court that day he "was afraid of Vinson's face."[22]

There Is No Inevitability: The First Conference

And so the matter had to be faced. On Saturday, December 9, the nine members of the Court met to seek a resolution to the "segregation cases." Outside the cloistered conference room the ground was also shifting.

In a matter of weeks the political culture of the Capital would change dramatically. Dwight Eisenhower had won the presidential election, defeating Adlai Stevenson. The Republicans would assume control of the White House for the first time in twenty years. As a retired military man Eisenhower had proven popular in the South. He had come out of an institution with very conservative social values, dominated at the officer levels for generations by Southerners. It was not at all clear what stance he or his justice department would take regarding the cases challenging a century of racial domination.

In addition, a complex of other political and social passions animated the times, some pulling toward finding against the defenders of segregation, others bidding caution.

On the one hand, the bitter cold war struggle with the Soviet Union and the stench attached to all forms of racism by the horrors of Nazism bid repudiation of segregation. As the struggle with the Soviets and their allies deepened in intensity and careened into open warfare in Korea the United States repeatedly found itself on the defensive in the face of Russian attacks on racial segregation. India, Indonesia, and a host of other former colonies had gained independence. European hegemony over the black, yellow, and brown peoples of the world was collapsing. As struggle between the two superpowers became increasingly a struggle for the hearts and minds of people of color the continued practice of racial segregation provided the Soviet Union with a club with which to continually beat the United States, the "leader of the free world."

Compounding this problem was the pall cast over state-sponsored racism by the revelations attending the collapse of Nazism. In the wake of exposure of Nazism's racial apocalypse even Hollywood, normally cautious about political content or social criticism, sensed a popular domestic market for films speaking to issues of tolerance and understanding. The 1947 Gregory Peck film "Gentleman's Agreement" condemned the taken-for-granted forms of antisemitism of the elite and professional classes in the United States. The film "Crossfire" centered on its cruder, more murderous expression among poorer, less-educated whites. Antiblack passions came under attack in "No Way Out" and "Home of the Brave."

The ground was shifting, but the mountain was still in place. Racism was still alive, but there was increasing support for the notion that race was not an appropriate yardstick by which to measure people.

On the other hand, there were very strong legal currents running in the other direction. The Supreme Court had never explicitly repudiated *Plessy's* separate-but-equal doctrine. Indeed, the Court had reaffirmed its validity in the years since it was first handed down. An appreciation of precedent as the foundation of responsible jurisprudence spoke to the need for caution in the face of demands that a doctrine on which a way of life had been erected be summarily rejected.

In addition, the judicial philosophy of the Roosevelt and Truman administrations suggested that its heirs, the members of this Court, might act with caution. Franklin Roosevelt's struggle with the Supreme Court, inherited upon taking office, had grown out of their repudiation of policies which he deemed necessary to cope with the crisis brought on by the collapse of the economy. He sought justices likely to be deferential to Congress and to other legislative bodies. If laws were foolish, unworkable, or unwise the people would turn their representatives out and elect new people. It was not the job of the Supreme Court to function as a superlegislature with justices upholding or repudiating laws in terms of their personal views of what constitutes a good society.[23]

There was no reason to believe that the majority of whites in the South did not support legal segregation. Whatever the personal views of the justices on the matter, precedent and a judicial philosophy favoring deference to legislative bodies spoke against the likelihood of a bold holding. And finally there was a grim reality. A holding overturning segregation in the schools might simply be defied. The white South was deeply and passionately committed to the system. Fiery voices in Virginia had already called for an end to public education. Other voices counseled open defiance. Mass defiance would yield a crisis of national and constitutional dimensions.

In the end the Supreme Court is a small group in a sociological sense. A small group needing a majority in order to act, but made up of autonomous individuals, requires leadership if it is to move to resolution on bitter and divisive issues. There was no issue more bitter and divisive than school segregation. The formal leader was the chief justice, Fred Vinson. If the matter was to move to decision Vinson had to be the force driving the Court, or there had to be someone else capable of exerting sufficient intellectual force and interpersonal charm as to be able to bring along at least four colleagues.

Events leading up to the decisive day in December had shown Vinson to be a man divided. J. A. DeLaine had not been entirely wrong in fearing what he had seen in Vinson's face as oral argument ended. On the one hand, Vinson seemed to lack the visceral antiblack sentiment of a James Clark McReynolds but, on the other hand, he seemed very hesitant to take judicial steps which would bring down on his head the wrath of fellow white Southerners. He had authored the comparatively progressive holdings of *McLauren*, *Sweatt*, and *Shelley*, but had wavered in later cases relating to race and rights,[24] perhaps in response to the ire of his erstwhile segregationist compatriots in Congress and in the state houses of the old Confederacy.

Kluger's recreation of the conference based on surviving notes indicates a man not prepared to confront the fundamental issue, the inherent destructiveness of state-sponsored segregation. He spoke first and resorted to original intent analysis as had John W. Davis in oral argument. There was nothing in the record suggesting that the Fourteenth Amendment was meant by its drafters to encompass schools. He also relied on precedent. The Court had upheld *Plessy*'s constitutionality in prior cases. Indeed, John Marshall Harlan had not mentioned schools in his *Plessy* dissent and three years later wrote the *Cummings* holding positing that public funding of a school for whites but not blacks did not present a constitutional problem. He was also drawn to the difficulties likely to be encountered by a decision abolishing segregated schools, the threats to abolish the public school system, the specter of massive white resistance. In the end it appeared that he was ready to affirm those lower-court holdings giving the deep South time to improve the quality of black schools within a framework of legal segregation.[25]

Hugo Black then spoke and also drew on his background as a Southerner. Both his reading of history and his experience as a son of the old South told him that segregation's only one purpose was to oppress and humiliate blacks. It rested on the premise of black inferiority. Surely the framers of the Fourteenth Amendment meant to put blacks on an equal footing with whites. There was no contemporary reading of the amendment which would reconcile that intent with the reality of legal school segregation. He did not doubt the difficulties attending overruling *Plessy* nor doubt the seriousness of the threats with regard to closure of the schools and civil disorder but those realities did not yield to the Court sufficient reasons for evading its responsibility.[26]

Stanley Reed spoke next. Earlier holdings suggested moderate views but he was, at heart, a Southern paternalist. Blacks collectively had made great strides but still lagged behind whites in level of culture. It was too soon to speak of desegregation of the schools. Segregation was grounded in objective social realities related to the differences between the races. Legal separation was not inherently unconstitutional. The equal protection concerns of the plaintiffs could be met through the upgrading of black schools within the framework of segregation.[27]

None of the justices save Felix Franfurter had ever drawn a breath as a member of a minority group, and for Frankfurter minority status complicated his jurisprudence. He brought the most complicated set of biographical issues to the table. He had been active in liberal and progressive causes before ascending to the high Court and was a supporter of both the NAACP and the American Civil Liberties Union. He had brought enormous intellect to the cause of the poor and the weak and the despised, and a passion perhaps born of empathy and the experience of membership in a group still subject to widespread discrimination in the United States and made the target of genocide in Europe.

But at the same time his consciousness of himself as a Jew moving in a world of powerful gentiles seems to have bread increasing caution and a circumspect approach to controversial issues. According to Kluger, he intimated to an associate in the late 1930s that "I have become a myth, a symbol, and promoter not of reason but of passion. I am the symbol of the Jew, the 'red' the 'alien.'"[28] Later, when his colleague Robert Jackson, perhaps meaning well, suggested that white supremacists might take less offense if the Court's *Smith v. Allwright* decision striking at the white primary were not seen as the work of a Jew he declined the chief justice's request to write the holding.[29]

His wish not be seen as the Court's Jewish "radical" combined with the preference of Roosevelt-nominated justices for granting deference to Congress and legislatures predisposed him to give the benefit of the doubt to the defenders of state laws and federal statutes. But in the context of the school cases this would mean affirming the legitimacy of legal segregation. According to Kluger, he was prepared to repudiate segregation but wanted the strongest possible legal reasons for doing so. The justices were not philosopher kings. For the good of the country and their own legitimacy they must proceed according to well-honed arguments derived from a plausible reading of the Constitution.

He had set his law clerk Alexander Bickel to the task of reading the voluminous debates attending the drafting of the Fourteenth Amendment. It could not be conclusively stated that its framers entertained meanings which could plausibly be said to have prohibited the states from assigning students to schools according to race.[30] The legal basis for overturning *Plessy* or finding segregation unconstitutional was not clearly there, at least in terms of original intent analysis.

Hence, he favored delay. Let the incoming Eisenhower administration submit briefs on the matter. Perhaps reargument could be scheduled in March, 1952. He understood the importance of a unanimous decision were segregation to be struck down and also understood that Fred Vinson was incapable of exercising the kind of leadership which would yield a unanimity. Delay might crystallize a clearer set of legal arguments and promote a dynamic more promising of a unified court.[31]

William O. Douglas had the self-assurance of a man who has been justified throughout his life in viewing himself as swifter than his fellows. Although he did not have an uncomplicated mind, he regarded many matters as uncomplicated, including the segregation cases. The classification of citizens by race for purposes of allocating public goods was not supportable. Segregation was an evil of constitutional dimensions and he was plainly ready to say so.[32]

Robert Jackson also brought a complicated biography to the table. He had presided at the Nuremberg trials of Nazi leaders and had seen the ultimate bitter fruit of racism as official state policy close. He appears not to have had any illusions about the destructive character of legal segregation in the American context. He had no sentimental attachment to the Southern way of life as did Vinson and Stanley Reed. Whereas Vinson moved in a small world populated by Southern cronies viscerally committed to white supremacy, Jackson strode on the world stage, an internationally known and respected figure as a result of his performance at the Nuremberg trials.

But as with Frankfurter he shrank from the view that the justices were philosopher kings empowered to interpret the language of the Constitution in terms of personal visions of the "just society." In the end he appears to have seen himself as confronted with the agonizing problem confronting Frankfurter.[33] Legal segregation was an evil of immense proportions, but it did not appear that conventional rules of statutory interpretation established that it was necessarily unconstitutional. Were the justices to act as individuals they might abolish it, but in their role as members of the Court they were constrained to read into the Constitution only what was plausibly there.

Whereas the views of Vinson and Reed reflected a rejection of the notion that segregation was inherently destructive, Jackson appears to have been convinced of its malevolent character but doubted that the Court could plausibly hold that the Constitution prohibited it. That a practice is evil does not necessarily mean that it is also unconstitutional. Ultimately it was up to Congress and the various state legislatures to address the practice. The Court might issue what amounted to an advisory opinion, but was not itself empowered to overrule the practice.[34]

Harold Burton was an uncomplicated man and he brought an uncomplicated position to the issue. The world had changed in the sixty years since *Plessy*. At the turn of the century honest men might have believed that "separate but equal" was both possible and consistent with the state's obligation to afford citizens the equal protection of the law. The experience of six decades established the inherently degrading nature of legal segregation. State-mandated racial segregation, in its nature, constituted a denial of equal protection of the law.[35]

As with Vinson, Reed, and Black, Tom Clark was from a state in which legal segregation ordered relations between black and white. And, as with Vinson and Reed, the Texan was free of visceral hostility to black concerns, but unlike Hugo Black he lacked a clear vision of racial justice and a commitment to using the court as an instrument, under the Constitution, to promote that vision. He would, perhaps, have preferred that school segregation did not exist. But it did exist. And, indeed, much of Southern life had been built around it. Were the Court to now abolish it, chaos would result. The resistance would be prolonged, bitter, and probably violent. Perhaps delay was best.[36]

Sherman Minton of Indiana was also an uncomplicated man. Lacking great intellect and a fixed ideology he appeared to be guided in his judicial role by two simple principles, deference to legislatures and respect for precedent. Neither of these principles would have committed him to side with the plaintiffs in the school segregation cases. He appears however to have been persuaded by the plaintiffs' briefs and arguments. A number of more recent cases had undermined the *Plessy* premise with regard state-based racial classification having a rational basis and benign consequences. State-mandated segregation of school children by race was unconstitutional.[37]

No vote was taken but it was clear that there was nothing approaching a consensus. Years later memories differed as to

whether a majority would or would not have voted to sustain segregation, but at the time an unsettling stalemate obtained. As winter turned to spring Vinson proved incapable of mobilizing the
Court in the face of the reality that they could not simply continue
to schedule rearguments and avoid ever reaching a decision.

Finally, as the term neared an end and the failure of the Court
to meet its responsibility loomed, Frankfurter offered that they put
the matter over yet once again. The parties would be invited back
in the next term to reargue, specifically addressing a set of questions which amounted to the following:

- Was there any reading of the debates, committee reports, and
  other records of the Congress that drafted the Fourteenth Amendment and submitted it to the states suggesting that it did, could,
  or might have intended to prohibit school segregation?
- Even if Congress did not, at that time, intend the immediate abolition of segregated schools, was there any evidence that they
  intended future Congresses to have the power to do so, or that the
  courts might have been so empowered in terms of changed conditions?
- Irrespective of what Congress intended, could the Fourteenth be
  construed in such a way as to confer the power to abolish school
  segregation on the courts?
- Assuming that school segregation violates the Fourteenth
  Amendment, would the immediate integration of the schools be
  ordered or would the courts mandate and monitor specific steps
  for gradual integration of the schools?[38]

The first questions entailed returning to matters already
addressed, the last to the matter of what would happen were the
plaintiffs to prevail. The specter of massive white resistance
loomed were the Court to rule school segregation unconstitutional.
That alone seemed to weigh so heavily on some that they shrank
from finding in the law sufficient reason for holding against continued segregation.

A grateful Court grasped at Frankfurter's straw. It delayed
matters. It offered the possibility of finding a path through the legal
wilderness and, importantly, it mandated a frank and sober review
of the role of the courts in the turbulent new world sure to follow
a decision favorable to the plaintiffs. But there was still Vinson and
the reality of the Court as a small group. Frankfurter had proposed
a strategy and the Court had accepted it. But in the end, without

leadership strong enough to bring the parties to a resolution, the outcome would be the same in the new term as it had been in the old.

And then Fred Vinson died.

The Coming of Earl Warren

A fatal heart attack in the early morning hours of September 8 ended a career that had carried the chief justice from poverty and small-town obscurity to the center of power in Washington. Whatever his strengths he appeared to be floundering in the face of the new challenges facing the Court. The new term was only a few weeks away, a number of important matters were on the docket, including the segregation cases. His death brought even greater uncertainty to the situation.

Eisenhower did not tarry in nominating a successor. A number of names were floated, including that of two-time Republican presidential nominee Thomas Dewey. But Eisenhower by-passed Dewey in favor of Dewey's 1948 vice-presidential running mate, California governor, Earl Warren.

Destined with *Brown* and other cases to make an indelible impact on American law and society, Earl Warren had never sat a day as a judge in any court in the land, but on Wednesday, September 30, 1953, he received a call from Dwight Eisenhower asking him resign as governor of California and assume the post of chief justice of the United States Supreme Court. Indeed, the request was that he assume his duties by the following Monday, October 5, the day the Court began its fall session. It was understood, of course, that he would be serving in an acting capacity, pending confirmation by the Senate.

Both the request and the acceptance are among the more baffling occurrences in the history of the Supreme Court. The president was asking the chief executive of what was at the time the second largest state in the union to change his life overnight, to move from the very public life of a governor to the cloistered life of a Supreme Court justice, to move from holding sway over vast bureaucracies to being master of one or two clerks and shepard to eight other justices, all of them deeply impressed with their own strengths and virtues. And finally he was being asked to do what he had never done before, render judgment as to the meaning of the Constitution's magisterial but often opaque language.

Eisenhower had met Warren a year earlier at the Republican convention where the California governor had played a key role in the seating of delegates pledged to the retired general. The abrupt circumstances of Warren's appointment did not suggest a political payoff however, nor was one suggested at the time. Indeed, it would have been hard to construe the offer and the required move across country as a payoff. A man of great accomplishment on the far side of middle age was being asked to give up his way of life, the places he knew, the friends he saw every day, the rhythms and pace of the life he had lived, and assume a new way of life in a distant place, among a sea of strangers.

In the end, however, the two men were also somewhat alike despite having pursued very different careers. Warren was an effective administrator in the best sense of the word. He was able to oversee a large and complex bureaucracy and weld together disparate interests in such a way as to achieve results. Eisenhower had done the same as commander and chief of allied forces in Europe. Neither man was an ideologue or an intellectual in the sense of being interested in ideas or grand theories. Neither expressed sentiments beyond the conventional pieties of small-town, middle-class America. Perhaps there similarities drew Eisenhower to Warren.

Neither his personal biography nor the details of his professional career suggested that Warren would break new ground on the Court. There was reason to believe that he would move the Court's business forward with greater efficiency than Fred Vinson but little reason to believe that he would lead the Court to new places. Of Norwegian immigrant stock, Warren had attended the University of California at Berkeley then gradually worked his way up the political ladder as a middle-of-the-road Republican, moving from district attorney of Alameda County to attorney general, acquiring along the way a reputation for honesty and effectiveness.[39]

Shortly after Pearl Harbor he had denounced Japanese-Americans living in California as a potential threat to national security and had supported their removal. Otherwise in his public life he had never appealed to racial or ethnic fears and, when elected governor, pushed for a state fair employment practices commission. His record as governor reflected sensitivity to civil liberties and a commitment to progressive social welfare policies, but within a framework of states' rights. He had denounced Senator Joseph McCarthy as a smear-mongerer but voiced concern about the threat of domestic Communism. He favored programs supporting the aged and the unemployed but under the authority of the states rather than the federal government.[40]

On October 5, 1953, he was sworn in as acting chief justice of the United States Supreme Court. As always the ascension of a new leader promised a new day for the Court, but few anticipated that it would be a day bringing enormous surprises as he began with fewer cards in his deck than most of the men who had preceded him. He had never been a judge nor was he a legal scholar or a person with strong intellectual or philosophical interests. Twenty or so years earlier he had appeared before the Court in oral argument on what turned out to be the day that Oliver Wendall Holmes announced his retirement, but he never claimed to be a great litigator or a constitutional scholar.[41]

Unlike Vinson however he brought enormous social intelligence to the post. He could read people and manage situations. He could interact with everyone from the humble to the mighty in such a way as to suggest that he appreciated their singular humanity.[42] In short order he had charmed his colleagues and allayed any misgivings they might have had about his fitness for the post. Hence, by December 7, 1953, the appointed day for reargument of the segregation cases, he had assumed leadership of the small group of men who were about to render a decision with regard to whether Lucy Brown should have been allowed to register for the third grade at the Sumner School.

The increasing tension generated by the reargument is reflected in a letter Walter White sent to Hugo Black "as a friend, not as secretary of the NAACP." White indicated that "no person will be admitted to the Court, such is the demand for seats, except members of the Supreme Court Bar and the plaintiffs. . . . As you know, I have been working for 35 years towards this day and wouldn't want to miss it."[43]

Again, the arguments were framed in terms of original intent. Again Marshall and the attorneys for the plaintiffs contended that the debates attending passage of the Fourteenth Amendment indicated that its framers never intended to exempt education from the sweep of its "equal protection" language. They also argued that the Supreme Court itself in *Gaines* and in *Strauder* had held that the rights protected under the Equal Protection clause were broad in scope. It followed therefore that the separation of school children by race pursuant to state law would per se be a violation of the Equal Protection clause. The Supreme Court itself could dismantle the system. It did not have to be left to the discretion of Congress.[44]

Appearing for the last time before the Supreme Court, John W. Davis again carried the burden for the South. Clearly, the Fourteenth Amendment had not been meant to disturb segregated education. The Congress that passed the Fourteenth Amendment had also appropriated monies for segregated schools in Washington, D.C. The Supreme Court itself had held in a number of cases that separation of the races by law did not offend the Equal Protection clause provided the strictures of *Plessy* were met. True, Virginia, South Carolina, and other states had fallen short of their duty to honor *Plessy*, but now herculean efforts were being made to make amends.

And at the end, driven perhaps by the thought that this might be his last appearance before the Court and by a deep commitment to state's rights and an indelible belief in racial difference, Davis brought passion to his argument. There was much at stake. The Court would speak not only to the meaning of the law but to what the country was. In the end he did not believe that it should be different from what it had been.[45]

On the third day of reargument Marshall provided a response, moving from legal argument to the realities of the matter. Davis had contended that segregation had been good for both races but, in truth, segregation had been imposed on blacks. It rested on the premise that blacks were inferior to whites and should the Supreme Court hold for the states it would be affirming that proposition. It was incumbent on the Court to find therefore that the Constitution did not permit state action predicated on a principle of racial inferiority.[46]

But at the end of the day the South felt good. Robert Figg believed that it would be close but that South Carolina would prevail. John Davis did not believe that it would even be close.[47]

The Court Decides

Three days later the nine justices met in conference to again take up the segregation cases. As per custom the chief justice spoke first. In an instant Warren cleared away the brush. The approach was clear and pragmatic. There were none of Frankfurter's intellectualized circumlocutions and intricacies or Vinson's evasions and hesitations. In a series of holdings, *Gaines* and *Sweatt* among them, the Supreme Court had itself eroded *Plessy*. All that really remained was whether the Court would address the issue of segregation itself. If they were to sustain segregation it could only be on the basis that blacks were inferior to whites, and if that is what they believed they should plainly say so. As for himself, there was no question but that the segregation laws in question must be struck down. The only question was how to frame the holding such as to secure the maximum of compliance and a minimum of resistance.[48]

Hugo Black. William O. Douglas, Harold Burton, and Sherman Minton had declared for the plaintiffs in the first conference. None had changed position. The majority was there.

Warren was moved by a further consideration however. The holding would turn the world upside down. It would strike at practices and beliefs that were deeply ingrained, however despicable. The mighty would not surrender meekly to the weak. Fierce and bitter resistance, always a possibility, would become a certainty were the Court not united. The slightest ray of legal hope would provide grounds for denying the legitimacy of the majority holding. Indeed, the legitimacy of the Court itself might be eroded were a split decision to become the instrument driving a political and social civil war. It was crucial that the Court speak with one voice.

It would be an uphill battle however. Stanley Reed spoke next and stuck to his position. True, South Carolina and many other states had shirked their duty under *Plessy*, but they were moving now to make amends. Assuming that black schools were made equal to white schools in terms of bricks and mortar it was not clear that there would be a basis for a claim of denial of equal protection of the law. He ignored Warren's observation with regard to a premise of racial inferiority being the only basis for sustaining the constitutionality of state-sponsored racial separation.[49] Warren had opened a window that Reed chose not to peer through.

Then Frankfurter spoke. He had made up his mind. He would vote for the plaintiffs. Original intent analysis did not provide guidance and the post-*Plessy* cases surely suggested that the doctrine of separate but equal was not inviolate.[50] Douglas concurred. He would vote for the plaintiffs.

Jackson was torn. He understood the barbarism attending legal segregation but doubted that conventional modes of legal analysis provided a basis for overturning more than half a century of law. It was a difficult and subtle position. If the Court had sanctioned and reaffirmed the constitutionality of a practice whose evil becomes manifest over decades, and if a way of life and institutions have grown up around that institution, may the Court simply declare it no longer constitutional even though not supported by either precedent or original intent analysis. They were after all judges bound by known modes of legal analysis and not philosopher kings. On the other hand, justice demanded a holding in favor of the plaintiffs. But the Court would be making a political decision and must so state.[51]

Harold Burton sided with Warren. There was no choice but to find for the plaintiffs.

Tom Clark had moved a distance on the matter. He would vote against continued segregation provided serious attention were given to the nightmare problems attending implementing the decision.

Sherman Minton continued to be strongly in support of the plaintiffs. The world had changed. Whatever *Plessy* might have meant at the end of the nineteenth century, it could not be relied upon for organizing relations between the races in the middle of the twentieth century. A potentially overwhelming majority was there, but not one voice. Reed was still to be won over. The crucial question of the exact language with which the Court would speak remained.

In the ensuing weeks a series of memos circulated among the justices reflecting anguish and a degree of calculation. Both Frankfurter and Jackson put pen to paper with regard to their personal abhorrence of segregation, but Frankfurter seemed more confident that there was a way of repudiating it without sacrificing the integrity of the Court. Jackson continued to be plagued by doubts that the Constitution clearly prohibited segregation even though segregation was an evil of gross dimensions.

Many years later a memo surfaced during hearings on William Rehnquist's nomination to the Supreme Court. Rehnquist had been one of Jackson's clerks at the time that *Brown* was being considered. The memo, bearing Rehnquist's initials, was a crude defense of the *Plessy* doctrine. Rehnquist alleged that he had drafted the memo at Jackson's request, that it reflected Jackson's views rather than his own, and that Jackson had intended at one point to uphold segregation. Others, privy to Jackson's thinking at the time, disputed this contention. Neither is there anything else in the record confirming Rehnquist's version of the facts. Jackson appears to have had a subtle and difficult view of the issues, and was preparing in his own way to speak against school segregation.

As time elapsed it appeared that even though there was a majority there might not be a single majority opinion, thereby providing an opening for malice and mischief to do their work in defense of segregation by obfuscating the meaning of the holding.

Stanley Reed still held out. He intended to write a dissenting opinion and set about formulating his arguments. Sometime in mid-February, 1954, a document appeared. Filled with nonsequiturs regarding the Equal Protection clause not requiring that every family have equal access to basic necessities, it failed to offer a sustained, coherent argument supporting the continued constitutionality of state-sponsored racial segregation in elementary and secondary schools.[52]

Perhaps a month later another vote was taken and Reed was again the only holdout. Nevertheless Warren set about writing a majority opinion. State-sponsored segregation of schools was to be found unconstitutional. The parties were to be invited back to Court for further argument on the mechanics of implementation. At the same time Jackson set to work on a concurrent opinion indicating the different path whereby he arrived at agreement with the majority.[53] Then, on March 30, Robert Jackson suffered a serious heart attack and was hospitalized.

In early May, Warren or his clerk hand delivered copies of his final draft to the justices. Warren personally went to the hospital to visit Jackson and solicit his views as to the document.[54] Suggestions were made for minor changes but to Warren's great relief his brethren were satisfied with the substance and style of the opinion.

Warren had never pressured or bullied Stanley Reed. The otherwise genial Southerner seemed to be moved by deep conviction. He believed that blacks had made great strides since the Civil War within the framework of segregation. He believed that outlawing school segregation would deeply inflame whites without helping blacks, and he believed that there was nothing in the Constitution that mandated dismantling school segregation. In the second week of May Warren confronted him however. He now stood alone. None of the other justices doubted the harsh and bitter reaction that would greet a finding for the black parents and their children. There was already talk of massive resistance and threats to close the public schools filled the air. None of the other justices doubted the need to build consideration for an orderly process of change into the decision. Opponents of the decision would seize any weapon to attack it and attack the Court. Would that be good for the nation? Did Reed want his dissent to be that weapon?[55]

On Saturday, May 15, the justices met in conference. The Warren opinion was approved without dissent.

Brown v. Board of Education

In the spring of 1896 the Supreme Court had rendered a decision that did not receive much attention at the time but which had enormous historical impact. Brute force and hostile sentiment had driven blacks to the margins of civil society. They were in the country but were less a part of it than the rawest immigrant, fresh from steerage, unable to speak English, the dirt of Calabria or Silesia still under his nails. They were not slaves, yet they were not a free. What rules would attend relations between this abject, lower caste and the white majority? On May 18, 1896, the Supreme Court provided an answer. Louisiana might properly exclude Homer Plessy from public carriers within the state provided it made some type of public transport available to people of color.

Fifty-eight years later, virtually to the day, the Supreme Court met to partially undue David Brewer's work. The *New York Times* indicated that "The eyes of the country will be on the Supreme Court more intently than at any time in recent years when it returns to the bench tomorrow,"[56] as the nation awaited the decision in the segregation cases.

At approximately noon the nine justices assumed their appointed places. Robert Jackson was present for the first time in seven weeks, drawn by the knowledge that the day's work would help define the nation. The presence of a number of distinguished and powerful persons in the courtroom intimated that something of historical proportions was about to occur even though there had been no public announcement that the Court was about to hand down its decision in the school segregation cases. The attorney general, Herbert Brownell, was present, as was the solicitor general, Simon Sobeloff, and Earl Warren's wife.[57]

A half hour was spent in the ceremony admitting attorneys to practice before the Supreme Court, then Tom Clark and William O. Douglas read the majority holdings in two anonymous cases. At approximately ten minutes to one, Earl Warren spoke. The Court's holding in the segregation cases was about to be read. He took about thirty minutes.

He began with a recitation of the posture of the case as it came to the Supreme Court: "In each of these cases other than the Delaware case, a three judge federal district court denied relief to the plaintiff's on the so-called 'separate but equal' doctrine announced by this Court in *Plessy v. Ferguson*."[58] He then moved to a declaration of the plaintiffs' essential claim: "segregated public schools . . . cannot be made "equal" . . . hence they are deprived of the equal protection of the law."[59] And at that point he commenced the recitation of the steps whereby the Court moved to a conclusion, given these irreconcilable positions.

Reargument and the Court's own efforts had not resolved the question of original intent. Without doubt some of the men who framed the Fourteenth Amendment meant for it to remove all barriers to full black participation in civil society while others intended that the language have only the most limited reach.

"An additional reason for the inconclusive nature of the Amendment's history, with respect to segregated schools, is the status of public education at the time."[60] The public school had not assumed the prominence and social role in the nineteenth century that it came to have in the twentieth. "As a consequence, it is not surprising that there should be so little in the history of the Fourteenth Amendment relating to its intended effect on public education."[61]

In some early decisions the Supreme Court had affirmed the relevance of *Plessy* in education without requiring separate to actually be equal, but in more recent decisions it had held the states to the second prong of the *Plessy* equation, and where the state was unable to provide equal facilities had ordered black admittance to graduate and professional schools. The cases before them posed a different issue: "Does segregation of children in the public schools solely on the basis of race, even though the physical facilities and other 'tangible' factors may be equal, deprive the children of the minority group of equal educational opportunity?"[62]

The answer came directly. "We believe that it does."

The first reason given for the holding related to the importance of access to education to life chances in the mid-twentieth century: "Today, education is perhaps the most important function of state and local governments . . . where the state has undertaken to provide it, it is a right which must be made available to all on equal terms."[63]

The second reason addressed the question of what did or did not constitute "equal terms": "To separate (black children) from others of similar age and qualifications solely because of their race generates a feeling of inferiority as to their status in the community that may affect their hearts and minds in a way unlikely ever to be undone."[64]

The formulation yielded the conclusion: "Separate facilities are inherently unequal."

In contrast to the quiet that had greeted *Plessy*, *Brown* broke like a thunderstorm across the nation and across the globe. Black voices were as jubilant as Frederick Douglas's had been despairing eighty years earlier after Justice Bradley had found constitutional defects in the public accommodations provisions of the Civil Rights Act of 1875. "The Supreme Court decision is the greatest victory for the Negro people since the Emancipation Proclamation. It will alleviate racial troubles in many other fields" declared the *Amsterdam News*.⁶⁵ The *Chicago Defender* heralded the end of a dual society: "Neither the atom bomb nor the hydrogen bomb will ever be as meaningful to our democracy as the unanimous declaration of the Supreme Court that racial segregation violates the spirit and the letter of our Constitution. This means the beginning of the end of the dual society in American life and the system of . . . segregation which supports it."⁶⁶ The *Pittsburgh Courier* saw an international impact: "This clarion announcement will . . . stun and silence America's Communist traducers behind the Iron Curtain. It will effectively impress upon millions of colored people in Asia and Africa the fact that idealism and social morality can and do prevail in the United States regardless of race, creed or color."⁶⁷ The *Atlanta Daily World* also saw an international impact: "This case has attracted world attention; its import will be of great significance in these trying times when democracy itself is struggling to envision a free world." And it also saw a major local consequence, indicating that the decision "has added significance to the citizens of Georgia, who are now confronted with a proposed state constitutional amendment to turn the schools from public to private hands, in the event the court did just what it has done. We now predict the defeat of the amendment."⁶⁸

The decision was seen as overwhelmingly important in the context of the cold war struggle between the Soviet Union and the United States. Within minutes the Voice of America was busy sending news of the decision around the world in thirty-four languages, aiming particularly at the Soviet Union and its satellites. "They have been told that the Negro in the United States is still practically a slave and a declassed citizen," according to a Voice official. News of *Brown* would indicate the United States's capacity to reform itself without "mob rule or dictatorial fiat."⁶⁹ George Meany, president of the American Federation of Labor, also saw the decision as stirring "new confidence in America on the part of millions of persons in Europe, Asia and Africa, and will prove of tremendous benefit in the fight against communism."[70]

And among the parties most immediately affected, Paul Wilson, who had argued the case for Kansas before the Supreme Court, predicted that segregation could be ended in two years "without any great problem except the assimilation of Negro teachers."[71] But other voices were more defiant. Seven years after turning back a request for modest assistance with transportation for black children to attend the black school in Clarendon County , L. B. McCord was still defiant. He did not think that the decision was good for either race. He did not foresee the day when "Negro and white children would go together."[72] And perhaps wary of white sensibilities, James Hinton, president of the South Carolina NAACP, advised blacks to "think much (about the decision) and talk little."[73]

Aftermath

Brown had consequences of enormous import. At the level of law it redefined the essential legal questions attending the meaning of freedom for African Americans. The decision affirmed the basic moral premise of the NAACP legal position. Racial distinctions in law were morally suspect and constitutionally illegitimate. The Constitution, in the oft-quoted words of John Marshall Harlan's *Plessy* dissent, is "color blind." *Korematsu* had cautioned the courts to subject racial distinctions to very close scrutiny, the thrust of *Brown* was to create a presumption of their illegitimacy.

The decision put the South on the defensive in political and moral terms and played a role in creating a national perspective that led to ever wider support for the bus boycotts, sit-ins, and freedom marches that ensued in the following decade.

Ten years after *Brown* Congress passed the Civil Rights Act of 1964, intended in some respects to undue the work of previous Supreme Courts in terms of emasculating the meaning of freedom, particularly with regard to public accommodations, and to create protections in new areas such as job discrimination by private employers.

In a larger sense, at the level of the Supreme Court, the decades following *Brown* have entailed a constant engagement with its basic meaning and premise. Ironically, and in a sense, tragically, the underlying premise with regard to the Constitution being color blind was transformed into an argument against further efforts to remove barriers to racial exclusion. Ultimately, as is indicated in the next chapter, the decision revealed the deep and tenacious nature of race hostility in the United States, and also established the essential role of the Supreme Court in determining the ultimate meaning of freedom in the United States.

Chapter 10

The Post-*Brown* Era

In December, 1964, the *Reporter* magazine carried an article entitled "preferential treatment for Negroes." Coming just months after the passage of the Civil Rights Act of 1964, the article addressed a new and potentially divisive issue posed by the relative success of the civil rights movement's long struggle to end legal discrimination. The essential moral claim of the movement had been that blacks and whites should be treated alike. There should be no distinctions in law based on color with regard to the rights enjoyed by citizens. Decades of struggle had been devoted to advancing the claim to equal treatment in a society in which both the law and popular sentiment supported unequal treatment and entrenched forms of racial subordination.

The *Reporter* article argued the case for transforming the agenda of the civil rights movement. A society that had consistently under-invested in black students ought to now adopt race-based policies aimed at helping young blacks overcome the deficits that had been perpetuated by segregation. It was not sufficient to adopt a "color blind" stance. The legacy of decades of systematic deprivation could be overcome only by color-conscious policies directed at the victims of that deprivation.[1]

The controversy engendered by the article foreshadowed the debate, which eventually pushed all other policy issues involving race and rights to the side in the post-*Brown* era. By the end of the twentieth century affirmative action had become the paradigmatic issue in the national struggle to accommodate racial difference to a national ethic of equality before the law. Opponents of affirmative action sought to seize the moral high ground by arguing that race-based policies betrayed the central ethical claim which drove the civil rights movement in its long struggle against legal segregation. And indeed, the moral assertion with regard to equal treatment had been at the heart of the claims the movements pressed before the Supreme Court in dozens of cases spanning five decades. The affirmative action issue crystallized in a series of cases coming before the Court in the post-*Brown* era.

This chapter focuses on the Court's role in the struggle for racial justice in the decades after *Brown*. As was urged in the preceding chapters, history is contingent rather than foreordained. The pre-*Brown* political dynamic yielded Supreme Court justices who shaped the nation's racial history and therefore its national destiny. The politics of judicial selection in the post-*Brown* years yielded a Court that had major consequence with regard to race and rights. Indeed the Rehnquist Court divided more sharply over race and rights than over any other issue. Over the first four years of Rehnquist's tenure as chief justice the Court divided five to four in almost 60 percent of race cases, while showing that split in only one-sixth of the nonrace cases.[2] Visions having profoundly different implications for the society were at war on the Court.

In chronicling the struggle on the Court this chapter draws on the discussion of preceding chapters. And indeed, there is continuity in the style of analysis and the underlying point of view between the conservative courts of the past and the conservative court that formed during the decade of the 1980s. A formalism reminiscent of *Bradley* became a mode of analysis adopted by some of the justices, masking affirmation of the racial status quo in a set of abstract and distilled propositions having little to do with the brutal facts attending racial subordination. Just as *Bradley* held that laws intended to overcome the legacy of centuries of slavery conferred special rights on blacks, so his conservative progeny on the Rehnquist Court one hundred years later declared that measures intended to overcome the consequences of a century of segregation gave blacks rights not enjoyed by whites.

The chapter is divided into four parts. The first section focuses briefly on the ten-year period from *Brown* to the passage of the Civil Rights Act of 1964, a period some have referred to as the "second Reconstruction." The second section examines the Court's initial response to the second Reconstruction and the evolution of the set of issues that came to be labeled "affirmative action." Part three focuses more closely on the Court yielded by the altered political scene following the election of Ronald Reagan as president in 1980, the new administration, according to some legal scholars, reflecting "a sharp change in the stance of the presidency on civil rights." The administration was said by these scholars to have "feigned support for civil rights" while attacking most measures intended to overcome the legacy of a century of segregation.[3]

And at the end of the chapter a step is taken back to look at the long history of the Court in relation to the even longer struggle for racial equity in the society. Some broad conclusions are drawn and lessons suggested about how the Court might be brought to be a more constant and faithful herald in the struggle to achieve racial justice.

From Brown to the Civil Rights Act of 1964

The *Brown* holding contributed to the erosion of the moral legitimacy of segregation. Following *Brown* the struggle to end segregation took on even greater urgency. Violent segregationist responses to peaceful protest lent a new moral authority to the civil rights movement. In 1957, blacks led by the young Martin Luther King, Jr., boycotted segregated buses in Montgomery, Alabama. In 1960, black students "sat in" at department store lunch counters calling for an end to the denial of service on racial grounds. In 1961, black and white "freedom riders" committed acts of civil disobedience by defying segregationist laws in interstate travel. And finally, in 1964, partly in tribute to the recently murdered John F. Kennedy, a sweeping civil rights bin was passed.

In its particulars the Civil Rights Act of 1964 had wider scope than any law or amendment enacted during Reconstruction. Title Two reversed Justice Joseph Bradley's majority holding in the *Civil Right Cases of 1883* by prohibiting racial discrimination in public accommodations, Congress deriving its power to reach the discriminatory acts of private entrepreneurs from the Constitution's Commerce Clause. Title Six, which later became the basis for Allan Bakke's suit against the University of California at Davis's affirmative action program on the grounds of "reverse discrimination" barred racial discrimination by educational institutions receiving federal monies. And Title Seven provided a federal "cause of action" for plaintiffs alleging discrimination in employment, providing for the first time a national law reaching racial, ethnic, gender, and religious discrimination by private employers.[4]

But even as the bill was being bitterly fought on the floor of Congress by segregationists and states' rights advocates such as Arizona Senator and 1964 Republican presidential candidate Barry Goldwater, the issues later crystallized in the affirmative action debate began to surface.

Advocates of tough sanctions against employers who discriminated were accused of covertly seeking quota hiring for minorities and women. The bill's supporters countered with explicit denials of the supposed dangers. Hubert Humphrey, longtime civil rights advocate and floor manager of the bill in the Senate, declared that the proposed Act "does not require an employer to achieve any kind of racial balance in his work force by giving any kind of preferential treatment to any individual or group." His ally in the fight, Senator Joseph Clark of Pennsylvania, also asserted that the purported danger was illusory: "Quotas are themselves discriminatory."[5]

Passage of the Civil Rights Act of 1964 represented a signal event in the history of the Republic, a victory for racial justice achieved after decades of struggle and at enormous cost against powerful and tenacious foes. Almost immediately it served to reduce the measure of indignity blacks received in simply going about their daily business. It held organizations to standards of racial fairness hitherto not demanded of them. And almost immediately the Supreme Court was called upon to respond to challenges to the Act and to the issues which evolved out of the new world created by the Act.

A series of challenges established the constitutionality of its major provisions. For example, *Heart of Atlanta* affirmed the power of Congress under the Commerce Clause to ban discrimination in public accommodations.[6] A flurry of school segregation cases also came before the Court revolving, essentially, around questions related to identifying official connivance in the perpetuation of segregated systems and defining the powers of federal judges to fashion sweeping and creative remedies to eradicate segregation. But even as these issues were being litigated the circumstances yielding the defining racial issue of the late twentieth century were forming.

The Coming of Affirmative Action

In August 1965, a bloody race riot erupted in the Watts section of Los Angeles. Although triggered by a police-civilian encounter, it highlighted ongoing problems of economic marginalization and political exclusion in Los Angeles and elsewhere. In 1967, a series of race riots swept the country, putting problems of the inner city on the national agenda. In April 1968, Martin Luther King, Jr., was assassinated, again triggering massive rioting and evoking a new sense nationally that something had to be done to cope with racial discrimination.

Concurrent with these social catastrophes was the emergence of a new way of looking at race and exclusion, generated in part by the attempt of the newly created Equal Employment Opportunity Commission to implement the Civil Rights Act and in part by scholars and activists addressing issues of race. The new law conceptualized discrimination as a malevolent act directed at an individual. Indeed, its proponents had stated that it was directed only at intentional acts of racial discrimination. As cases of alleged racial discrimination came before the EEOC however, it became increasingly clear that black exclusion might in given instances, be as much a function of the way in which an employer traditionally did business as of an intent to discriminate. The networks ordinarily tapped and the tests ordinarily used might generate exclusion as effectively as intentional discrimination. Nondiscrimination was not enough. Nondiscrimination might still leave many blacks outside the mainstream, marginally employed, semieducated.

The new social and intellectual reality crystallized in three propositions which came to serve as the basis for a new social policy.

1. Blacks were excluded from full participation in the society by intentional discrimination and by what came to be called "institutional racism." The latter involved neutral policies which nevertheless generated racial exclusion. In the legal context, institutional racism relative to employment was called "disparate impact" discrimination and involved racial, ethnic, or gender exclusion generated by hiring criteria having a disparate and negative impact on a "protected class" without being job related in the sense of predicting successful or unsuccessful job performance.

2. Bringing minorities into the mainstream required going beyond the mere forbidding of discrimination. It was necessary also to take affirmative steps to break down subtle institutional and cultural barriers to full and equal participation in society.

3. Breaking down institutional barriers entailed reexamining some of the criteria conventionally used to mediate access to schools, colleges, universities, and the workplace.

These propositions departed from the century-long moral claim of the black struggle to repudiate race as an element in public decision making. Over time they were codified in a series of affirmative action policies at the federal and state levels.

Although political parlance tended to cite something called "affirmative action," in reality a number of different programs and policies came into existence, having somewhat different purposes and consequences and supported by different legal and sociological theories.

At the federal, state, and municipal levels, so-called set-aside programs were established. Typical, set-aside programs sought to direct a percentage of public spending to minority or female vendors either directly or by requiring primary contractors to allocate a certain percentage of the value of the contract to minority or female subcontractors. As policy, set asides evolved in response to evidence of discrimination in the allocation of public contracts and in recognition of the fact that the legacy of discrimination left many minority and female vendors genuinely unable to show the kind of track record or bonding capacity necessary to be viable competitors for public contracts under traditional rules.

At the state level a number of programs evolved in the area of higher education intended to increase minority presence on campus. At the City University ofNew York a program was inaugurated aimed at facilitating access for "disadvantaged" students. The State University of New York launched an Equal Opportunity Program directed at economically and educationally disadvantaged students, but was widely understood to be a vehicle for increasing black and Puerto Rican enrollment.

Other states and institutions developed similar programs, some having an explicit racial or ethnic focus. Mary Washington College instituted a minority scholarship fund. Florida State University funded programs to recruit and retain minority students. Califomia moved to take race and ethnicity into account, along with other factors, in the allocation of places in its undergraduate and professional schools.[7]

The crystallization of affirmative action as policy generated enormous controversy. Former segregationists adopted the language of the civil rights movement with regard to the Constitution being color blind. Other opponents were moved by philosophical considerations. The Washington Legal Foundation became a major player in the legal battle against affirmative action in higher education, and sought out cases that allowed them to "assert the principle that racial classifications are wrong."[8]

The fundamental question posed in the key cases that came before the Court challenging affirmative action related to the constitutionality of racial distinctions in law. They also related to the question of whether any effort would be made to address the legacy of decades of discrimination. The 1964 *Reporter* article, an argument for affirinative action before there was a policy, rested on the premise that racial discrimination as legal practice and cultural norm for most of the nation's history had given whites such disproportionate advantage with regard to power, privilege, and opportunity that neither a change in the law nor an easing of white animus would yield significant black mobility. The instruments of racial oppression were no longer necessary to sustain racial stratification. They had done their work. Without a race-conscious effort to undo that work, racial stratification would simply persist.

The Burger Court and the New World of Race

Pursuing a "southern strategy" Richard Nixon won the presidency in 1968, building on the move started in 1964 by Barry Goldwater to portray the Republican Party as an entity sympathetic to the white South's resistance to the black movement. Chief Justice Earl Warren became an issue in the campaign, the "Warren Court" being attacked as liberal claque, given to imposing its own value preferences and passions on the nation. Nixon promised to appoint "strict constructionists" to the bench, justices less inclined to give an expansive reading to the Constitution, less inclined to see it as an instrument for correcting the ancient evils afflicting the nation, less inclined to see merit in ancient black claims.

A year into the Nixon presidency Earl Warren retired, giving his fellow Californian the opportunity to nominate sixty-two-year-old Warren Burger as the new chief justice. A lifelong Republican, former Justice Department assistant attorney general during the Eisenhower years, and member of the United States Court of Appeals for the District of Columbia, Burger attracted Nixon's attention when he spoke of the importance of heeding the needs of law enforcement as well as the rights of the accused in criminal matters, and cautioned respect for settled law and established precedent.

Perhaps unknown or disregarded by Nixon were certain facts in Burger's background that suggested that he might bring a sensibility to matters of race and rights at odds with the conservative stance of the administration. Decades earlier in his native Minriesota he had helped found and became the first president of the St. Paul Council on Human Relations, directed at fighting racial discrimination. And with the onset of World War II he had spoken out against the forced relocation of Japanese citizens and had taken a Japanese family into his home in the face of enormous criticism.[9]

Burger assumed leadership of a Court made up of justices nominated by presidents who had responded to or been swept along by the civil rights revolution. William Brennan, an Eisenhower nominee, had proven to be a fierce advocate of racial reform. Hugo Black and William O. Douglas, Roosevelt nominees, had been instrumental in driving the Court forward from the days when the defenders of segregation stood in the Court's well to an era where repudiation of legal segregation was a settled matter. And symbolic of all that had happened and all that had changed in thirty years was the presence of Thurgood Marshall on the bench as a colleague.

Issues of race and rights came to engage the Burger Court almost immediately and as the Court's stance evolved over a period of years three principles emerged, sometimes with the agreement of the chief justice, sometimes with the chief justice in the minority.

In the *Griggs* case the Court expanded the definition of "discrimination" to embrace seemingly neutral practices by an employer which have a disproportionately harmful impact on blacks without being job related. In *Griggs*, Duke Power, required a high school diploma and used a variety of tests in recruiting its entry-level workforce. The doleful history of the local area with regard to support for black schools decreased the percentage of blacks with the high school diploma, thereby excluding them from consideration. And for those blacks who did become part of the employer's pool, tests alleged to assess "aptitude" proved to be a significant barrier. The case was significant in advancing the concept of "disparate impact" type discrimination, thereby allowing the law to become a more effective instrument in addressing the legacy of decades of legal discrimination.[10]

Second, the Burger Court came to recognize that an argument for a "color blind" approach to public policy could mask malevolent motives or freeze into place advantages and disadvantages yielded by decades of legal discrimination. The North Carolina *Swann* decision occurred in the midst of a storm of ongoing litigation involving efforts to implement *Brown* by dismantling North Carolina's dual school system. Fifteen years after *Brown*, many schools in the state remained segregated in fact though not by law. In resistance to court efforts to desegregate the system via mandated busing, the North Carolina legislature passed a law forbidding the use of race as a criterion in assigning students to schools for any purpose, including the establishment of "racial balance."[11] Implicit in the Court's rejection of the North Carolina argument was recognition of the fact that the Fourteenth Amendment does not prohibit government from making *any* decisions based on race, and that a consideration of race might be proper where necessary to overcome the disadvantages yielded by prior discrimination.

Third, in the *Weber* and *Bakke* cases the Burger Court addressed the matter of whether race might be made an aspect of policy where there had been neither a judicial finding of prior discrimination nor an admission by an employer or a school that it had engaged in discrimination. In other words, to what extent could voluntary affirmative action programs be accommodated by the law and by the Constitution?

Bakke began with a set of facts providing the model for "reverse discrimination" challenges to affirmative action programs. Alan Bakke had applied to the medical school at the University of California at Davis and had twice been denied entrance. In seeking redress in the courts he argued that the University had set aside sixteen of the one hundred spots in the first-year class for minority applicants. He also argued that he was better qualified according to traditional criteria than many of the minorities admitted under the special program and that he therefore had been rejected solely because he was white in violation of his rights under Title Six of the 1964 Civil Rights Act, and his right to the equal protection of the law. The California Supreme Court ordered Bakke's admission to the medical school and prohibited the university from using race as a factor in the admissions process.

At stake in the case was the fate of voluntary affirmative action programs. The Supreme Court had allowed government to take race into account in a remedial context, but the University of California at Davis had never discriminated against minorities in the admission process, nor had it been accused of doing so. The use of race as a factor in the allocation of a scarce but desired good could not, therefore, be justified in remedial terms.

In June, 1978, a bitterly divided Court yielded a holding which came to constitute the rules of the affirmative action process until placed in jeopardy by the holdings of the Court dominated by Burger's successor, William Rehnquist. The *Bakke* holding rejected the use of hard and fast numbers in minority recruitment but allowed race to be taken into account as one factor among many in the admission process. The pursuit of diversity was recognized as a legitimate objective. However, an institution might have a problem if it segregated minority applicants from others and rated them only against each other.[12]

Bakke was a watershed in terms of affirmative action admissions in higher education. Most programs were voluntary. Many were subject to restructuring in the fight of the decision, but the process survived the court challenge. Shortly after *Bakke*, the Burger Court spoke to the issue of voluntary affirmative action in the employment context. Prodded by the civil rights community, Kaiser Alunfmum and the Steelworkers Union entered into an agreement under which, without admitting fault or prior discrimination, they established a series of training programs intended to increase the number of black workers at skilled and craft levels. Pursuant to this agreement, the Kaiser plant in Gramercy, Louisiana, stablished a program open to both black and white workers who were selected on the basis of seniority from separate fists, one for blacks, the other for whites. Brian Weber, a white worker, applied to the program in his plant but was rejected despite having more seniority than some of the blacks who were selected from the other list.

Weber brought a suit under Title Seven, alleging that he was the victim of racial discrimination. Eventually the matter reached the Supreme Court where sharp and bitter language separated the majority from the minority. The issue was one of statutory interpretation. Did the literal language of Title Seven indicate that Congress intended to prohibit voluntary affirmative action programs? In a vitriolic dissent, William Rehnquist accused the majority of taking an Orwellian approach to the law, contending that the plain language of Title Seven prohibited the use of race as a factor in employment decisions and that Brian Weber's rights had been shamelessly violated.

The majority countered by going to the minutes of the Congressional meetings and conferences from which Title Seven had emerged. The intention of the people who drafted the law, according to the Court majority, had been to bring blacks into the mainstream. It would be ironic indeed if an employer were now to be barred from voluntarily pursuing the law's objective via programs that were temporary, narrowly tailored to reach proximate goals, and that did not injure white workers.[13]

Weber provided constitutional support for voluntary affirmative action programs in an employment context provided certain rules were followed. Programs that were temporary, narrowly tailored, and did not injure white workers in terms of any proprietary interest such as loss of job or loss of legitimate seniority rights would survive challenge.

One year after *Weber*, Ronald Reagan was elected president. Philosophically closer to Barry Goldwater than Richard Nixon, Reagan's nominees to the Court brought a different sensibility to issues of race and rights. Of greatest consequence with regard to race and the law was his nomination of William Rehnquist to be chief justice following the retirement of Warren Burger. In Chapter Two it was stated that Joseph Bradley's nearest equivalent on the Court at the end of the twentieth century was William Rehnquist. The post–Civil War Court, driven by Bradley on issues of race and rights, played a significant role in shaping an America which institutionalized racial subordination. In the post–*Brown* era the Rehnquist Court also spoke powerfully in similar tones to the nation's fate with regard to race. In the last two sections of this book, analysis focuses on the Rehnquist Court and matters of race, and on the process whereby the Court might be brought to be a more constant and effective force for the pursuit of racial justice.

The Rehnquist Court and the Conservative Vision

In 1986 Warren Burger retired and William Rehnquist was nominated by Ronald Reagan to succeed him as chief justice. Just as Burger's background suggested certain sensibilities with regard to matters of race and rights, so also did Rehnquist's. Following his original nomination to the Court by Richard Nixon charges had been made and denied regarding his having harassed black voters in his home state of Arizona in the 1960s. In addition, a memo surfaced, written when he was law clerk to justice Robert Jackson and bearing his initials, urging support of *Plessy*'s separate-but-equal doctrine against the claims of black parents in *Brown*, then being considered by the Court. His nomination in jeopardy, Rehnquist denied bad motives, claiming that he had merely been laying out the alternative arguments for Jackson.[14] It also emerged that while head of the Office of Legal Council in Nixon's Justice Department he had strongly urged not giving the Equal Opportunity Commission expanded cease-and-desist authority relative to employment discrimination claims on the grounds that the agency was too "client oriented."[15]

As a sitting justice Rehnquist brought a singular and distinct vision to issues of race and rights, and in the Reagan years he was joined by justices who shared that vision. With the addition of Anthony Kennedy, Sandra Day O'Connor, and Antonin Scalia to the Court the dimensions of a conservative majority on matters of race and rights began to form. The conservative mode of analysis emerged in sharp relief in cases embracing race and rights across a spectrum of concerns other than affirmative action. In its particulars it embraced the following.

1. Federal Courts were likely to be deemed to have exceeded their authority where remedial measures in the interest of black plaintiffs were ordered but not have exceeded their authority where such measures were delimited or eliminated.

In *Missouri v. Jenkins* a federal district court's orders requiring the state to take certain measures in support of a magnet school concept to promote desegregation was held by Rehnquist and his ideological cohorts to be "beyond the court's remedial authority."[16]

In *Board of Education v. Dowell* a conservative majority supported the claim of Oklahoma City Board of Education that the 10th Circuit Court of Appeals held them to an excessively stringent standard with regard to whether they had taken all feasible steps to elirninate school segregation. As was indicated by one legal scholar, the conservative majority advanced the view that the "rule, which makes terminating a federal injunction very difficult, should not apply to desegregation cases . . . ," allegedly because it was inconsistent with the tradition of local control of schools.[17]

In *Pasadena Board of Education v. Spangler* Rehnquist led a divided Court in holding that the United States District Court for the Central District of California had acted improperly in ordering measures to ensure that particular schools within the district not become minority schools.[18]

On the other hand, in *Freeman v. Pitts* a District Court's partial withdrawal from oversight of a Georgia school system which had not yet fully met desegregation objectives was found to be a proper exercise of discretion.[19]

The conservative impulse to limit the remedial powers of federal courts relative to the claims of black plaintiffs extended beyond school desegregation cases and the presumed sanctity of local school boards. In *Spallone v. United States* Rehnquist, joined by O'Connor, Scalia, Kennedy, and White, held that the United States District Court for the Southern District of New York had abused its discretion in imposing contempt sanction against members of the Yonkers City Council who continued to resist court orders relative to steps necessary to overcome city-imposed racial segregation in housing.[20]

2. Constitutional and statutory language is given a narrow and restrictive reading relative to the claims of black plaintiffs.

In *Moose Lodge v. Irvis*, one of his earliest opinions, Rehnquist found that the United States District Court for the Middle District of Pennsylvania had erred in revoking the liquor license of a local lodge that refused to serve the black guest of a member: "the licensing of the lodge to serve liquor, did not . . . implicate the state in the lodge's discriminatory guest policies, so as to make the regulation and licensing state action which would fall within the ambit of the equal protection clause."[21]

In *St. Mary's Honor Center v. Melvin Hicks* Scalia led a five-to-four majority in asserting that Title Seven of the 1964 Civil Rights Act did not entitle a black plaintiff to victory in a racial discrimination suit even though the district court, acting as the trier of fact, had concluded that the employer lied with regard to the purported reasons for Hicks's demotion and discharge. Title Seven required that Hicks prove bias as the reason for his discharge, according to Scalia and his associates, it did not permit the inference that the employer had lied to conceal a biased motive. Perhaps, asserted the majority, he had lied to cover up something else, and race was not the reason after all.[22]

And in *Patterson v. McLean Credit Union* an impulse to read remedial statutes narrowly was combined with a kind of negative judicial activism directed at overturning precedent cases and prior decisions that had expanded the legal rights of blacks fighting discrimination. Having been harassed by her supervisor on racial grounds, Brenda Patterson brought suit under the Civil Rights Act of 1866, which gave blacks the same right to make contracts as whites. In conference following initial oral argument before the Court, Rehnquist asked his colleagues to summon the attorneys to come before the Court for reargument but, this time, to also address the question of whether a prior case—*Runyon v. McCrary*—had been correctly decided.

The legal community was stunned. *Runyon* had affirmed the right of blacks to sue private parties under Section 1841 of the United States Code but had not been a factor in *Patterson*, in the sense that neither party had relied on it. The request came out of nowhere but seemed to portend an effort driven by a conservative Court to cripple remedial laws and overturn progressive holdings that it had not even been asked to consider.

The resulting firestorm led to a retreat on *Runyon* but the outcome for Brenda Patterson and others similarly situated was not as positive. Formalist analysis characterized the holding read by Anthony Kennedy for the Rehnquist wing of the Court. The Civil Rights Act of 1866 gave blacks the right to "form a contract" but did not offer legal grounds for pursuing enforcement of the contract. And, in any event, maybe Title Seven of the 1964 Civil Rights Act was an adequate vehicle for pursuing redress.[23]

3. There is extreme reluctance to grant the sufficiency of evidence establishing racial bias as systemic rather than the acts of individual bigots.

In *Rizzo v. Goode* Rehnquist led a majority in finding that the federal courts below had exceeded their authority in ordering remedial steps relative to a finding that the Philadelphia police department had shown a "pervasive pattern of unconstitutional police mistreatment of minority citizens." At best, according to Rehnquist, a few bad cops had abused the rights of particular people.[24]

Twenty years later in *Armstrong v. United States* Rehnquist held that the United States Attorney's office in Los Angeles did not have to open its records relative to allegations of selective prosecution by black defendants, given that every person charged was black while a substantial number of the felons committing the same crime were white.[25]

The conservative vision of race in America is ahistorical yet the most fundamental issues regarding race and rights in the United States cannot be grasped apart from their historical context. Affirmative action as public policy rests on certain premises regarding American history, and, in particular, on the assumption that formal, legal discrimination yielded pervasive, ongoing "structural discrimination" as real in its consequences as the former system of explicit, overt discrimination. The distinguished legal historian Ronald Dworkin defined structural discrimination as "the intractable social and economic patterns of American society, created by generations of injustice, through which poorer education, lower expectations and instinctive and unacknowledged prejudice insure that race continues to be a dominant pervasive factor affecting the lifetime prospects of individual citizens."[26]

The conservative vision does not recognize the existence of structural discrimination and in a sense, therefore, does not acknowledge that historical facts may have present consequences. Yet the constitutional status of affirmative action policies rests on the assumption that an end to legal discrimination is hollow if no steps are taken to address the practices and habits that sustain white racial privilege with a degree of effectiveness that make legal segregation unnecessary.

The profoundly different implications of the alternative visions and uses of history played themselves out in *Croson.* This book closes with a review of this case and with a discussion of the alternative roles the Court may play in the future regarding race and rights.

Croson and the Conservative Uses of History

In the 1989 case *Croson v. Richmond* the Supreme Court addressed the constitutionality of a law by which the Richmond, Virginia, City Council had mandated that prime contractors on construction projects allocate at least 30 percent of the dollar value of contracts with the city to minority subcontractors, subject to a waiver were this to prove not feasible. By implication, the constitutionality of similar "set aside" laws at the municipal and state levels nationwide was at stake.

Richmond had been the capital of the Confederacy. But by April, 1865, as Lee's Army of Northern Virginia collapsed, it remained only as the last citadel of a domain shrunken to patches and remnants of futile resistance. The sun had set on a strange and cruel world. Jefferson Davis's cavaliers had fought and died for the freedom to keep others in bondage. And as the train left, carrying the leaders of the erstwhile slave empire to their various fates, the city went up in flames. Civilians and Confederate soldiers, now bereft of an army and a country, took to pillage, uncertain of their fate and fearing what was to come.

In the years following defeat and humiliation Richmond had been rebuilt and became a bastion of the new, post–Civil War racial order. It was as rigidly segregated as any city in the South. It housed the Museum of the Confederacy and along Monument Avenue displayed statues of Confederate heroes, Robert E. Lee, J. E. B. Stuart, and "Stonewall" Jackson. As was customary in the decades during which segregation prevailed, the instruments and services of government were used primarily to benefit the city's white population. Naturally, this extended to the letting of city contracts for goods and services. Minority vendors did not participate. They were not the beneficiaries of public spending.

The decade of the 1960s brought change to Richmond as it did to the rest of the South and the country. A combination of changes in the racial composition of the city and the Voting Rights Act of 1965 eventually yielded a black majority on the city counsel. And this majority moved to change a number of city policies, including policy with regard to the letting of city contracts. On April 11, 1983, Richmond adopted a Minority Business Utilization Plan which required prime contractors doing business with the city to subcontract at least 30 percent of the dollar amount of the contract to one or more minority-owned businesses.

On September 6, 1983, the city issued an invitation to bid on a contract to provide and install plumbing fixtures in the city jail. On September 30, Eugene Bonn, regional manager for the J. A. Croson Company, a mechanical plumbing and heating firrn, submitted a bid. The unsealing of bids two weeks later revealed J. A. Croson to be the only bidder. One week later Croson sought a waiver from the set-aside provision of the contract, arguing that it could not find a qualified minority subcontractor. On November 2, the city denied the waiver request, giving Croson ten days to adjust its bid to include minority vendors identified as being capable of doing the subcontracting work. Early in December, counsel for Croson wrote to the city asking for a review of the waiver denial but was informed that the city had decided to rebid the contract. Shortly thereafter Croson brought suit under Article 42 of the United States Code, Section 1983.

Ironically, the statute under which Croson sued traced back historically to the post–Civil War period. On April 20, 1871, the House of Representatives passed the Ku Klux Klan Act intended to protect the newly freed black population from Klan terror and from abuse by rebel sympathizers holding office at local and state levels. The language provided a civil cause of action to anyone suffering "deprivation of any rights, privileges or immunities secured by the Constitution or the laws" as a consequence of the actions of any person acting "under cover of any statute, ordinance, (or) regulation."[27]

Thus, J. A. Croson brought suit against the black-dominated

city council under a statute which traced back to a federal effort to provide protection for blacks against official connivance in Klan terror.

The company argued that the statute was unconstitutional on its face and that it violated the Equal Protection clause of the Fourteenth Amendment. Applying the language of the law to its predicament Croson contended that Richmond was constitutionally prohibited from writing any statute which made preferential distinctions based on race relative to the distribution of public goods and services.

Richmond defended the new law on two grounds. A prior Supreme Court holding had affirmed the constitutionality of set-asides in terms of federal contracts, given substantial evidence of widespread racial discrimination in the construction industry at the local, state, and national levels. Equally persuasive evidence could be advanced with regard to Richmond specifically. In the years immediately preceding the passage of the new law less than 1 percent of city contracts had gone to minority vendors, and, in addition, local contractors' associations had virtually no minority membership. The Associated General Contractors of Virginia and the American Subcontractors Association had no black Richmond-area members, while the Professional Contractors Estimators Association and the Central Virginia Electrical Contractors associations had one each, and the National Electrical Contractors Association had two black members.

The city had, perhaps, also relied on various members of the Court having a background understanding of segregation, what it was about and how it worked. In the capital of the old Confederacy, in a self-proclaimed proud citadel of segregation, government had, without question, systematically excluded minority businesses from participating in the contracting business.

In addition to resting on legal precedent and evidence, the Richmond argument also rested, most importantly, on a sense of history, on a grasp of the essential nature and consequences of segregation, as indeed do most forms of affirmative action as policy. The essence of formalist judicial analysis from Bradley in the *Civil Rights Cases of 1883* through Justice Sandra Day O'Connor in *Croson* is to wrench the black experience out of historical and social context. In that sense there is continuity between the judicial mode which eviscerated the Reconstruction statutes and the analytic approach taken by the Rehnquist Court to affirmative action cases. *Croson* reflected that continuity.

Justice O'Connor began by acknowledging that, in principle, a "the city of Richmond (had) legislative authority over its procurement policies, and can use its spending powers to remedy private discrimination, if it identifies that discrimination with the particularity required by the Fourteenth Amendment."[28]

But the "particularity required by the Fourteenth Amendment," as defined by the conservative majority, virtually precluded the possibility of ever finding circumstances sufficient to justify race-based remedial policy. The Richmond justification for the set-aside program had been supported by evidence going to the ongoing consequences of historical discrimination. Much of the analysis of the conservative majority went to denying the reality of the history Richmond described.

There were, they claimed, "numerous explanations" for the near total absence of minority representation in Richmond's contractor associations, of which prior discrimination was only one, others might be "black and white career and entrepreneurial choices. Blacks may be disproportionately attracted to industries other than construction." Or in other words, the citadel of resistance to integration along a number of fronts might have had integrated contractors' associations, had not blacks simply chosen to pursue other interests.

Further, "for low minority membership to be relevant, the city would have to link it to the number of local MBEs (minority business enterprises) eligible for membership. If the statistical disparity between eligible MBEs and MBE membership were great enough, an inference of discriminatory exclusion could arise." In other words, if there was a large number of minority businesses eligible for membership in the professional associations but only a small number that were actually members, then possibly an inference of discrimination might be drawn.

Again, the majority approach was ahistorical. Richmond argued that a century-long history of racial bias in public spending had stunted the growth of black businesses. There was no parallel universe of black contractors who had flourished irrespective of being excluded from a major portion of the market. Institutionalized bias had consequences. The analytic model proposed by the majority presupposed either that systematic exclusion existed but had no consequences or that it never existed at all.

In his dissent Thurgood Marshall attacked the formalist approach taken by the majority. "They had taken "the disingenuous approach of disaggregating Richmond's local evidence, attacking it piecemeal, and thereby concluding that no *single* piece of evidence adduced by the city 'standing alone' . . . suffices to prove past discrimination. But items of evidence do not, of course, 'stand alone' or exist in alien juxtaposition; they necessarily work together." The majority had, according to Marshall, taken a "myopic view" of the historical facts and had refused to acknowledge that "The more government bestows its rewards on those persons or businesses that were positioned to thrive during a period of private racial discrimination, the tighter the dead hand grip of prior discrimination becomes on the present and the future."[29]

Aftermath

Croson had immediate and long-range consequences. As regards the immediate consequnces, the decision was handed down on June 9, 1989. The more than two hundred state and local set-aside programs in existence immediately became constitutionally suspect. The tangible impact of *Croson* went far beyond Richmond. In 1974 Atlanta, Georgia, had initiated a program to channel a percentage of city contract dollars to minority and female vendors. By 1989 these firms were receiving 35 percent of the city's contract dollars. Within six months of *Croson* contracting with minority and female-owned vendors fell to 15 percent. In Philadelphia the minority share of the city's contracts fell from 25 percent to between 3 percent and 4 percent. By 1991 two dozen cities accross the nation had suspended their set-aside programs as had a number of states.

The less tangible but equally important consequence of the holding went to a matter of national mood. The decisions of the Supreme Court constitute political and moral affirmations of particular positions in addition to being legal pronouncements. The decision supported, sustained, animated, and energized hostility to affirmative action programs, allowing some of the proponents of abolition to cloak bad motives in moral language. The momentum of the antiaffirmative movement in the 1990s received moral and political impetus from the holding of the Supreme Court on the eve of the final decade of the twentieth century as the Court played its historic role of shaping the nation.

In the last decade of the twentieth century the United States stood at a crossroads as regards race and rights. Open and avowed racism was anathema, but covert racist practice and coded racist speech bespoke deep reservoirs of hostility and a barely damned urge to racial atrocity. At the same time an impulse to overcome the violence and racial tragedy of the past impelled efforts to struggle and sacrifice in the interest of racial reform. And as ever the Supreme Court's role in the life of the nation gave it a peculiar power to move the nation toward one destiny or the other.

The Supreme Court and Race and Rights in the Twenty-First Century

The analysis taken here views history as contingent, not quite a series of accidents but not operating according to any grand law or fundamental principle either. *Cruikshank* was not inevitable, nor was *Reese*, but both had profound consequences for the direction race and rights took in the United States well into the twentieth century. Had the Enforcement Acts and the Fifteenth Amendment not been undermined, the United States would not have moved toward a new eden in terms of race and rights in the decade after the Civil War. The grip of custom with regard to racial subordination was too strong, the psychological and social benefits yielded to the white majority by having a despised and brutalized black minority in its midst were too great. Decisions going the other way would have generated a different racial dynamic however, giving greater potential for the values and vision underlying the reform laws and new amendments to gain strength and move the country along a path less tortured and painful than the one down which it was propelled by the Bradleys, Brewers, and Melville Fullers.

And so at the end of the twentieth century the country stands again at a crossroads. The Court in some respects is eerily reminsecent of the Court in the decades of the 1870s and 1880s. A conservative majority in thrall to its own simplistic view of racial history offers up formalist evasions as pentrating judicial analysis. But history is emergent rather than determined. Although William Rehnquist is reminiscent of Jopseph Bradley on matters of race and rights, there is no law of history which mandates that Rehnquist must create the world that Bradley helped create.

The past informs the future. To the extent that it is understood that Rehnquist casts the same shadow as Bradley, that his mode of judicial analysis is equally formalist, equally evasive of the squalid facts of racial subordination, equally hostile to any law or policy that would seem to compromise in any degree the historic and customary privileges of the white majority, to that extent there is a basis for holding that the United States in the twenty-first century cannot, for its own sake, afford a Bradley or a Rehnquist.

The twenty-first century promises to pose issues of race and rights in more complex form. A larger percentage of the nation's population will be nonwhite, the population of the country will be much more heterogeneous ethnically and racially, the various racial and ethnic groups will be highly stratified internally as regards wealth and income, reflecting in varying degrees sharpening class divisions in the population as a whole, the cultural fabric of the country will be more diverse, and the dichtomous black-white framework within which issues of race and rights played themselves out historically, already outmoded and collapsing from the 1960s onward, will become largely obsolete early in the twenty-first century.

The Supreme Court's historic charge to interpret the constitutional rules of the game will be extraordinarily difficult. The faithful discharge of their constitutional responsibility will also be important to the survival of the United States. Diversity is both a promise and a danger. The promise lies in the kind of cultural richness and economic dynamism which propelled the country to the forefront among developed nations; the danger lies in the the absence of the kinds of common cultural commitments and shared values crucial to holding a society together. The extraordinarily difficult task confronting the Supreme Court will lay in crafting a conception of justice that shows a commitment to a recognition of a need at the policy level to acknowledge racial or ethnic difference where necessary to overcome biased practice or where desirable in terms of the benefits it may yield.

The blinkered and shuttered courts that gave the nation *Cruikshank, Reese, Plessy,* and *Corregan* served the nation badly. The formalist evasions of the Waite, Fuller, and Rehnquist Courts on matters of race and rights substitute pretense for the kind of close and disquieting examination of ugly realities necessary to moving the nation away from its grim racial past. But history is contingent and the Court has from time to time played a noble role, and if a John Marsha Harlan and a Charles Evans Hughes and a Hugo Black and a Thurgood Marshall once sat on the Court there is no reason to doubt that their like will come again.

Notes

Chapter One
Introduction: The Supreme Court and Civil Rights

1. *Blyew v. United States*, (Dec. 1871) Sup Ct. 591.

2. Op. cit., pp. 597–98.

3. Op. cit., p. 599.

4. Transcripts of the *Blyew* proceedings, located in the Nation Archives, provide a vivid feel for the time and covey a sense of the horrific nature of the crime.

5. *Black Courage: 1775–1783: Documents on Black Participation in the American Revolution*, Richard Ewell Green, National Society of the Daughters of the American Revolution.

6. Ibid.

7. Gary Wills in *Lincoln at Gettysburg* (New York: Simon and Schuster, 1992), and David Herbert Donald in *Lincoln* (New York: Simon and Schuster, 1995), discuss the legacy of Jefferson's ambiguity on race and the compromise relative to the Declaration of Independence. The citation in the text comes from the *Dictionary of Afro-American Slavery*, Randall Miller and John David Smith, editors (New York: Greenwood Press, 1988), pp. 174–75.

8. Kelly Miller, the celebrated black intellectual at the turn of the century, saw Jefferson as torn between ambition and conscience. See *Race*

Adjustments, Kelly Miller (New York and Washington, D.C.: Neale Publishing, 1908), p. 231, republished by Arno Press and *New York Times*, New York, 1968. The citation in the text is from the *Jeffersonian Cyclopedia*, V. 2, John P, Foley, editor, Russel and Russel, New York, 1967, p. 811.

9. David Brion Davis, Sterling Professor of History at Yale, has written extensively on slavery in Western culture.

10. "Slavery and Anti-Slavery," Sylvia Frey, *The Blackwell Encyclopedia of the American Revolution*, Jack P. Green and J. R. Pole, editors (Cambridge, Mass.: Basil Blackwell, 1995).

11. *Slavery in the Courtroom*, Paul Finkleman (Washington, D.C.: Library of Congress, 1985).

12. The Finkleman book provides a sense in which slavery as a system was supported by deeply held assumptions as well as by force.

13. Op. cit., p. 46.

14. *Dred Scott v. Sandiford*, 19 How., 393, 60 U.S., 15 L.Ed., 691 (U.S. Mo.,Dec.Term 1856).

15. *The Tempting of America*, Robert Bork (New York: The Free Press, 1990), p. 130.

16. *Buchanan v. Warley*, 245 U.S. 60, 1917.

17. *Public Opinion and the Supreme Court*, Thomas Marshall (Boston: Unwin Hyman, 1989).

18. *Patterson v. McLean*, 485 U.S. 617 (1988).

19. *The Gallop Poll: Public Opinion 1935–1971*, George Gallop (New York: Random House), p. 783.

20. Patricia Williams, *The Alchemy of Race and Rights* (Cambridge: Harvard University Press, 1991).

21. See *Reconstruction and Reunion, 1864–88*, Part Two, Charles Fairman (New York: Macmillan, 1987), p. 564, p. 279.

22. Ibid.

23. "Looking to the Bottom: Critical Legal Studies and Reparations," Mari Matsuda, *Harvard Civil Rights—Civil Liberties Law Review*, vol. 22, no. 2, Spring 1987, p. 328.

24. Frederick Douglas's bitter words can be found in the *Frederick Douglas Papers*, Series One: Speeches, Debates, and Interviews: vol. 5, John Blassingame and John McKivigan, editors (New Haven: Yale University Press), p. 122.

25. *The Supreme Court Compendium*, Lee Epstein, Jeffrey Segal, Harold Spaeth, and Thomas Walker, Congressional Quarterly, Washington D.C. (1994), p. 336.

26. *In Re Turner*, Fed. Case No, 14, 247 (1867).

Chapter Two
The Meaning of Freedom

1. See *The Civil War Day By Day: An Almanac 1861–1865*, E. B. Long and Barbara Long (Garden City, N.Y.: A Da Capo, 1971), for a sense of the war as a living event.

2. See the *Statutory History of the United States: The Civil War:* Bernard Schwartz, editor (New York: McGraw Hill, 1970), pp. 42–48, for the full text of Wood's defense of slavery.

3. Ibid., pp. 48–54.

4. The Schwartz compilation and *The Civil Rights Record: Black Americans and the Law, 1849–1920*, Crowell Publishers, provide an excellent map of the mental terrain of the period.

5. *New York Times*, March 22, 1864, indicated that money for the relocation of blacks to Haiti had been appropriated.

6. For the story of Jackson, the vice president's escaped slave, see *The Reminiscences of Levi Coffin* (Cincinnati: Robert Clark, 1898), reprinted by Arno Press and *New York Times*, 1968.

7. See "American Caste and Common Schools," J. H. Townsend, *The Anglo-African Magazine*, 1859, Arno Press and *New York Times*, pp. 80–81.

8. Op. cit., pp. 222–23.

9. See also *The Civil War and Reconstruction in Florida*, Wm. Watson Davis, Columbia University, 1913, pp. 420–21, for a discussion of the content and purposes of the black codes.

10. See *New York Times*, June 3, 1865, p. 4.

11. *New York Times*, December 22, 1863.

12. "State Sovereignty and State's Rights," L. Tribe, *Oxford Companion to the Supreme Court of the United States*, J. Ely, J. B. Grossman, and W. Wiecks, eds. (New York: Oxford University Press), 1992.

13. *New York Times*, January 7, 1866, p. 8.

14. *The Black Abolitionist Papers V,* C. Peter Ripley, ed. (Chapel Hill and London: University of North Carolina Press), p. 152.

15. *The Abraham Lincoln Encyclopedia,* M. Neely, editor (New York: McGraw-Hill, 1982), p. 218.

16. See David Donald's *Lincoln* in terms of his evolving ideas on race.

17. *New York Times,* January 7, 1866, p. 8.

18. Ben Flanders's as quoted in Eric Foner's monumental work *Reconstruction: America's Unfinished Business,* Harper and Row, 1988, p. 199.

19. The *Colored American* can be found in the Howard University Library.

20. For contemporaneous accounts of the Black Codes see *Documentary History of Reconstruction,* vol. I, W. Fleming, ed. (Glouster, Mass.: P. Smith, 1960).

21. See *New York Times,* Feb. 12, 1868, p. 4, and Foner regarding motives for the codes.

22. See Foner's *Reconstruction,* p. 129, regarding the planter view of the role pf Black labor.

23. *New York Times,* August 19, 1865.

24. *Documentary History of Reconstruction,* vol. 1, 249.

25. "The Civil Rights Bill—The Veto," *New York Times,* April 7, 1866.

26. Johnson's veto message, delivered March 27, 1866, attacked the bill as antiwhite.

27. *U.S. v. Rhodes,* (Cas. No. 16,151), Fed. Cas. P. 785 (1866).

28. "The 14th Amendment That Wasn't," Andrew Krull, *Constitution,* Winter 1993, pp. 68–70.

29. John Armor Bingham, 1815–1900, was a key player. The language of the equal protection clause was a compromise. It placed constraints on state action but accommodated some of the racial distinctions made by Northern states, including Bingham's Ohio.

30. See *New York Times,* August 27, 1866, for an account of the rioting.

31. *Documentary History of Reconstruction,* p. 483.

32. See *The White Terror: The Ku Klux Klan Conspiracy and Southern Reconstruction*, Allan W. Trelease (New York: Harper and Row), pp. 95, 113, 119, 129, and 136.

33. The Republican Party had never received a majority of the white vote as the 1868 election approached. Concern for the black vote was, in part, a matter of self-interest.

34. See Records of the U. S. Senate, 42d Cong., 1st Sess., Nat. Archives, Wash., D.C.

35. See *The Fiery Cross: The Ku Klux Klan in America*, W. Wade (New York: Simon & Schuster).

36. *The Fiery Cross*, p. 72.

37. See the *Tulane Review*, V. 67, Appendix A, 1993, pp. 2225–29.

38. "The Klan Act," ibid., pp. 2226–27.

39. *The White Terror*, pp. 399–418.

40. The Civil Rights Act of 1875 captured a particular sensibility. Its proponents sought to address the everyday abuses and insults attending being black. In effect they were claiming a right to "dignity." In the context of the times it was not a widely accepted view.

41. *Documentary History of Reconstruction*, p. 247.

Chapter Three
The First Cases

1. The Bradley letter, dated October 30, 1876, can be found in the Bradley papers, New Jersey Historical Society, Newark, New Jersey, and in *Reconstruction and Reunion, 1864–88*, part 2, Charles Fairman (New York: Macmillan, 1987), pp. 279, 564.

2. *Reconstruction and Reunion, 1864–88.*, XIV, "The Legal Tender Cases," p. 679.

3. *Lincoln*, David Herbert Donald (New York: Simon and Schuster, 1995), p. 264.

4. Carl Schurz remarked that Chase "looked as you would wish a statesman to look," ibid.

5. See *Reconstruction and Reunion*, Foner's *Reconstruction*, and Donald's *Lincoln* on Chase.

6. This and other comments about Chase can be found in *History of the Supreme Court of the United States: Reconstruction and Reunion 1864–88*, Charles Fairman (New York: Macmillan, 1987), p. 540.

7. Chase celebrated his own moral rectitude in a letter to H. Barney, May 29, 1868, ibid., p. 541.

8. See "Joseph P. Bradley: An Aspect of Judicial Personality," A. Champagne and D. Pope, *Political Psychology*, vol. 6, no. 3, 1985, pp. 481–93, and the Bradley papers, New Jersey Historical Society, Newark, New Jersey.

9. *Civil Rights Cases of 1883*, 3 S. Ct. 18, 1883.

10. "Joseph P. Bradley: An Aspect of Judicial Personality," p. 492.

11. "An Apect of Judical Personality," op. cit., p. 485.

12. Champagne and Pope refer to Bradley's "desire for omniscience" and his "extreme interest in control over his envirnoment," p. 481.

13. See the Bradley Papers, New Jersey Historical Society, Newark, New Jersey.

14. *Bradwell v. Illinois*, (1873).

15. See the Bradley Papers, New Jersey Historical Society, Newark, New Jersey.

16. "Joseph P. Bradley: An Aspect of Judical Personality," op. cit. pp. 485–86.

17. See Bradley's June 4, 1871, letter, New Jersey Historical Society, Newark, New Jersey.

18. "William Strong," Michael B. Dougan, *Oxford*, p. 486.

19. *The Nation*, July 11, 1872, pp. 22–23.

20. "The Negro Problem in Virginia," *The Nation*, February 20, 1873, p. 131.

21. Ibid.

22. See *White Terror*, p. 399.

23. Ibid., pp. 402–407.

24. Herbert Spencer toured the United States giving well-received lectures on Social Darwinist theory. Elites were pleased to be viewed as the finest achievement of the evolutionary process.

25. *The Slaughterhouse Cases*, 16; *Wallace Reports*, 36, 67 (1873).

26. Ibid., p. 71.

27. Ibid., p. 77.

28. Ibid., p. 78.

29. Ibid., p. 80.

30. "The Supreme Court Righting Itself," *The Nation*, April 24, 1873, p. 281.

31. *Reconstruction and Reunion, 1864–88, VI: Judicial Response to New Legislation II*, p. 413.

32. Ibid., pp. 263–64.

33. See *The Nation*, April 24, 1873, for contemporaneous accounts of the massacre.

34. *Judicial Response to the New Legislation*, p. 267.

35. Ibid., pp. 263–64.

36. *Reconstruction and Reunion, 1864–1888*, part 2, pp. 267–68.

37. For the Bradley letter see *Reconstruction and Reunion, 1864–1868*, p. 564.

38. *Reconstruction and Reunion, 1864–1888*, vol. 7, part 2, C. Fairman (Macmillan, 1963), p. 111.

39. Ibid., pp. 168–71.

40. *Morrison R. Waite: The Triumph of Character*, P. Magrath (New York: Macmillan, 1963), p. 100.

41. Ibid., pp. 168–71.

42. "Judicial Response to the New Legislation," note 153, p. 273.

43. *U.S. v. Cruikshank*, 91 U.S. 542 (1876); 25 F.Cas 707 (C.C.D.La. 1874) No. 14,879.

44. Quoted in "Federal Civil Rights," *Tulane Law Review*, V. 67, 1993, p. 2155.

45. *Reconstruction and Reunion, 1864–1868*, part 1, p. 1377.

46. *United States v. Reese*, 92 U.S. 214 (1876).

47. See *Reese* file, National Archives, Washington, D.C.

48. This language is taken from the *Reese* file.

49. "Judicial Response to the New Legislation II," p. 277.

50. See the above regarding the government's concern over the impact of an adverse *Reese* decision on pending cases.

51. *United States v. Reese*, 92 U.S. 214 (1876).

52. Sources of data include A. Trelease, *White Terror*, which summarizes data from other works including William Davis, *Enforcement Acts* (New York: Columbia University Press, 1914), p. 224, and E. Swinney, "Enforcement of the Fifteenth Amendment," *Journal of Southern History*, vol. 28, pp. 202–58.

53. *New York Times*, November 15, 23, 27, and 29 (page 2), 1876.

54. *The History of the Supreme Court of the United States: Five Justices and the Electoral Commission of 1877*, C. Fairman (New York: Macmillan), p. 123.

55. Ibid., pp. 123–24.

56. Ibid., 165.

57. Ibid., 167.

58. See Foner, *Reconstruction*, p. 581.

59. For a discussion of Hayes ascension see Foner, *Reconstruction*, pp. 575–87.

60. *The Nation*, as quoted by Foner in *Reconstruction*, p. 581.

Chapter Four
From Pace to Plessy: If Not Slavery—What?

1. *Reconstruction and Reunion, 1864–1868*, part 2, p. 521.

2. Ibid., p. 498.

3. Ibid., p. 586.

4. See note 28 in *Reconstruction and Reunion*, part 2, p. 231.

5. *Virginia v. Rives*, 100 U.S. 313 (1880) and *Strauder v. West Virginia*, 100 U.S. 303 (1880).

6. *New York Times*, November 25, 1879, p. 8.

7. See ch. 11, "The Civil Rights Cases of 1883," in *Reconstruction and Reunion, 1864–1888*.

8. *Civil Rights Cases of 1883*, 109 U.S. 3, 13 (1883).

9. Ibid., pp. 24–25.

10. Harlan's dissent promotes an understanding of formalism as a mode of judical analysis that evades the intent of civil rights legislation via a type of verbal analysis that abstracts words from the brutal realities they are intended to reflect.

11. Ibid., p. 61.

12. See *The Frederick Douglas Papers*, Series One, J. Blassingame and J. McKivigan, eds. (New Haven: Yale University Press, p. 122). For Bishop Turner see *The Black Man's Doom*, J. A. Rodgers, Philadelphia (1896).

13. *North Carolina Republican*, May 22, 1884, Howard University, Washington, D.C.

14. See "The Civil Rights Cases," *Reconstruction and Reunion*, pp. 571, 574.

15. *The Triumph of Jim Crow:Tennessee Race Relations in the 1880s*, J. H. Cartwright (Knoxville: University of Tennessee Press), p. 168.

16. Ibid., p. 166.

17. *Strauder v. West Virginia*, 100 U.S. 303 (1880).

18. See the Melville Fuller Papers, Manuscript Division, Library of Congress, Washignton, D.C.

19. See The David J. Brewer papers, Yale University Library, New Haven, Connecticut.

20. *Louisville Railway v. Missippi*, 133 U.S. 587 (1889).

21. *Kentucky Bulletin*, Sept. 24, 1881, Howard University Library, Wash., D.C.

22. *North Carolina Republican*, May 22, 1884, Howard University Library, Wash., D.C.

23. See Harlan's *Louisville* dissent relative to the inconsistency between it and *Hall*.

24. *Louisville*, p. 591.

25. *The Plessy Case:A Legal Historical Interpreation*, C. Lofgren (New York: Oxford University Press, 1987).

26. *State ex rel Abbott*, 44 La. Ann. 770 is discussed in *The Plessy Case*.

27. *The Plessy Case*, p. 149.

28. *Benjamin Harrison: Hoosier President*, H. J. Sievers, Bobbs-Merrill, New York, p. 151.

29. *Plessy v. Ferguson*, 163 U.S. 537, 551–52 (1896).

30. Ibid., p. 544.

31. Ibid., p. 550.

32. Harlan's dissent yielded the phrase "the Constitution is color blind." As is indicated in chapter 2, Congress rejected language that would have made it color blind. Ironically, the phrase fueled the civil rights movement and in the post–civil rights era is used by the foes of affirmative action.

33. *Cummings v. Board of Education*, 175 U.S. 528, 537 (1899).

34. Ibid., p. 545.

35. See commentary on Harlan's holding in "Principle and Prejudice: The Supreme Court in the Progressive Era," B. Schmidt, *Columbia L.Rev.*, V. 82, No. 3, April 1982, p. 470.

36. See the *Cummings* case file, National Archives, Wash., D.C., for the Edmund's letter.

Chapter Five
American Apartheid

1. See the *Buchanan v. Warley* case file, National Archives, Washington, D.C.

2. Kelly Miller, "Everlasting Stain" (Washington, D.C.: Associated Publishers, 1924); reprinted by Arno Press and *New York Times*, pp. 226–29.

3. See U.S. Census Bureau, *The Negro Population in the United States:1790–1915*.

4. *Crisis*, November 1910, vol. 1, no. 1.

5. Ibid.

6. *The Judiciary and Responsible Government, 1910–1921*, A. Bickel and B. Schmidt, eds. (New York: Macmillan, 1984).

7. *Literary Digest*, vol. 3, March 18, 1916.

8. Baltimore and other cities filed in support of the Louisville apartheid statute.

9. Thomas Dixon and others were part of a cultural offensive with regard to a revisionist view of the South, which culminated thirty years later with the publication of *Gone with the Wind.*

10. See, the National Archives, Washington, D.C., Dept. of Justice, File 152961–3.

11. Bickel and Schmidt, op. cit., p. 740.

12. Ibid., p. 736.

13. Ibid., p. 38.

14. See *Justice Oliver Wendall Holmes: Law and the Inner Self,* G. E. White (Oxford University Press, 1993).

15. *Muller v. Oregon,* 208 U.S. 412 (1908) raised this issue relative to women's rights.

16. *Lochner v. New York,* 198 U.S. 45 (1905) is an example of this type of jurisprudence.

17. *Giles v. Harris,* 189 U.S. 475 (1903).

18. White, op. cit. P. 318.

19. Ibid., p. 319.

20. See *Charles Evans Hughes,* vols. 1 & 2, M. Pusey (New York: Macmillan, 1952).

21. *Bailey v. Alabama,* 219 U.S. 219 (1911).

22. Ibid., p. 244.

23. Ibid.

24. Ibid., pp. 244–45.

25. See the Holmes dissent in *Bailey.*

26. Bickel and Schmidt, op. cit., p. 783.

27. *McCabe v. Atchison,* 235 U.S. 151 (1914).

28. Bickel and Schmidt, op. cit., pp. 781–82.

29. *Cozart* and *Airline* are cited in Bickel and Schmidt, op. cit., p. 777.

30. *Chiles v. Chesepeake and Ohio,* 218 U.S. 71 (1910).

31. See discussion of *Butts* and related issues in Bick and Schmidt, op. cit., pp. 477–95.

32. *McCabe v. Atchison*, 235 U.S. 151 (1914).

33. Ibid.

34. Ibid.

35. "The Latest Phase of Negro Disenfranchisement," *Harvard Law Rev*, 1910, pp. 42–63.

36. See Bickel and Schmidt, op. cit., p. 909.

37. Ibid., p. 920.

38. "The Latest Phase of Negro Disenfranchisement," p. 43.

39. Bickel and Schmidt, op. cit., pp. 927–49.

40. See *Guinn v. United States*, 238 U.S. 347, 348–50 for Bailey's argument.

41. See *Jack Johnson: In the Ring and Out* (London: Proteus Publishers, 1977).

42. *Mutual* denied film First Amendment protection and was not reversed for forty years.

43. *Myers v. Anderson*, 238 U.S. 368 (1915), *United States v. Mosley*, 238 U.S. 383 (1915).

44. *Guinn V. United States*, pp. 364–65.

45. *The Literary Digest*, July 3, 1915, p. 5. There was widespread coverage of the decision, with acknowledgment that an Oklahoma victory would have rendered the Fifteenth Amendment moot.

46. McReynolds was a racist and an antisemite, unloved in his time and forgotten later.

47. See *Justice on Trial: The Case of Louis D. Brandeis*, A. L.Todd (New York: McGraw Hill, 1964).

48. Ibid., p. 57.

49. Bickel and Scmidt, op. cit., pp. 789–917.

50. See Louisville city attorney P. Beckely's March 2, 1916, letter in the *Buchanan v. Warley* file, National Archives, Washington, D.C.

51. See the *Buchanan* file for the *Harris* pleading.

52. *Berea v. Kentucky*, 211 U.S. 45 (1908).

53. See Beckley's letter in the *Buchanan* file, National Archives, Washington, D.C.

54. The Louisville argument in favor of its apartheid statute can be found in summary form in *Buchanan v. Warley*, 245 U.S. 60, 61–64 (1917).

55. The Blakey and Storey arguments can be found for summary in *Buchanan v. Warley*. 245 U.S. 60, 61–61 (1917).

56. See *Columbia University Law Rev.* V. 82, 1982, pp. 511–17.

57. For a fuller understanding of *Buchanan* see record of prior proceedings in the case file.

58. Bickel and Schmidt, op. cit., pp. 800–803; see also *The Literary Digest*, November 24, 1917, for the jubilant black reaction to the *Buchanan* decision.

59. The impulse to create racial zones did not die with *Buchanan*. For the next twenty years various cities and towns sought to zone by race, efforts invariably found unconstitutional.

Chapter Six
The Court and the "Golden Age of Segregation"

1. *New York Times*, June 27, 1923, p. 40.

2. "Black Businessman Has Been Cleared," *New York Times*, October 26, 1996.

3. "The Ocoee Riot," Zora Neal Hurston, reprinted in *Essence*, February 1989.

4. *New York Times*, March 11, 1927, p. 2.

5. *The Harlem Renaissance*, Nathan Huggins (New York: Oxford University Press, 1971), p. 270.

6. Ibid., p. 280.

7. *Blacks in Blackface: A Source book on Early Black Musical Shows*, H. T. Sampson (Metuchen, N.J.: ScareCrow Press, 1980), p. 133.

8. See *Terrible Honesty: Mongrel Manhattan in the 1920s*, Ann Douglas, ed. (New York: Farrar, Straus and Giroux, 1995), for a discussion of the varied and complex relations between black artists and white patrons during the 1920s.

9. *New York Times*, August 21, 1929, p. 33.

10. *New York Times*, May 23, 1921.

11. Ralph Ginsburg's *Lynching*, a compilation of contemporary newspaper accounts, establishes the taken-for-granted nature of lynching during that era.

12. Douglas, op. cit., p. 326.

13. *Crisis*, December 1925, pp. 63–65.

14. See the Taft bio, *Oxford Companion to the Supreme Court of the United States*, p. 855.

15. *Truax v. Corrigan*, 257 U.S. 312 (1921).

16. *Bailey v. Drexel*, 259 U.S. 20 (1922).

17. *New York Times*, May 31, 1923.

18. See "Justice Sutherland," G.Leedes, *Journal of Supreme Court History*, 1995, pp. 137–51.

19. *New York Times*, May 16, 1923, p. 21.

20. "Pierce Butler," D. Burner, *Justices of the Supreme Court*.

21. 142 University of Pennsylvania Law Review, 1891, 1899, note 22.

22. *Ozawa v. United States*, 260 U.S. 178 (1922).

23. *Totyota v. United States*, 268 U.S. 402 (1924).

24. *Gong Lum*, 275 U.S. 78 (1927).

25. *New York Times*, January 4, 1926, p. 7.

26. *New York Times*, January 9, 1926.

27. *Corrigan v. Buckley*, 271 U.S. 323 (1926).

28. See *Corrigan v. Buckley* file, National Archives, Washington, D.C.

29. See files of the NAACP, Library of Congress, Washington, D.C.

30. *Nixon v. Herndon*, 273 U.S. 536 (1927).

Chapter Seven
From *Scottsboro* to *Gaines*

1. Without question the Scottsboro Boys would have been lynched save for the promise that the law would do the job for the mob.

2. *Amsterdam News*, June 6, 1936, p. 4.

3. Black newspapers of the time give a feel for the context in which protest was mounted.

4. Scottsboro: *A Tragedy of the American South*, D. Carter (Baton Rouge: Louisiana State University Press, 1969). See note 20 for newspaper comment, p. 20.

5. Ibid., p. 18.

6. Ibid., p. 19.

7. Ibid., p. 48.

8. See *New York Times*, April 12, 1930, p. 1 and April 13, p. 1 regarding opposition to Parker.

9. *Scottsboro, OpCit.*, pp 53–54.

10. *Stories of Scottsboro*, J. Goodman (New York: Pantheon Books, 1994).

11. The case assumed prominence beyond the actors involved as It moved to the world stage.

12. *Stories of Scottsboro*, p. 156.

13. See "Argument for Respondent," in *Powell v. Alabama*, 287 U.S. 45, 47–49 (1932).

14. See *New York Times*, Nov. 8, 1932, regarding the tension attending reading the decision.

15. *Powell v. Alabama*, 287 U.S. 45 (1932).

16. The differences between Hughes and Holmes points up the fallacy of looking for simple factors.

to explain different judicial approaches to race and rights. Holmes and Hughes had a great deal in common, yet Hughes brought a reality to racial jurisprudence from the beginning that Holmes moved to only very late.

17. *Scottsboro: A Tragedy of the American South*, pp. 181–82.

18. Ibid., pp. 194–96.

19. Ibid., p. 215.

20. Ibid., pp. 265–67.

21. Ibid., pp. 278–84.

22. *Norris v. Alabama*, 294 U.S. 587 (1934); *Patterson v. Alabama*, 294 U.S. 600 (1934).

23. *Hale v. Kentucky*, 303 U.S. 604 (1938).

24. *Pierre v. Louisiana*, 306 U.S. 354 (1939).

25. *Smith v. Texas*, 311 U.S. 128 (1940).

26. See *The Supreme Court Reborn*, W. E. Leuchtenburg (New York: Oxford University Press, 1995), pp. 26–52, for a discussion of the struggle between the railroads, Congress, and the Court.

27. See *The Supreme Court Reborn* and "The Court-Packing Scheme," *Oxford Companion to the Supreme Court*, for a discussion of the dynamics yielding the scheme.

28. See the Hughes File, Manuscript Division, Library of Congress, Washington, D.C.

29. *Moorehead v. Tibaldi*, 298 U.S. 587 (1936).

30. For details of the plan, see *The Supreme Court Reborn*, pp.132–63.

31. See *Mr. Justice Black: The Man and His Opinions*, J. Frank (Westport, Conn.: Greenwood Press). Any public dissent from segregation would have ended Black's Senate tenure.

32. For discussion of the storm re Black's Klan membership see *Mr. Justice Black*, pp. 95–108.

33. Ibid.

34. Ibid.

35. For White's letter, see the Black Papers, Manuscript Div., Library of Congress, Washington, D.C.

36. For White's telegram see Black's Papers, Manuscript Div., Library of Congress, Washington, D.C.

37. The history of labor's efforts to organize is complicated and is cross-cut by the history of labor as another institution compromised by accommodation to racism.

38. See Reed's bio in *The Oxford Companion to the Supreme Court of the United States*, F. O'Brien, pp. 712–13.

39. *The New Negro Alliance v. Sanitary Grocery*, 303 U.S. 560 (1937).

40. See files of the NAACP, Manuscript Division, Library of Congress, Washington, D.C.

41. See files of the NAACP, Manuscript Division, Library of Congress, Washington, D.C.

42. See *Simple Justice*, Ralph Kluger (New York: Vintage Books, 1977), p. 189.

43. Ibid., pp. 187–95.

44.

45. See files of the NAACP, Manuscript Division, Library of Congress, Washington, D.C.

46. Ibid.

47. Ibid.

48. Ibid.

49. Ibid.

50. *Gaines v. Canada*, 305 U.S. 337 (1938).

51. Ibid., p. 351.

52. Ibid., p. 352.

53. See files of the NAACP, Manuscript Division, Library of Congress, Washington, D.C.

54. Ibid.

55. Ibid.

56. *New York Times*, February 13, 1940, p. 1.

57. See *New York Times*, February 13, 1940 for text and commentary on *Chambers*.

58. *Chambers v. Florida*, 309 U.S. 227 (1940).

59. *New York Times*, February 13, 1940, p. 1.

60. Ibid.

61. *Charles Evans Hughes*, M. Pusey (New York: Macmillan, 1952), p. 790.

Chapter Eight
The Road to *Brown*

1. See the *Mitchell v. United States* case file, National Archives, Washington, D.C.

2. Ibid.

3. Ibid.

4. *Mitchell v. United States.*

5. *New York Times*, August 26, 1946.

6. *New York Times*, June 2, 1943, p. 2.

7. *New York Times*, June 17, 1943.

8. Ibid.

9. *New York Times*, June 22, 1943, p. 1.

10. *Grovey v. Townsend*, 295 U.S. 45 (1936).

11. *Smith v. Allwright*, 321 U.S. 649 (1944).

12. See *The Rise of Industrial America*, vol. 6, P. Smith (New York: Penguin Books, 1984), pp. 175–76.

13. See the Douglas Papers, Manuscript Division, Library of Congress, Washington, D.C.

14. *Tunstall v. Brotherhood*, 323 U.S. 210 (1944), *Steele v. Louisville*, 323 U.S. 192 (1944).

15. "The Saboteurs Case," D. J. Danelski, *Journal of Supreme Court History*, 1996, vol. 1, pp. 61–83 16. *New York Times*, May 7, 1945.

17. *Justice at War*, Peter Irons (Oxford University Press, 1983), p. 93.

18. *Hirabayashi v. United States*, 320 U.S. 81 (1943).

19. *Korematsu v. United States*, 323 U.S. 214 (1944).

20. Ibid., pp. 233–47.

21. Ibid., p. 216.

22. For a brief revealing bio of Vinson see Kluger's *Simple Justice.*

23. *Morgan v. Virginia*, 328 U.S. 373, and see also *New York Times*, June 4, 1946, for a sense of what the case meant to the actors at the time.

24. Ibid., pp. 389–93.

25. *New York Times*, February 14, 1947.

26. *Bob-Lo Excursion Co. V. Michigan*, 333 U.S. 29 (1947).

27. "This Contract of Conviction," *The Courage of Their Convictions*, Peter Irons, pp. 65–66.

28. *Shelley v. Kraemer*, 334 U.S. 1 (1948).

29. See *Sweatt v. Painter*, National Archives, Washington, D.C. re scholarship policy statement.

30. See "Scholarship Aid Fund for Negro . . . Students," *Sweatt v. Painter*, case file.

31. *Sweatt v. Painter*, 339 U.S. 629, 632 (1950).

32. Sworn statements by Texas officials regarding establishing a law school for blacks can be found in the *Sweatt* case files.

33. See *Simple Justice* for an account of how *Sweatt* moved up to the Supreme Court.

34. A letter from Texas Attorney General Price Daniels, December 28, 1949, referring to the rejection of the Council of Churches inquiry, can be found in the *Sweatt* case file.

35. See *Sweatt* case file for a copy of the Greenhill telegram to Arthur Goldberg, March 22, 1950 refusing to agree to submission of a friend of the court brief.

36. *Sweatt v. Painter*, op. cit., p.634.

37. Ibid., p. 636.

Chapter Nine
Brown v. Board of Education

1. See *Simple Justice*, Ralph Kluger (New York: Vintage Books, 1977) for the best and most thorough account of Oliver Brown's fateful visit to the all-white school.

2. Ibid., pp. 371–80.

3. Ibid., p. 394.

5. *Crusaders in the Courts*, Jack Greenberg (New York: Basic Books, 1994), pp. 126–32.

6. *Simple Justice*, pp. 3–27.

7. Ibid., p. 16.

8. Ibid., p. 18.

9. Ibid., p. 23.

10. Ibid., pp. 141–44.

11. Ibid., p. 304.

12. Ibid., pp. 345–48.

13. See *Crusaders in the Courts*, pp. 123–24, and *Simple Justice*, pp. 315–46, for accounts of the testimony of Kenneth Clark and other social scientists.

14. *Simple Justice*, pp. 365–66.

15. Ibid., p. 366.

16. *Crusaders in the Courts*, p. 156.

17. Ibid., p. 130.

18. Ibid., p. 131.

19. Ibid., pp. 149–50.

20. Ibid., pp. 150, 156.

21. Ibid., p. 581.

22. Ibid.

23. In a different guise the tendency of justices to read their own preferences into the Constitution took the form of "Lochnerism" after the case in which the Court found that the document protected the property interests of the monied class.

24. A Supreme Court justice has a social circle. Vinson's circle was probably offended by the crude racism of the poor white, but was not prepared to entertain notions of white-black social equality.

25. *Simple Justice*, pp. 587–91.

26. Ibid., pp. 591–95.

27. Ibid., pp. 595–96.

28. Ibid., p. 597.

29. Ibid., p. 598.

30. Ibid., p. 599.

31. Ibid., pp. 600–601.

32. Ibid., pp. 602–603.

33. Ibid., pp. 603–605. Rehnquist clerked for Jackson at the time of *Brown*. Years later he gave unconvincing explanations for a prosegregationist memo found in the file bearing his initials.

34. Ibid., pp. 607–10.

35. Ibid., pp. 610–11.

36. Ibid., pp. 611–12.

37. Ibid., pp. 612–13.

38. "Brown . . . Revisited," Herbert Brownell, *Journal of Supreme Court History*, 1993, p. 23.

39. *Simple Justice*, p. 660.

40. *Ibid*, p. 652.

41. Warren's impact on the Court speaks to the complexity of leadership. Undoubtably there were men on the Court more intellectually gifted, but he had the kind of social intelligence that yielded effective leadership.

42. This book suggests that the differing capacity of justices to interact effectively with colleagues translated into different potentiality for being effective with regard to Judaical objectives.

43. See the Hugo Black Papers, Manuscript Division, Library of Congress, Washington, D.C.

44. *Simple Justice*, pp. 667–70.

45. Ibid., pp. 671–72.

46. Ibid., pp. 673–75.

47. *Crusaders in the Courts*, p. 194.

48. *Simple Justice*, pp. 678–80.

49. Ibid., p. 680.

50. Ibid., pp. 680–81.

51. Ibid., p. 681.

52. Ibid., pp. 691–93.

53. Ibid., p. 694.

54. Ibid., p. 697.

55. Ibid., p. 698.

56. *New York Times*, May 17, 1954, p. 1.

57. *New York Times*, May 18, 1954, and Kluger, *Simple Justice*, p. 701.

58. *Brown v. Board of Education*, 347 U.S. 483, 484 (1954).

59. Ibid., 488.

60. Ibid., p. 489.

61. Ibid., p. 490.

62. Ibid., p. 493.

63. Ibid.

64. Ibid., p. 494.

65. *New York Times*, May 18, 1954, p. 19.

66. Ibid.

67. Ibid.

68. Ibid.

69. *New York Times*, May 18, 1954.

70. Ibid.

71. Ibid., p. 20.

72. Ibid.

73. Ibid.

Chapter Ten
After *Brown*

1. "Preferential Treatment for Negroes," F. Hechinger, *The Reporter*, December 3, 1964.

2. The divided nature of the Rehnquist Court is discussed in 66 *Tulane L.Rev*, 1267, 1277.

3. The exact quote is stark: "The Reagan administration feigned support for civil rights while declaring its opposition to race-conscious remedies. . . . The . . . administration specifically targeted affirmative action . . . and began a public campaign . . . against 'special interest groups' such as African Americans," 47 *University of Miami L.Rev* 469, 487.

4. Title Seven also created exemption categories under the rubric "bonafide occupational qualifications," for example, a relevant religious affiliation for pastoral work.

5. *Legislative History of Titles VII and IX of the Civil Rights Act of 1964*, Washington, D.C., U.S. Government Printing Office, n.d., p. 3005.

6. *Heart of Atlanta*, 379 U.S. 241 (1964).

7. *Bakke* came from the California effort to expand minority enrollment in medical school.

8. "Providing the Punch for the Right's Rhetoric," M. Shabazz, *Black Issues in Higher Education*, November 17, 1994.

9. "Memorable Tribute to Chief Justice Burger," *The Supreme Court Historical Society Quarterly*, V. XVI, No. 2, 1996, pp. 8–9.

10. *Griigs v. Duke Power Company*, 401 U.S. 424 (1971).

11. *Swann v. Charlotte-Mecklenburg*, 402 U.S. 1 (1971).

12. *Bakke v. Board of Regents*, 438 U.S. 265 (1978).

13. *Steelworkers v. Weber*, 99 S.Ct. 2721 (1979).

14. For a discussion of the memo, see Kluger and 31 *Tulsa Law Journal*, 251, 255.

15. See 1995 *The Utah Law Review*, 51, 64, for a discussion of this episode.

16. *Missouri v. Jenkins*, 515 U.S.—(1995).

17. *Board of Education v. Dowell*, 498 U.S. 237 (1991).

18. *Pasadena Board of Education v. Spangler*, 427 U.S. 424 (1976).

19. *Freeman v. Pitts*, 503 U.S.—(1992).

20. *Spallone v. United States*, 493 u.s. 265 (1990).

21. *Moose Lodge v. Irvin*, 407 U.S. 163 (1972).

22. *St. Mary's Honor Center v. Melvin Hicks*, 509 U.S.—(1993).

23. *Ward's Cove* and other cases also handed down in 1989 led, eventually, to the Civil Rights Act of 1991.

24. *Rizzo v. Goode*, 423 U.S. 362 (1975).

25. *United States v. Armstrong*, 517 U.S.—(1996).

26. Dworkin is quoted in note 156, 66, *Tulane Law Review* 1267.

27. The historical origins of the Klan Act were recounted in chapter 2. It is a matter of supreme irony that the act would serve a century later to bring charges against a city council seeking to change the world the Klan created.

28. *Richmond v. Croson*, 488 U.S. 469 (1989).

29. *Richmond v. Croson*, 102 L.Ed. 854, 913 (1989).

Bibliography

Books, Journals, and Newspapers

Bickel, A., and Schmidt, B. 1984. *History of the Supreme Court of the United States: The Judiciary and Responsible Government.* New York: Macmillan.

Blassingame, John, and John McKivigan. *The Frederick Douglas Papers*: Series One: Speeches, Debates, and Interviews, vol. 5. New Haven: Yale University Press.

Bork, Robert. 1990. *The Taming of America.* New York: The Free Press.

Carter, D. 1969. *Scottsboro: A Tragedy of the American South.* Baton Rouge, La. State University Press.

Cartwright, J. H. *The Triumph of Jim Crow: Tennesee Race Relations in the 1880s.* Knoxville, University of Tennessee Press.

Champagne, A., and D. Pope. 1985. "Joseph Bradley: An Aspect of Judicial Personality." *Political Psychology,* vol. 6, no. 3, pp. 481–93.

Coffin, Levi. 1898. *The Reminiscences of Levi Coffin.* Cincinnati: Robert Clark. Reprinted by Arno Press and the *New York Times,* 1968.

Cover, Robert. June, 1982. "The Origins of Judicial Activism in the Protection of Minorities," *Yale Law Journal,* vol. 91, no. 7.

Crisis. "Baltimore," November 1910, vol. 1, no. 1.

Currie, David P. February 1986. "The Constitution in the Supreme Court: 1921–1930," *Duke Law Journal.*

Danelski, David. 1996. "The Saboteurs' Case." *Journal of Supreme Court History,* pp. 61–82.

Delgado, Richard. Spring, 1987. "The Ethereal Scholar: Does Critical Legal Studies Have What Minorities Want." *Harvard Civil Rights—Civil Liberties Law Review,* vol. 22, no. 2.

Donald David Herbert. 1995. *Lincoln.* New York: Simon and Schuster.

Dougan, Michael. 1992. "William Strong." *Oxford Companion to the Supreme Court of the United States.* J. Ely, J. B.Grossman, and W. Wiecks, eds. New York: Oxford University Press.

Douglas, Ann. 1995. *Terrible Honesty: Mongrel Manhattan in the 1920s.* New York: Farrar, Strauss and Giroux.

Epstein, Lee, Jeffrey Segal, Harold Spaeth, and Thomas Walker. 1994. *The Supreme Court Compendium.* Washington, D.C.,: Congressional Quarterly.

Fairman, Charles. 1987. *History of the Supreme Court of the United States: Reconstruction and Reunion: 1864–88: Part Two.* New York: Macmillan.

———. 1988. *History of the Supreme Court of the United States: Five Justices and the Electoral Commission of 1877.* New York: Macmillan.

Finkleman, Paul. 1885.*Slavery in the Courtroom.* Washington, D.C.,: Library of Congress.

Fleming, W. 1960. *Documentary History of Reconstruction.* Glouster, Mass.: P. Smith.

Foley, John P. 1967. *Jefferson Cyclopedia.* New York: Russel and Russel.

Foner, Eric. 1988. *Reconstruction: America's Unfinished Revolution.* New York: Harper and Row.

Frank, J. *Mr. Justice Black: The Man and His Opinions.* Westport, Conn.: Greenwood Press.

Frey, Sylvia. 1995. "Slavery and Anti-Slavery." *The Blackwell Encyclopedia of the American Revolution.* Jack P. Green and J. R. Pole, editors. Cambridge, Mass.: Basil Blackwell.

Gallup, George. *The Gallup Poll: Public Opinion 1935–1971.* New York: Random House.

Goodman, J. 1994. *Stories of Scottsboro.* Pantheon Books.

Green, Richard Ewell, *Black Courage:1775–1783: Documents of Black Participation in the American Revolution.* Washington, D.C., National Society of the Daughters of the American Revolution.

Greenberg, Jack. 1994. *Crusaders in the Courtroom.* New York: Basic Books/Harper Collins.

Hall, David. 1990. "Contradictions, Illusions, Ironies and Inverted Realities: The Historical Relevance of the *Richmond v. Croson* Case," *The Urban League Review.*

Hechinger, Fred. December 3, 1964. "Preferential Treatment for Negroes." *The Reporter.*

Higginbotham. A. Leon, and William C. Smith. 1992. "The Hughes Court and the Beginning of the End of the 'Separate But Equal' Doctrine." 76 *Minn L. Review* 1099.

———, and Greer C. Bosworth. 1991. "Rather Than the Free: Free Blacks in Colonial and Antebellum Virginia," *Harvard Civil Rights—Civil Liberties Law Review,* vol. 26.

Huggins, Nathan. 1971. *The Harlem Renaissance.* New York: Oxford University Press.

Hurston, Zora Neal. 1989. "The Ocoee Riot." Reprinted in *Essence,* February, 1989.

Johnson, Jack. 1977. *Jack Johnson: In the Ring and Out.* London:Republished Proteus Ltd.

Irons, Peter. 1988. *The Courage of Their Convictions.* New York: Free Press.

———. 1983. *Justice at War.* New York: Oxford University Press.

Kluger, Richard. 1976. *Simple Justice.* New York: Alfred A. Knopf.

Krull, Andrew. Winter, 1993. "The Fourteenth Amendment That Wasn't." *Constitution.*

Legislative History of Titles VII and IX of the Civil Rights Act of 1964, Washington, D.C. U.S. Government Printing Office, n.d. p. 3005.

Les Benedict, Michael. 1978. "Preserving Federalism: Reconstruction and the Waite Court," *The Supreme Court Review,* Philip Kurland and Gerhard Casper, eds. Chicago: University of Chicago Press.

Leutchtenburg, William. 1995. *The Supreme Court Reborn.* New York: Oxford University Press.

Lewis, David Levering. 1993. *W. E. B. DuBois.* New York: Henry Holt and Company.

The Literary Digest. "End of the Grandfather Clause," July 3, 1915, p. 5.

The Literary Digest. "Negro Segregation in St. Louis," vol. 3, March 18, 1916, p. 702.

The Literary Digest. "The Negroes' Right of Residence," November 24, 1917, pp. 17–18.

Lofgren, C. 1987. *The Plessy Case: A Legal-Historical Interpretation.* New York: Oxford University Press.

Long, E. B., and Barbara Long. 1971. *The Civil War Day-by-Day: 1861–1865.* Garden City, N.Y.: A. Da Capo.

Magrath, P. 1963. *Morrison R. Waite: The Triumph of Character.* New York: Macmillan.

Marshall, Thomas. 1989. *Public Opinion and the Supreme Court.* Boston: Unwin Hyman.

Matsuda, Mari. Spring, 1987. "Looking to the Bottom: Critical Legal Studies and Reparations." *Harvard Civil Rights—Civil Liberties Law Review,* 22.

Miller, Kelly. 1908. *Race Adjustments.* New York and Washington, D.C.: Neale Publishing. Republished by Arno Press and the *New York Times,* 1967.

Miller, Randall, and John David Smith, editors. 1988. *Dictionary of Afro-American Slavery.* 1988. New York: Greenwood Press.

Monnet, Julien C. 1910. "The Latest Phase of Negro Disfranchisement," *Harvard Law Review,* pp. 42–63.

Neely, M., Editor. 1982. *The Abraham Lincoln Encyclopedia.* New York: McGraw-Hill.

The Nation. "The Rice Negro As an Elector," July 11, 1872, pp. 22–23.

The Nation. "The Negro Problem in Virginia," February 20, 1873, p. 131.

The Nation. "There has been a horrible massacre in Louisiana . . . ," April 24, 1873.

New Amsterdam News. "Where Hope Lies," June 6, 1936.

New York Times. Editorial on the Franchise for Freedmen, June 3, 1865, p. 4.

New York Times. "The Real Question As to the Future Political Status of the Negro," August 19, 1865, p. 4.

New York Times. "Southern Sentiment: A Georgian on the Freeman and Reconstruction," January 7, 1866, p. 8.

New York Times. "The New Orleans Riots—The Official Record," August 27, 1866.

New York Times. "Editorial," February 12, 1868.

New York Times. "Her Body One Mass of Wounds—Story of a Colored Election Officer," November 29, 1876.

New York Times. "The Color Prejudice: A Young Negro Refused Admission to the Grand Opera House," November 25, 1979, p. 8.

New York Times. "Negro Production Opens at Sixty-Third Street Music Hall," May 23, 1921.

New York Times. "Labor Leaders Hit Wage Law Decision," May 16, 1923.

New York Times. "The Supreme Court and Partisan Passion," May 31, 1923.

New York Times. "Jersey Negroes Fight School Segregation," March 11, 1927.

New York Times. "A Negro Talking Picture," August 21, 1929, p. 33.

New York Times. "New Trial Ordered by Supreme Court in Scottsboro Case" ,November 8, 1932.

New York Times. "Texas City under Martial Law as Races Clash in Beaumont Riots," June 17, 1943.

New York Times. "Bias Decision Awaited," May 17, 1954, p. 1.

New York Times. "High Court Bans Pupil Bias," May 18, 1954, p. 1.

New York Times. "Businessman Has Been Cleared," October 26, 1996.

North Carolina Republican. May 22, 1884.

Pusey, Merlo. 1952. *Charles Evans Hughes.* Vols 1 and 2. New York: Macmillan.

Ripley, C. Peter. 1981. *The Black Abolitionist Papers.* Chapel Hill: University of North Carolina Press.

Sampson, H. T. 1980. *Blacks in Blackface: A sourcebook on Early Black Musical Shows.* Metuchen, N.J.: Scarecrow Press.

Schwartz, Bernard. 1970. *Statutory History of the United States: The Civil War.* New York: McGraw Hill.

Schmidt, Benno. April, 1982. "Principle and Prejudice: The Supreme Court in the Progessive Era," *Columbia Law Review*, vol. 82, no. 3.

Shabazz, M. November, 1994. "Providing the Punch for the Right's Rhetoric." *Black Issues in Higher Education.*

Sievers, H. J. 1952. *Benjamin Harrison—Hoosier President.* New York: Bobbs-Merrill.

Smith, Page. 1984. *The Rise of Industrial America: A People's History of the Post–Reconstruction Era.* Vol. 6. New York: Penguin.

Todd, A. L. *Justice on Trial: The Case of Louis D. Brandeis.* New York: Notable Trials Library/Gryphon Editions.

Townsend, J. H. 1859, "American Caste and Common Schools." *The Anglo-African Magazine.* Reprinted by Arno Press and the *New York Times.*

Trelease, Allan W. 1971. *The White Terror: The Ku Klux Klan Conspiracy and Southern Reconstruction.* New York: Harper and Row.

Tribe, Lawrence. 1992. "State Sovereignty and State's Rights." *Oxford Companion to the Supreme Court of the United States.* J. Ely, J. B. Grossman, and W. Wiecks, eds. New York: Oxford University Press.

Turner, H. M. 1891. *The Black Man's Doom: Two Barbarous and Cruel Decisions of the United States Supreme Court.* Philadelphia: James A. Rodgers.

U.S. Bureau of the Census. 1968. *Negro Population of the United States: 1790–1915.* Arno Press and the *New York Times.*

Watson, William. 1913. *The Civil War and Reconstruction in Florida.* New York: Columbia University.

White, G. Edward. 1993. *Justice Oliver Wendall Holmes: The Law and the Inner Self.* NewYork: Oxford University Press.

Williams, Patricia. 1991. *The Alchemy of Race and Rights.* Cambridge: Harvard University Press.

Wills, Gary. 1992. *Lincoln at Gettysburg.* New York: Simon and Schuster.

Cases

Bailey v. Alabama, 219 U.S. 219 (1911).
Bailey v. Drexel, 259 U.S. 20 (1922).
Bakke v. Board of Regents, 483 U.S. 265 (1978).

Berea v. Kentucky, 211 U.S. 45 (1908).
Blyew v. U.S. (Dec. 1871), Sup. Ct. 591.
Board of Education v. Dowell, 498 U.S. 237 (1991).
Bob-Lo Excursions Co. v. Michigan, 333 U.S. 29 (1947).
Bradwell v. Illinois, (1873) 16 Wallace 130.
Brown v. Board of Education, 347 U.S. 483 (1954).
Buchanan v. Warley, 245 U.S. 60 (1917).
The Civil Rights Cases of 1883, 3 S. Ct. 18 (1883) .
Chambers v. Florida, 309 U.S. 337 (1938).
Chiles v. Chesepeake and Ohio, 218 U.S. 71 (1910).
Corrigan Buckley271 U.S. 323 (1926).
Cummings v. Board of Education, 175 U.S. 528 (1899).
Dred Scott v. Sandford, 20 How. 1 (1856).
Freeman v. Pitt, 503 U.S. 467 (1992).
Gaines v. Canada, 305 U.S. 337 (1938).
Giles v. Harris, 189 U.S. 475 (1903).
Gong Lum, 275 U.S. 78 (1927).
Griggs v. Duke Power Company, 401 U.S. 424 (1971).
Grover v. Townsend, 295 U.S. 45 (1936).
Guinn v. U.S., 238 U.S. 347 (1914).
Hale v. Kentucky, 303 U.S. 604 (1938).
Heart of Atlanta, 379 U.S. 241 (1964).
Hirabayashi v. U.S., 320 U.S. 81 (1943).
In Re Turner, Fed. Case No. 14,247 (1867).
Korematsu v. U.S., 323 U.S. 214 (1944).
Lochner v. New York, 198 U.S. 45 (1905).
Louisville Railway v. Mississippi, 133 U.S. 587 (1889).
McCabe v. Atchison, 235 U.S. 151 (1914).
Missouri v. Jenkins, 515 U.S.—(1995).
Mitchell v. U.S. 313 U.S. 80 (1940).
Moorehead v. Tibald, 298 U.S. 587 (1936).
Moose Lodge v. Irvin, 407 U.S. 163 (1972).
Morgan v. Virginia, 328 U.S. 373.
Muller v. Oregon, 208 U.S. 412 (1908).
Myer v. Anderson, 238 U.S. 368 (1915).
Nixon v. Herndon, 273 U.S. 536 (1927).
Norris v. Alabama, 294 U.S. 587 (1934).
Ozawa v. U.S. 260 U.S. 178 (1922).
Pasadena Board of Education v. Spangler, 427 U.S. 424 (1976).
Patterson v. Alabama, 294 U.S. 660 (1934).
Patterson v. McClean, 485 U.S. 617 (1988).
Pierre v. Louisiana, 306 U.S. 354 (1939).
Plessy v. Ferguson, 163 U.S. 537 (1896).
Powell v. Alabama, 287 U.S. 45 (1932).
Richmond v. Croson, 488 U.S. 469 (1989).
Rizzo v. Goode, 423 U.S. 362 (1975).

Saint Mary's Honor Center v. Melvin Hicks, 509 U.S. 502 (1993).
The Slaughterhouse Cases, 16 Wallace Report 36 (1873).
Shelley v. Kraemer, 334 U.S. 1 (1948).
Smith v. Allwright, 321 U.S. 649 (1944).
Smith v. Texas, 311 U.S. 128 (1940).
Spallone v. U.S., 493 U.S. 265 (1990).
Steele v. Louisville, 323 U.S. 649 (1944).
Steelworkers v. Weber, 99 S. Ct. 2721 (1979).
Strauder v. West Virginia, 100 U.S. 303 (1880).
Swann v. V. Charlotte-Mecklenburg, 402 U.S. 1 (1971).
Sweatt v. Painter, 339 U.S. 629 (1950).
Toyota v. U.S., 268 U.S. 402 (1924).
Truax v. Corrigan, 257 U.S. 312 (1912).
Tunstall v. Brotherhood, 323 U.S. 210 (1944).
U.S. v. Armstrong, 517 U.S.—(1996).
U.S. v. Cruikshank, 91 U.S. 542 (1876).
U.S. v. Moseley, 238 U.S. 383 (1915).
U.S. v. Reese, 91 U.S. 214 (1876).
U.S. v. Rhodes, Fed. Case No. 16,151 (1866).
Virginia v. Rives, 100 U.S. 313 (1880).

Index

R

S